ECOTOURISM AND SUSTAINABLE TOURISM

New Perspectives and Studies

ECOTOURISM AND SUSTAINABLE TOURISM
New Perspectives and Studies

Edited By
Jaime A. Seba

Research Specialist, Hospitality and Tourism Service;
Holland-America Cruise Lines, Seattle, Washington, U.S.A.

Apple Academic Press

TORONTO   NEW YORK

© 2012 by Apple Academic Press, Inc.

International Standard Book Number: 978-1-926692-93-7 (Hardback)

This book contains information obtained from authentic and highly regarded sources. Reprinted material is quoted with permission and sources are indicated. Copyright for individual articles remains with the authors as indicated. A wide variety of references are listed. Reasonable efforts have been made to publish reliable data and information, but the authors, editors, and the publisher cannot assume responsibility for the validity of all materials or the consequences of their use. The authors, editors, and the publisher have attempted to trace the copyright holders of all material reproduced in this publication and apologize to copyright holders if permission to publish in this form has not been obtained. If any copyright material has not been acknowledged, please write and let us know so we may rectify in any future reprint.

Library and Archives Canada Cataloguing in Publication

Ecotourism and sustainable tourism: new perspectives and studies/[edited by] Jaime A. Seba. —1st ed.

Includes index.
ISBN 978-1-926692-93-7
1. Ecotourism–Case studies. 2. Sustainable tourism–Case studies. I. Seba, Jaime

G156.5.E26E25 2011   338.4'791   C2011-905383-7

Trademark Notice: Registered trademark of products or corporate names are used only for explanation and identification without intent to infringe.

Apple Academic Press also publishes its books in a variety of electronic formats. Some content that appears in print may not be available in electronic format. For information about Apple Academic Press products, visit our website at **www.appleacademicpress.com**

Preface

All over the world, technological advances are being made at the speed of light, and the hospitality and tourism industry is growing and changing just as quickly. Customers can get a special rate when they follow a hotel on Twitter. They can book tour reservations online with a simple click. Cruise destinations around the world can be explored without leaving home, and bloggers on different continents share dining recommendations. Travelers can even plan a vacation that allows them to commune with nature while printing e-mails from their smartphones.

In order to stay competitive in an international market, businesses must adjust to these emerging social trends and respond to the ever-changing needs of their customers. The traditional focus on customer service and guest loyalty has become intertwined with rapidly progressing technological enhancements influencing all areas of the industry, including sales, marketing, human resources, and revenue and asset management. The result is a visitor experience personalized to each specific guest, through strategic data collection, market trend research, and the capabilities of integrated online self-service. This means knowing what matters most to consumers and recognizing emerging innovations that will be the next big thing for the next generation of customers.

One such movement is the worldwide recognition of the need for environmentally friendly "green" initiatives, which are becoming significantly reflected in the hospitality industry. There has been an increased interest in ecotourism and sustainable tourism, which provide travelers with destinations and activities that have a lower negative impact on the environment. This trend is evidenced by the growing prevalence of green conferences that attract everyone from hotel general managers and tour operators to the tourists themselves. Ecotourism, responsible tourism, jungle tourism, and sustainable development have become prevalent concepts since the late 1980s, and ecotourism has experienced arguably the fastest growth of all sub-sectors in the tourism industry. The popularity represents a change in tourist perceptions, increased environmental awareness, and a desire to explore natural environments.

We live in an interconnected world today, and this reality has enormous bearing on the hospitality and tourism industry. Considering these impact and meaningful trends, the future of the industry will depend on a skilled workforce that can react quickly to rapid changes at the forefront of global culture.

— **Jaime A. Seba**

List of Contributors

Carolyn A. Afolami
Department of Agricultural Economics and Farm Management University of Agriculture Abeokuta, P. M. B. 2240 Abeokuta, Nigeria.

Sukhiin Amgalanbaatar
Research Biologist with the Institute of Ecology at the Mongolian Academy of Sciences, President of the Argali Wildlife Research Center, and a Research Associate with the Denver Zoological Foundation.

Marc Ancrenaz
Kinabatangan Orangutan Conservation Project, Hutan, Sandakan, Sabah, Malaysia.

Elena Angulo
Ecology, Systematics and Evolution, UMR CNRS 8079, Universite Paris-Sud, Orsay, France.

Eugene J. Aniah
Department of Geography and Regional Planning, University of Calabar, Calabar, Nigeria.

Blessing E. Asuquo
Mission Director, US Forest Service, International Programs, Washington, DC, USA.

Mohammad Zaki Ayob
Faculty of Business Management, Universiti Teknologi Mara (UiTM) Kedah, P.O. Box 187, Merbok, 08400 Kedah.

Andrew Balmford
Department of Zoology, University of Cambridge, Cambridge, UK.

Donald J. Bedunah
Professor of Rangeland Resource Management, Department of Forest Management, College of Forestry and Conservation at The University of Montana, Missoula, MT.

James Beresford
Department of Zoology, University of Cambridge, Cambridge, UK.

Ralf Buckley
International Centre for Ecotourism Research, Griffith University, Southport, Queensland, Australia.

Leigh Bull
Ecology, Systematics and Evolution, UMR CNRS 8079, Universite Paris-Sud, Orsay, France.

Michael Cherry
Associate professor in the Department of Botany and Zoology at the University of Stellenbosch in Stellenbosch, South Africa.

Stuart Cottrell
Department of Natural Resource Recreation and Tourism, Colorado State University, 1480 Campus Delivery Fort Collins, CO 80523, USA.

Franck Courchamp
Ecology, Systematics and Evolution, UMR CNRS 8079, Universite Paris-Sud, Orsay, France.

Lisa Dabek
Tree Kangaroo Conservation Program, Woodland Park Zoo, Seattle, Washington, USA.

Hongmei Dong
School of Management, Xi'an University of Science and Technology, Xi'an 710054, Shaanxi, China.

College of Tourism and Environmental Sciences, Shaanxi Normal University, Xi'an 710062, Shaanxi, China.

Eugene E. Ezebilo
Southern Swedish Forest Research Centre Swedish University of Agricultural Sciences, P.O. Box 49, 230 53 Alnarp, Sweden.

Jeremy Firestone
Center for Carbon-free Power Integration, College of Earth, Ocean, and Environment, University of Delaware, Newark, DE, 19716, USA.

Karen Gaul
Karen Gaul, Cultural Anthropologist, Lake Clark National Park, National Park Service, Anchorage, AK, USA.

Kristy Graham
Degree holder in eco-tourism and is currently is a research student at School of Environmental and Information Sciences at Charles Sturt University in Albury, Australia.

Jonathan Green
Department of Zoology, University of Cambridge, Cambridge, UK.

Richard J. Hall
Ecology, Systematics and Evolution, UMR CNRS 8079, Universite Paris-Sud, Orsay, France.

Zaliha Hj Hussin
Faculty of Business Management, Universiti Teknologi Mara (UiTM) Kedah, P.O. Box 187, Merbok, 08400 Kedah.

Kamaruzaman Jusoff
Department of Forest Production, Faculty of Forestry, Universiti Putra Malaysia, 43400 UPM Serdang, Selangor, Malaysia.

Willett Kempton
Center for Carbon-free Power Integration, College of Earth, Ocean, and Environment, University of Delaware, Newark, DE, 19716, USA.

David W. Look
Cultural Resources Team, Pacific Great Basin Support Office, National Park Service, San Francisco, California, USA.

Meredith Blaydes Lilley
Center for Carbon-free Power Integration, College of Earth, Ocean, and Environment, University of Delaware, Newark, DE, 19716, USA.

Andrea Manica
Department of Zoology, University of Cambridge, Cambridge, UK.

Leif Mattsson
Southern Swedish Forest Research Centre Swedish University of Agricultural Sciences, P.O. Box 49, 230 53 Alnarp, Sweden.

Yves Meinard
Ecology, Systematics and Evolution, UMR CNRS 8079, Universite Paris-Sud, Orsay, France.

Craig A. Miller
Warnell School of Forestry and Natural Resources, University of Georgia, Athens, GA, USA.

Robin Naidoo
Conservation Science Program, World Wildlife Fund–US, Washington, DC, USA.

List of Contributors

Henry Nicholls
Freelance science writer based in London, UK.

Susan O'Neil
Tree Kangaroo Conservation Program, Woodland Park Zoo, Seattle, Washington, USA.

Judith E. Otu
Department of Sociology, University of Calabar, Calabar, Nigeria.

M. Rahmatian
Department of Economics California State University, Fullerton, USA.

Richard P. Reading
Director of Conservation Biology at the Denver Zoological Foundation and Associate Research Professor at the University of Denver, Denver, CO, USA.

Philippe Rivalan
Ecology, Systematics and Evolution, UMR CNRS 8079, Universite Paris-Sud, Orsay, France.

Fatimah Mohd. Saman
Faculty of Business Management, Universiti Teknologi Mara (UiTM) Kedah, P.O. Box 187, Merbok, 08400 Kedah.

Ryan L. Sharp
Warnell School of Forestry and Natural Resources University of Georgia, Athens, GA 30602, USA.

Fujun Shen
College of Forestry and Horticulture, Henan Agricultural University, China.

Laetitia Signoret
Ecology, Systematics and Evolution, UMR CNRS 8079, Universite Paris-Sud, Orsay, France.

H. Soleimanpour
Natural Environment and Biodiversity Division, Department of the Environment, Tehran, Iran.

Dirk H. R. Spennemann
Associate professor at Charles Sturt University in Albury, Australia.

Min Tong
School of Economics and Management, Northeast Forestry University, Ha'erbin 150040, China.

M. A. Ushie
Department of Sociology, University of Calabar, Calabar, Nigeria.

Jerry J. Vaske
Colorado State University.

F. J. (Freek) Venter
Conservation Services, Kruger National Park, South Africa.

R. A. Voeks
Environmental Studies Program, California State University, Fullerton, USA.

Matt Walpole
Fauna and Flora International, Cambridge, UK.

Hongshu Wang
School of Economics and Management, Northeast Forestry University, Ha'erbin 150040, China.

Pengfei Zhu
Beihai College of Beihang University, Beihai, Guangxi 536000, China.

List of Abbreviations

AAE	Anthropogenic Allee effect
AEM	Averting expenditure method
ANCSA	Alaska native claims settlement act
ANILCA	Alaska national interest lands conservation act
BMPs	Best management practices
CB	Contingent behavior
CBD	Convention on biological diversity
CERCOPAN	Centre for education, research and conservation of primates and nature
CFI	Comparative fit index
CHM	Clearing house mechanism
CNMI	Commonwealth of the Northern Mariana Islands
CRNP	Cross river national park
CRS	Cross river state
CRSFC	Cross river state forestry commission
CRSG	Cross river state government
CRSTB	Cross river state tourism bureau
CSD	Commission on sustainable development
CUIS	Cumberland island national seashore
CVMs	Contingent valuation methods
DEDO	Delaware economic development office
FFI	Flora and fauna international
FGN	Federal government of Nigeria
GDP	Gross domestic product
GIS	Geographic information system
HPM	Hedonic pricing method
HVNP	Hoge Veluwe national park
ILO	International labour organization
IMB	International multi-stakeholder body
IUCN	The international union for the conservation of nature
KNP	The Kruger national park
KOCP	Kinabatangan orang-utan conservation project
MWTC	Mean willingness to contribute
NBI	National botanical institute
NBT	Nature-based tourism

NBTA	Nature-based tourism areas
NGOs	Non-governmental organizations
NMB	National multi-stakeholders body
NNPS	Nigerian national park service
NPQM	Northern piedmont in the Qinling Mountains
NPS	National park service
NPV	Net present value
OD	Okwangwo division
OECD	Organization for economic and co-operation development
OICI	Opportunities industrialization centers international
OLSs	Ordinary least squares
PAs	Protected areas
PNG	Papua new guinea
PPA	Power purchase agreement
PPP	Purchasing power parity
PRATIO	Parsimony ratio
PRM	Participatory research method
PSA	Programa de Pago de Servicios Ambientales
RAE	Red ape encounters
RMSEA	Root mean square of approximation
SANBI	South African national biodiversity institute
SCI	Safari club international
SE	Standard error
SEM	Structural equations modeling
SPACE	Sustainable practices in agriculture for critical environments project
SWD	Sabah wildlife department
TCM	Travel cost method
TIES	The international ecotourism society
TKCP	Tree kangaroo conservation program
TLI	Tucker-Lewis index
TMP	Transportation management plan
UMENGO	Union of Mongolian environmental, nongovernmental organizations
UNCTAD	United Nations conference on trade and development
UNEP	United Nations environment programme
USAID	United states agency for international development
USFS/IP	US forest service department of agriculture, international programs office
USG	United states government

WCED	World commission on environment and development
WCS	Wildlife conservation society
WSSD	World summit on sustainable development
WTA	Willingness to accept
WTC_i	Individual's willingness to contribute
WTO	World tourism organization
WTP	Willingness to pay
WWF	World wide fund for nature
YUS	Yupno, Uruwa, and Som local-level government region

Contents

1. Tourists' Satisfaction with Ecosystem Services 1
   R. A. Voeks and M. Rahmatian

2. Legal Implications for Nature-based Tourism 17
   H. Soleimanpour

3. Trends in Nature-based Tourism 30
   Andrew Balmford, James Beresford, Jonathan Green, Robin Naidoo, Matt Walpole, and Andrea Manica

4. Community Participation in Environmental Management of Ecotourism 38
   Hongshu Wang and Min Tong

5. Environmental Issues and Best Practices for Ecotourism 45
   USAID

6. Effect of Wind Power Installations on Coastal Tourism 54
   Meredith Blaydes Lilley, Jeremy Firestone, and Willett Kempton

7. Role for Local Communities in Biodiversity Conservation 73
   Marc Ancrenaz, Lisa Dabek, and Susan O'Neil

8. Value of Rare Species in Ecotourism 83
   Elena Angulo and Franck Courchamp

9. Rarity Value and Species Extinction 92
   Franck Courchamp, Elena Angulo, Philippe Rivalan, Richard J. Hall, Laetitia Signoret, Leigh Bull, and Yves Meinard

10. Parks and Tourism 103
    Ralf Buckley

11. The Conservation Business 106
    Henry Nicholls

12. Ecological Sports Tourism Resources and Its Industry 112
    Pengfei Zhu

13. Ecotourism in the Northern Piedmont in the Qinling Mountains 118
    Hongmei Dong

14. Heritage Ecotourism in Micronesia 125
    Dirk H. R. Spennemann, David W. Look, and Kristy Graham

15. Economic Value of Ecotourism in the Nigerian Rainforest Zone 129
    Eugene E. Ezebilo, Leif Mattsson, and Carolyn A. Afolami

xvi   Contents

16. **Visitor Access to Cumberland Island National Seashore, Georgia**............ 140
    Ryan L. Sharp and Craig A. Miller

17. **Sustainable Development of China's Ecotourism**... 147
    Wei Chen and Wenpu Wang

18. **Ecotourism in Protected Areas in Cross River State, Nigeria**................... 154
    Jeffrey J. Brooks, John Neary, and Blessing E. Asuquo

19. **Kilim River Mangrove Forest Ecotourism Services**..................................... 189
    Mohammad Zaki Ayob, Fatimah Mohd Saman, Zaliha Hj Hussin, and Kamaruzaman Jusoff

20. **Wilderness Stewardship in the Kruger National Park, South Africa**........ 198
    F. J. (Freek) Venter

21. **Sustainable Tourism Development in Cross River State, Nigeria**............. 203
    Eugene J. Aniah, Judith E. Otu, and M. A. Ushie

22. **Conserving Biodiversity on Mongolian Rangelands**................................... 212
    Richard P. Reading, Donald J. Bedunah, and Sukhiin Amgalanbaatar

23. **Predictors of Sustainable Tourism in Holland and China**.......................... 236
    Stuart Cottrell, Jerry J. Vaske, and Fujun Shen

24. **Subsistence, Tourism, and Research**.. 244
    Karen Gaul

25. **Biodiversity Science in South Africa**... 253
    Michael Cherry

    Permissions.. 262

    References.. 265

    Index... 288

Chapter 1

Tourists' Satisfaction with Ecosystem Services

R. A. Voeks and M. Rahmatian

INTRODUCTION

Natural ecosystems provide an array of critical but largely undervalued goods and services. Because these are seldom included in benefit-cost calculations of land use change, the value of wild land development nearly always appears greater than protecting wild nature. The following chapter introduces a theoretical framework within which environmental economists evaluate ecosystem services. This is followed an assessment of three types of ecosystem services with particular relevance to the developing world pharmaceutical drug development from native plants, the economics of non-timber product extraction, and the benefits and costs of ecotourism as a development strategy. We conclude with an overview of recent attempts to provide a global estimate of the value of nature's services.

Ecosystem services include those processes and conditions within which nature sustains and otherwise meets the needs material and otherwise of humankind. These include tangible goods, such as timber, fiber, fuelwood, foods, and medicines, as well as the array of environmental services that support life on earth, such as water purification, carbon dioxide absorption, biogeochemical cycling, and many others. In spite of the obvious value of these goods and services in supporting and improving the human condition, many of these values are customarily ignored in the course of development projects. Even when cost-benefit analyses are incorporated into planning and decision-making, many of the less tangible services provided by ecosystems are omitted from the calculus. The result of these omissions is that the economic benefits of development, such as replacing forest with pasture, or draining wetland for agricultural expansion, nearly always appear to outweigh the costs of environmental protection.

In recent publications, (Daily, 1997) attempted to correct this omission by synthesizing the vast array of scattered publications dealing with the economic valuing ecosystem services. They recognize, however, that this endeavor is fraught with difficulties (Gatto and De Leo, 2000). For example, assigning an economic value to many of these life-support systems may seem too "trivial" for consideration how meaningful, for example, is it to identify the value of oxygen production by plants to human life? Moreover, unlike traditional goods and services whose values are captured in commercial markets, many ecosystem services seem to defy rational accounting. For example, in South America the iroko tree is considered the "sacred" dwelling place of an ancient forest god (Voeks, 1997). Is it a useful endeavor to attempt to monetize the value of people's religious beliefs? Economic evaluations of nature are seen by others, particularly those that ascribe to a "deep ecology" view, as part and parcel to the problem, rather than the solution. Is it acceptable to value the existence of a nondescript species, such as a spider or flea, over a more visually and emotionally appealing species, such as a tiger or elephant? In spite of these conflicting issues, these authors contend that the gravity of the environmental problem demands, at least, that an attempt be made at quantifying these benefits at the global level.

The objectives in this chapter are to introduce the concept of valuing ecosystem goods and services. After examining the theoretical framework within which environmental goods and services are valued, we review three areas of nature valuation with relevance to the developing world. These include:

- The value of folk medicinal plants in pharmaceutical drug development;
- The value of petty resource extraction from natural landscapes;
- The value of ecotourism as a development strategy for developing countries; and
- Finally, summarizing the work of (Daily, 1997), an estimate of the combined global value of ecosystem goods and services is provided.

THEORETICAL FRAMEWORK

In order to evaluate environmental goods and services, the key is to recognize that the relevant measure is the change in damage reductions brought about by a policy. These changes are called incremental benefits and can be defined as the reduction in health, ecological, and property damages associated with an environmental policy initiative. To identify these incremental benefits, the analyst must compare the actual or expected benefits to society after some policy is implemented to a baseline of current conditions.

These benefits are of two kinds primary and secondary. A primary environmental benefit is a damage reducing effect that is a direct consequence of implementing an environmental policy. Examples include human health benefits, a more stable ecosystem, and improved aesthetics where they all are direct outcome of environmental policy. Secondary environmental benefits are characterized as providing an indirect gain to society associated with the implementation of environmental policy. Examples could include higher worker productivity resulting from the primary benefit of improved health. The overall environmental benefits evaluations include (but are not necessarily limited to):

- Economic values (e.g., improved soil productivity and increased value of other natural resources, increase in international tourism),
- Environmental opportunities (e.g., increased recreational values of lakes, rivers, beaches and forests for the population), and
- The value of healthy life and well being of the population (e.g., life saved, avoidance of pain and suffering from illness, cleaner environment, etc.).

In this chapter the value of environmental goods and services is frequently expressed as a percentage of gross domestic product (GDP) in order to provide a sense of magnitude. It is also often useful to compare these values to GDP in order to assess their relative magnitude over time. If the value of environmental benefits as a percentage of GDP is growing over time, it suggests that the welfare increase from environmental improvement is growing faster than GDP.

The environmental benefits are valued conceptually since there are no explicit markets for environmental quality. Thus, we need to draw inferences about how society derives value or utility from the environmental goods. From a purely conceptual point, it is generally recognized that the society derives utility from environmental quality through two sources of value, user value, and existence value.

User value is the utility or benefit derived from physical use or access to an environmental well which consists of direct user value and indirect user value. Direct user value is derived directly from consuming services provided by an environmental good. Indirect user value is derived from indirect consumption of an environmental good. Existence value on the other hand is the utility or benefit received from an environmental good through its continuance as a good or service. Total valuation of environmental quality is the sum of user value and existence value, which is referred to as "Preservation Value."

METHODOLOGICAL APPROACHES TO MEASURING ENVIRONMENTAL BENEFITS

The process of estimating the value of environmental amenities involves a three-step process:

- Quantification of environmental amenities (e.g., monitoring of ambient air quality, river/lake/sea water quality, and soil pollution),
- Quantification of the consequences of a change in the amenities (e.g., changes in soil productivity, changes in forest density/growth, reduced natural resource based recreational activities, reduced tourism demand, and health impacts of air pollution); and
- Monetary valuation of the consequences (e.g., estimating the cost of soil productivity losses reduced recreational values, ill health).

Environmental science, natural resource science, health science, and epidemiology, economics (and frequently other sciences) are often used to quantify environmental degradation/conditions and its consequences. For valuation of the consequences, environmental economics, and natural resource economics are applied. This chapter has attempted to collate available information on the quantification of environmental valuation in the world, and information that has been available on the consequences of degradation.

In order to materially estimate the environmental qualities of various areas of the environment, the analysis and estimates are generally organized by means of the following categories: water; air; soil; waste; coastal zones; and cultural heritage and the global environment.

Techniques that assess responses immediately related to environmental changes are broadly categorized as direct and indirect methods. The direct method uses political referendum and contingent valuation methods (CVMs). Indirect methods are those that examine responses not about the environmental good itself, but about some set of market conditions related to it. This method uses averting expenditure, travel cost, and hedonic pricing methods (HPMs).

Direct Estimation Methods Under the Behavioral Linkage Approach

The behavioral linkage approach is based on the observations of behavior in the markets or consumer responses about hypothetical markets for environmental goods. This method estimates the environmental benefits according to responses or observed behaviors directly tied to environmental quality. There exist two broad categories in this approach:

The Political Referendum Method

This method uses voter responses to political referenda on environmental issues to make inferences about society's valuation of the associated benefits. Inferences drawn from a single referendum provide only a qualitative assessment about environmental benefits. To use the political referenda data to quantify incremental benefit, the analyst must monitor voter's reaction to a series of proposals that will convey how changes in environmental quality are valued. This method is often used to confirm findings of other estimation approaches or to test the predictive power of methods that use hypothetical markets.

The Contingent Valuation Method (CVM)

Economists consider the appropriate value of environmental amenities to be what an individual would be willing to pay to preserve it. This should reflect the value of foregone consumption and leisure time and the loss of contact with loved ones. Willingness to pay (WTP) can be estimated using the CVM. The CVM estimates the WTP or willingness to accept (WTA) for a change in the quantity and/or quality of a good by using survey techniques (Hoevenagel, 1994; Mitchell and Carson, 1989). In the questionnaire a hypothetical change is described and the respondents are asked directly for their WTP or WTA for the proposed change.

The CVM is used when the market data are unavailable or unreliable. Surveys are employed to inquire about individual's WTP for some environmental policy initiative. This method is favored by researchers of its applicability to variety of environmental goods and services because of its capacity to assess existence value as well as user value. The following are some of the applications of CVM.

- Measures society's WTP for water quality improvements
- Incremental benefits from air quality
- Value ecological benefits, such preventing endangered species.

Because CVM is a costly and complex method, studies have been conducted in only a limited number of countries for a limited number of environmental goods and services. In the United States and Europe numerous CVM studies have been conducted on the WTP for whole array of environmental amenities. Where WTP/WTA is not available for a particular country, one can estimate these values for risk reduction through "benefit transfer" of WTP studies performed outside that country.

Benefit transfer is an application of monetary values from a particular valuation study in one area to a policy decision setting in another geographic area (Navrud, 1999). When transferring values, it is important to know when data from other studies can be used and under what conditions. The value that people attach to environmental improvement depends on the type and magnitude of risk (low probability, high impact), the extent to which the risk is experienced voluntarily, on cultural settings, income, and the futurity of the risk. The most important factors for applying benefit transfer are the level of real per capita income, represented by purchasing power parity (PPP) per capita income, and the income elasticity of WTP. Where estimates of WTP for environmental amenities are not available, it is therefore necessary to transfer these estimates from countries where WTP studies have been conducted. When extrapolating estimates of WTP from one country to another, adjustments must be made for the effect of income on WTP. For instance, in transferring estimates from country A to country B the formula used is:

$$WTP_B = WTP_A [Income_B/Income_A]^\varepsilon$$

where ε represents the income elasticity of WTP (the percentage change in WTP corresponding to a 1% change in income). It should be acknowledged that there is considerable uncertainty regarding estimates of the income elasticity of WTP, as well as uncertainty regarding the estimates of WTP themselves. This uncertainty can be handled in two ways. First, several estimates of the income elasticity of WTP such as 1.0 and 0.4 are used. Holding WTP_A constant, the 0.4 elasticity results in a larger WTP estimate for the country in question than the 1.0 elasticity. Indeed, when WTP estimates from the US are transferred to another country using PPP adjusted income; an income elasticity of 0.4 implies a very large WTP for that country that is about the size of WTP in the US. Therefore WTP estimates based on an income elasticity of 0.4 as upper bound estimates, and estimates based on an income elasticity of 1.0 as central case estimates. Second, to handle uncertainty about the size of WTP, a conservative, lower bound estimates of the value of environmental amenities are being presented.

Indirect Estimation Methods Under the Behavioral Linkage Approach
The behavioral linkage approach explores the relationship that exists between the implicit prices of environmental characteristics that differentiate closely with related products. There are several methods where the marginal implicit price of environmental goods or services can be estimated.

Averting Expenditure Method (AEM)
The AEM method uses changes in an individual's spending on goods that are substitutes for a cleaner environment to estimate the value of environmental qualities and services. The motivation here is that exposure to pollution causes damages that negatively affect an individual's utility. There are two critical assumptions:
1. A systematic relationship can be identified between the quality of the overall environment and that of an individual's personal environment.
2. Goods may act as substitutes for environmental quality.

One drawback of AEM is jointness of production. Whereas some averting expenditures yield benefits beyond those associated with a cleaner environment. Although there are some disadvantages of using AEM, this approach has been used to value statistical life of wearing seat belts in automobiles in an effort to reduce mortality risk.

Travel Cost Method (TCM)
The TCM uses the complementary relationship between the quality of a natural resource and its recreational use value. A disadvantage of using TCM is that it is capable of estimating only user value and not existence value. Due to this limitation, the TCM is commonly used only to estimate the value of improvements to water bodies used mainly for recreational activity.

Hedonic Pricing Method (HPM)
The HPM uses the estimated hedonic or implicit price of an environmental attribute to assign value to policy driven improvements in the environment. It is based on the theory that a good or service is valued for the attributes or characteristics that it possesses. The HPM uses regression analysis to determine the implicit price of any environmental variable. Hedonic pricing estimates the WTP/WTA through:

- The difference in the value of the same property located in different areas with different environmental risks (property value differential) or
- The wage differential people are willing to pay (or accept) for a decrease (or increase) in risk of death related to a job.

This method of evaluation is used only due to the fact that it approaches the problem of monetizing incremental benefits in a logical way, directly using market prices. Unfortunately it relies on a fairly complicated empirical model. Also the model calls for extensive data or product characteristics, which are often unavailable or incomplete. The HPM has been used for estimating a variety of pollution control benefits.

In the following sections we present several approaches to estimating the value of environmental goods and services in global production. Our purpose is to present some economically logical valuations that might be included in future green GDP accounts. Most of the estimates are based on the assumption that a hypothetical market exists where these environmental amenities are exchanged and the population is being charged for its use. Zero on the lower end and gross world output at the upper end bound all of these estimates logically. The underlying message of this calculation is clear; including the value of ecosystem goods and services would dramatically alter current GDP estimates.

Valuing Local Plant Pharmacopoeias

In the last few decades there has been a renewed interest in the healing properties of nature, in particular the social and economic benefits of bioprospecting for pharmaceutical drug plants. It is well known that plants maintain a host of defensive secondary compounds saponins, phenols, terpenes, alkaloids, and others and that many are bioactive in humans. Over the centuries, many plant compounds have been tested and ultimately developed into modern pharmaceuticals. Quinine derived from the bark of the Peruvian cinchona tree (*Cinchona ledgeriana*) is used to treat malaria. Pilocarpine from the Brazilian herb (*Pilocarpus jaborandi*) is used to treat glaucoma. Diosgenin from Mexican yams (*Diascorides* ssp.) is used as a female contraceptive. In the most celebrated example, the alkaloids vincristine and vinblastine derived from the Madagascar periwinkle (*Catharanthus roseus*) were developed into a cure for Hodgkin's disease and childhood leukemia (Balick and Cox, 1996; Soejarto and Farnsworth, 1989). More recently, several plant derived products, including the protein MAP30 from the bitter melon (*Momordica charantia*) and prostratin from the Samoan mamala tree (*Homalanthus nutans*) have shown anti-HIV activity in *in vitro* studies Cox (2000); Kell (2001); and Myers (1997) estimates that 30,000 American lives are saved each year by anti-cancer drugs derived from plants.

The developing world represents a particularly rich source of potential medicinal species. Secondary compounds are more concentrated in tropical regions, as is the biological diversity of plant species (Levin, 1976; Pitman and Jorgensen, 2002). Just as important, the traditional societies that sustain these cognitive relations with nature are much more likely to survive in developing as opposed to industrial countries.

Economic projections of the potential value of medicinal plant resources, both to private pharmaceutical corporations and to society in general, underscore the value of this endeavor (Adger et al., 1995; Myers, 1997). According to (Soejarto and Farnsworth, 1989), 25% of all prescription drugs sold in the US in the 1980s contained compounds that were extracted from plants, totaling over US $8 billion in annual retail sales. A few years later recalculated this figure. Noting again that one-quarter of drugs currently on the US market were originally derived from plant compounds, and multiplying this by the current prescription sales in the US (US $62 billion/yr), he estimated that the value of plant-derived drugs averages US $15.5 billion/yr.

Principe (1991) reconsidered these calculations in terms of societal benefits of potential new plant-derived drugs. First, he estimated that roughly 500,000 Americans contract cancer per year. He then notes that anti-cancer drugs, of which 40% are of plant-derived origin; cure about 15% of these cases. This yields about 30,000 Americans per year who owe their continued existence to plant-derived drugs. He then considered the "value of life" of each of these individuals, and used the average figure of US $8 million. Multiplying this figure by the 30,000 saved lives yields a total economic value to American individuals of US $240 billion/yr.

The economic value of potential drug plants can be examined as well by considering individual drug discoveries. In the 1960s, the Eli Lilly Pharmaceutical Corporation began examining the pharmacological properties of the Madagascar periwinkle (*Catharanthus roseus*). The discovery of the efficacy of two of its 76 alkaloids vincristine and vinblastine in the treatment of acute lymphoblastic leukemia, lymphosarcoma, Hodgkin's disease, and other tumors, was a major catalyst for renewed interest by pharmacological companies in plant derived medicines. The idea to explore the medicinal properties of this particular species was provided by a traditional healer, who recommended its use to treat diabetes (Balick and Cox, 1996). Sales from this single drug by Eli Lilly are estimated to generate US $100 million/yr.

Finally, what is the potential value of the many as yet undiscovered drug plants? The case of tropical forests species is instructive. It is estimated that there are between 310,000 and 422,000 plant species on Earth (Pitman and Jorgensen, 2002). Of this total, roughly 125,000 are thought to inhabit tropical forest landscapes. On average, three plant parts (usually leaves, bark, and roots) per species are tested. There are, on average, two extraction methods used for each plant part, yielding a total number of plant extractions of 750,000 total extractions (125,000 × 2 × 3). Pharmacological screens of plant extractions average between 50 and 75. This produces 38–56 million possible screens from the total tropical flora of the world. On average, between one in 50,000 and one in 1 million screens produces a commercial drug. Applying this success rate to the total number of possible screens (38–56 million) yields a general figure of roughly 375 commercially valuable species waiting to be discovered. There have, however, already been 47 drugs produced from tropical species. Subtracting these previous discoveries from 375 yields distribution, and interest rates, the estimated economic value of each of these undiscovered species is US $94 million (Mendelsohn and Balick, 1995).

As noted by many ethnobotanists, these potential drug discoveries are threatened by an array of factors. Habitat loss has been linked to decreasing access to traditional plant medicines in Samoa, Kenya, eastern Brazil, (Cox, 1999; Jungerius, 1998; Voeks, 1997). In other locations, such as Sierra Leone, Cameroon, and India, valuable medicinal taxa are declining due to excessive plant extraction to supply national and international markets (Anyinam, 1995; Lebbie, and Guries, 1995; Pandey and Bisaria, 1998). The most pressing threat to medicinal plants and their knowledge profiles, however, appears to be declining medicinal knowledge among rural communities (Cox, 2000). Religious conversion (Caniago, and Siebert, 1998; Voeks and Sercombe, 2000), entrance of western medicine (Milliken, et al., 1992; Urgent, 2000), economic improvement (Benz et al., 2000; Voeks and Nyawa, 2001), and enhanced access to formal education (Voeks and Leony, 2004) have all been linked to declining knowledge of nature.

Economics of Petty Resource Extraction

Petty resource extraction represents one of the least explored land use options for developing countries. It is based on the idea that collection of wild, non-timber products by rural people fruits, nuts, latex, fibers, rattans, medicinal, and others represents a viable alternative for natural area protection. Long perceived as a symptom of "underdevelopment," and reflective of past boom-and-bust economic cycles, petty extractive activities are most often viewed by the developing world as a form of economic retardation and backwardness.

Beginning in the 1980s, environmental scientists and economists began to reconsider the possible value of the "extractive option" for nature conservation. Most of these efforts have been directed at tropical countries, where traditional extractive activities have a long pedigree, and where ongoing environmental destruction is acute. The reasoning is that, under the best of circumstances, petty extraction:

- Generates revenue at the local and national level,

- Leads to minimal levels of environmental damage,
- Maintains and supports the traditional livelihoods of local rural populations, and
- Encourages local people to serve as de facto nature stewards.

An example of this activity comes from the eastern forests of Brazil, where Voeks (1996a) investigated the ecology and extractive economy of the piassava palm (*Attalea funifera*). This species has supplied durable leaf fiber for the production of ropes, roofing thatch, and brooms and brushes for at least 2 centuries. Although originally collected by cutting and killing the palm, during the 20th century forest collectors switched to a sustainable method of removing fiber on an annual basis. This activity appears to have minimal impact on forest diversity. A study carried out in a single piassava extractive area Voeks (1996b) revealed a high level of floristic diversity (Simpson Ds = 0.78). Moreover, economic revenue had steadily climbed over most of this century. From a low of roughly US $200,000 in sales in 1910, passive production had climbed to nearly US $20 million by 1990.

The most successful example of the role of extraction in nature conservation comes from Amazonian Brazil. Since the mid-19th century, this region has been prized for its natural population of Brazilian rubber trees (*Hevea brasiliensis*). Many thousands of rural rubber tappers base their livelihoods on the collection and sale of latex from the forest. Responding to increasing levels of forest removal for the creation of cattle ranches, rubber tappers, and environmentalists encouraged the Brazilian government to establish "extractive reserves." This proposal was finally given serious attention after the assassination of Chico Mendez, leader of the rubber tappers, by a local cattle rancher.

Today there are four other rubbers extractive reserves, where latex and extractive products continue to support the local population, but where forest removal is prohibited. There are a limited number of economic studies on the viability of extractive economies. In a classic study carried out in Peru, Peters et al. (1989) and censuses the economically valuable extractive products in a one-hectare plot of forest. Seventy-two species had market value 60 timber species, 11 food species, and one latex species. Utilizing the mean retail value of the non-timber extractive products, including the cost of labor and transportation, they calculated that the net present value (NPV) of fruit and latex collection was US $6,330/ha of forest. Although the immediate value of timber extraction was higher, the long recovery time necessary for forest trees to grow back to harvestable size translated to a relatively low NPV of US $490. Although there were methodological errors in this calculation, and non-use ecosystem good and services were omitted from the calculation, it suggests nevertheless that extraction should be considered as an economic option to habitat destruction.

In another economic analysis, this in Belize Balick and Mendelsohn (1992) examined the extractive value of plants used by locals in traditional healing and sold in local markets. They collected the medicinal species in two small plots, one of 0.28 ha, the other of 0.25 ha. The two sites yielded 86.4 and 358.4 kg (dry weight biomass), respectively. Projecting this to a full hectare yielded 308 and 1433 kg, respectively. The estimated gross revenue from these two sites was US $864 and $4,014, respectively.

Including estimated labor and transportation costs into the calculation yielded values of US $564 and $3,054/ha. The authors compared these values to alternative land uses clearance for agriculture (corn, beans, and squash), and pine plantation development, which were estimated to yield US $339 and $3184/ha, respectively. The results of this study suggest that allowing natural areas to be deployed as medicinal plant extraction zones compares favorably with more destructive forms of land use. Godoy et al. (1993) reviewed economic analyses of extractive enterprises done to date, and found them lacking in several ways. They note that each study uses different economic assessment methods, none includes the value of both animals and plants, and all assume without evidence that these activities are environmentally sustainable. They suggested the following methods: randomized village samples, accurate biomass weighing systems, photographing species that cannot be collected, and using GPS and GIS techniques for field mapping of extractive zones. Regarding economic analysis methods, they recommended: using actual local market value of goods (including barter value), distinguishing goods that are consumed in the village from those transported to markets, adjusting for relevant taxes and subsidies, including cost of material, labor, and discount rate, and including value of non-use ecosystem services in the calculation.

In a later publication, incorporated most of these suggestions in a study of extraction in rural Honduras villages. They worked in two villages, identifying the value of fish, game, and other forest products gathered in the vicinity. The two villages averaged US $91,041 and $3,920, respectively, per year in extractive products. Calculating this per unit hectare yielded figures of US $2.50 and $9.05. These values are much lower than those achieved in earlier studies, suggesting that other studies may have over-valued the extractive enterprise in their respective areas. It also underscores the economic motivation for local populations to switch to more destructive land uses, such as agriculture and forestry, which produce higher immediate economic returns.

Whether or not petty extraction represents a viable alternative to destructive land use is problematic. Research on the topic has produced mixed results. Importantly, none of these studies incorporated ecosystem values, such as carbon sequestration, erosion control, and others, that tend to benefit the global rather than local community. If non-use ecosystem values are to be incorporated into rural economic assessment, it seems clear that global stakeholders, who are likely to accrue most of its benefits, must bear some of the costs of protecting rural ecosystems in the developing world.

Ecotourism and Nature's Economic Services

Ecotourism is widely touted as a viable development strategy for the developing world. It can be defined as "responsible travel to natural areas that conserves the environment and sustains the well-being of local people" (Honey, 1999). In addition to appreciating the natural qualities of the region dramatic landscapes, native wildlife, and endemic plants visitors are often drawn as well to observe local cultural traditions. While often based on romanticized notions of the relations between rural people and nature, ecotourists nevertheless often wish to observe how traditional societies live with nature their subsistence agricultural methods, hunting and fishing techniques, religious ceremonies, and healing practices.

The allure of ecotourism for developing countries is that:
- It requires minimal infrastructural investment,
- It causes limited environmental impact compared to other options, and
- It generates significant foreign exchange. Indeed, the tourist industry has exploded in recent decades.

In 2000, there were an estimated 702 million international tourists, generating an estimated US $621 billion in revenue. Roughly 8% of the world's population is employed, directly or indirectly, in tourism-related activities. Ecotourism, which represents the fastest growing tourism sector, generates an estimated US $50 billion in global revenue in 2000 (Fennell, 1999). In Tanzania, where ecotourism represents the largest source of revenue, gross receipts totaled US $322 million in 1996. Kenya realized $502 million in gross receipts in 1997, while South Africa received $2.2 billion in earnings in 1995 (Honey, 1999). Clearly, there is a significant economic motive to embrace ecotourism development.

Under the best of circumstances, ecotourism provides benefits at the local, regional, national, and international levels. At the local level, people benefit as visitors purchase locally produced foods and crafts, lodge in locally owned hostels, employ local guides, and otherwise encourage local people to remain in rural settings rather than migrating to cities. At the regional level, jobs are produced and locally produced goods are marketed. At the national level, tax revenues and user fees are collected, foreign exchange is generated, and capital investment is captured rather than exported to the developing world. Finally, because ecotourism encourages nature protection in the developing world, globally significant ecosystem services are protected rather than destroyed.

In spite of these potential economic benefits, ecotourism development is also accompanied by a host of social and economic challenges. For example, Costa Rica established the Tortugeira National Park in the 1970s in order to stimulate ecotourism and to protect rare and endangered sea turtles that nest along the immediate coast. Although these environmental and economic expectations were realized, the impact on local communities was mostly negative. Land speculation and the rising cost of living forced most of the original local population to migrate away from the area (Place, 1991). In India, national park expansion to meet the needs of ecotourists has occurred at the expense of local farmer access to land.

Moreover, "leakage" or revenue plagues many ecotourism efforts. While the host country bears most of the costs of ecotourism, it is often foreign companies that realize most of the profits. This is particularly true as more and more ecotourists opt for package tours organized in their home country staying in foreign-owned hotels, eating and drinking imported luxury goods, and employing foreign guide services. Culture change can be a particularly insidious dimension of ecotourist development. Malaysia, Thailand, and elsewhere, tourist attraction to more exotic elements of the local religion and culture has led a form of "cultural co modification." Tribal societies in Thailand dress up in traditional attire to meet the expectations of visitors, while in Malaysia and Brunei Darussalam the interior tribal groups perform dances and other cultural activities at times and place to meet the needs of tourists. Over time, the cultural significance of long-established rituals and ceremonies is defined more by its attraction for visitors than by its original cultural meaning.

National efforts to better capture foreign revenue include: collection of user fees (e.g., park entrance), concession fees charged to tour companies, royalties from souvenir sales, taxes, and donations. Bhutan, for example, charges US $200 per day for foreign visitors, and limited annual visitation to only 5,000 visitors. Rwanda charges a flat rate of US $250 for a 60-min visit to their mountain gorilla preserve. But these extreme models are not likely to be repeatable in less sought-after locales.

The small Central American nation of Costa Rica has banked heavily on ecotourism as a means of advancing nature protection and generating sorely needed foreign revenue. Possessing a high degree of natural values, from coral reefs and beaches to tropical rainforests and highland cloud forests, Costa Rica also has the burden of a high level of rural poverty and unemployment. Since the 1990s, the principal national revenue has shifted from coffee cultivation to ecotourism. With a total population of only three million people, Costa Rica now hosts over one million tourist visitors per year (Honey, 1999).

The evolution of one of its various parks, Monteverde National Park, underscores the economic impact of tourist development. With on 471 visitors in 1974, the park had increased visitation to 26,600 by 1990. Utilizing the travel cost method to measure the economic value of ecotourism, Menkhaus and Lober (1996) determined that the cost of travel for ecotourists ranged from a low of US $800 to a high of $8,000. Multiplying the average travel cost to ecotourists, US $1150, and assuming that ecotourists visited other areas of Costa Rica, the determined that the value of ecotourism to Monteverde National Park was on the order of US $4.5 million/yr.

In the Cuyabeno Wildlife Reserve in Ecuador, Wunder (2000) examined economic benefits to various local communities. Presently, about 5,000 ecotourists arrive at the protected area per year. Using semi-structured interviews, demographic studies, and cash and subsistence evaluations, Wunder (2000) examined the relative success of five separate ethnic groups in capturing capital. Unlike other studies, this author discovered that significant economic benefits were accrued by the various local groups. One group realized US $49,430 during a single year, representing 100% of their total cash income, while another group received $31,753, representing 97.5% of their cash income for the year. In this case, ecotourism development led to positive economic benefits for the local communities.

As a strategy for developing countries, ecotourism provides divergent prospects and problems. In many cases, significant levels of foreign revenue are realized at the local and national level. Nevertheless, strategies need to be pursued in order to diminish the effects of revenue leakage.

The Social and Cultural Impacts of Nature's Goods and Services: A Global Assessment

Economic assessment of the global significance of ecosystem services requires a division of the Earth's ecosystems into a logical set of geographical units. To simplify the bewildering diversity of ecosystems, aquatic, and terrestrial, the approach taken in is to work at the biome level. Coastal and marine biomes include:

- Open ocean,
- Estuaries,
- Sea grass beds,
- Coral reefs, and
- Continental shelves.

Terrestrial biomes included:
- Tropical forest,
- Temperate/boreal forest,
- Grassland/rangeland,
- Wetlands,
- Lakes/rivers,
- Deserts, and
- Tundra.

Some of these ecosystems have been the subject of environmental economic analysis; others have received no attention whatsoever. This obviously biases the final results, and should serve as motivation to expand research efforts into these under-represented subsets of nature.

Although ecosystem services overlap considerably, for convenience these are reduced to seventeen classes of goods and services.

These include:
- Gas regulation (e.g., maintaining the CO_2/O_2 balance);
- Climate regulation (e.g., precipitation regimes);
- Disturbance regulation (e.g., flood control);
- Water regulation (e.g., irrigation);
- Water supply (e.g., access to potable water);
- Erosion control (e.g., loss of topsoil);
- Soil formation (e.g., rock weathering);
- Nutrient cycling (e.g., nitrogen fixation);
- Waste treatment (e.g., pollution control);
- Pollination (e.g., crop reproduction);
- Biological control (e.g., sustaining keystone species);
- Refugia (e.g., waterfowl habitat);
- Food production (e.g., fishing);
- Raw materials (e.g., lumber);
- Gene resources (e.g., locally-endemic cultigens);
- Recreation (e.g., ecotourism); and
- Cultural (e.g., aesthetics).

What follows is a sample of the ecosystem goods and services that are rendered by nature, a sample of the threats to these values, and an attempt at economic valuation of each.

Open Oceans

Open oceans represent the largest of Earth's biomes, with an area of 33,200 ha × 10^8. These areas are particularly important on a global scale in regulating gas exchange. This includes especially the production of oxygen from surface plankton; as well a sink for carbon dioxide, the principal compound involved in anthropogenically forced global warming. Open oceans also provide important zones of nutrient cycling, particularly for nitrogen and phosphorus. Of course, the ocean is also a major contributor of fish to the global market place. The estimated economic value of these goods and service is US $252/ha/yr. Multiplied by the total area of open oceans; this translates to an annual value of US $8.3 billion.

Coastal Marine Environments

The interface between land and water represents an especially important resource and ecosystem service zone. Upwelling zones, such as off the coast of Peru, Namibia, and California provide the most productive commercial fish resource zones in the world. These zones are also noted for their recreational value to boating, swimming, surfing, and sport fishing. Coral reefs likewise represent a high value material and cultural resource in the coastal zone. They are important sources of waste treatment, biological control, recreation, and research. They are also important sources of commercial fish and lobster, including aquarium fish. Although often harvested by unsustainable means using dynamite and cyanide poisoning, the aquarium fish trade is estimated to yield between US $20 and $40 million dollars in revenue per year (Hoagland et al., 1995). Summing the value of these and other coastal environments yields an estimated value of US $4,052/ha/yr, or a total of US $12.3 trillion/yr for all coastal marine ecosystem goods and services.

Tropical Forests

Tropical forests cover roughly 1,900 ha × 10^8. Given their high levels of plant productivity and extreme levels of biodiversity, this biome generates significantly valuable ecosystem services. They are especially important in terms of climate regulation, erosion control, nutrient cycling, raw materials (especially hardwoods), and tourism. Deforestation in the tropical zone has been implicated in global warming, due to release of carbon dioxide from burning, as well as regional shifts in rainfall, evapo-transpiration, and temperature. Krutilla (1991) used the replacement cost method to estimate the economic value of tropical forests as sinks for carbon dioxide. He determined that replacement costs for all tropical forests would run to about US $223 billion/yr. Combining these values with the plant and animal existence values, tropical genetic resources are estimated to be worth US $41 billion/yr. The total economic value of all tropical forest goods and services averages US $3.8 trillion/yr.

Temperate/Boreal Forests

Temperate forests occur from subtropical zones to the edge of the arctic. They cover an estimated 2,955 ha × 10^8. Primary ecosystem services include climate regulation, waste treatment, food production, recreation, and forest raw materials. Although often managed under conditions not considered to be sustainable on a long-term basis, most temperate forests are managed with this objective. On a global scale, the economic value of timber resources alone is estimated at between US $10 and $73/ha/yr. Calculated for all timberlands, the global economic value of timber harvest is roughly US $26 billion/yr. This figure included WTP figures for recreational forest habitat. Determined, for example, that the average California resident was willing to pay US $73 to protect the forest habitat of the northern spotted owl. This translated to a statewide figure of US $760 million, far more than the estimated market value of the timber. In this case, endangered species protection appears to outweigh the public's interest in raw materials. Taking into consideration all of the economic goods and services provided by temperate zone forests, their global value is placed at US $894 billion/yr.

Grasslands/Rangelands
Grasslands and associated shrub lands comprise roughly 3,989 ha × 10^8. These are located mostly between 200 and 450 north and south latitude. Their principal ecosystem services include erosion control, food production, waste treatment, and nature tourism (in Africa). Given the high productivity of the soils, mostly moll sols, this biome represents the breadbasket of many civilizations. Burke et al. (1989) examined the economic value of grasslands as sinks for carbon dioxide. They determined that the average grassland that was converted to agriculture lost the ability to absorb 1.0 kg/m of carbon dioxide. Assuming a cost of CO_2 emissions (as a factor in global warming) of US $0.10/ha, they estimated the global value of CO_2 fixation by grasslands at US $7 billion/yr. Including all relevant ecosystem services, grasslands are valued at US $906 billion/yr.

Wetlands/Floodplains
Wetlands and floodplains represent a particularly important source of nature's services. Although constituting only 165 ha × 10^8 ha in area, these ecosystems provide a host of essential environmental values. These include gas regulation, waste treatment, environmental disturbance regulation, water supply, wildlife refugia, recreation, and others. The presence of riparian vegetation along streams and rivers, for example, dramatically diminishes the impact of natural flood cycles. In the US, the estimated economic value of the avoided costs of flood control damage reaches US $7,240/ha/yr. Wetlands are equally important as sources of natural pollution control, and as refuges for endangered and threatened plants and animals. Pollution control services of wetlands in the US are estimated at US $1,659/ha/yr. The total global value of wetlands and floodplains is estimated to be US $4.9 trillion/yr.

Lakes and Rivers
Inland lakes and rivers are often centers of human population. Although they cover only 200 ha × 10^8 of the Earth's surface, they include an array of essential goods and services. These include water regulation, water supply, waste treatment, recreation, and food. These ecosystems have in many cases suffered massive alteration, often dramatically diminishing their natural services. Once representing an important commercial fishery, the Aral Sea has lost 60% of its area in the last 30 years due to irrigation

withdrawal. Lake Chad in West Africa has suffered a similar fate, with withdrawal for irrigation reducing the area extent by over 90% in the previous 2 decades. Considering all relevant environmental services, lakes, and rivers are calculated to generate on average US $1.7 trillion annually.

Deserts and Tundra

Deserts and tundra cover 1,925 ha $\times 10^8$ and 743 ha $\times 10^8$, respectively. They clearly provide significant environmental services; however there have been no attempts to date to quantify them. They are thus omitted from the global calculation.

Total Value of Nature's Services

Combining the calculated value of ecosystem goods and services for all the world's biomes yields a mean estimate of US $33 trillion/yr. This figure ranges from a low of US $16 trillion/yr to a high of US $54 trillion/yr. Comparing it to total world GNP reveals the significance of this sum. Using 1977 figures, ecosystem goods and services on a global scale are estimated to contribute 1.8 times more than the total global GNP. Nature's services clearly need to be integrated into cost-benefit analyses of environmental modification.

KEYWORDS

- **Ecosystem services**
- **Ecotourism**
- **Environmental economics**
- **Non-timber products**
- **Pharmacopoeia**

ACKNOWLEDGMENTS

This chapter was presented in Spring 2003 at the "International Workshop on Environmental Economics: An Essential Tool for Sustainable Development" in Tehran, Iran. The authors would like to give special thanks to Dr. Majid Abbaspour and Dr. Farideh Atabi for organizing the workshop.

Chapter 2

Legal Implications for Nature-based Tourism

H. Soleimanpour

INTRODUCTION

Nature-based tourism (NBT) as an effective instrument for sustainable use of biodiversity is an interesting issue to be studied in order to evaluate response of international community to the interaction between developmental and environmental pillars of sustainable development. Various international endeavors have been carried out with considerable outcomes to address NBT in different forms and manifestations. As a result, the international community has attained many successful achievements and valuable experiences. There is an urgent need for an internationally accepted instrument to address the existing gaps and overlaps appropriately. Such an instrument should respond to lake of adequate environmental and developmental rules and regulations at international scale. Careful study of major international environmental and developmental achievements related to NBT could provide the international community with an appropriate legal framework to address such an environmentally fragile, economically viable, and a culturally sensitive issue. The NBT, as a new phenomenon in the relationship between environment and development, has potential adverse effects if it is not properly planned and implemented. However, well planned NBT could while it is recognized as highly instrumental in conservation and sustainable use of the biodiversity. To this end phenomenon, the main endeavors of international environmental and developmental instruments should be reviewed. This review should focus on the post Rio activities and policymaking of these instruments in order to understand their approaches, main achievements, gaps and overlaps, and to evaluate their contribution in regulating NBT activities. On one hand NBT has its roots, in the tourism industry with more than 11% contribution to the world's GDP as one of the most appropriate means of generating income and employment in many developing countries while providing nearly 8% of the total global workforce, (one in 16 jobs and 7% of capital investment) (Shackleford, 1995; WTO/OMT, 1998). The NBT is an important component of the worldwide international and domestic tourism industry, which has been expanding rapidly over the past two decades, and further growth is expected in the future. Overall, depending on the region, nature, and wildlife tourism accounts for 20–40% of international tourism (Giongo, 1993). The scale of this kind of tourism is even larger if domestic tourism is taken into consideration. On the other hand its roots are in the conservation and sustainable use of environmental features including its biodiversity and aesthetic values. Therefore, NBT is a major issue on the interaction of developmental and environmental issues. It should be properly governed to maximize its benefit to local communities and minimize its adverse effects on nature.

Although tourism was not in the agenda of Earth Summit in Rio 1992, the Commission on Sustainable Development (CSD) as the UN body responsible for the implementation of Agenda 21 in its seventh session in 1999 and based on the final outcome of Rio+5, made a landmark decision to establish an international work program on sustainable tourism. The decision 7/3 opened up a new political space at the international and national levels to bring tourism development in line with the commitments undertaken in Rio.

In the 2002 World Summit on Sustainable Development (WSSD), the achievements of the so-called Rio Process were evaluated and new strategies planned. Such strategies were needed given the failure of the international community to implement most of the promises and hopes of Rio, not least in tourism, which in recent years has become one of the world's leading industries. The WSSD offered an opportunity for a re-oriented tourism to be integrated into the strategies for sustainable development. This re-orientation of the tourism industry towards environmentally and socially responsible behaviors and leisure activities, is needed for sustainable development, but it faces many challenges.

One of major challenges in the re-orientation era of NBT is the lack of a comprehensive, integrative, and cross-sectoral policy making framework for a new approach of tourism. Such an approach needs a coherent, responsible, and equitable cooperation among all stakeholders, including local communities, indigenous peoples, political and/or local authorities, the tourism industry, tourists, and civil society. Benefiting from the outcome of two major international summits in 2002, the Quebec Summit on International Year of Ecotourism and WSSD, this chapter tries to find out the appropriate way to address NBT by introducing basic legal forms to regulate and coordinate as far as possible the international behavior on NBT.

METHODOLOGY

The methodology used in this research is based on international archival research, containing detailed analysis of international documents on instruments and organizations for development such as the CSD and United Nations Conference on Trade and Development (UNCTAD) as well as international environmental agreements and instruments United Nations Environment Programme (UNEP), the Convention on Biological Diversity (CBD), and some relevant international, regional, intergovernmental, or UN specialized agencies like World Tourism Organization (WTO/OMT), and European Commission. Moreover, the outcome of major UN conferences and relevant international agreements has been studied. Archival research has been complemented by data gathering, reviewing the most recent and successful experience of relevant international organizations and the collection of information pertaining to NBT. From legal point of view, major principle in international law, particularly environmental law, has been studied. More than 55 principles and rules of international law reflected in treaties, binding acts of international organizations, state practices, and soft law commitments has been gathered and made contribution to compile final suggestion.

Definition of NBT

The definition of tourism was proposed by the WTO in 1991 and officially adopted by the United Nations Statistical Commission in 1993. It states that "Tourism comprises the activities of persons travelling to and staying in places outside their usual environment for not more than one consecutive year for leisure, business and other purposes" (Holden, 2000).

Many academicians in 90s emphasized the behavioral and impact aspects of tourism. As an example, Bull defined tourism as a human activity, which encompasses human behavior, use of resources, and interaction with other people, economies, and environments (Bull, 1991). The concept of sustainable tourism was introduced in the late 1980s. It was the tourism industry's reaction to the Brundtland Report on our common future as an outcome of World Commission on Environment and Development (WCED) in 1987 (Brundtland website, 1987). Having in mind the notion of sustainability in WCED, sustainable tourism development can be defined as tourism that meets the need of the current generations without compromising the ability of future generations to meet their needs (Weaver, 2001).

The definition of NBT differs from specialized tourism components such as ecotourism or adventure tourism (Whelan, 1991) due to the activities involving the direct use of a destination's natural resources as either a setting or an attraction (Ceballos-Lascurian, 1997; Fennell, 1999; Goodwin, 1996).

Weaver and Lawton (2001) defined NBT as a form of tourism that maintain a dependent, enhancive, or incidental relationship with the natural environment, or some aspect thereof, in terms of its utilization of attractions and/or setting. It includes the 3S tourism (sea, sand, and sun), adventure tourism, ecotourism, consumptive tourism, captive, and health tourism as various forms of NBT (Table 1). As far as this chapter concerns, NBT's main characteristics are; (a) community-based tourism,

Table 1. The outstanding achievements of the NBT through decision 7/3.

Categories	Issues	Descriptions
First category	Concepts	This category mainly focused on definition
Second category	Strategy setting and policymaking	This category includes the creation of a framework and instruments, the drafting and implementing of a master plan, locally integrated planning approaches, and design with nature in mind
Third category	Socio-cultural Issues	This category includes consultation with major groups and local educational initiatives and responsible tourism commumtles, behaviour, tourism information awareness, sexual exploitation, in- flight education videos, and art and music
Fourth category	Economic Issues	This category includes the eradication of poverty, and small and medium size enterprise iss1:1es
Fifth category	Environmental Issues	This category includes voluntary initiatives, eco-efficiency, waste reduction and management, the development of indicators, and coastal zone fragility
Sixth category	Procedural Issues	This category includes capacity building, the dissemination of information, the exchange of information on services, the research and study on needed areas, and the establishment of global networks
Seventh category	Institutional Issues	This category includes international cooperation, an ad-hoc informal open-ended working group on tourism, the implementation and enforcement of standards and guidelines related to tourism, the development of guiding principles for sustainable tourism development, international guidelines on tourism activity in sensitive areas, and a supporting Global Code of Ethics for tourism

(b) non-consumptive form of tourism, (c) low impacts on the environment and culture of the destination, (d) compatibility with the carrying capacity and economic factors of destinations, (e) designed to fulfill visitors' desires, (f) implemented in a learning environment.

Therefore, NBT means any form of sustainable nature and community-based, non-consumptive, low environmental, and cultural impact tourism according to the carrying capacity and economic generation of the destination, which fulfills the wishes and aspirations of all kinds of visitors in a learning environment.

LITERATURE REVIEW

Agenda 21 did not pay direct attention to sustainable tourism development as one of the leading industries. It is because of the novelty of such an industry and the traditional procedures of UN developmental bodies, which normally need sufficient time to consider a new and emerging phenomenon in their agenda of work. As a result of such circumstances, sustainable tourism development was ignored on the working agenda of the international community and thus the appropriate action on this important issue, in which all three pillars of sustainable development are involved, was postponed. The CSD as a UN body responsible for the follow up of Agenda 21 addressed sustainable NBT, first in the framework of sustainable development of Small Islands Developing States and then in the context of the working program of its seventh session in 1999.

A couple of years back, the environmental instruments of international community, particularly UNEP, recognized the importance of issues and tried to address such need. One of the institutional initiatives of UNEP regarding sustainable (nature-based) tourism is the UNEP draft principle on sustainable tourism, which was initiated in 1995 and after a series of negotiations presented to the CSD7. With its approval the final draft was published in early 2000. The main intention of the UNEP principle is to provide a framework on which international environmental agreements related to tourism can further develop their work programs. The time of launching the UNEP initiative coincided with CSD7 and the adoption of decision 7/3. The content of the principle, as an international reference document, demonstrates its own capacity to deal with NBT. The principle approach is towards environmental considerations in contrast with decision 7/3 and may be regarded as an environmental approach to tackle NBT.

One of the innovations of the UNEP principle on sustainable tourism is formatting of the titles and categorizing issues in a useful and concrete manner. It contains four main groups of subjects and each one examines related sub-titles. However, in the developmental institutions, CSD7 approved the landmark decision of sustainable tourism in its decision 7/3 in February 1999 (CSD website, 1999).

Despite many achievements, decision 7/3 fails to address several important issues related to sustainable tourism in general and NBT in particular. The main conceptual shortcomings of decision 7/3 include the lack of a comprehensive clarification of the rights and obligations of the major stockholders, the lack of a comprehensive provision on policy and planning including integrated planning, and environmental and development policies. Other major shortcomings of decision 7/3 are the lack of tools and policies for implementation and coordination mechanisms such as EIAs, monitoring and reporting procedures, carrying capacity issues, Clearing House Mechanism (CHM), and ESTs.

The main procedural shortcoming of the CSD on sustainable tourism development as well as NBT is the lack of adequate follow-up. Procedure although the CSD7 on several occasions refers to its next sessions for considering reports on the progress and implementation of specific parts of decision 7/3, none of the post-CSD7 sessions consider tourism substantially. Although decision 7/3 has not been followed up adequately by other relevant organizations, it has shown the need for the international community to address procedural setting and the legal framework on which sustainable tourism development and particularly NBT are to be based. At the same times, the UN General Assembly for reviewing of the implementation progress of Agenda 21, in its special session (Rio+5) tried to deal with Sustainable tourism and for the first time addressed the issue at a summit level very briefly. The NBT was recognized as an issue which needs to be addressed by relevant international forums including WSSD. Thereafter in 2002, WSSD considered sustainable tourism development among the issues interlinked with the protection of the environment, poverty alleviation, and social concerns of the local community. Chapter 41 of the Plan of Implementation refers to promoting sustainable tourism development, including non-consumptive and NBT/ecotourism, as a means to increase the benefits of tourism resources for the population in host communities while maintaining the cultural and environmental integrity of those communities and enhancing the protection of ecologically sensitive areas and the natural heritage. This Chapter also proposed a plan of action for sustainable tourism development (WSSD website, 2002).

The most direct actions recommended by Chapter 41 are to "develop programmes, including education and training programmes, that encourage people to participate in eco-tourism, enable indigenous and local communities to develop and benefit from eco tourism, and enhance stakeholder cooperation in tourism development and heritage preservation, in order to improve the protection of the environment, natural resources and cultural heritage."

This Chapter 41 made references to two recent achievements at the international level to formulate the international activities towards sustainable tourism development; the Quebec Declaration and the Global Code of Ethics for Tourism. The Quebec Declaration on Ecotourism is the result of 3 consecutive year of preparatory programs with 18 preparatory meetings at the international level before and during the International Year of Ecotourism in 2002. The Declaration is the outcome of a multi-stakeholder dialog, although it is not a negotiated document. As stated in the preamble of the Declaration, its main purpose is the formation of a preliminary agenda and a set of recommendations for the development of ecotourism activities in the context of sustainable development (WTO/OMT website, 2002). The Declaration produced 49 recommendations to governments, the private sector, non-governmental organizations, community-based associations, academic and research institutions, intergovernmental organizations, international financial institutions, development assistance agencies, and indigenous and local communities as well as WSSD. Another reference guideline of Chapter 41 of Plan of Implementation of WSSD on sustainable NBT is the Global

Code of Ethics for tourism (WTO/OMT website 1, 2000). The Code is the result of a follow up to the 1997 WTO General Assembly resolution in Istanbul. After 2 year of consecutive and extensive consultation, the WTO General Assembly meeting in Santiago in October 1999 approved the Code unanimously. The Articles of the Code outline the "rules of the game" for destinations, governments, tour operators, developers, travel agents, workers, and travelers themselves. As Francesco Frangialli, Secretary General of the WTO pointed out (WTO/OMT website 2, 2000), the Code sets a frame of reference for the responsible and sustainable development of world tourism at the dawn of the new millennium.

Needs and Characteristics of International Instrument on NBT

As it is obvious, the main challenge facing international community is to move from the existing ad hoc approaches, to an instrument that can integrate the current social, economic and environmental programs, funds and initiatives, and evolve new patterns for management of NBT in a more systematic and dynamic way. The main arguments behind the need for such an instrument are:

1. to provide the legal framework to support the integration of the various aspects of sustainable use of natural resources and biodiversity related to NBT,
2. to propose an agreed single set of basic principles which may guide states, the tourism industry, local communities, intergovernmental organizations, civil society, and individual tourists,
3. to assist the consolidation of various sectoral approaches and codes into a single legal framework,
4. to facilitate institutional and other linkages between existing internationally accepted codes of conduct and related international organizations,
5. to fill in the gaps in international law, by placing principles on NBT in a global context, and
6. to draft a universal basis for NBT upon which future lawmaking efforts might be developed. Main characteristics of international instrument on NBT layout in Table 2.

Table 2. Main characteristics of international instrument on NBT.

(a)	Conservation of ecosystem structure and functioning
(b)	Sustainable tourism in ecosystems conserving their structure and fimctioning
(c)	Fair and equitable sharing ofbenefits
(d)	Information sharing and dissemination ofbest practices and experiences
(e)	Restoration of past damage
(f)	Technical assistance and Capacity building
(g)	Enhancement of global and regional coordination
(h)	Governing international behaviour and approach on nature based tourism
(i)	Fair distribution of international funds available on the issue
(g)	Priority setting for state members

DISCUSSION

Having above facts in mind, to provide an internationally accepted legally binding instrument for governing international behavior on NBT, there is a need to explore and explain legal bases as well as main innovations of such instrument. Both issues will be discussed in this part, namely; (a) Legal bases of international instrument on NBT and, (b) Required innovations.

Legal Bases of International Instrument on NBT

The proposed instrument should build on principles and concepts that have already been developed through the relevant principles of international environmental law and principles of international law relevant to developmental issues and tourism as well as international practice processes. It should also focus on practical guidance to facilitate its implementation, and linkages between sustainable economical developments and the protection and conservation of environmental and cultural heritage by sustainable NBT. Sands (1995) believes that the general principles and rules of international environmental law reflected in the treaties, binding acts of international organizations, and state practices are potentially applicable to all members of the international community across the range of their activities in respect to the protection of all aspects of the environment. Most general rules and principles have broad support and are frequently endorsed in practice. They include the following: the principle of the state sovereignty over its natural resources and the responsibility not to harm or cause damage to the environment of other states; the principles of preventive action and good neighborliness and international cooperation; the precautionary principle; the polluter pays at principle; the principles of common but differentiated responsibility and human rights; and the principle of sustainable development comprised of inter-generation, intra-generation, integration of environment, and development and the sustainable use of natural resources.

Boyles and Birnie (2002) believe that sustainable development, as reflected in the outcomes of the Rio Summit, contains both substantive and procedural elements. The substantive ones are mainly the sustainable use of natural resources, the integration of environmental protection into the economic development, the right to development, intra- and inter-generation equality, and polluter pays principle. These are reflected in Principles 3–8 and 16 of the Rio Declaration. The procedural principles include public participation in decision-making, EIAs, and access to information. These are reflected in Principles 10 and 17 of the Rio Declaration.

All relevant principles declared by 1992 Rio Declaration and the 1972 Stockholm Declaration as well as main legal principles used by the 2000 IUCN Draft Covenant on Environment and Development should be employed. To compile a draft of international instrument on NBT. The IUCN Draft Covenant on Environment and development is a recent endeavor of the international community to harmonize environmental and developmental issues (see Table 3).

It is not a negotiating text although it is the result of the work of international experts and academics based on international environmental law and other relevant international law.

Table 3. Main principles on international developmental and environmental law relevant to NBT.

Accepted principles on international law	References in main international instruments
Principle of preventive action	Principles 11 and 14 of the Rio Declaration and 6, 7, I 5, I 8, and 24 of the Stockholm Declaration and Articles 6, I 2.2 and 23 of IUCN Draft Covenant
Principle of good neighbourliness and mutual cooperation	Principles 19 and 27 of the Rio Declaration and 24 of the Stockholm Declaration
Principle of inter-generation and intra-generation equality	Principles 3 ofthe Rio Declaration and 1 of the Stockholm Declaration and Article 5 of IUCN Draft Covenant
Principle of common but differentiated responsibility	Principles 7 of the Rio Declaration and 23 of the Stockholm Declaration and Article 3 of TUCN Draft Covenant
Principle of integration of development and environment	Principles 4 of the Rio Declaration and 13 and 14 of the Stockholm Declaration and Article 5 of TUCN Draft Covenant
The precautionary principle	Principle 15 of Rio declaration
Principle of human rights	Principles 1, 3, and 10 of the Rio Declaration and I of the Stockholm Declaration and Article I 2. I of iUCN draft Covenant
Principle of the right to development	Principle 3 ofthe Rio Declaration and Article 8 of TUCN Draft Covenant
Principle of poverty alleviation and equitable benefit sharing	Principles 5, 8, and I 2 of the Rio Declaration and Article 9 and 13.1 of I UCN Draft Covenant
Principle of carrying capacity	Principle 9 of the Rio declaration
Participatory principle	Principles 10, 20, 21, and 22 of the Rio Declaration and Article 7 of IUCN Draft Covenant
Principle of sustainable production and consumption patterns	Principle 8 of the Rio declaration
Principle of environmental impact assesment	Principle 17 of the Rio declaration
Principle of the use of environmentally sound technology	Principle 7 and 9 of the Rio declaration
Principle of sovereignty over natural resources	Articles 11.1, 11.2, and 15.1 of IUCN Draft Covenant
Polluter pays principle	Article 11.6 ofiUCN Draft Covenant
Principle of sustainable use of natural resources	Articles 1.3, 12.6, 17, 18, 19, and 34 ofiUCN Draft Covenant
Principle of conservation and the sustainable use of biodiversity	Articles 2, 21.1, 21. 2, and 30.2 ofiUCN Draft Covenant
Principle of careful activity in sensitive and protected areas	Articles 20.1, 20.2 and 52 bis of IUCN Draft Covenant
Principle of waste disposal and waste management	Articles 14, 15.2, 24, and 25 ofiUCN Draft Covenant
Principles of spatial planning and the aesthetic value of nature	Articles 21.1, 22, and 34 ofiUCN Draft Covenant
Principle of integrated sustainable NBT planning	Article 13.2 ofiUCN Draft Covenant
Principle of the need for sustainable indicators and standards	Article 38 ofiUCN Draft Covenan
Principle of environmental awareness and education	Articles 12.3, and 44 ofiUCN Draft Covenant

The following principles of international developmental and environmental law should be used in the drafting of an international covenant on NBT. The basic legal arguments used by the relevant international conferences, meetings, and workshops relevant to NBT on drafting or setting out final outcomes, agreements, codes of conduct, or guidelines should also be taken into consideration. Some of the well established principles used to compile tourism's international legal instruments are; the principle of the right to rest and leisure, and the principles of tourism safety and of equal access, and non-discrimination in the Tourism Bill of Rights and the Tourist Code, the principles of common natural heritage and the preservation of cultural identity in the 1972 WHC, the principle of cultural heritage and landscape and the principle of spatial planning in the 2000 European Landscape Convention. The principles of integrated sustainable NBT planning, destination management, committed tourism industry, carrying capacity, and tourist safety are all included in the 1999 WTO Global Code of Ethics. While the 1992 CBD sets out the principles for obligatory restoration of disturbed ecosystems, incentive measures and voluntary initiatives, the development of suitable indicators, and the restrained development of fragile ecosystems.

Required Innovations
Almost all of the above mentioned principles made a significant contribution to the drafting of various environmental or developmental international instruments. They are the basis of international forums on negotiation and either form new instruments or amend existing ones. They also could provide a very useful input to the rule making and procedures for NBT. On the other hand and as a result of reviewing and analysis of existing international instruments concerning NBT, could deduced that, there is a need to design innovative mechanism to deal with particular shortcomings or resolve problems or provide with updated ideas and instruments to achieve the sustainable development objectives related to NBT. Based on this study, some of the notable innovations that should be taken into account on the drafting NBT instrument such as international covenant are suggested as follows:

The Establishment of Nature-based Tourism Areas (NBTA)
The main attractions of NBT can be found in the rich, beautiful, and most environmentally and socio culturally sensitive areas. These areas normally include national parks and reserves, protected areas in the land and seas which contain outstanding environmental, social, cultural, historic, scientific, aesthetic, and wilderness values. Having in mind that NBT and the environmental quality of the sites have a permanent interaction, the preservation and conservation of these areas have a high priority in NBT agenda. One of the important innovations of the proposed covenant is the establishment of NBTA. The NBTAs should be created using specific criteria. There should be a national system of NBTAs and the management should be based on an ecosystem approach. The NBT activities in these areas should be conditional and restricted. The establishment of geographical areas for particular use was employed only in the 1972 World Heritage Convention and the 1991 PEPAT of the Antarctic Treaty.

Multi-stakeholders' Involvement in all NBT Activities by Establishing a National Multi-stakeholders Body (NMB)
The active participation of the all stakeholders in NBT should be addressed as one of the main shortcomings of the existing international instruments. Such participation will guarantee the achievement of the social development objectives, protection

of environmental assets, and preserve cultural values. In addition, it will provide for the equitable distribution of benefits in the NBT destination. To achieve such a goal, the proposed covenant should come up with the new idea of establishing NMB as a participative planning mechanism. This mechanism should guarantee the maximum possible participation of the local community, tourism industry, government authorities, vulnerable groups, scientists, and academics in NBT activities. The NMB should provide transparency, accountability, and participatory factors at all levels of rule setting, decision-making, implementation, management, EIAs, monitoring, and reporting processes. By using NMB, every single social sector has its voice in the NBT process. This will provide it with an environment to secure its interests and to lead NBT activities towards a more balanced approach. The NMB will also increase the responsibility of all stakeholders.

Establishing an International Multi-stakeholder Body (IMB)
The NMB is an instrument to working at national level. There is a need to provide major stakeholders with an international forum to express their views and influence and shape the decision-making process at international level. The international forums are normally the place to coordinate governments' positions. There are quite a few international organizations where major stakeholders have a voice. The International Labour Organization (ILO) is well established and the oldest one in which government representatives, the trade union representatives, and the representatives of labor union are active in the decision-making process. To a certain extent there is an immense gap within international environmental and developmental instruments regarding the involvement of major stakeholders in the decision-making process. Therefore, the proposed covenant should envisage a coordinated policy approach in the form of a consultative body within new instrument.

Providing the Local Community with Major Roles in NBT Activities
One of the main objectives of the proposed covenant should be facilitating and enhancing the participation of local communities and indigenous people in and around NBT areas. It should provide a suitable mechanism to serve the other objectives of the proposed covenant including the protection and sustainable use of NBT areas, the preservation of cultural and social values in the destination, the equitable distribution of benefits, and generally contribute to the sustainability of the NBT areas. It should identify the rights and obligations of the local community and define the responsibilities of the government in respect of the local community. The right of the local community to participate in all NBT process should be expressed. By using the NMB, the local community empowers to participate in high level decision-making, rule setting, implementation, and management of any NBT development. The proposed covenant should also provide them with the right to oversee the tourism industry regarding requesting the state members to ensure the local community's representation on the responsible national bodies.

Tourism Industry Involvements, its Rights, and Obligations
The tourism industry has an important role in this economic sector. In some countries with an advanced tourism sector, the industry has a decisive role compared with the

national authorities. One of the innovations of the proposed covenant should prepare the ground for more meaningful involvement and responsibility of the industry in decision-making and norm setting as well as the implementation and management of NBT by identification of its rights and obligations. It should provide the tourism industry with an environment to hear and be heard, to deal with the concern of other major stakeholders and to resolve its problems through an international instrument. By this involvement the cooperation between all stakeholders and the harmony in the development and management of NBT will improve.

Proposing EIA Procedures
For almost 3 decades the international community and individual countries, particularly developed ones, have tried to formulate Environmental Impact Assessment procedures. Before the 1992 Rio summit, the 1982 World Charter for Nature in its Para 11 and the 1982 UNCLOS in Article 206 address the issue to some degree, while the US in the 1969 NEPA tried to sort out a set of regulations for IEAs. It was addressed by principle 17 of the Rio Declaration and hereafter the international community had a more integrated approach towards IEA procedures (Boyle and Birnie, 2002). The proposed covenant should make a series of innovations on the implementation and management of the IEA process within the tourism industry. It should categorize NBT areas as marine or land areas. For both of them, the employment of prior EIA procedures at the commencement of any new development or activity should be obligatory in order to determine whether or not the impacts are minor or transitory. This procedure should assess the likelihood of any significant adverse impact on the buffer zones. The proposed covenant should also identify the character and functional factors of EIAs. The activity may proceed forthwith if classified as having less than a minor or transitory impact. Otherwise, an initial environmental evaluation shall be prepared to recognize if the activity has more than a minor or transitory impact. In this case there is a cumulative impact and alternative proposals should be introduced. If the initial environmental evaluation procedures find that the proposed activity has no more than a minor transitory impact, the activity may proceed under proper monitoring. Otherwise, a comprehensive EIA shall be employed. The proposed covenant shall describe the technical aspects of the process. If the implementation of the proposed activity is approved, it should be carried out under regular and verifiable monitoring using key environmental indicators. To assist the implementation of the above EIA procedures, the proposed covenant could suggest the designation of responsible national authorities to control the national aspects of the implementation of the EIA.

Introducing a Compensation Mechanism
In the case of significant harm to the natural resources of NBT areas, the covenant should propose a system of compensation to re-establish the situation by providing a remedy for the incurred damages. It includes rehabilitation and restoration measures, research and capacity building, and contribution to the socio–cultural development of the damaged site. This process should be monitored by relevant international organizations and if the harm is serious the perpetrator should be punished by establishing sanctions and implement fines, confiscation, suspension, and any other measures. The proposed covenant should also provide its members with a system of compensation for the shared

NBT areas or deliberate acts. In the case that damage is caused by individuals, it should set out measures to ensure the re-establishment of the site by appropriate remedies and/or proper compensation to victims of the environmental harm. In the case of serious environmental harm, the state of which the perpetrator is a national is responsible.

Introduction of NBT Awards

This initiative is a result of the more obligatory use of the voluntary initiatives approach of the proposed covenant. The covenant should put an emphasis on the development and wider use of incentive measures including awards. The NBT Award may design to serve the ample use and implementation of the objectives and content of the covenant. It should be granted to selected stakeholders that have made a remarkable contribution to the protection and sustainable use of the NBTA. The achievement of the award should be taken into account by the international community as a sign of the eligibility and commitment of the recipient.

Introduction of a Clearing House Mechanism (CHM)

The proposed covenant should provide a CHM mechanism to address the needs of its members for the enhancement of technical and scientific cooperation in NBT. The bases for the action of the proposed CHM are the development of information networks and the dissemination of information, best practices and techniques, and establishing joint research programs. It also facilitates capacity building, regional cooperation, the transfer of ESTs, cooperation among stakeholders, and early warning systems.

Providing a Mechanism to Confront Tourism Seasonality and Achieve Sustainability and Awareness

Destination countries and societies are always confronted with the seasonality in their tourism planning and management. This is a major challenge and notable barrier to achieving tourism sustainability. Seasonal mass tourism ignores the carrying capacity limitation of the destination, destroys cultural and environmental assets, puts pressure on precious natural resources, creates job uncertainty, and generates unsustainable conditions in the destinations. The NBT has the ability to remove such segments from its market. The proposed covenant should provide an innovative measure by recommending state parties to allow the leave of absence of students each year during term-time to enjoy NBT activities with their families and provide other students with information obtained, disseminate information among the youth and so increase their respect for the environment and local communities' culture. It could also advise the improvement of the system of annual leave with pay for the same purpose.

Defining the Criteria for Sustainability in NBT

The identification of the criteria for sustainability in the NBA should be other important step forwards in the proposed covenant. It has to address the core issues of NBT and provide a proper legal basis for further activities and actions under the umbrella of the covenant. The main criteria are that NBT should be ecologically bearable, environmentally viable, and socially equitable. Other criteria for NBT include increasing local community benefits, contributions to the protection of NBTA, carrying capacity of the destination and confronting seasonality issues, planning with nature in designing NBT products, enhancement of tourists' awareness, and profitability for all stakeholders.

Proposing a Compliance Measure Mechanism
Many new legally binding international instruments employ compliance measures as tools to ensure the implementation of the obligations of each party. To the extent of the author's knowledge, there is not an international tourism related instrument with compliance measures as an integral part. The proposed covenant should provide the provision of obligatory compliance measures including strengthening reporting requirements and enquiry procedures. It should also establish different types of visits to sites to verify any breach of regulations observed by the proposed covenant. These visits could be categorized as voluntary visits where the concerned party invites the selected officials to pay a visit to the NBTA, the periodical visits that will be organized through appropriate decisions and measures and, fact-finding missions which are more restricted visits.

There are other requirements such as addressing shared NBTA, creation of a system of NBT at national level, defining carrying capacity of NBTA, setting up guidelines for NBT strategy and planning, and management and sustainability measures on production and consumption patterns, to make the propose covenant more effective.

CONCLUSION

Despite various attempts made by international environmental and developmental organizations and relevant specialized agencies to propose an adequate framework to deal with the new phenomenon of NBT, lack of an internationally accepted comprehensive, integrated, legally binding agreement based on existing international law and practice is obvious. Such an instrument could fill the gap and properly address one of the outstanding areas of the new convergence of environmental and developmental pillars of sustainable development in the area of sustainable use of natural resources and biodiversity.

Such instrument, based on the previous experiences and relevant international law, should be dealt with the rights and obligations of each major stakeholder in NBT including governments, tourism industry, local communities, and others. It should provide a variety of facilities for its members while regulating and harmonizing their activities regarding the protection and sustainable use of resources related to NBT. In addition, it will provide appropriate mechanisms for the participation of all stakeholders and the distribution of benefits in an equable and sustainable manner.

KEYWORDS

- **Agenda 21**
- **Commission on Sustainable Development**
- **Environmental law**
- **Legal instrument**
- **Nature-based tourism**
- **Sustainable development**
- **UNEP**

Chapter 3

Trends in Nature-based Tourism

Andrew Balmford, James Beresford, Jonathan Green, Robin Naidoo, Matt Walpole, and Andrea Manica

INTRODUCTION

Reports of rapid growth in nature-based tourism (NBT) and recreation add significant weight to the economic case for biodiversity conservation but seem to contradict widely voiced concerns that people are becoming increasingly isolated from nature. This apparent paradox has been highlighted by a recent study showing that on a per capita basis, visits to natural areas in the US and Japan have declined over the last two decades. These results have been cited as evidence of "a fundamental and pervasive shift away from nature-based recreation" but how widespread is this phenomenon? We address this question by looking at temporal trends in visitor numbers at 280 protected areas (PAs) from 20 countries. This more geographically representative dataset shows that while PA visitation (whether measured as total or per capita visit numbers) is indeed declining in the US and Japan, it is generally increasing elsewhere. Total visit numbers are growing in 15 of the 20 countries for which we could get data, with the median national rate of change unrelated to the national rate of population growth but negatively associated with wealth. Reasons for this reversal of growth in the richest countries are difficult to pin down with existing data, but the pattern is mirrored by trends in international tourist arrivals as a whole and so may not necessarily be caused by disaffection with nature. Irrespective of the explanation, it is clear that despite important downturns in some countries, nature-related tourism is far from declining everywhere, and may still have considerable potential both to generate funds for conservation and to shape people's attitudes to the environment.Across Southern Africa, NBT reportedly now generates roughly the same revenue as farming, forestry, and fisheries combined (Scholes and Biggs, 2004). Worldwide, tourism as a whole has been estimated to account for roughly 10% of gross domestic product (GDP) (World Travel and Tourism Council, 2007), with wildlife viewing and outdoor recreation (much of it centered on PAs) reportedly making up one of its fastest growing sectors (Davenport et al., 2002; Goodwin, 1996; Mastny, 2001). Though statistics like these are rarely supported by detailed data, they underpin widespread recognition that NBT is an important ecosystem service (Millennium Ecosystem Assessment, 2005), capable of generating substantial resources for both conservation and local economic development (Boo, 1990; Goodwin, 1996; Gossling, 1999). This is particularly significant given that PAs are under increasing pressure to provide economic justification for their existence (Ceballos-Lascurain, 1996; Walpole et al., 2001; West, 2006; Wilkie and Carpenter, 2002).

This positive perspective stands in sharp contrast to growing concerns about an emerging disconnect between people and their natural environments. Increasing urbanization and the rise of sedentary, indoor pastimes (such as television, the Internet, and video games) have been linked to a reduction in informal, outdoor recreation (Pyle's "Extinction of Experience" (Pyle, 2003)), with potentially serious consequences for childhood development, mental and physical wellbeing, and environmental knowledge and concern (Balmford, 2002; Barnes, 2007; Kahn and Kellert, 2002; Kareiva, 2008; Louv, 2005; Nabhan and Trimble, 1994; Pyle, 1993; Zaradic and Pergams, 2007). Many see this as a major challenge for biodiversity conservation (Balmford and Cowling, 2006; Kareiva, 2008; Pyle, 1993, 2003): if people no longer experience and know their natural environments, how can they be expected to care about them?

These worries have been further fueled by a recent and widely publicized data examining trends in 16 measures of outdoor recreation (14 from the US, plus one each from Japan and Spain (Pergams and Zaradic, 2008)). This analysis showed that, expressed per head of population, visits to natural areas in the US and Japan (as well as participation in duck-hunting and fishing in the US, but not hiking, camping, or other hunting) have declined since the late 1980s (though for contrasting US figures, see (Reed and Merenlender, 2008)). From these per capita trends the authors conclude there has been "...a fundamental and pervasive shift away from nature-based recreation" (Kareiva, 2008; Pergams and Zaradic, 2008; Williams, 2008). However, the data produced no evidence of declines outside the US and Japan (and per capita national park attendance in Spain, the only other country sampled, has not declined), raising the possibility that the reported shift may not be universal.

To date, lack of data has meant no study has looked at trends in NBT across more than a handful of countries. Here, we use newly compiled information on visitor numbers to 280 PAs in 20 countries (Australia, Canada, Chile, China, Ecuador, Ghana, India, Indonesia, Japan, Korea, Madagascar, Peru, Philippines, Rwanda, South Africa, Sri Lanka, Tanzania, Uganda, UK, and US) between 1992 and 2006 to explore the generality of the US and Japan results and to understand the apparent mismatch with the claim that globally, NBT is on the rise. Importantly, because we are interested in trends in nature tourism as a whole as well as individual interest in nature, we analyze changes in both total visit numbers and visit numbers corrected for national population size. The latter are a better reflection of per capita interest in a country's PAs (Pergams and Zaradic, 2008), but the former are a more sensible proxy for trends in the overall benefit derived from nature tourism as an ecosystem service.

MATERIALS AND METHODS

Somewhat surprisingly, there is no global database or consistent set of national statistics summarizing trends in NBT. Instead, like previous authors (Pergams and Zaradic, 2008) we infer changes in the sector as a whole from visits to PAs. We compiled information on annual visitor numbers to terrestrial PAs (including any listed in (World Conservation Union and United Nations Environment Programme-World Conservation Monitoring Centre, 2007)). The PA visits are among the most frequent forms of nature-based recreation recorded in the US (Pergams and Zaradic, 2008), and we suggest they are likely to account for an even greater proportion of nature recreation in other countries, where alternatives are less developed. We collected data from as many sources as possible: the grey and published literature, personal contacts, and especially the World Wide Web. The methods used to record visitors were rarely reported in detail, but varied widely, including dedicated studies, gate receipts, and traffic counts (Eagles, 2002). There are also likely to be biases in some datasets, with corruption, for example, perhaps leading to systematic under- (and in some cases, maybe over-) reporting of visitor numbers (Cochrane, 2003). These problems may confound estimation of absolute visitor numbers, but will have less impact on within-PA changes in visitor numbers over time, and so here we used all available information.

In total we were able to collate ≥6 year data (between 1992 and 2006) for 280 PAs from 20 countries. We then expressed visitation trends at each PA in two ways—using total visit number, as a measure of the overall tourism benefit provided by the PA; and (as in (Pergams and Zaradic, 2008)) using visit number divided by national population size in that year (from (World Bank, 2008)), as a measure of per capita use of the PA. For PAs with large numbers of nondomestic visitors, tracking per capita use by dividing by national population size is imperfect (and data on visitor origins are too patchy for any more sophisticated adjustment by population size). However, data we obtained for 190 PAs (many lacking time series information and so excluded from our core analysis) indicate that, for all except one continent, a mean of >70% of visitors are nationals, so that errors caused through adjusting by national population size are relatively limited. The exception is Africa, where on average only ~30% visitors are nationals. For this continent, adjustment by national population growth (which is also generally higher than elsewhere) is probably excessive and so negatively biases estimates of trends in per capita visit rates.

For each PA we next performed linear regressions of total visit number and per capita visit number on year, and derived standardized measures of rates of change (ranging from +1 to −1) as (slope/maximum total (or per capita) visit number predicted by the regression during the 15-year range). We explored geographical variation in trends in our two measures of visit numbers by calculating median standardized rates of change across continents, and across countries. We compared the latter with per capita GDP adjusted for purchasing power parity (PPP) (for 2005, from (World Bank, 2008)), using linear regression weighted by the number of PAs sampled in each country. As an additional check to see whether our results for total visit number were confounded by changes in national population size, we performed an equivalent weighted regression of national median change in total visit number versus annual population growth (for 1990–2006, from (World Bank, 2008)). Last, to see whether our findings were specific to nature-related tourism, we also obtained data on trends in all foreign arrivals between 1995 and 2005 (again from (World Bank, 2008)), and compared standardized national rates of change (calculated in the same way as for PA visits) with per capita GDP and with median standardized rates of change in total visit numbers.

DISCUSSION

Our dataset on PA visits has far broader geographical coverage than any others we are aware of, yet yielded no evidence to support the idea of a consistent global decline in nature-based recreation. Instead it appears that falling visitation is mostly restricted to a few well-off countries. When we adjusted visit numbers for population growth to examine individual participation in nature recreation we were able to replicate previously reported declines in per capita visit number in the US and Japan (Pergams and Zaradic, 2008), but also found that in most other countries population-adjusted visit numbers have been increasing.

These patterns were more marked when we looked at trends in PA visitation as a whole, using total numbers of PA visits. We found these are growing on four out of six continents and in 15 of the 20 countries for which we could get data. These changes in average visit rates are quite well predicted by wealth, but are unrelated to national population growth confirming the finding from the per capita analysis that it is not the case that visitation is increasing simply where populations are growing rapidly. Instead, it appears that PA visitation is generally growing, but at a progressively lower rate (eventually falling below zero) with rising affluence.

We do not have a ready explanation for this negative link between visit growth and wealth, and believe this will be hard to unravel from correlational analyses alone. It could be related to the emergence of "videophilia" (Zaradic and Pergams, 2007), or to other aspects of growing urbanization or increasingly sedentary lifestyles (Kareiva, 2008; Louv, 2005; Pyle, 1993). These ideas are plausible, but direct evidence for them is sparse. Given that very many potential drivers co-vary with one another and with time, causality may be difficult to establish until more detailed data become available, or an experimental approach is adopted.

One nonexclusive alternative explanation for the patterns of changing PA visitation that we see could be that many formal PAs in richer countries are becoming increasingly crowded and thus less attractive to nature enthusiasts (J. du Toit, personal correspondence). Overcrowding and the perception of overcrowding have been noted as a concern of visitors to many larger US National Parks for over a decade (Anonymous, 2007; Fretwell and Podolsky, 2003). If would-be visitors are instead switching to less publicized sites where visitors are not counted, overall visit rates to natural areas in these countries could be stable or even growing, yet still recorded as declining.

One other explanation for the pattern we see could be that there is a shift in preference away from domestic destinations as nature-focused tourists become wealthier and alternative wildlife attractions in less costly developing countries become more accessible (Ceballos-Lascurain, 1993; Prosser, 1994). Strikingly, the patterns we uncovered for PA visitor trends are echoed by those for international tourism more generally: standardized national rates of change in all foreign arrivals (from (World Bank, 2008)) co-vary positively with median changes in total and per capita PA visit numbers (for total visit numbers, Figure 1A; regression weighted as in Figure 2A, $r^2 = 0.34$, n = 19 countries excluding Rwanda, for which no arrival information was available: $F_{1,17} = 10.2$, $p < 0.01$; for per capita visit numbers, Figure 1B; weighted regression: $r^2 = 0.25$, n = 19, $F_{1,17} = 7.0$, $p < 0.05$). Changes in foreign arrivals also show a negative relationship with per capita GDP, falling to zero growth in the US. These results suggest that trends in nature-based recreation might be less driven by attitudes to nature *per se* and more to do with how rising wealth and the emergence of new destinations influence the dynamics of recreation as a whole (Butler, 1980; World Tourism Organization, 2002). To resolve this, more data would be needed than we were able to obtain on the nationalities and motivations of visitors to individual PAs.

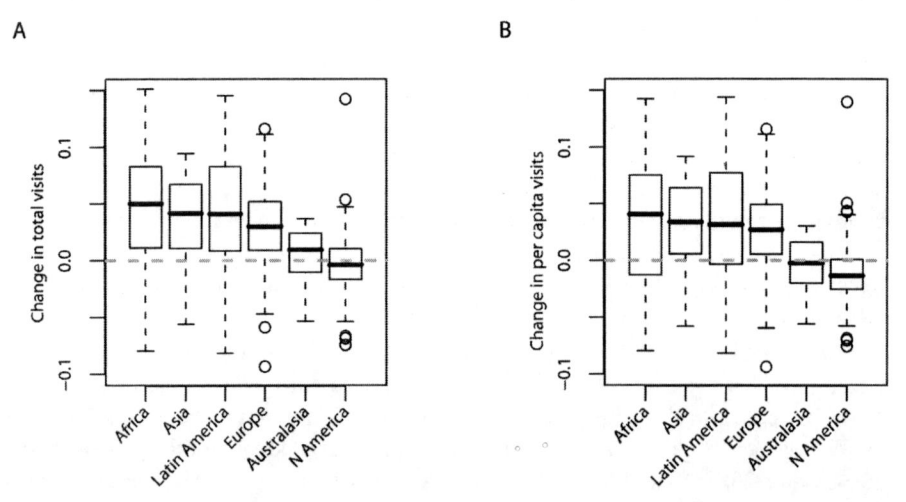

Figure 1. Median national rates of change in numbers of visits to PAs in relation to standardized annual change in foreign arrivals (1995–2005); symbols as in Figure 2.

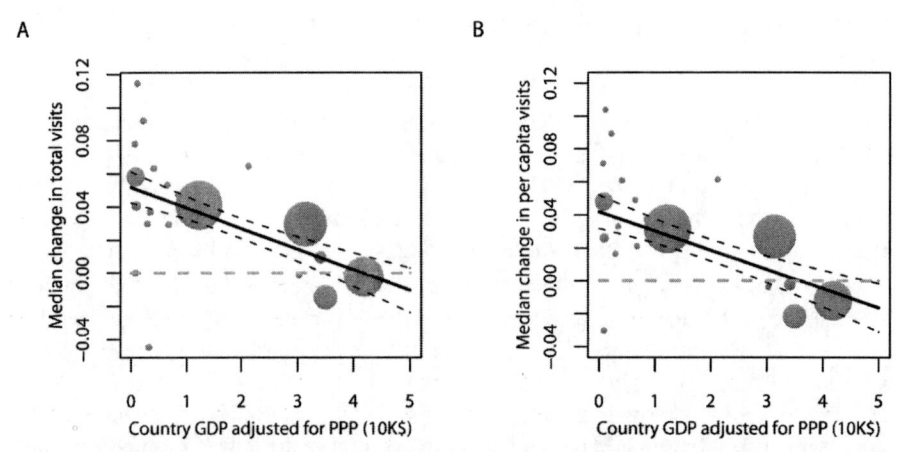

Figure 2. Median national rates of change in numbers of visits to PAs in relation to per capita GDP (in 2005), adjusted for PPP; the number of PAs sampled per country is reflected in point size, and used to weight the regression; solid line represents the best model, dark dashed lines represent ±1 standard error (SE). (A) Changes in total visit number; (B) Changes in per capita visit number.

Regardless of the underlying drivers, our analyses indicate that it is premature to conclude that PA visit data indicate a general and pervasive shift away from nature tourism. This is apparently occurring in a few developed countries, where it is worrying, and where it certainly demands more attention. But in contrast, in most developing countries visits to PAs are growing at rates that mirror general increases in tourism and travel—in many cases by more than 4%/year (Figure 2A). This is especially significant for conservation, given that, unlike other nonconsumptive uses of ecosystems, NBT produces tangible financial flows that can, if carefully developed, be of direct benefit to local decision-makers (Boo, 1990; Ceballos-Lascurain, 1996; Gossling, 1999; Walpole and Leader-Williams, 2001; Walpole and Thouless, 2005).

Tourism can often provide a strong incentive for protection in biodiversity-rich areas (Gossling, 1999), and formal designation of such sites can raise their profile and influence tourism visitation (Buckley, 2004). However, increasing visitor numbers alone is no guarantee that tourism revenues will be reinvested in conservation (Wells, 1993). Equally, recording visitor numbers does not equate with the much less common practices of monitoring or managing tourism impacts (Buckley et al., 2008). International nature tourism raises other important worries—about CO_2 emissions, about its vulnerability to changing fashions, about disturbance to wildlife and nearby people, and about how far its revenues filter down to local communities (Anonymous, 2007; Bookbinder, 1998; Butler, 1980; Butynski and Kalima,1998; Ceballos-Lascurain, 1993; Fretwell and Podolsky, 2003; Kiss, 2004; Prosser, 1994; Reed and Merenlender, 2008; Walpole and Goodwin, 2000; Walpole and Leader-Williams, 2001; Walpole and Thouless, 2005; Williams, 2008; World Bank, 2008; World Tourism Organization, 2002). The NBT is only likely to be sustainable under certain conditions of effective planning, management, and local participation (Boo, 1990; Eagles, 2009; Kruger, 2005; Plummer and Fennell, 2009). However, to the extent that these concerns can be addressed, our results argue that far from having a diminishing role, nature-based recreation has the potential in many parts of the world to make a growing contribution to both conservation and sustainable development.

RESULTS

Our analysis of standardized rates of change in PA visit numbers provides limited support for the previously reported declines in nature-based activities in the US. Using total visit numbers, only 14 out of 51 US PAs for which we could get data showed significant decreases in visit number (at $p < 0.05$), while 11 exhibited significant increases. Adjusting for changes in national population size, the number of US PAs experiencing significant declines rose to 27 and the number with increasing attendance fell to just six. Clearly, the decline in per capita visitation to US PAs we could sample is real, but arises largely because absolute attendance has been almost static despite a growing national population. In Japan, the only PA for which we had data showed a non-significant decline in visits, whether expressed in terms of total or per capita visit numbers.

More interestingly, these weak declines in two countries are far from globally typical: instead, visitor trends show marked geographical variation. When we pooled standardized rates of change within continents, rather than being negative we found that trends in total visit numbers were not significantly different from zero in North America or Australasia, and were on average positive in Africa, Europe, Asia, and Latin America (Figure 3A; $F_{5,274} = 10.2$, $p < 0.001$; in post hoc tests only Australasia and North America had rates of changes not significantly different from zero at p < 0.05). There was similar broad-scale variation when we compared trends in per capita visit numbers across continents (Figure 3B: $F_{5,274} = 10.4$, $p < 0.001$, with significant positive trends again everywhere apart from Australasia and North America).

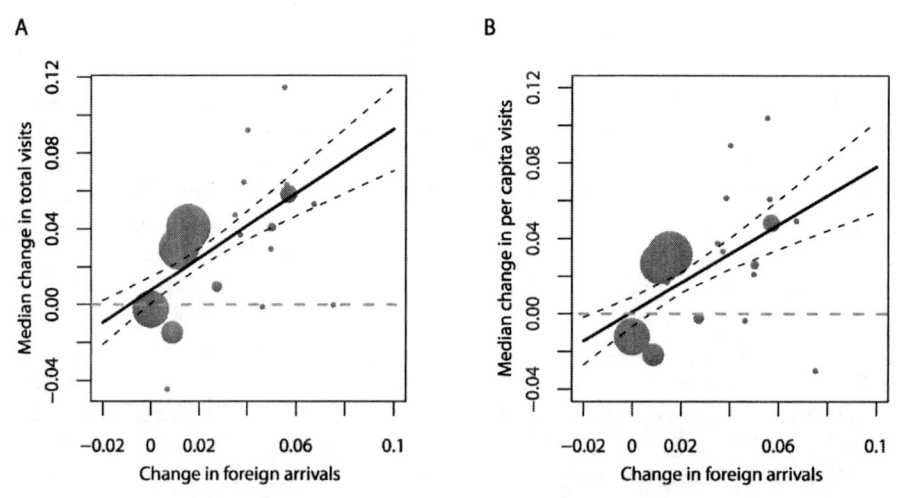

Figure 3. Comparisons across continents of rates of change in numbers of visits to protected areas, 1992–2006; lines, boxes, error bars, and circles show medians, interquartile ranges, minima and maxima (excluding outliers), and outliers (which deviate from the median by >1.5x interquartile range), respectively. (A) Changes in total visit number; (B) Changes in per capita visit number.

These patterns of spatial heterogeneity were confirmed when data were analyzed by country. Total visit numbers to PAs on average grew in 15 out of the 20 countries sampled and fell in four (with Uganda showing no change). Even allowing for population growth, per capita visit numbers rose in 14 countries (with Uganda and Australia added to the list of countries showing falling visitation). The only country we sampled outside the Organization for Economic and Co-operation Development (OECD) with consistently falling PA visitation was Indonesia.

National rates of change are closely associated with wealth. In contrast to the US and Japan, poorer countries typically had increasing numbers of PA visits, with median standardized rates of growth in total visit numbers showing a clear negative relationship with per capita GDP (Figure 2A; regression weighted by number of PAs sampled per country: adjusted $r^2 = 0.52$, n = 20 countries, $F_{1,18} = 21.8$, $p < 0.001$). This result was not due to correlated variation in population growth, because the negative link with rising wealth held when visit numbers were adjusted for changes in population size (Figure 2B; weighted regression of median standardized rates of change in per capita visit numbers against per capita GDP: adjusted $r^2 = 0.43$, n = 20, $F_{1,18} = 15.5$, $P < 0.001$). As a further check for any confounding effects of population growth, we compared changes in total visit numbers with national population growth rates, but found no association between the two. The tendency for PA visitation to be increasing in poorer countries appears to be independent of population growth.

CONCLUSIONS

The NBT is frequently described as one of the fastest growing sectors of the world's largest industry, and a very important justification for conservation. However, a recent, high profile report has interpreted declining visit rates to US and Japanese national parks as evidence of a pervasive shift away from nature tourism. Here we use the largest database so far compiled on trends in visits to PAs around the world to resolve this apparent paradox. We find that, while visit rates measured in two different ways are indeed declining in some wealthy countries, in roughly three-quarters of the nations where data are available, visits to PAs are increasing. Internationally, rates of growth in the number of visits to such areas show a clear negative association with per capita income, which interestingly is matched by trends in foreign arrivals as a whole. Our results therefore suggest that, despite worrying local downturns, nature-related tourism is far from declining everywhere, and may still have considerable potential to generate funds for conservation and engage people with the environment.

KEYWORDS

- **Gross domestic product**
- **Per capita**
- **Protected areas**
- **Tourism**

AUTHORS' CONTRIBUTIONS

The author (s) have made the following declarations about their contributions: Conceived and designed the experiments: Andrew Balmford, Robin Naidoo, Matt Walpole, and Andrea Manica. Performed the experiments: Andrew Balmford, James Beresford, Jonathan Green, Robin Naidoo, Matt Walpole, and Andrea Manica. Analyzed the data: Andrew Balmford, James Beresford, Jonathan Green, and Andrea Manica. Wrote the chapter: Andrew Balmford, Robin Naidoo, and Andrea Manica. Obtained grant: Andrea Manica.

ACKNOWLEDGMENTS

We are very grateful to Abishek Behl, Graham Burton, Janet Cochrane, Ian Craigie, Phil Dearden, Dubiure Umaru Farouk, Richard Jenkins, Afan Jones, Chris Kirkby, N. Aldrin D. Mallari, Heather McNiff, Julia Ohl, Maria Otero, Lydia Napitupulu, Joep Stevens, Claudia Townsend, and others for providing visitation data; Emily Adams for retrieving socioeconomic information; and Ralf Buckley, Peter Kareiva, Agi Kiss, and Johan du Toit for commenting on previous versions of this chapter.

Chapter 4

Community Participation in Environmental Management of Ecotourism

Hongshu Wang and Min Tong

INTRODUCTION

Ecological environment is the material base of the development of ecotourism. The ecotourism cannot develop well without high quality ecotourism environment. The goal of ecotourism development is to protect ecological environment, which is also the essential characteristic of ecotourism different from other kind of tourism. This chapter tries to discuss the community participation in environmental management of ecotourism, aims to improve the awareness of participation and environmental protection among community residents and, to establish the mechanism of community participation in environmental management of ecotourism. In this way, can the community residents be benefit from ecotourism; and at the same time, the communities provide strong motive to protect the resources and environment of ecotourism well.

Ecotourism is sustainable tourism, which is based on the ecological principle and sustainable development theory. Its aim is to conserve resources, especially biological diversity, and maintain sustainable use of resources, which can bring ecological experience to travelers, conserve the ecological environment, and gain economic benefit. Ecotourism establishes a harmonious symbiotic relationship between sightseeing visit and environmental protection, which can make the negative influence of travel to ecological environment be reduced to minimum extent by strict management, so as to ensure the everlasting utilization of resources. Ecotourism is very popular to travelers for its bases that emphasize on natural ecological environment and pay attention to ecological environment protection.

As early as 1982, Zhangjiajie National Forest Park had been built, which is the first forest park in China. Subsequently, the ecotourism activities had begun to appear and develop in China. Especially, depending on natural landscape superiority, the forest parks, and nature reserves regard ecotourism as pillar industry of sustainable utilization of resources. However, although the development of ecotourism has brought economic interests to tourism destination, it has caused great influences to local ecological environment, such as too many artificial sceneries, the influx of tourists and tourism transport facilities in short time, more and more waste of water, gas and residue discharged by industry, and so on. All of them have exceeded tourist environment capacity, which results in damage and pollution to ecological environment. Furthermore, a high rise of garbage packing has destroyed the natural landscape and illustrated water body in tourist scenes, that is, water eutrophication. According to related organizations investigation on 100 nature reserves above the provincial level, there has been 22% of nature reserves causing environment destruction because of ecotourism development, and 11% of them appearing tourism resources degradation.

Good ecological environment is not only the premise and basis of ecotourism, but also the important guarantee of state ecological safety. Therefore, in order to develop the ecotourism well, the ecological environment should be depended on, so as to promote the ecotourism development. Well how to promote ecotourism to develop healthy and coordinate is a new subject to us all.

THE ESSENCE AND CONNOTATION OF ECOTOURISM

Strictly speaking, to date, there has not been a uniform final conclusion on the definition of ecotourism among the scholars at home and abroad. The reason is not only that the understanding and comprehension of people toward ecotourism is continuously deepened, but also that many researchers, developers, and business administrators artificially take their respective needs and garble a statement. Since 1980s, the studies on ecotourism have been prevailed all over the world.

Ecotourism is the necessary choice of the tourism development in certain phase; it is the best form of sustainable tourism; it is the concrete application of the principle of sustainable tourism in natural areas and certain social cultural regions.

This study argues that the connotation of ecotourism mainly embodies in the following aspects:

First, the destination of ecotourism is refers to the natural regions that are subjected less interferences and pollutions.

Second, the progress of ecotourism emphasizes on the principle of ecological protection. Ecotourism pays much attention to the protection during its development and uses development to promote protection, which is the harmony and unification among economic benefit, social benefit, and environmental benefit

Third, ecotourism is the green industry of high scientific and technological content, which needs multidisciplinary kinds of guiding and argumentation from ecologist, economist, and sociologist, and needs to considerate the enduring ability of ecological environment and tourism resources; it is a kind of unique sustainable tourism and responsible tourism form that pays more attention to the continuity of ecology and cannot result in the environmental destruction or the decrease of the environmental quality.

Fourth, ecotourism pays much attention to the economic development of tourism destinations and the improvement of the living standard of local residents; the income of ecotourism should not only be used to protect the ecological environment but also benefit the local residents.

Fifth, ecotourism gives prominence to the educational function of ecological environment; the life style and environmental view of tourists can be changed through ecotourism activities, and the consciousness of protecting resources and environment can be improved.

In all, ecotourism should regard environmental education, science popularization, and spiritual civilization construction as the core content, and really let itself be a grand school of people studying nature, loving nature, and protecting nature.

RELATIONSHIP BETWEEN ECOTOURISM AND ECOLOGICAL ENVIRONMENT

Ecological Environment is the Foundation of Ecotourism

Environment is the material base of survival and development of human society. Man's materials production should be based on the exploitation and utilization of the environmental resources. Tourism is a kind of human's higher-level need that meets individuals' spiritual needs. It is a wild wish to travel when social productivity is low or material life is not abundant. With the fast developing of economies and the rising standard of living, people began to have a well-off life after solving the food-and-clothing problems. In the premise that the basic survival conditions are satisfied, people have surplus money to pay traveling expenses. Meanwhile, people need novel, rich, and enriched spiritual life to meet their enjoyment desire after the material living conditions getting greater improvement. The aim of travel is to add leisurely and carefree mood to human life, such as leisure, entertainment, and vacation, thus the environment of tourism scenic spots is very important. Tourism environment is the one on which tourism industry rely for existence; environmental quality is the foundation of the existence of tourism. The development of tourism should be based on graceful sky, water, and mountain, as well as environment protection. Only when the environment be protected well and natural landscape and humanities landscape be in a virtuous circle, can the travel desire of people be inspired and changed into real tourism demand.

So is the development of ecotourism. Ecotourism activities, ecotourism resources, and ecotourism industry are all based on ecological environment. There is no ecotourism without graceful ecological environment. Graceful ecological environment is the material base of the ecotourism development. Chinese have a saying: "With the skin gone, what can the hair adhere to?" Therefore, the ecological environment can be seen as life source of the ecotourism. There is no ecotourism without high quality ecotourism environment.

Ecological Environment Protection is the Goal of Ecotourism

Ecotourism is the inevitable choice of the tourism development in certain phase. It is a best kind of sustainable tourism. The ecotourism development model is based on the sustainable development view, and its targets are human development and social progress. Meanwhile, the ecotourism development emphasizes on the harmonious development among economy, society, human being, and nature, which is completely satisfied the criterion of sustainable development view. Besides, the ecological environment protection is also the essential characteristic of ecotourism different from other kind of tourism. Ecotourism is not only one kind of simple, ecological, and natural tourism pattern, but also is the one that increases our responsibly on natural resources protection through tourism activities. Therefore, the connotation of ecotourism puts more emphasis on the conservation of natural landscape. It is one kind of high-grade tourist activity and education activity with sense of responsibility. The responsibilities of ecotourism include the protection of tourism resources, the respect for the economy, society and culture of tourism destination, the promotion of sustainable development of tourism destination, and so on. The basic aim of ecotourism is to be close to nature, to protect nature, and to maintain the ecological balance. The most important characteristic of the real ecotourism is protection. By developing ecotourism, we can maximally follow the natural law of biodiversity, and fully embody the harmonies and unified ecological relationship between man and nature, and put an end to short-term economic activities, and seek for the unity coordinated with economics, society and ecology, and at last maintain the sustainable development of the resources and environment of tourism.

ENVIRONMENTAL MANAGEMENT OF ECOTOURISM AND COMMUNITY PARTICIPATION

Community Participation is the Important Character of Ecotourism

Ecotourism has three typical characteristics by protection, economy, and community participation, all of which are related to communities of tourist destination. The protection of ecotourism means protecting the environment and resources of ecotourism destination—including local communities. The economy of ecotourism means developing the economy of local communities of tourist destination. Both the protection and economy are the targets of ecotourism development; well the community participation is the effective method to realize the targets mentioned above. Ecotourism impliedly includes the model of community participation in tourism development, whose aim is to make the tourism development meet the demand of local development, and to make the communities appropriately set and market the norms of tour and industry's operation as well as reasonable financial source acquirement, so as to promote the quality of the resources and environment of communities. According to the ecotourism practice in all countries, community participation is an important part of ecotourism activities both in developed countries and developing countries.

Community Participation Provides a Powerful Motivation for Resources Protection of Tourism Areas

Local community is an important tie of binding the protection to the economic income and social benefit, and it is the core of stakeholders of ecotourism. The existence and development of local inhabitants are based on the resources and environment of ecotourism areas. The local inhabitants are both the beneficiaries after environmental optimization and the victims after ecological environment broken by ecotourism development. Community participation in ecotourism can make a positive promotion to the protection of ecotourism environment For example, it can avoid the neglect of environmental and social benefits, and prevent from such phenomena as acquiring short-term benefit by sacrificing long-term benefit and environmental protection; meanwhile, it can also make the damage caused by tourism development be controlled in the limits of assimilation and self-purification of ecological environment, which keeps the ecosystem stable, so as to resolutely avoid the ecological environment deterioration possibly caused by unplanned predatory management or over-exploitation.

Community participation can mobilize all the social resources to administer the environment of the ecotourism destination. First, community participation itself has the feature by behavior style of internal convergence; all members of the community will construct a whole network of environmental protection construction under organizing coordination, which can closely supervise every community member and community unit. Second, the community can maximally call on the local residents to take part in the environmental protection activities. Besides, if the environmental protection consciousness is changed into social morality, the community members who have destroyed the ecological environment will be disdained by all other members; therefore, it is easy to be recognized that environmental protection regulations of the ecotourism destination is the common behavior criterion.

MEASURES OF COMMUNITY PARTICIPATION IN ENVIRONMENTAL MANAGEMENT OF ECOTOURISM

Improve the Consciousnesses of Participation and Environmental Protection of the Community Residents

We can develop widespread community education among the community residents, cultivate the community residents' sense and ability of participation, improve their positive cognition of ecotourism development, and environmental awareness of rights and obligations. Therefore, we should take some measures. First, we should let the community residents know what local environment and resources mean to them, and how many benefits the ecotourism protection can bring them, so as to stimulate their enthusiasm of participating in the ecotourism protection. Second, we should let them correctly understand the environment problems, and set up good environmental awareness, and keep civilized environmental behavioral habits, so as to devote themselves into controlling environmental pollution and improving the ecological environment.

Let the Community Residents Share the Benefits Brought by Ecotourism

During developing ecotourism activities, we should not only protect the fragile local ecological environment, but also benefit the local residents, both of them are more and more inseparable. Besides, we should absorb the community residents to take part in the ecotourism operation actively, increase the economic income, improve the living conditions, and share the benefits brought by ecotourism development. Under the driving of economic interests, the local residents participated in ecotourism may recognize that their income stems from the development of tourism industry. Well good natural environment and the continuation of biodiversity are the premise conditions of tourism development; protecting environment is to protect one's own economic interests. Therefore, we should change the habit of the community residents from living on consuming resources to living on developing, marketing, and managing resources, so as to not only relieve the pressure to resources protection, but also form relevant interest groups and resultant forces to biodiversity and ecological environment protection.

Propose the Communities to Change to the Life Style of Environmental Protection Type

Community residents' daily life and work, economic activities, traditional customs, and so on are close related to the ecological environment around as well as animal and plant resources in the natural reserve. For a long time, the residents in the ecotourism destination have lived on nature resources consumption; the abundant nature resources in ecotourism area have supplied them material basis for survival. These not only have caused environmental destruction and pollution, but also have been unfavorable to biodiversity protection. Therefore, the government should actively spread and apply new energies of environmental protection type, such as biogas, solar energy, power, briquette, and so on, build the wastewater treatment plant for communities; to form the life style of environmental protection type and realize the virtuous circle of environmental protection and community development

Establish Decision-making Mechanism in Planning of Ecotourism Participated by Communities

The community residents, especially those who long engage themselves in tourism activities, have a more intuitional understanding on the needs of tourists, can give some advice to the planners on the development of the ecotourism project and the distribution of facilities; meanwhile, they can offer useful reference to the environmental protection in ecotourism development process according to their long-history fit in the environment and, what's more, if they have participated and accepted the ecotourism project, they will be friendly and provide high quality service, which will improve the tourists' satisfaction to the ecotourism project, so as to achieve a better travel effect. Therefore, the management departments of tourism development should establish full-time branches of community management, and consider fully the interests of inhabitants, and guarantee the participation channel unimpeded, and form bulletin system and consultation system for significant happenings during the development and planning of tourism, and form veto system for improper important decisions in some tourism areas, and at last make sure that every tourism decision is discussed and studied by all parties.

Innovate the Mechanism of the Operation and Management of Ecotourism Resources

The kind of internal incentive mechanism, which is able to stimulate the community residents consciously to take part in the protection of ecological resources they live by, is needed to protect the ecotourism environment and make the sustainable development of ecotourism come true. The mechanism should not only have the encouraging function of stimulating the community residents to participate in the ecological protection, but also be available to achieve the optimal management of the resources and the sustainable development of the community. Well the community residents carry out share cooperation of ecotourism with the ecotourism resources and the establishing of labor stock, thus they are both the shareholders and laborers in the development and management of ecotourism. All of them make those come true that the ecotourism resources change from "public" to "common," and the community residents become the real masters and actively participate in the ecotourism decisions and consciously maintain the ecotourism resources they live by. The basic aim of share cooperation of ecotourism is to arouse the enthusiasm of the participation of the community residents, so as to achieve aim to ecological environmental protection.

CONCLUSIONS

Ecological environment is the necessary condition and foundation of the ecotourism development. Well the community participating in ecotourism is favor of ecotourism environmental protection; the level of community participation in environmental management of ecotourism is based on the self-development of the community. Therefore, effective measures should be carried out. First, the government should supply teaching and training services, so as to improve the sense and ability of the participation of the residents. Second, we should establish the mechanism of community participation in environmental management of ecotourism; let the community residents benefit from ecotourism, so as to arouse their enthusiasm in participating in ecological environmental management and consciously maintain the resources and environment of ecotourism, and at last achieve the aim to ecological environment protection. Third, we should set up laws and regulations, which should be representative enough to influence the decision and to ensure the rights that the community residents participate in ecotourism and community development, so as to realize the legalization and institutionalization of the rights.

KEYWORDS

- **Community participation**
- **Ecotourism**
- **Environmental management**
- **Resource protection**
- **Sustainable development**

Chapter 5

Environmental Issues and Best Practices for Ecotourism

USAID

INTRODUCTION

Brief Description of the Sector

Ecotourism has become a significant part of the tourist industry in Latin America and the Caribbean. Increasingly, tourists are seeking out opportunities to experience undisturbed natural areas where they can observe and enjoy unusual scenery, unique plants and animals, and cultural and historical features. Ecotourism can contribute to economic development and the conservation of protected areas by providing local employment and community ownership while generating revenues that can be used to sustainably manage protected areas. But careful planning and management is required to avoid adverse impacts and balance ecological, social, and economic objectives.

The Nature Conservancy and the World Conservation Union have both adopted the following definition of ecotourism: "Environmentally responsible travel to natural areas, in order to enjoy and appreciate nature (and accompanying cultural features both past and present) that promote conservation, have a low visitor impact, and provide for beneficially active socio-economic involvement of local people" (see http://nature.org/aboutus/travel/ecotourism/). Key to this definition is the concept that successful ecotourism involves "mutually supporting partnerships among three key elements: the natural environment, the local communities, and the tourism system" (IUCN 1997).

Beyond ecotourism, United States Agency for International Development (US-AID's) activities should promote community-based natural resource management—increasing socioeconomic benefits to communities and landowners while sustainably managing the environment. It can also increase awareness and support conservation, boosting the capacity to conserve, and manage natural resources outside protected areas. If local communities can benefit from the use of their land, water, forests, and other natural resources, they will want to participate in supporting actions that conserve and sustain them.

Table 1. Sample Visitation Rates to Selected Nature-based destinations in Latin America and the Caribbean.

Country	1990	1999	Total Increase	Average Annual
Costa Rica	435,000	1,027,000	136%	9.0%
Belize	88,000	157,000	78%	6.0%
Ecuador	362,000	509,000	41%	3.5%

Source: WTO 2000.

Potential Environmental Impacts

The impact of ecotourism is similar to the impact of small-scale construction, water and sanitation, and roads, but there is added concern for sensitive environments. Potential adverse impacts include:

- Soil erosion or compaction from: poorly designed roads and trails that do not follow natural contours; off-road movements to avoid wet, rutted, or gullied areas; off-road or off-trail traffic to view unique wildlife or resource features; and poorly planned infrastructure or excessive use in areas such as camp sites and tour routes.
- Deterioration of water resources and quality due to inappropriate design and sitting of latrines, septic tanks, and solid waste.
- Deforestation from firewood harvesting, camping, and construction.
- Destruction of unique flora.
- Changes in animal behavior due to human interference.
- Pollution from litter, oil residues, or vehicle exhaust.

Local resource users living near protected areas can also be affected adversely. Tourists can have a significant impact on a community's cultural and economic integrity. The seasonal nature of tourism can conflict with labor needs for crop planting and harvesting, and enhanced protection of an already protected area can conflict with a community's traditional use of the area for non-timber products (fuelwood, medicinal plants, and game meat).

At the same time, the potential benefits of ecotourism can adversely affect the environment of the protected area. An increase in employment, infrastructure (roads, electricity, and telecommunications), technical assistance, or services (education and healthcare) can stimulate people to migrate to the vicinity of a protected area. Also, improved economic conditions are often accompanied by increased production of solid waste.

PROGRAM DESIGN—SOME SPECIFIC GUIDANCE

Adverse environmental impacts often result from poor planning and coordination. Ecotourism should be based on a national tourism plan and protected-area management plans, which would be useful in catalyzing soundly designed ecotourism programs. This plan can be used as a guide to establish regulations, policies, and responsibilities for tour operators and other users. In addition, management plans should be developed for specific protected areas before initiating tourism activities. Standards for environmentally sound design and operation of camps and lodges need to be promulgated and legally required for all potential developers and operators.

The staff in protected areas should be trained in managing resources, materials, equipment, personnel, and budgets. Aside from enhancing the enjoyment and educational experience of visitors, properly trained staff can ensure that tourists stay within designated areas and use facilities—water resources, fuelwood, and camping sites—in a sustainable manner.

Limits of Acceptable Use

The maximum level of visitor use an area can sustain without sacrificing visitor experience or ecological, aesthetic, or natural resource values. Limits of acceptable use can be based on number of visitors per day, number of beds allowed in a zone, number of vehicles per kilometer, or other measurements. Whatever measures are selected, they must be easy for protected area staff to track and act on if exceeded.

Concessions for Tourism Services in Costa Rica

In the early 1990s the Costa Rican National Park System established a tourism concession program in the Irazu and Poas National Parks. Concessions for tourism-related services such as entrance fee collection, tour guides, groundskeepers, security guards, food and beverage, and souvenir stands are competitively bid to local small businesses and residents living in the buffer zones of these parks. These commercial concessions, generally awarded for a 3-year period, are a real and effective way in which communities can participate and benefit from protecting a natural area. The FUNDECOR, a national environmental NGO, administers the concessions program for the Costa Rican National Park Service, and provides oversight and quality control of the concessions. Concessionaires pay a percentage of their gross profits to a fund (co-administered by FUNDECOR and the National Park Service) that finances capital improvements for the parks and training and equipment for staff. Currently there are more than 80 concessionaires working in the two parks.

The concession mechanism has greatly improved the facilities and services provided in the national parks and has contributed to their financial sustainability. Most importantly, surrounding communities have formed a strong alliance with the park service in protecting the biological resources of the national parks, which provide many of them with an alternative source of income. During 1995–2000, the concession mechanism generated more than $250,000, which has been reinvested in the management and operations of the two parks.

MANAGEMENT PLANS

Develop protected-area management plans. Based on social and ecological field assessments, these plans should incorporate limits of acceptable use for specific protected zones. Protected-area management plans should also establish criteria governing access to sensitive ecological, scenic, or cultural sites, including minimum distances for roads and the degree of foot access allowed. They should designate areas specifically reserved for research, wilderness, roads, trails, social preservation, visitor facilities, and overnight posts. The ecological assessment should identify sites to be avoided as well those to be developed, and the type and amount of infrastructure considered permissible-lodges, camps, roads, visitor centers, administrative offices, staff housing, and the like.

In many cases the most significant impacts are associated with roads and trails that provide visitor access. Existing plans should be revisited to determine whether roads might be relocated or replaced by trails. Increasingly, managers and developers recognize that visitor experience is often enhanced by experiencing natural environments on foot, rather than from vehicles.

Plans should incorporate environmental and social assessments to provide information on how local communities use protected areas. Many communities in Latin America and the Caribbean harvest (or use or depend on) resources from protected areas, including fuelwood, construction materials, game meat, fish, birds, insects, medicine, ornamental plants, and fruits and berries. Social assessments identify the people who use the protected areas and how their activities affect ecosystems and visitor experience. They can also be used to determine the potential for establishing sustainable partnerships between tourism managers and local communities.

Once the ecological and social assessments are completed, a tourism plan can be developed that sets parameters for infrastructure development (roads, trails, and camp sites), the number and location of tourist visits, and responsibilities for implementing and monitoring the plan. Consider the following while establishing management guidelines:

- Decide on the primary audience—general visitors, tour operators, and user groups.
- Identify the theme or key thrust—environmental protection and increased cultural awareness.
- Include guidance for visitor behavior and use—campgrounds, hiking, and boating.
- Consult with guides and drivers who escort tourists into target areas.
- Obtain technical assistance from scientists who have studied tourism impacts.
- Organize meetings or workshops with stakeholders in tourism development, and form a committee of residents, resource managers, guides, commercial operators, lodge owners, service personnel, tour drivers, and local vendors.
- Use guidelines from other countries as models.
- Set objectives and formulate a way to evaluate whether the objectives have been met—improved views and decreased soil erosion.
- Develop a draft document that can be reviewed by technical specialists, and create a distribution plan for the guidelines.
- Establish official regulations based on the guidelines (requires enforcement and research personnel to make recommendations supported by data on visitor impacts on soil, water, endangered species, and habitat).

Develop Tourism Concession Programs

Designed to regulate development on protected lands, tourism concession programs can require that proposals and agreements follow specific guidelines for environmentally sound design and management. Within established limits of acceptable use, management plans determine which visitor activities and camping and lodging facilities will be allowed and can lay out the terms and conditions of commercial leases. A well-structured tourism concession plan provides a stable administrative environment for concessionaires, fair market value and reimbursement costs for protected-area management services, and quality visitor facilities and services for the public.

Concession agreement leases are normally set for a limited number of years and monitored by periodic inspections. The information obtained from monitoring is used by protected area managers to determine whether to continue or terminate a concession. The information can also be used to determine whether a concessionaire should be allowed to build or operate additional facilities within established limits of acceptable use. A concession application should include specific information on the monitoring and implementation of the activity. The government, private sector, tour guides, interpretive workers, NGOs, donors, and local communities should agree on information and restrictions to be included in a concession contract.

Guidelines on concession operation and implementation should provide environmental standards that will reduce visitor impacts. If a protected area has a concession system, its requirements can be mandated before a business is allowed to operate in the area. Without a concession system, adverse impacts from the management of tour operations, lodges, and all other enterprises in the area may be difficult to prevent.

Guidelines should also be developed for tourists, who need and usually appreciate information how to use and conserve protected area resources. Much of the environmental and cultural damage that tourists cause results from lack of information and understanding.

Table 2. Environmental Mitigation and Monitoring Issues.

Issue or aspect of activity	Impact The activity may	Mitigation Note: Mitigations apply to specified project phase planning and design (P&D), construction (C), or operation and maintenance (O&M)
General Planning and Design		
Defining use limits	• Exceed limits of acceptable use (LAUs) for the protected area	• Develop management zone plans to set LAUs and the processes that will be employed to ensure that LAUs are not exceeded. • Employ the principle of minimum tool needed to provide emergency access to sensitive or wilderness areas. (P&D) (C) (O&M)
Selecting infrastructure site	• Cause loss of tropical forest and habitat necessary for maintenance of biodiversity • Adversely affect threatened or endangered species • Result in poor siting of infrastructure, roads • Adversely affect viewsheds and aesthetics	• Carry out environmental assessments or detailed mitigation strategies to avoid or mitigate adverse impacts on tropical forest, biodiversity, or threatened and endangered species • Use a multidisciplinary team hydrologist, geo-technical engineer, soil scientist, ecologist, tourism specialist to determine the nature of proposed infrastructure and site locations buildings, roads, camp sites, observation points (see Chapter 2: Small-Scale Construction in this manual) (P&D) (C) (O&M)
Providing access to protected area	• Unnecessarily alter natural setting and viewsheds • Siting too close to wetlands, rivers, water bodies, tropical forests, or sensitive areas • Adversely affect viewsheds and aesthetics	• Develop integrated road and trail network plans, emphasizing use of trails near sensitive exceptional resources, such as habitats for rare, threatened, or endangered species, tropical forests, and cultural, archeological, scenic, historical, or paleontological sites • Locate lodges, camps out of view of protected area visitors • Carefully analyze soil and subsurface geology. Incorporate correct siting and design within specifications (see Chapter 3: Rural Roads in this manual)

Table 2. *(Continued)*

Issue or aspect of activity	Impact The activity may	Mitigation Note: Mitigations apply to specified project phase planning and design (P&D), construction (C), or operation and maintenance (O&M)
Quarrying for road surface maintenance and construction materials	• Adversely affect viewsheds and aesthetics	• Develop a quarry and borrow pit management plan for extracting construction materials. Plans should include assessments of quantity and quality of material from potential sites, in sufficient detail to also plan for restoration (see Chapter 2: Small-Scale Construction and Chapter 3: Rural Roads in this manual)
Selecting construction materials	• Result in over-dependence on imported construction materials	• Incorporate local materials as much as possible in designs, without depleting available resources or adversely affecting the environment tree re-planting or careful restoration of local quarries or borrow pits (see Chapter 2: Small-Scale Construction in this manual)
Supplying long-term water requirements	• Result in excessive water consumption that competes with protected area demands of fauna and flora, especially in arid and semi-arid areas	• Estimate protected area water demands for all future uses. Develop surface and groundwater budgets based on historical meteorological records and assessments of ground water flows. Select water conserving and purifying technologies (see Chapter 2: Section B Water Supply and Sanitation in this manual)
Determining site locations for human waste disposal and selecting human waste disposal system	• Place latrines and septic systems too close to wells and water supplies • Create human waste disposal problems spread of disease and odor, loss of potential soil nutrients	• Carefully analyze soil and subsurface geology. Incorporate correct placement and leachfield design into specifications w Establish a comprehensive schedule for disposal and reuse of accumulated human waste. For latrines, require ventilated improved pit designs; for campers provide instruction in soil mining (digging a pit for human waste and covering immediately after use) where pit latrines are not feasible. Establish a long-term plan for the removal and reuse of sludge (see Chapter 2: Section B Water Supply and Sanitation in this manual)
Selecting energy sources	• Increase dependence on nonrenewable energy resources	• Employ solar water heat in low cloud-cover regions; employ photovoltaics for lighting, radio, and cold-chain storage in areas without access to grid electricity • Incorporate passive solar cooling and heating into designs • Investigate wind and small-scale hydro energy and employ where cost-effective • Develop and implement energy conservation plans (see Chapter 6: Renewable Energy in this manual)
Choosing solid	• Cause solid waste accumulation at disposal sites	• Develop management plans for disposal of solid waste and recycling of wet wastes (organics), paper, metal, plastics, and waste oil. Require all visitors, concessionaires, and tour operators to bag and remove all solid waste from the protected area. Where feasible, employ check-in/check-out systems for all food consumed by visitors • Minimize incineration. Centralize it outside the protected area, or locate incinerator away from visitors and animal populations • Include design specifications to reduce access of potential disease vectors insects, birds, rodents to solid waste, requiring screening or regular covering (see Chapter 5: Section A Management of Solid Waste in this manual

Table 2. *(Continued)*

Issue or aspect of activity	Impact *The activity may*	Mitigation Note: Mitigations apply to specified project phase planning and design (P&D), construction (C), or operation and maintenance (O&M)
Equipment Operation		
Fueling and servicing vehicles and equipment	• Create noise problems hearing loss for equipment users, undesirable aesthetics for visitors, alteration of animal behavior • Give insufficient attention to contamination of soil and water	• Place generators and pumps below ground or in sound buffered earth mounds or sheds. Require earplugs or other hearing protection for workers • Design fueling and equipment maintenance areas to minimize fuel spillage and prevent gasoline and waste oil from contaminating soil or water (see Chapter 3: Rural Roads in this manual)
Developing financial management plan	• Generate insufficient revenues for sustainable operation	• Emphasize high value, low-impact tourism with fees and lodging cost structures adjusted to provide for sustainable management
Providing for local economic and social benefits	• Insufficiently benefit local communities	• Establish local employment requirements in concession agreements • Include community revenue and benefit-sharing clauses in concessions or trust agreements
Construction		
Creating road-sand trails	• Lead to excessive road and trail networks • Contribute to soil erosion	• Ensure protected area management observes the long-term comprehensive road and trail network plan (see Chapter 3: Rural Roads in this manual)
Constructing hotels and lodges	• Contribute to unsustainable use of local materials • Result in excessive use of imported materials • Contribute to soil erosion and siltation of riparian systems	• (See Chapter 2: Section A Small-Scale Construction in this manual)
Quarrying roadsurface maintenance and construction materials	• Adversely affect viewsheds and aesthetics	• Ensure extraction follows the long-term quarry and borrow pit management plans for building construction and roads. Carry out phased and systematic restoration/reclamation (see Chapter 2: Section A Small-Scale Construction and Chapter 3: Rural Roads in this manual) (P&D) (C) (O&M)
Excavating for road or building construction	• Damage or remove paleontogical, archeological, or cultural artifacts	• Inspect site periodically. Establish severe penalties for damage or theft of artifacts. Encourage preservation with education and incentives (P&D) (C)
Siting construction camps	• Spread HIV/AIDS	• Periodic follow-up education with construction workers, communities, and protected-area staff
Construction and operational safety	• Create potential hazards to workers and communities (injury, disease, human-animal encounters) • Create potential hazards to visitors	• Prepare a health and safety plan for the protected area and environs, including appropriate safety for workers masks for dust, gloves for exposure to waste oil, earplugs for high decibel equipment use. Provide health and safety training • Protect against human-animal interactions. • Develop mitigation plan to reduce speeding (see Chapter 3. Rural Roads in this manual) (P&D) (O&M) (C)
Operation		
Protected area visits	• Exceed visitor LAUs	• Enforce limits of acceptable use for protected area zones. Conduct annual protected area reviews of compliance with limits of acceptable use and the need for any additional action (P&D) (O&M)

Table 2. *(Continued)*

Issue or aspect of activity	Impact *The activity may*	Mitigation *Note: Mitigations apply to specified project phase planning and design (P&D), construction (C), or operation and maintenance (O&M)*
Vehicle or foot traffic in protected area	• Result in off-road or off-trail visitor movement • Create multiple tracks • Change animal behavior	• Regularly schedule field inspection by designated ecologist or inspector
Visitor use	• Cause loss of tropical forests and habitats necessary for maintenance of biodiversity • Adversely affect threatened or endangered species	• Revise annual workplans, management plans, and strategies
Visitor and community natural resource extraction	• Result in illegal extraction beyond established limits for sustainable use for fauna and flora	• Provide budget and training for local community residents and local staff to act as protected area resource monitors for flora and fauna to ensure observance of extraction limits and for archeological, paleontological, historical, or cultural sites • Provide awards or incentives for exemplary performance of resource monitors and concessionaires. Use strong disincentives (loss of concessions or employment, visitor or tour operator fines) for illegal extraction or damage to resources of special significance and sensitive area • Regularly schedule field inspection by designated inspectors or resource monitors
Providing potable water for eco tourism activities	• Result in excessive water consumption that competes with protected area demands of fauna and flora, especially in semi-arid and arid areas.	• Schedule site inspections to ensure water supply and use rates are as predicted and that water supply technologies are being used effectively. Monitor water supply to ensure that proper health practices are observed (see Chapter 2: Section B Water Supply and Sanitation in this manual)
Visitor and staff human waste disposal	• Contaminate water and soil with human waste	• Periodically test water and soil. Schedule field observations (see Chapter 2: Section B Water Supply and Sanitation in this manual) (P&D) (O&M)
Visitor and staff solid waste disposal	• Contaminate water and soil with solid waste	• Regularly schedule field observations (see Chapter 5: Section A Management of Solid Waste in this manual) (P&D) (O&M)
Visitor interactions with local communities	• Alter local cultural values	• Arrange educational sessions and materials for tourconcessionaires, tour operators, and visitors (P&D) (O&M)
Sex worker and local community interacting with laborers, truck drivers, tourists	• Spread HIV/AIDS	• Periodically follow up education with laborers, hotel staff, communities, and protected area staff (P&D) (O&M)
Operation of equipment	• Insufficiently train staff in equipment operation and maintenance • Create excessive noise, affecting equipment operators, other staff, visitors, and communities	• Provide budget and conduct periodic retraining of staff in maintenance and operation of equipment. Emphasize the need for accurate operation and maintenance logs on equipment • Schedule field observations (P&D) (O&M)

Table 2. *(Continued)*

Issue or aspect of activity	Impact *The activity may*	Mitigation *Note: Mitigations apply to specified project phase planning and design (P&D), construction (C), or operation and maintenance (O&M)*
Administrative- and financial management	• Insufficiently train staff in administrative and financial management • Infringe on traditional land use by local communities • Prompt in-migration to ecotourism sites or protected areas • Contribute to natural population increase in the area over time	• Provide budget and periodically retrain staff • Design and implement a community support service program employing protected area staff. Work with district governments, villages, and nongovernmental organizations to develop regional assessments of land use outside the protected areas and regional environmental assessments and regional plans for reducing population pressures. Carefully assess cumulative impacts • Develop and institute companion health and family planning services and non-farm employment initiatives • Ensure establishment of a licensing, permit, or quota system for residents in or near the area (P&D) (O&M)
Decommissioning		
	• Erode abandoned roads and trails • Adversely affect aesthetics of abandoned infrastructure	• Include plans and budget for decommissioning in original planning and design and incorporate in design and construction specifications
	• Create hazards from abandoned infrastructure, quarries, and borrow pits	• Inspect site at time of decommissioning to ensure abandoned infrastructure does not adversely affect aesthetics or pose safety or health hazards (see Chapter 2: Section A Small-Scale Construction and Chapter 3: Rural Roads in this manual) (P&D) (O&M)

Partnerships and shared commitments should be forged among communities, the government, and the private sector to strengthen ecotourism ventures, plan the sustainable use and management of resources, boost business and community marketing, and build financial and organizational skills. These partnerships must provide equitable tourism benefits to communities and the private sector to ensure their sense of responsibility to sustainable management.

KEYWORDS

- **Community**
- **Ecological**
- **Ecotourism**
- **Tourism**

Chapter 6

Effect of Wind Power Installations on Coastal Tourism

Meredith Blaydes Lilley, Jeremy Firestone, and Willett Kempton

INTRODUCTION

We surveyed more than 1,000 randomly sampled, out-of-state tourists at Delaware, USA beaches in 2007. After providing respondents with wind turbine project photo-simulations at several distances, we inquired about the effect development would have on visitation. Approximately one-quarter stated that they would switch beaches if an offshore wind project was located 10 km from the coast, with avoidance diminishing with greater distance from shore. Stated avoidance is less than: avoidance with a fossil fuel power plant located the same distance inland; attraction to a beach with offshore wind turbines; and the percentage stating they would likely pay to take a boat tour.

Beginning in 1980 with a "few experimental turbines" (Toepfer, 2002) and expanding to more than 25,000 MW of installed capacity (American Wind Energy Association, 2009), the domestic wind power industry has exceeded even the most optimistic expectations held in the early 1990s for its potential growth (Toepfer, 2002). During the past 4 years, the US has led the world in installed wind energy capacity (Roach, 2008; US and China in Race to the Top of Global Wind Industry, 2009; Wiser and Bolinger, 2007).

Offshore wind is of particular interest today in the Eastern US, because it is a very large resource close to urban load centers that lack other large, cost-effective renewable resources (Kempton et al., 2007). Despite offshore wind power's technical viability, proven in 19 years experience in Europe, the US has yet to commission an offshore wind project. The delay is due in part to anticipated public objection to any offshore project, following the widely publicized Cape Wind proposal, with its well-funded and politically connected public opposition (Firestone et al., 2007, 2009; Kempton et al., 2005). Nevertheless, other states have begun moving forward with offshore wind development. Texas first approved offshore wind development in 2005, and 2008 was a breakthrough year, with Delaware, Rhode Island, and New Jersey all accepting bids for offshore wind power. In Delaware specifically, Bluewater Wind, LLC has recently entered into a power purchase agreement (PPA) with the regulated utility, Delmarva Power and Light, for the purchase and sale of energy from an offshore wind farm to be constructed and operated offshore by Bluewater. The wind turbines would be located approximately 22 km from the Delaware coast.

The Local Economic Importance of Coastal Tourism

One oft-claimed, but as yet unsubstantiated, criticism of wind power is its perceived negative impact on local tourism. For example, a 2005 study found that a sizeable percentage of Cape Cod residents (more than 40%) believe the Cape Wind project will negatively impact local tourism (Firestone et al., 2007). However, as described below, this effect has not been observed at European offshore wind sites, and indeed, evidence suggests that offshore wind power actually boosts local economies by drawing increased numbers of visitors.

Any effect on local tourism must be distinguished from the effect of offshore wind farms on tourism more generally. While a wind farm might decrease tourism in the locality, tourism would presumably increase in another location, and although overall revenues would not necessarily change, there would be a loss in consumer surplus among those that switch beaches (Parsons and Massey, 2003). In future work, we may examine that issue; here we are focused on the local effects—that is, the effect on the adjacent community and the state.

Greater clarity as to the potential impact of offshore wind power on beach tourism revenues would be valuable given that beach tourism contributes substantially to the economies of numerous US coastal states. Indeed, beaches are the nation's lead tourist destination, and due to this tremendous popularity, coastal states garner approximately 85% of tourism-related revenues (Houston, 2008). In Delaware's economy, tourism plays a critical role. Expenditures from out-of-state, US visitors to Delaware reached $2.4 billion in 2006, comprising 75% of the state's total tourism sales (2008). Also in 2006, economic activity in the Delaware travel and tourism sector created approximately 38,000 jobs, both direct and indirect, accounting for 8.7% of total state employment and ranking tourism as the state's 5th largest employer (2008).

Moreover, the majority of these tourism revenue and employment gains are attributable to Delaware's beach region, with beach tourism expenditures in 2004—$627 million—representing 40.6% of total tourism expenditures (2008). In 2001, Delaware's ocean beaches received an estimated 4.8 million person trips, generating $665 million in expenditures and $409 million in consumer surplus (Kent and Jones, 2007). In 2004, the majority of out-of-state trip expenditures in Delaware's beach region fell in the lodging sector (as compared to the food, shopping, entertainment, and transportation sectors) with tourists spending $296 million (47% of total expenditures) on accommodation (2005).

As an economic comparison, Bluewater indicated that a 600 MW wind project off the coast of Delaware would employ 500 workers for 2 years during the construction phase and 80 on an ongoing basis. Proponents of wind power therefore point to the employment benefits of projects as an economic plus for the local economy. On the other hand, there might be local job losses if tourists are diverted out of state, but a 2% drop in tourism, for example, would not necessarily result in a 2% drop in local employment. Moreover, although a 600 MW project would generate approximately $200 million/yr ($2007) in electricity sales, much of the revenues would likely be utilized to pay off loans that would have been put toward the purchase of wind turbines, which would mostly likely have been manufactured in Europe.

Research Objectives
State and local governments in the US, and national and local governments in the European Union, are typically concerned about job retention and economic policies.

Public policy decisions require good data on the negative effects of offshore wind development and potential economic losses as well as economic gains. The purpose of this study is thus to improve the estimates of the likely effects (positive and negative) of wind development on local tourism. Although this study examines this question in the context of wind power development off of the Delaware coast, it may more broadly shed light on the expected economic effects of wind power development at other tourism-dependent sites, given the dearth of analysis of this question at land-based, offshore, installations.

The findings complement those of a 2006 mail survey eliciting the same views and opinions on offshore wind power held by Delaware residents (Krueger, 2007) and thus in tandem the two present a more complete picture of the implications of such development. This chapter will compare the findings of this out-of-state tourist survey with those of its counterpart Delaware resident survey.

Previous Studies Examining Tourism and Offshore Wind Power

Studies of observed behavior in response to offshore wind turbines reveal either no effect or a positive effect on tourism. However, given climate and tourist expectations in adjacent communities, as described below, the applicability of these studies to the US experience is somewhat limited. Surveys examining expected behavior in response to hypothetical or proposed offshore wind turbines have more mixed results, with a number showing expected increases in tourism, others little to no effect, and one indicating a potential decline in tourism. Unfortunately, a number of these studies have not employed rigorous scientific methods (Dudleston, 2000).

Given that the only offshore wind installations in the world are in European waters, it is fitting to first assess post-construction tourism effects there. Empirical information in this regard is limited to two case studies, Horns Rev in Denmark and Scroby Sands in England. The discussion then turns to an examination of surveys conducted in mainland Europe, the UK, and the US to better elucidate the potential tourism effects (positive and negative) of offshore wind turbines that may be constructed in the future.

Observed Changes in Tourism Behavior—the European Experience

Denmark's Horns Rev, one of the world's largest offshore wind farms, is situated in the North Sea 14–20 km (Kannen, 2005) off the coast of the Blavand Strand, a scenic, miles-long sweep of public beach (Harrington, 2006).

Before construction of Horns Rev, local authorities and businesses opposed it, fearing declines in tourism, a chief component of the local economy. Kuehn (2005), however, found neither a decrease in the community's tourism levels nor any reduction in the price of summerhouse rentals 1 year following construction. The absence of any effect on tourism is thought to have largely led to a noticeable movement away from opposition towards acceptance among the residential population (Kuehn, 2005). Further, experiences at Scroby Sands, one of the UK's first utility-scale offshore wind farms, suggest a positive impact on tourism. There, the on-site, educational visitor center welcomed 30,000 visitors within its first 6 months of opening (British Wind Energy Association, 2006).

While the finding of no overall effect on tourism in Denmark is promising for the wind industry, some have questioned its applicability to tourist sites in the UK and the US. According to Cook (2004), Denmark is a small, fairly developed and urbanized country with a high density of land-based wind turbines. Tourists visiting Denmark's coastal area do not visit for the "wilderness experience and unspoilt nature of the country" (Cook, 2004). However, visitors to Scotland, according to groups concerned about the effect of wind farms on tourism, do visit for that reason. Moreover, in the European Union, areas with high numbers of coastal tourists, such as resorts in the Mediterranean, have "generally not been targeted for offshore wind development" (Firestone, 2005, p. 98); Conversely in the US, offshore wind installations have been proposed at sites that experience high levels of recreational and tourism use (including Cape Cod; Block Island, Rhode Island; southern Delaware; and Atlantic City, New Jersey) (Firestone, 2005). Thus, wind farms off the US Atlantic coastal region might be expected to generate more objections on aesthetic grounds than those sited off the coast from less populated areas, with ties to non-tourist, commercial uses such as those found in Denmark (Santora et al., 2004).

Studies on Potential Changes in Tourism Behavior
Studies on tourist attitudes, perceptions, and potential changes in behavior have been conducted in both Europe and the US. A survey in Germany, prior to the construction of any offshore wind farms, found general acceptance by tourists and residents, provided that the wind farms were not sited too close to the coastline. Offshore wind turbines were also favored over those onshore (Institut für Tourismus- und Bäderforschung in Nordeuropa (N.I.T.), 2000), a trend also uncovered by Ladenburg (2009a). Further, studies in Sweden show higher levels of acceptance among local residents than among tourists (Devlin 2002; Soerensen et al., 2003). A 2006 survey likewise found a higher percentage of Delaware residents (84%) than tourists, sampled herein, reporting they would be likely to visit a new beach to see an offshore wind farm (Firestone et al, 2009).

The debate regarding the effect of wind farms on tourism revenues has grown contentious, with inconclusive evidence to confirm the claims of either side. Dalton et al. (2008) surveyed tourists at hotels in Australia, asking for their views on renewable energy and showing them on- and offshore wind farm simulations, among other options. Only 40% responded favorably to the offshore simulation, yet the simulated turbines appear both unrealistic (the turbines in the offshore wind farm simulation appear elongated and otherwise disproportionate, as compared to those in the onshore simulation) and much closer to shore (within 5 km) than most in existence today (Firestone et al., 2009). Conversely, MORI, a respected research organization in Scotland, polled over 300 visitors in a tourism-dependent town for their opinions on local, land-based wind farms. Fifty-five percent of the sample reported a positive to completely positive impression, whereas only 8% reported a negative one. Moreover, 80% of those surveyed stated interest in visiting an educational center at a wind farm during their trip. Yet, while widely cited as evidence for wind power's lack of adverse impacts on tourism, even in areas treasured for their beautiful scenery, the results of this study have been discounted as biased toward wind developers, who paid MORI to conduct the research.

According to Strachan et al. (2006) "broader evidence" is needed to conclude that wind farms are a source of economic development.

Additional studies carried out in the UK and in the US provide further insight into the effect of wind farms on tourism levels and, in turn, revenues. Yet, in all of them, respondents were not randomly chosen. The NFO World Group's interviews of visitors to Wales reveal that the large majority is generally positively disposed toward wind farms. Upon viewing simulations of offshore wind farms, negative responses decreased with increasing distance from shore, an intuitive finding. Interestingly, tourists reported a distinct preference (83%) for siting wind farms offshore rather than onshore, largely due to the perception of reduced aesthetic and environmental impacts in offshore locations. This finding may indicate a low likelihood of offshore wind farms deterring tourists in Wales. The study also uncovered some evidence of wind farm attraction of tourists, with 21% reporting that wind facilities would be "an added attraction... in popular tourist areas" (Lieberman Research Group, 2006; NFO, 2003, p. 4, 18–19). Mills and Rosen (Lieberman Research Group, 2006) uncovered similar results in a non-random convenience poll of New Jersey beachgoers, reporting that 14.6% would be more likely to visit a beach with a wind farm 10 km offshore, whereas only 9.2% would be less likely. Last, among tourists at onshore wind sites in England, Aitchison (Aitchison and Fullabrook, 2004) found little effect on tourism, with slightly higher numbers of visitors reporting they would be drawn to the wind farm (7.2%) rather than deterred from it (6.1%).

In sum, evidence supports both sides of the tourism debate, but geographic differences between existing and proposed offshore wind sites in the European Union and the US confound comparability, and few scientific studies have been conducted. With regard to the effect of offshore wind farms on local tourism activity and revenues, the jury is thus still out (Devlin, 2002; Kannen, 2005; Strachan and Lal, 2004; Strachan et al., 2006).

METHODS

Survey Development

The survey design commenced in February 2007. The survey instrument underwent 16 iterations over the course of its development. Duplication of some questions from a previous study of Delaware residents (Firestone et al., 2008) allowed for comparison across the two surveys. Protocols for developing and administering the survey drew from Dillman's Tailored Design Method (Dillman, 2007).

The survey instrument was pretested with 91 respondents at one Delaware beach on June 21 and July 2, 2007. Pretesting proved critical for improving question wording, clarity, and order, and for refining formatting and length.

The final survey instrument, printed as a booklet, had five sections. The first section elicited general opinions of both onshore and offshore wind power. The second primarily investigated how beach visitation behavior might change if wind turbines were added to the seascape. These contingent behavior (CB) questions are discussed further below. The third section tested knowledge of the impacts of carbon dioxide emissions on the coastal environment, as well as perceptions of wind power's potential contribution to mitigating climate change. The fourth section asked about respondent's current trip, including duration, lodging distance from shore, and lodging expenditures. The final section elicited demographic data.

Professionally simulated photos of wind farms were employed, as they provide concrete visual examples for respondents to more realistically estimate their reactions to potential changes in the ocean view, an important consideration when undertaking surveys on perceptions and opinions of wind projects. The simulations in this study may visually overstate the impact of offshore turbines on the ocean view and thus produce conservative results. First, respondents received simulations of turbines that encompassed the entire ocean horizon (see the supplementary materials for the simulations), a framing that exaggerates the extent to which they would be visible. In a recent study, Global Insight (2008) noted that at about 5 km off the coast, a wind farm would occupy only 45% of the ocean vista, and at 10 km, only 22.5%. Second, Bishop and Miller (2007) found that perceived visual impacts decrease with decreasing wind turbine contrast against the horizon (during hazy or cloudy versus clear weather conditions, or under back versus front lighting). They also uncovered a significant difference in perceived visual impacts between simulations of moving versus stationary blades, with the latter consistently generating more negative responses. Our simulations show a wide field of turbines, are front-lighted, and as still photos, show stationary blades, all factors that might increase negative reactions.

Contingent Behavior
A primary focus of the research was to gain an understanding of how tourist beach choice would be affected by the presence of wind turbines, or a fossil power plant, as a function of the distance of those facilities from the beach. Beach choice could be measured using either stated preference (contingent valuation or CV, and CB) or revealed preference techniques. Because we are examining behavior in response to a hypothetical wind farm, and considering the absence of offshore wind farms in the US, we use reported or stated choices of how an individual is likely to behave as opposed to an individual's actual (revealed) choices made after the development of a wind farm (Grijalva et al., 2007). While validity studies, which compare, inter alia, respondents' observed behavior post-policy with their stated behavior pre-policy, have been more commonly conducted with CV studies, Grijalva et al. (2007) conducted a validity test with a CB study. They found that surveyed individuals did "not appear to overstate changes in trip behavior when presented with hypothetical questions" about access restrictions to a site they visited (Grijalva et al., 2007).

In contrast to CV studies, which elicit willingness to pay estimates, CB studies derive demand behavior estimates for a nonmarket good (Carson and Hanemann, 2005). Because we are interested in how changes in an attribute of a good (in this case, the placement of a wind farm) may affect tourism expenditures, CB was employed. Given that out-of-state tourists generate 75% of Delaware's tourism revenues, the majority of which are ascribed to the state's beach region (2005, 2008), reported beach visitation in this study serves as a proxy for local tourism revenues.

With CB, proper research design and methods—which include carefully designing the survey questions to elicit truthful responses, pretesting the survey instrument, and randomly selecting respondents—are essential for obtaining sound data (Thur, 2003). We further discuss the methods we employed in the next section.

Sampling Strategy and Pretesting

Delaware's compact, Atlantic Ocean coastline extends only about 40 km (2008) yet has a wide cross-section of beaches. Some are highly developed (with oceanfronts lined with hotels, restaurants, boardwalks, and shops) whereas others are state parks with more natural surroundings (only a simple shower and changing area, a snack bar, and lifeguards). To plan the full survey sample, we conducted beach reconnaissance trips on May 15, 2007 and July 2, 2007. Criteria recorded included the size and availability of parking as well as the presence of other beach amenities such as bathhouses and lifeguards. We also informally interviewed local persons with knowledge of beach tourism—state park officials, representatives from local chambers of commerce, town managers, and the tourism director at the Delaware Economic Development Office (DEDO). Based on information gathered, we stratified the sample to include: developed beach sites at three coastal towns—Rehoboth Beach (and its boardwalk), Dewey Beach, and Bethany Beach (and its boardwalk); and beaches at three state parks—Cape Henlopen State Park, Delaware Seashore State Park, and Fenwick Island State Park.

Based on pretests, we systematically intercepted beachgoers using a geographic-transect method to obtain a probability sample. This process involved walking along the beach parallel to the shore. At regular, predetermined intervals (depending on the density of beachgoers) the surveyor would turn to face the ocean and walk in a straight line to the water. The closest individuals (one per group) within 6 feet of that transect were then asked two screening questions: whether they were out-of-state residents; and, if qualifying age was in doubt, whether they were at least 18 years old. Eligible adults who agreed to participate were handed the survey on a clipboard with laminated offshore wind simulation pictures. Refusals and acceptances were tallied. This selection process was systematically repeated along the length of the beach. On boardwalks, we intercepted individuals seated on benches in the most highly trafficked area—where the boardwalk and the town center coincide—always selecting the adult seated to one pre-determined side (e.g., the person furthest to the right). Both the geographic-transect method for beaches and the bench selection process for boardwalks proved to be minimally disruptive. These approaches, along with the advantage of communicating in person with unoccupied beachgoers on vacation, allowed for a high response rate.

Implementation, Response Rates, and Weighting

A total of 10 survey researchers took part in the data collection during two trips. The first spanned 3 weekdays and 2 weekend days (from Wednesday, July 18th through Sunday, July 22nd); the second occurred on the weekend of August 4th and 5th. We sampled in July and August, during the expected height of the Delaware beach tourist season (given school vacations and the fact that the highest air temperatures are experienced during those months). Leisure and business travel visitor trends in Sussex County, which includes Delaware's main state beaches, provide further support for the selection of July and August (2008). At each beach site, sampling took place over 2 days, 1 weekday, and 1 weekend day. Each boardwalk location was sampled on 1 weekend day.

Of the 1,716 adult beachgoers approached, 386 were Delaware residents and thus ineligible to take the survey. Of the 1,330 eligible, 1,076 agreed to participate, yielding an overall response rate of 81%; the response rate was lower on the boardwalks, where people are more transient, although still robust (Table 1). We collected a minimum of 100 surveys at each beach, with larger numbers at the two locations with the most visitors, Rehoboth and Bethany beaches; we collected slightly fewer surveys at both boardwalks. The survey responses were coded and entered into a database. In total, more than half of the surveys (with 55 data points apiece) were double-checked and corrected, as needed (with an error rate of less than 0.1% found).

We weighted each sampled beach according to its beach visitation rate (Falk et al., 1994) in relation to the total visitation of all sampled beaches. The Bethany and Rehoboth boardwalk locations were grouped with their adjacent beach. The more often a tourist visited a sampled beach, the greater the probability of he or she had of being selected to participate in the survey. As a result, for a portion of the analysis, we evaluated the data in two ways: (1) weighting solely by beach location and (2) weighting by both beach location and the inverse of the number of days a respondent reported to have visited Delaware beaches in the last 12 months. The first better accounts for visitor-days by allowing more frequent visitors to be sampled more often. The latter better samples tourists on an individual basis, regardless of how often they visit the beach.

Table 1. Surveys completed and response rates by sampling location.

Sampling location	# Completed surveys	Response rate
Rehoboth Beach	173	81.6%
Rehoboth Boardwalk	74	61.7%
Bethany Beach	190	87.2%
Bethany Boardwalk	72	72.0%
Dewey Beach	165	79.7%
Cape Henlopen State Park	145	81.9%
Fenwick Island State Park	116	87.2%
Delaware Seashore State Park	141	86.5%
TOTAL	**1,076**	**80.9%**

RESULTS AND DISCUSSION

This section reports: (1) demographic and trip characteristics; (2) wind power attitudes and perceptions; (3) reported changes in beach visitation, contingent upon a wind farm at varying distances from shore or the presence of an inland fossil fuel power plant;

and (4) potential economic development associated with attraction to a beach with a wind farm. We also discuss the significant factors influencing beach choice, uncovered through CB modeling.

Demographic and Trip Characteristics

Of the 1,040 out-of-state respondents who provided their state or country of primary residence, 99.2% are from the US. Over two-thirds visited from three adjacent states: Pennsylvania (39.5%), Maryland (28.5%), and Virginia (10.9%). Lower percentages traveled to Delaware beaches from New York (5.9%), New Jersey (4.0%), the District of Columbia (2.3%), and Ohio (1.2%). The remaining 7.8% of US respondents traveled from 25 other states, each comprising less than 1% of the total.

Table 2 displays demographic and trip characteristics of the sample population. The majority of respondents are female (58.5%) with the median education level being a bachelor's degree. The mean age is 46, while median household income falls within the range of $75,000–$99,999. Further, 17.2% own property in a Delaware beach community as a second home. Compared to the population of Delaware residents (Firestone et al, 2009) the sampled tourists are similarly educated, but on average younger and wealthier.

When asked about their previous visits for pleasure or recreation to Delaware beaches, respondents reported visiting an average of 19.4 total days in the past 12 months. On their present trip, those staying only for the weekend comprised 16%, and day-trippers 12%, of the sample. The 88% who reported staying overnight in Delaware stayed an average of 7.4 nights. They spent slightly more than $1,100 for lodging, which was on average 5 km from the beach. More visitors (20.9%) rented a beach house than any other type of lodging (e.g., motel, campground, and so on).

Table 2. Sample characteristics (means, unless indicated otherwise).

Variables	Sample values
Individual attributes	
Age	46
Male tourist	41.5%
Median education	Bachelor's degree*
Median household income	$75,000 to $99,999
Own property in Delaware	17.2%
Trip attributes	
Days visited Delaware beach in past year	19.4
Staying for weekend	15.5%
Staying overnight	87.6%
Nights in Delaware	7.4
Number in lodging group	4.8
Trip lodging cost	$1,106
Lodging distance from shore	5km

For further background information on what out-of-state beachgoers expect from their beach experience, we asked respondents to rank the desirability of different beach features or amenities. The means for these beach features are ranked in order from most to least desirable (4 = most desirable; 0 = least desirable) in Table 3. Here and in the remaining presentation of the data descriptively, the results have been weighted by both location and beach visitation.

Table 3. Mean desirability of beach features (n = 953).

Beach feature	Mean desirability
Adequate parking	3.5
Wide sandy beach	3.4
Lifeguards	3.3
Bath house facilities	3.2
Boardwalk	3.1
Undeveloped, natural beach	3.1
Big waves	2.6
Fishing	2.1
Vehicle access on the beach	1.9
Wind farm 10 km from shore	1.8
Many people	1.5

As illustrated in Table 4, 85% of respondents perceive wind power in general as either positive or very positive. Conversely, less than 1% holds a negative to very negative view of wind power. When asked about the effect of wind turbines on the "environment" (without ascribing a particular meaning to the term such as wildlife, health, or climate) 80% similarly reported a positive effect. But when asked about the effect on landscape appearance, more than half are neutral, with equal percentages positive or negative.

Table 4. Attitude toward and perceived effects of wind power.

Response	General attitude (n = 1,036)	Effect of wind turbines on the environment (n = 1,035)	Effect of turbines on appearance of landscape (n = 1,035)
Very positive	45.4%	37.6%	4.3%
Positive	39.3%	41.9%	17.4%
Neutral	14.9%	17.3%	56.5%
Negative	0.4%	3.1%	20.0%
Very negative	0.0%	0.0%	1.7%

The overall positive attitude toward wind power also applies to sea-based wind power, as displayed in Table 5. Only 2.6% of visitors stated that it should be prohibited. In contrast, 86% stated that ocean siting of wind turbines should be allowed in appropriate circumstances (with "appropriate" being undefined), or encouraged and promoted. This level of support from out-of-state beachgoers is not significantly different from that of Delaware residents who live near the ocean (80.7%), but is significantly less than the level of support among Delaware residents statewide (91.7%) (Firestone et al, 2009). This finding is consistent with Ladenburg (2009b), who observed that people who use the coastal zone more frequently—either as tourists who visit the beach often or as residents who live close to the coast—appear to associate higher visual disamenities and environmental costs with offshore wind farms than those who have weaker connections to coastal areas. However, we did not find statistically significant, finer gradations of support based on frequency of beach visits.

Table 5. Support to place turbines in the ocean (n = 1,034).

Response	Percentage
Encouraged and promoted	35.0%
Allowed in appropriate circumstances	51.0%
Tolerated	5.7%
Prohibited in all instances	2.6%
Not sure	5.7%

REPORTED CHANGES IN BEACH VISITATION

Descriptive Statistics

The survey posited wind farms at different distances: 1.5 km from the coast, 10 km, 22 km, and too far out to see (which we refer to here as "out of sight"). We present the results in tabular and in graphic form, Table 6 and Figure 1, respectively.

Table 6. Reported visitation at varying wind farm distances (n = 983).

Respondent beach choice	1.5km	10km	22km	Out of sight
Same beach	55.3%	73.9%	93.7%	99.4%
Different beach in Delaware	35.0%	18.9%	4.3%	0.3%
No Delaware beach	9.7%	7.2%	2.0%	0.3%

The reported loss of tourism at the closest distance (1.5 km) is substantial, with almost 45% stating they would switch to another Delaware beach or not go to a Delaware beach at all. With increasing wind farm distances from shore, however, progressively fewer respondents report diversion from Delaware beaches. These results are consistent with those of Krueger (2007), and are also predictable considering that visual impact is one source of opposition to wind power (Logan and Kaplan, 2008) and that the ocean view is presumably one amenity sought by beachgoers given advertisements for and higher prices of accommodations with an ocean view. Some diversion to another beach, albeit marginal, is still reported when the turbines are "out of sight," suggesting reasons for opposing offshore wind other than visual aesthetics.

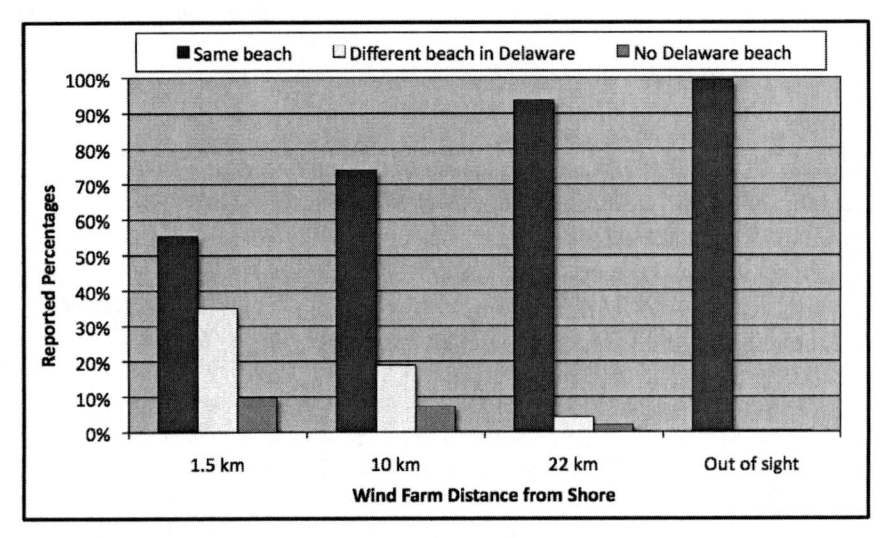

Figure 1. Reported visitation at varying wind farm distances (n = 983).

A 2006 survey asked Delaware residents a similar question regarding the potential effect of a wind farm situated 10 km offshore on their beachgoing behavior (Firestone et al, 2009). Here we compare responses to questions across these two surveys, which used the same visualizations, but with slightly different wording (500 vs. 200 turbines; and asking respondents to recall their most recent beach visit versus the present one).

Almost identical percentages of out-of-state beachgoers (93%) and Delaware residents (94%) indicate that they would continue to visit a beach in Delaware if a wind farm existed 10 km from shore. However, a smaller percentage of out-of-state beachgoers (74%) than Delaware residents (89%) reported that they would have gone to the same Delaware beach. Of those saying they would either move to another beach in Delaware or to a beach in another state, a greater percentage of Delaware residents (51%) report that they would likely switch to a different Delaware beach than out-of-state tourists (28%) (Firestone et al, 2009). These findings make sense. First, presumably, Delaware residents are more likely to take more frequent and shorter trips to local beaches due to their closer proximity to them than out-of-state beachgoers. Typically traveling greater distances, those from out-of-state are more likely to plan less frequent, but longer trips, and may therefore be more selective when choosing their annual holiday beach location. Second, switching to non-Delaware beaches may present more of an economic hardship in terms of additional travel costs (measured in time and out-of-pocket outlays) for Delaware residents than, for example, Maryland, Pennsylvania, or New Jersey residents. Third, Delaware residents also may have a sense of greater fealty to Delaware beaches than out-of-state visitors. Finally, although both residents and tourists are exposed to the perceived visual disamenity, local residents stand to benefit from employment at a nearby wind farm or from the profit-sharing venture of allowing wind turbines to operate on their property, whereas temporary residents or tourists, who tend to be financially independent of the region, do not (Devlin 2002; Soerensen et al., 2003).

For each of these beach amenity characteristics, denoted above in Table 3, we conducted a difference-of-means test between those who would go to a Delaware beach with an offshore wind farm and those who would switch to an out-of-state beach. None of the means were significantly different from each other except for the desirability of vehicle access on the beach. Those who would continue visiting a Delaware beach with an offshore wind farm value vehicle access on the beach significantly more than those who would not continue visiting a Delaware beach. This finding is reasonable; respondents who desire vehicle access understandably would be more amenable to additional uses of the coast, such as offshore wind development, compared to those looking for a more pristine beach not subject to multiple uses. Additionally, there may not be good substitutes for beaches with vehicle access in neighboring states.

Furthermore, stated visitation if there were an offshore wind farm, and the attitudes toward and perceived effects of offshore wind power (presented in Table 4) are positively and significantly correlated (at the 1% level) with each other. These findings are intuitive, illustrating that as wind power attitudes and perceived effects among respondents become more positive, reported visitation at Delaware beaches with offshore wind development increases as well.

Figure 2 graphs the percentage of respondents choosing "same beach" as a function of distance when wind turbines are in view. It can thus be used to predict the number of tourists who would report switching at any given distance within the range. For example, at 22 km offshore (the approximate distance proposed for Delaware's Bluewater Wind, LLC development) an estimated 8% would report that they would switch to another beach if shown a similar simulated view at that distance, although a much smaller percentage (~2%) would shift out-of-state. This estimate is high, however, because the Bluewater wind farm will be further than 22 km from some beaches, and indeed, will not be visible from some. According to Figure 2, an offshore wind farm constructed 16 km from shore would result in 17% of beachgoers visiting another beach, although again, the majority of these shifts would occur within, rather than beyond, Delaware. This estimate is likewise high, given that the data upon which it is based assumes that the wind farm would be located adjacent to each Delaware beach.

Although the surveys of Delaware residents (Krueger et al., (under review)) and tourists indicate that wind farms present visual disamenities, the decision of whether to locate a new wind farm cannot be made in isolation but must consider the tradeoffs among various means of generating electricity (Jarvis, 2005; Lilley and Firestone, 2008). When respondents were presented with two different beach visit scenarios—(1) a wind farm located 10 km from shore; and (2) a coal or natural gas power plant located the same distance inland—73.6% stated they would visit the same beach with the wind farm, whereas 61.1% stated they would visit the same beach with the coal plant. It is worth noting that a large coal power plant exists approximately 14.5 km from the Delaware coast (Firestone et al, 2009). Even though the wind farm would be more intrusive on the ocean view, the posited coal or natural gas power plant thus reduces visitation by 12.5% more than does the hypothetical offshore wind farm. This difference in beach avoidance is statistically significant. These results account for respondents who may have known about the nearby coal plant and chose to visit the beach anyway, whereas other beachgoers, not sampled in this survey, may have visited another beach to avoid it. Thus, the coal-plant diversion effect may be greater than 61.1%.

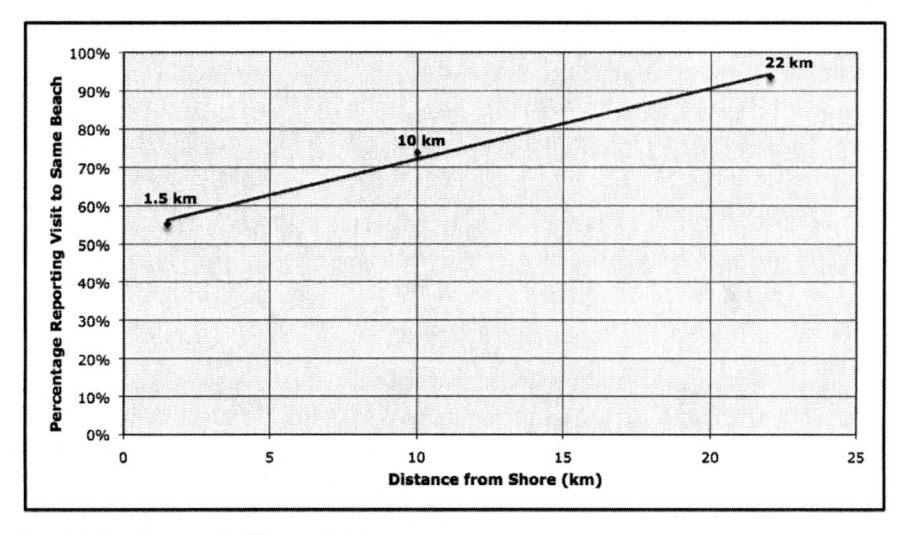

Figure 2. Acceptance of offshore wind in view.

An alternative explanation of this inconsistency—whereby people say they would avoid a beach with a nearly coal plant, even though they were on such a beach when interviewed—is that some fraction of respondents use this type of visitation question to "vote" against various types of energy development. If the "voting" explanation is correct, then our finding can be interpreted as meaning that more people are opposed to a nearly coal plant they cannot see than are opposed to a wind development in their ocean view.

Contingent Behavior Modeling

The following multivariate logistic regression model predicts a given tourist's reported likelihood of visiting a Delaware beach with a wind farm 10 km from shore, based on trip-related and demographic factors. Due in part to Delaware's small coastline, state policy regarding the tourism effects of offshore wind power is likely to consider any tourism loss statewide, rather than in-state tourism losses or shifts. Thus, we model whether or not a visitor is likely to switch to an out-of-state beach. More specifically, the dependent variable is assigned a "1" if a tourist reported he or she is likely to visit either the same beach or another beach in Delaware and a "0" if otherwise. Given that there is more variation in the dependent variable at 10 km than at 22 km, and 10 km represents a reasonable distance at which development might occur, we model this question based on responses at 10 km. Table 7 presents the model's coefficient estimates and other regression statistics.

Table 7. Logit regression of the likelihood of visiting a Delaware beach if a 10-km wind farm existed off the coast of sampled tourist destination.

Variable	Coefficient	Odds ratio	Standard error	p-value
No lodging cost	-0.055	0.946	1.313	0.966
Mean lodging cost (natural log)	-0.216	0.805	0.183	0.237
Mean income (natural log)*	-0.923	0.397	0.508	0.069
Own property	-0.991	0.371	0.867	0.253
Age below30**	2.221	9.215	0.869	0.011
Have seen wind turbine before	0.356	1.427	0.537	0.508
Surveyed on a boardwalk***	2.298	9.950	0.842	0.006
Surveyed at Cape Henlopen**	2.065	7.889	0.995	0.038
16 or 17 year old in group**	1.238	3.450	0.620	0.046
Constant**	13.838		5.498	0.012
	N	542†		
	Chi-square	48.71		
	P value	0.0000		
	Pseudo R2	0.1581		

The model fits the data well, with a likelihood ratio statistic significant at the 0.0001 level. Excluding the constant, the model has one significant variable at the 1% level, three at the 5% level, and one borderline significant at the 10% level.

We generated histograms for expenditures (lodging cost—a proxy for trip expenditures) and income to examine whether those measures' probability distributions are more log normal or linear normal. We found lodging expenditures to be bimodal in distribution due to a large component of sampled tourists who spent no money for lodging on their beach trip. When this zero-expenditure group is excluded, the lodging-cost distribution appears log normal. Income likewise appears log normal. We therefore logged the variables for income and lodging expenditures and included them in the model, with a dummy variable to control for those who did not spend any money on lodging (day-trippers). The negative yet insignificant coefficients on the "No lodging cost" and "Mean lodging cost" variables imply the lack of an effect of trip expenditures on the likelihood of continuing beach visits. Higher income, however, may reduce that likelihood, as the effect is borderline significant (p = 0.069). Interestingly, logistic modeling results (not presented here) further reveal that beachgoers with higher income are significantly less likely (p = 0.041) to visit a beach not typically or never before visited, to see a wind farm. Thus, individuals who have higher incomes are less likely to visit both familiar and unfamiliar beaches with offshore wind farms, all else constant.

The variable measuring whether a respondent has previously seen a wind turbine (land or sea-based) has a positive yet insignificant coefficient. The odds of continuing to visit a Delaware beach increase significantly, by a factor of 9.2 (since the logit is the log of the odds, the exponential of the logit provides the odds of the outcome—in this case, a visit to either the same beach or another beach in Delaware—and thus exp (2.221) = 9.2 (Long, 1997), when the respondent is below 30 years of age, holding all else constant. In a survey examining the visual impacts of offshore wind turbines, Bishop and Miller (2007) found a similar age effect, with the youngest age group having significantly more positive responses than the oldest. This effect may be attributable to the overall negative correlation between increasing age and environmental concern (Booth, 2002). Younger generations also may not have as much of an attachment to place, and further, may be more willing to embrace, or at least be less risk averse to, new technology.

The boardwalk survey variable is the most significant and influential predictor in the model, with the odds of continuing to visit a Delaware beach increasing by a factor of about 10 if the respondent was sampled on the boardwalk, as opposed to on the beach (Cape Henlopen State Park is the only exception). This finding is intuitive, considering that tourists on the boardwalk presumably tend to be less focused on the seascape than those on the beach, and instead more focused on other beach area attractions such as shops and restaurants.

Similarly, the odds of visiting a Delaware beach significantly increase by a factor of about eight if the respondent was sampled at Cape Henlopen State Park rather than at the other beach locations, all else constant. Given that out-of-state visitors to Delaware's three state parks (Cape Henlopen, Delaware Seashore, and Fenwick Island) seek more natural beach characteristics than those found at more developed Delaware beaches (e.g., Rehoboth, Bethany, and Dewey beaches) we analyzed the routes that tourists most likely traversed from their points of origin to reach Cape Henlopen, Delaware's northernmost state park. If distance traveled affected the beach choice decision, Delaware Seashore State Park could serve as a convenient substitute for Cape Henlopen. Cape Henlopen, however, differs from Delaware Seashore (and Fenwick Island) State Park in that those visiting it are less likely doing so solely for the beach experience. Compared to the other Delaware state parks, Cape Henlopen offers a more diverse range of outdoor activities for visitors, including hiking and biking along forest trails and ponds, whereas the other state parks, primarily (if not exclusively) attract tourists who visit specifically to sunbathe, swim, surf fish, and so on. The significantly greater likelihood of visiting Cape Henlopen if a wind farm was built 10 km offshore, compared to the other Delaware beaches, may therefore be attributable to the lack of adequate, proximate substitutes to Cape Henlopen, given its unique and diverse natural amenities.

Last, for each additional 16- to 17-year old in a family, the odds of visiting either the same beach with turbines 10 km from shore or another beach in Delaware increase by a factor of 3.45, all else held constant. Contrastingly, neither the number of children (from 0 to 15 years) nor the presence of any children (yes or no) in a given household was significant (neither variable was included in the final model). Older teenagers may have strong beach preferences irrespective of whether a wind farm is present (e.g., they may have preferences for non-beach amenities in the adjacent town or their teenage friends may vacation in the beach/town they are visiting) and their parents may not wish to override those preferences.

Excluded Variables and Diagnostics Employed

Neither sex nor education significantly influenced the likelihood of visiting a Delaware beach with a wind farm 10 km from shore. Similarly, due to their insignificance, none of the variables measuring either the frequency of beach visits (number of days spent visiting a US beach in the past year, number of days spent at a Delaware beach in the past year, and number of trips made to Delaware that included a beach visit in the past 5 years) or the duration or timing of the present trip (number of days, number of nights, and weekend trip) were included in the model presented. Given Ladenburg's finding that attitude formation toward offshore wind power is closely associated with the frequency and type of beach visits (Ladenburg, 2009a), this finding may at first appear surprising. However, his study examined attitudes among Danish residents toward existing offshore wind farms, whereas none of the out-of-state tourists in this study have had any experience with offshore wind turbines, at least not along Delaware's coast.

Finally, a number of variables measuring attitudes toward and perceived effects of wind power were not included in the beach visitation model because those variables were endogenous. Endogeneity occurs when the relationship between the dependent variable and the specified independent variables is bidirectional, or simultaneous; in such cases, the variables in the model are jointly, or mutually, determined (Gujarati, 2003). Additional endogenous variables excluded from the model are those measuring the desirability of beach amenities or features (presented in Table 3) as well as the perceived effect of wind power on climate change.

The variance inflation factor (VIF) diagnostic was used to formally test for multicollinearity among the explanatory variables specified in the offshore wind beach visitation model. None was found.

Tourism Economic Development Associated with Offshore Wind Farms

In isolation, the results presented so far—that visible wind farms would likely deter some visitors—suggest a strong argument for locating offshore wind turbines at distances greater than 16 km from shore, if not out of sight. However, the results have not yet accounted for any increase in beach visitation that may result from a wind farm. Table 8 illustrates the potential benefit to beach tourism resulting from an offshore wind farm. Approximately 66% of out-of-state tourists say they would be very or somewhat likely to visit a beach they do not typically visit, at least once, if a wind development were to be built 10 km offshore. This visitation effect is stronger among Delaware residents, sampled in 2006, with 84% likely to visit such a beach (Firestone et al, 2009). This discrepancy could be due to proximity, pride, place attachment, or other local factors.

In any case, these results demonstrate a strong attraction to a beach with visible turbines. Importantly, the number attracted is a majority of both Delaware residents and out-of-state tourists. Even among out-of-state tourists the percentage attracted (66%) is over twice the percentage reporting they would not visit the same beach (26%) and more than nine times the percentage reporting they would switch to an out-of-state beach (7.2%). Given the large percentage of visitors to Delaware beaches who indicate that they would likely visit a beach with a visible wind farm, one can surmise that some number of beachgoers who typically visit beaches in neighboring Maryland and New Jersey, and regional travelers not currently visiting any Delaware beach (and thus not in our sample), would also be inclined to visit such a beach. Further, although the question asked about visiting "at least once," some first-time visits could spark additional trips to the same beach, especially if attractive beach amenities are available, or if tourists should travel with more than one group of relatives or friends (Firestone et al, 2009).

Thus, despite the uncertainties regarding reported behavior and whether a question about "at least one visit" can be compared with potentially ongoing avoidance of wind turbines, the attractive effect appears to be stronger than the avoidance effect. That is, although evidence is not firm, there is a good chance that a wind development 10 km offshore would increase beach tourism rather than reduce it.

The question above about the attractive effect of an offshore wind farm does not consider that entrepreneurs or the local tourism industry may try to make it a tourism attraction. We thus asked about one such possibility—a boat tour of the wind development. Forty-four percent of out-of-state beachgoers report they would likely pay to take a boat tour of an offshore wind facility (Table 8).

Table 8. Likelihood of visiting a new or different beach at least once to see an offshore wind farm located 10 km from shore or of taking a boat tour.

Response	New or different beach (n = 495)*	Boat tour (n = 1,010)
Very likely	35.5%	15.9%
Somewhat likely	30.2%	28.5%
Somewhat unlikely	15.6%	23.1%
Very unlikely	18.6%	32.4%

In sum, reported avoidance of beaches with offshore wind turbines:
- diminishes with greater turbine distance from shore;
- is less than avoidance of beaches with a fossil fuel power plant located the same distance inland;
- is less than reported attraction to them;
- is less than the number of beachgoers reporting they would likely pay to take a boat tour.

Given these results, we suggest that, as a novelty and a tourist attraction, an offshore wind farm could pave the way for new tourist activities and services, such as a visitor center and opportunities for marketing the offshore wind site beyond the state, in addition to offshore wind boat tours asked about in the survey (Firestone et al, 2009).

CONCLUSIONS

Based on the CB findings of tourist's stated beach visitation, we would not advise developers of offshore wind to claim that there will be no negative impact on tourism. Some beachgoers report that they would avoid beaches with visible turbines, as one may anticipate from the general literature and industry perceptions. Considering that the reported avoidance effect diminishes with greater distance from shore, locating offshore wind turbines further out to sea would mitigate this outcome. Examining the avoidance question in isolation from other offshore wind farm tourism effects, however, would yield a misleading picture. We also find a reported avoidance of beaches with a fossil fuel power plant located the same distance inland, and that avoidance is stronger than the avoidance of offshore wind. More important is the presence of a countervailing effect—respondents' attraction to both offshore wind boat tours and to beaches themselves in order to see wind turbines is substantially greater than reported avoidance of beaches with visible wind turbines.

KEYWORDS

- **Beaches**
- **Delaware beaches**
- **Offshore wind farms**
- **Out-of-state**
- **Tourist**

ACKNOWLEDGMENTS

The authors wish to thank the anonymous reviewers for their insightful comments on the manuscript. Further, both the survey questions and this chapter have benefited from comments received from George Parsons and Jonathan Lilley. We are also grateful for the contributions of Jesse Fernandes, Andrew Krueger, Jacqueline Piero, Joana Flor Tavares, Phil Whitaker, Kelley Appleman, Amardeep Dhanju, and Peter Edwards for their assistance with survey design and development, pretesting, administration, and/or data entry. Diane and William Hanson's hospitality in providing accommodations for us during our survey sampling and collection efforts was very helpful and most appreciated. We also thank the Cape Wind developer, Energy Management, Inc., for granting us permission to use the photo simulations, as well as Delaware/NOAA Sea Grant for funding this research.

This chapter was prepared under award NA09OAR4171041 from the National Oceanic and Atmospheric Administration (NOAA) US Department of Commerce. The statements, findings, conclusions, and recommendations are those of the authors and do not necessarily reflect the views of NOAA or the Department of Commerce.

Chapter 7

Role for Local Communities in Biodiversity Conservation

Marc Ancrenaz, Lisa Dabek, and Susan O'Neil

INTRODUCTION

There is little debate that unchecked human population growth and the development of "modern" societies are responsible for the current biodiversity crisis. To stop the growing loss of biodiversity, global conservation efforts have mostly focused on creating protected areas free of human influence (Hogkins et al., 2006). But many of these protected areas are also in crisis. In most cases, their long-term viability depends on the integrity of complex ecological processes that stretch well beyond their geographical boundaries. Efficient conservation initiatives need to be undertaken at the landscape level, incorporating multiple-use habitats where people and wildlife co-habit (Mace et al., 1998). Since most traditional conservation efforts were typically designed to exclude human residents, they have often failed to actively involve groups of people living within or near protected areas. This failure to consider the interests of local communities has resulted in a general lack of support for conservation and subsequent degradation of protected areas (Borrini-Feyerabend et al., 2004). Theories, rationales, and underlying principles about ways to integrate conservation and development are fueling passionate debate at many levels, but convincing documentation of successful implementation is still scarce (Borrini-Feyerabend et al., 2004; Child, 2004; Oates, 1999). Since substantial biodiversity is still occurring outside of protected areas, we believe that poverty eradication and biodiversity conservation are intimately interconnected. Addressing these two challenges simultaneously remains one of our best hopes for achieving tangible and durable results (Phillips, 2003). Here we describe two cross-cultural and inclusive community-based conservation programs in Borneo and Papua New Guinea (PNG) that were designed with these factors in mind.

THE KINABATANGAN ORANG-UTAN CONSERVATION PROJECT

The two extant orang-utan species, *Pongo pygmaeus* in Borneo (Figure 1) and *Pongo abelii* in Sumatra, are facing extinction due to the loss of the ecological integrity of the islands' lowland ecosystems (IUCN, 2007). The Malaysian state of Sabah (north Borneo), which is one of the species' major strongholds, harbors 11,000 orang-utans (Ancrenaz et al., 2004), about one-fifth of the Bornean population. About 60% of the animals are surviving outside of protected areas, in secondary forests that are exploited by indigenous communities and local industries, resulting in a direct conflict of interest between the needs for preserving this iconic species and the needs for human development.

Figure 1. At 8-years old, orang-utans like Etin, who lives in the KOCP intensive study site in the Lower Kinabatangan Sanctuary, start wandering alone in the forest to find a new territory.

In the Kinabatangan floodplain (east Sabah), past and recent exploitation of the natural resources (timber extraction, conversion to agriculture, etc.) have destroyed more than 80% of the original forest cover, degraded, and fragmented natural ecosystems, caused environmental problems such as river pollution, depleted timber and wildlife resources, increased human-wildlife conflicts, and reduced the area available for the development of new economic activities. Yet the remaining forests still support a remarkably high abundance and diversity of wildlife, including 10 primate species (including 1,100 orang-utans (Ancrenaz et al., 2005)), Bornean elephants, estuarine crocodiles, and more than 300 bird species. These species live in a mosaic of agriculture (mostly palm oil plantations), human-made habitat, and natural forests under different levels of degradation.

Until recently, the absence of in-depth field studies on the relationships between orang-utans and disturbed habitats impaired efforts to design and implement sound conservation strategies for this species in non-primary forests. In 1998, Hutan (a French nongovernmental organization (NGO)) and the Sabah Wildlife Department (SWD) initiated the Kinabatangan Orang-utan Conservation Project (KOCP) to rectify this situation. A small research center was established in the village of Sukau, and a permanent study site was set up in the forest. Today, KOCP employs 40 full-time research assistants, all from the local community.

At first, our research activities met resistance from most villagers. With their means of subsistence seriously degraded (by water pollution and the depletion of fisheries resources and forest products), most people viewed the proposed Lower Kinabatangan Wildlife Sanctuary as an attempt to lock up scarce resources that are essential for their own survival. And because crop-raiding elephants and orangutans upset the frail economy of many households, villagers viewed these species as pests, a sentiment that was further exacerbated when elephants devastated local graveyards by trampling down and pulling out tombs. Many Kinabatangan inhabitants asked, "Why give land to the orang-utans and elephants, and not to people?"

Since orang-utans cannot survive outside of natural forest, it became clear that preserving this species in Kinabatangan would require the development of ecosystem management programs that embraced a wider perspective than the species itself and considered the needs and aspirations of the local communities. A prerequisite for local support of wildlife preservation is the recognition of the intrinsic value and uniqueness of species that inhabit the area. To build support for the project, the KOCP local research assistants organized in-depth consultations with community members to identify major challenges as well as the threats posed by local wildlife. With villagers' input, the KOCP started to implement an integrated and multidisciplinary strategy, combining scientific research, community engagement, capacity building, education, and policy formulation. This process involves in-depth training sessions in field research (Figure 2), community participation techniques, sustainable development, environmental education, computer skills, English language skills, and project management. These efforts have produced an effective network of Sabahan partners in government agencies, NGOs, and research institutions, as well as involving private stakeholders.

Figure 2. The KOCP conducts orang-utan ecological fieldwork during a joint program with staff from Sabah parks in the Lower Kinabatangan Wildlife Sanctuary.

Since the project started, we have witnessed a gradual decline of illegal and nonsustainable use of the remaining natural resources of Kinabatangan by indigenous people. Most encroachments today originate from outside the local communities (private industry and nonresident people). More importantly, community members gradually started to realize the importance of preserving the last forests for their own wellbeing and to support the creation of the Lower Kinabatangan Wildlife Sanctuary through local media and other means. In 2005, 26,000 ha of forests were eventually protected and placed under the jurisdiction of the SWD. We attribute this positive change in attitude to education campaigns raising awareness about the importance and uniqueness of wildlife species found in the area (orang-utans being the major icon), and in large part to encouraging local community members' active participation in conservation efforts and strategy.

For example, 20 KOCP research assistants were officially recognized as honorary wildlife wardens to help the SWD enforce the new Sanctuary Management Plan. Wardens patrol the area to control human encroachments within and beyond the sanctuary, monitor wildlife, and mitigate conflicts, and they hold events to raise conservation awareness in schools and the community. This alliance between a state agency and community members lays the foundation for securing the long-term management of the sanctuary. Financial losses resulting from wildlife crop-raiding activities were a major impediment to building local support for wildlife conservation. In 2000, a team of seven KOCP research assistants created the elephant conservation unit to alleviate wildlife conflicts and to increase tolerance for wildlife-induced damages. This community-based squad implemented nonlethal control strategies consisting of both active and defensive mitigation measures (see (Woodroffe et al., 2005)), trained local farmers in mitigation techniques, and allocated micro-loans to small-scale landowners to build fences. The unit also investigates the ultimate causes for raiding activities through scientific studies of elephant ecology—including feeding strategies, home range patterns, and identification of bottlenecks—to prevent future raids. These control activities engendered a better acceptance of the animals—leading to a complete halt of elephant shooting as a means of crop protection and an 80% reduction of economic losses due to crop-raiding activities in the area of Sukau over 5 years.

Nature-based tourism provides another opportunity to give the local community a stake in conservation. However, in most cases, "ecotourism" ventures are commercially run by private operators and result in indirect and sometimes negligible benefits to local communities (Lascurain, 1996). In 2001, the SWD, Hutan, and the community of Sukau, with the initial funding from the Danish Cooperation Agency, launched Red Ape Encounters (RAE), a community-based ecotourism model for integrating wildlife preservation with local economic development through orang-utan viewing. The SWD awarded the community the exclusive right to use a part of the sanctuary to develop ecotourism activities, and a for-profit company owned by the people of Sukau was registered in 2005. A transparent benefit-sharing mechanism ensures that the revenues generated by RAE ecotourism activities profit all its members, not just RAE's personnel. Further integrating the ecotourism project into the local economy, RAE contributes 4% of its tourism revenue to two funds (the community tourism development fund and the community conservation fund), each managed by a different village committee (Rajaratnam et al., 2007).

Conservation initiatives in Kinabatangan currently focus on implementing a general bio-monitoring program in order to assess the general health of the ecosystem (forest coverage and regeneration), as well as orang-utan and other wildlife population trends. Our current results show that orang-utans can survive in the degraded forests of Kinabatangan, that the elephant population has almost doubled over a 10-year period, and that forest loss due to human encroachments is decreasing. Although it is still too early to quantify precisely how the ecosystem benefits from all these efforts, the partnerships developed between village members, government agencies, and other players active in Kinabatangan provides the best possible long-term sustainable model that simultaneously considers the needs of the communities and those of wildlife.

THE TREE KANGAROO CONSERVATION PROGRAM

On the Huon Peninsula of PNG, the conservation issues are very different, but the strategy is the same community involvement. With more intact forest than other tropical countries, PNG is considered by Conservation International to be one of three remaining tropical wilderness areas (Mittermeier et al., 2003). The Huon Peninsula is a remote and incredibly diverse region of PNG with a steep elevation gradient from coral reefs to cloud forests a rare habitat worldwide with over 60% of the total area in Asia Pacific and a significant portion of that in PNG (Bubb et al., 2004). Many forested regions of PNG have been exploited by outside private industries for timber and mining resources. On the Huon Peninsula, however, the rugged terrain has discouraged road building, and thus encroachment by outside industries has been minimal, although the potential for commercial extraction activities is increasing. Future threats include large-scale logging and mineral extraction as world demand increases and new areas are targeted (Betz, 2001). Current threats to the Huon Peninsula are more localized, and include increasing village populations, subsistence hunting, and small-scale subsistence logging and resource extraction.

When the Tree Kangaroo Conservation Program (TKCP) started working on the Huon Peninsula in 1996, we found that although the endemic Matschie's tree kangaroo (*Dendrolagus matschiei*) was endangered (Flannery, 1995), there was still time to prevent commercial over-exploitation of resources, with locally focused solutions. Conservation depended on local education and outreach to raise awareness about the threats to tree kangaroo survival and to identify ways the local community could help sustain the populations. The indigenous people have a stake in maintaining healthy tree kangaroo populations, because the animals are part of the local diet and their fur is used for ceremonial dress. The TKCP's priority on the peninsula is to create a locally managed conservation area to prevent habitat destruction and wildlife species decline.

The endangered Matschie's tree kangaroo, which is endemic to the cloud forest on the Huon Peninsula, is the flagship species for this community-based conservation program. Other threatened Huon Peninsula species include the endangered long-beaked echidna (*Zaglossus bruijni*), the New Guinea harpy eagle (*Harpyopsis novaeguineae*), the vulturine parrot (*Psittrichas fulgidus*), and the endemic bird of paradise species *Huon astrapia* (*Astrapia rothschildi*) (Dabek et al., 2007). In 2001 and 2003, biodiversity inventories were conducted at different elevations within the proposed conservation area to provide baseline data for monitoring species presence. Tree kangaroo population densities have been surveyed at three sites using distance sampling techniques. The TKCP will also be implementing a series of biodiversity and cultural metrics to monitor success of the conservation area and provide measures to monitor tree kangaroo populations (Figure 3) and to evaluate biodiversity benefits. Surveys of local project assistants completed before and after the biodiversity studies indicated that involvement in these conservation projects changed their perception of the intrinsic value of the habitat and species unique to the area and increased their commitment to conserving the wildlife (unpublished data).

With over 95% of the land in PNG owned by the indigenous people (Lea, 2004), conservation programs must win the support and involvement of local people to succeed. Ecotourism is not a viable option in these communities, due to their remoteness and lack of transportation infrastructure, which also limits access to government services. The TKCP has worked with the landowners of the Yupno, Uruwa, and Som rivers (YUS) local-level government for over 10 years, aided by staff recruited from local university graduates and the YUS community. Through these alliances, TKCP explored social or human service benefits that would work within the existing landscape and culture and decided to focus on improving local education and healthcare.

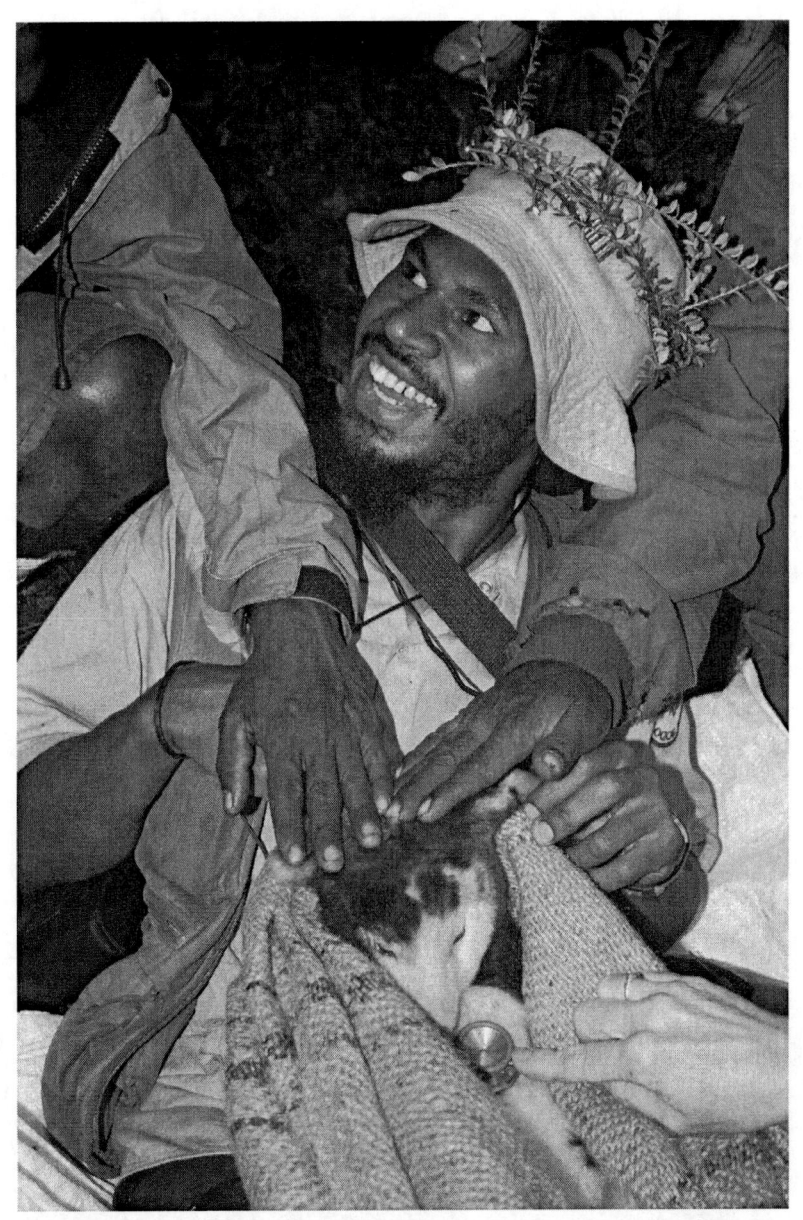

Figure 3. Gabriel Porolak of PNG prepares to outfit a tree kangaroo with a radio collar.

The TKCP provides both immediate resources and long-term investment in education within the communities, mostly funded by outside grants to TKCP. The project sponsors local students at a teacher training college with the agreement that after graduating, they will teach in YUS village schools for at least 6 years. Sponsoring local students to obtain the necessary education to return to their community not only addresses the difficulty of recruiting educated outsiders to this remote area, but also builds the educational foundation of the local community. With more teachers in the community, at least three new schools have been able to reopen. Also, the local-level government and the YUS Education Committee have agreed to financially invest in the program to help even more students receive training each year and to alleviate the local teacher shortage.

These staff members then help plan and implement an annual teacher training workshop in the villages sponsored by TKCP. The YUS teachers define the annual themes with TKCP staff and receive training in teaching methodology, environmental education, and conservation curriculum. Similar to KOCP, capacity building and training are integrated into all TKCP activities with staff and community members, including university programs, training workshops, conferences, and exchange visits with other communities and conservation programs.

Following the success of the education projects, TKCP visited villages and worked with the provincial healthcare workers in 2005 to identify outstanding health care needs. Many villages have no access to outside doctors, forcing the community to deal with most health care issues. The TKCP is sponsoring workshops with the Provincial Health Department to train midwives and community health workers through an initiative called "Healthy Village, Healthy Forest," which acknowledges that conservation programs must address the health of the human community so the community can address the health of the environment.

In exchange for TKCP's support, local land owners have pledged portions of intact habitat on their land to establish the country's first conservation area, which now covers over 60,000 ha from sea level to 4,000 m, which are off limits to hunting, resource extraction, and forest conversion of any sort (no large- or small-scale logging). Landowners have primarily pledged intact habitat at higher elevations or greater distances from a village, setting aside other areas of their forest for subsistence hunting. Landowners explain that this strategy creates "wildlife banks" areas safe for wildlife to reproduce that generate "interest": offspring dispersing into hunting areas. This strategy is consistent with historical local cultural practices of leaving certain forest areas untouched and treated as "taboo" a traditional conservation approach that had previously been curtailed by missionaries. Land near the villages continues to be used for subsistence farming and resource extraction. As a result of these pledged areas, TKCP staff and YUS landowners have reported an increase in tree kangaroo evidence (based on sightings, scat, and scratch marks on trees) and the return of wildlife species not seen on their land for generations (unpublished data).

The Conservation Areas Act of PNG, originally passed in 1978, provides the legal foundation for protecting sensitive species and habitats. Once landowners pledged their land to conservation, TKCP staff began working with the local, district, provincial, and national government, along with other NGOs and the PNG Department of Environment and Conservation, to formalize the YUS conservation area. Following approval of the conservation area by the national government, the management plans for the conservation area must be finalized. To achieve long-term species and habitat protection, local landowners have been involved in all aspects of developing the management plans including the mapping (geographic information system boundary mapping and locations of culturally and naturally significant areas), management rules, and fines. To ensure the community can successfully manage the conservation area over the long-term, TKCP is helping YUS establish a community-based organization, which will maintain the link between conservation, education, and healthcare services. Acting as the liaison between the YUS communities and various government agencies, TKCP has the resources to implement the education, healthcare, and conservation projects that are driven by local decision making but hampered by lack of access to government bodies and urban centers.

LESSONS LEARNED

The KOCP and TKCP have different conservation issues in very different landscapes, yet both embrace a similar process and philosophy of involving local communities in directing their missions. The TKCP is working in a relatively intact area conserving species and forests, which would otherwise be affected by gardening and resource use, while working to avoid future conflicts between the communities and outside pressures. Meanwhile, KOCP is working in a highly fragmented landscape with current human-animal conflicts and with intense human pressure placed on the last natural resources of the area. Meeting human needs and respecting biodiversity in both areas is the means to a conservation end.

The Kinabatangan experience shows that in the absence of hunting (traditionally, local communities do not hunt wildlife for pet trade or for food except deer), a wide array of wildlife (including orang-utans) can survive in relatively small patches of degraded and fragmented multiple-use forests. Hunting remains the major threat to wildlife in tropical forests worldwide where this activity goes uncontrolled. Since orang-utans depend directly on natural forests, their long-term survival depends on protecting the various forest remnants from further destruction. Financial incentives brought by conservation and ecotourism activities are important factors explaining the increasing support for orang-utan conservation in Sabah. However, making the orangutan a symbol of the state's natural heritage was even more effective in attracting interest from various stakeholders (local communities, private industries, and land deciders alike) and in raising awareness about the species' fate. Eventually building a trustful collaboration with government agencies and empowering selected community members in the management of their natural resources appears to be the most promising approach to securing the future of Kinabatangan. The ongoing monitoring will provide the necessary data to document the measurable impacts of all these efforts on the general ecosystems and biodiversity.

For the Huon Peninsula, the primary benefit for the local community is that TKCP can serve as a link between their remote region and the different levels of government in PNG. The TKCP is helping the YUS community receive desperately needed and deserved human services in exchange for managing their forests in a sustainable manner. Because the YUS conservation area will be the first of its kind in PNG, the YUS community is now also seen as a leader in the country and is receiving unprecedented attention nationally and internationally.

For community-based conservation approaches to succeed, they must make a long-term commitment, allow for flexibility in responding to new situations and opportunities, and, more importantly, establish a strong physical presence on the ground. Sharing and experiencing the daily conditions of community life, learning the vernacular language, respecting the local traditions, understanding current and historic use of the forests, and above all valuing the dignity, knowledge, and connection of the people to their land and their survival are essential tools to forge alliances and develop trust with local people and, more generally, to eventually demonstrate the value of conserving wildlife and its habitat. Last but not least, we need to recognize that a strategy is successful in a given scenario at a given time is not necessarily replicable to other situations. Although it is crucial to draw conclusions from the different grassroots conservation initiatives existing today, it is unlikely that a simple and unique path exists for reconciling human development and biodiversity conservation.

KEYWORDS

- **Kinabatangan Orang-utan Conservation Project**
- **Orang-utan species**
- **Tree Kangaroo Conservation Program**
- **Yupno, Uruwa, and Som rivers**

ACKNOWLEDGMENTS

The KOCP wants to thank the SWD as well as the Economic Planning Unit for granting research authorization in Sabah. This project would not exist without the commitment of all KOCP research assistants and the long-term support of our partners: zoos (Apenheul, Chester, Ouwehand, La Palmyre, Beauval, Columbus, Cleveland, Pittsburgh, Houston, Philadelphia, Bush Gardens, Lowry Park, and Woodland Park), Foundations (Abraham, World Women Work, Shared Earth, Arcus, and LEAP), the Australian Orangutan Project, the US Fish and Wildlife Department, the Orangutan Conservancy, BOS-NL, the World Wildlife Fund, Elephant Family, and all supporters. The TKCP thanks the TKCP staff and community of YUS, all of our partners and funders, in particular Woodland Park Zoo; Conservation International Global Conservation Fund; Conservation International—Melanesia Center for Biodiversity Conservation; National Geographic Society; the Shared Earth Foundation; the International Foundation; Conservation, Food & Health Foundation; individual donors; and zoos (Calgary, Cleveland, Columbus, Kangaroo Conservation Center, AZA Marsupial and Monotreme Taxon Advisory Group, Milwaukee, New Mexico, Oaklawn Farm, Oregon, Pittsburgh, Quebec, Roger Williams Park Zoo, Saint Louis, Santa Fe Community College Teaching Zoo, Sedgwick, and Toronto). We also thank the Papua New Guinea Department of Environment and Conservation, University of Papua New Guinea, and University of Technology. For helpful comments and suggestions, we thank Benoit Goossens and anonymous referees.

Chapter 8

Value of Rare Species in Ecotourism

Elena Angulo and Franck Courchamp

INTRODUCTION

It has recently been postulated that the value humans place on rarity could cause the extinction of rare species. This is because people are willing to pay the high costs of exploiting the last individuals. Many hobbies, such as ecotourism or the keeping of exotic pets may cause this effect—known as the anthropogenic Allee effect. However, the entire theory relies on the insofar undemonstrated assumption that people do value rarity.

In order to quantify how much people valued rare species relative to common ones, we created online slideshows of photographs of either rare or common species on the Internet website. The slideshow with photographs of rare species attracted more visitors, and visitors spent, in general, more time waiting to view it.

We provide evidence that people value rare more than common species. As we did not target consumers of a specific market, this finding suggests that the anthropogenic Allee effect is likely be driven by a large part of the population. Given the substantial participation in our online experiment, we highlight the potential of the World Wide Web resource as a tool for conservation action. However, the evidence presented here that the general public value rare species, combined with the assumption that anthropogenic Allee effect is operating, implies that conservationists should be prudent when using rarity to promote conservation.

The exploitation of rare and endangered species may result in their extinction, if people who greatly value rarity can drive an increase in the economic incentives to exploit the last individuals, thereby creating a positive feedback loop (Brook and Sodhi, 2006). This recently described concept, known as the anthropogenic Allee effect, shows how humans attributing value to rarity could precipitate the extinction of rare species (Courchamp et al., 2006). Historically, economic theory suggested that rare species would be safe from overexploitation, as the costs of exploiting rare species would prevent a viable economic market (Clark, 1990). However, under the anthropogenic Allee effect theory, less abundant species could suffer disproportionately from exploitation if their rarity makes them systematically more valuable (Courchamp et al., 2006; Hall et al., 2008).

Different activities may drive an anthropogenic Allee effect: collections and trophy hunting, in which the rarity of a species is directly related into an exponential increase in their value (Barnes, 1996; Rivalan et al., 2007; Slone et al., 1997); luxury items, traditional medicine, and exotic pets, in which the perception of rarity increases the owners prestige and, in turn, increases people willingness to pay even high prices

(Duarte-Quiroga and Estrada, 2003; Jepson and Ladle, 2005; Yi-Ming et al., 2000); negative impacts of ecotourism on species via disturbance would be mostly focused on fashionable species, most of which correspond to already endangered species (Courchamp et al., 2006). Such higher value of rare species remains, however, to be demonstrated.

The difficulty in demonstrating high value of rarity stems from three main points. The first is the metrics of the value itself. The most obvious choice is currency (e.g., Euros), but several studies have shown that willingness to pay is not a satisfactory metric to assess the value people invest in goods. The second difficulty is to identify a good for which a value can be attributed in the framework of an experimental design, and which can be compared for rare and common species, without endangering the species concerned. The third difficulty is the need to obtain unbiased and honest responses from a sufficiently high number of subjects, implying that they must not be aware that their choices are being monitored. These three main obstacles may explain why, despite its seemingly intuitive straightforwardness, the higher value attributed to rarity in living species has never been demonstrated.

Here, we performed an experiment to quantify the hypothesized higher value attributed to rare species compared to a common one (all other things being equal). We created online slideshows of photographs of either rare or common species on the Internet website. We distinguished three different indications of value: attractiveness of each slideshow (measured by the percentage of visitors to each slideshow), perseverance to download it (measured by the number of attempts for each slideshow), and finally patience while waiting to download it (measured by the time spent for each slideshow). While visitor's attraction measures directly the value of a given species (rare or common), time spent, and number of attempts are a way of estimating personal investment, which we assumed proportional to the value given to each species. Our results unambiguously confirm the added value of rarity and the likely generality of the concept of the anthropogenic Allee effect.

MATERIALS AND METHODS
Online Slideshow Experiment Design
We created a web page (http://www.ese.u-psud.fr/diapos/) to which visitors were invited to view high quality images of rare and common animals. To access the slideshow pages, visitors had to first go through a page consisting of a very short questionnaire asking their sex, age (six categories: less than 15 years old; 15–25; 25–35; 35–50; 35–65, and more than 65 years old), and education level (four categories: no degree; general degree; bachelor degree, and master degree). Upon reply, the slideshow page appeared offering the possibility to view two different slideshows. The only indication of the slideshows' contents was that one was showing rare species and the other common species. The slideshow links were just two similar buttons labeled with the words "rare" or "common." The two links were positioned to minimize bias in the first selected choice and the position of the two links (upper-left or lower-right) was randomly generated each time the page was loaded. Clicking on either of the slideshow links opened as small window with a cancel button in which a progression bar

indicated the proportion of the slideshow that had been downloaded as well as a cancel button. The progression of the download was rapid until halfway so as to encourage visitors to stay, but then slowed exponentially. The bar was entirely filled after 6 min, but nothing happened (the slideshow still appeared to be downloading). The visitors could cancel the downloading at anytime, in which case they were redirected to an error page indicating that they had canceled the downloading before completion, and they were given a link to the rare/common slideshow page to try again.

We recorded automatically the response of the short questionnaire together with the time and date, the slideshow position, the selected slideshow (s), and the duration from choice to cancelation for each attempt. We automatically coded the IP number so that we could differentiate attempts from each machine, which we supposed to represent a single visitor. After authorization by the ethical committee of the CNRS and the University Paris Sud, we sent emails to the students and staff of the university, as well as to many newsgroups of nature, sport or photography users, asking them to forward the message as much as possible. The test lasted for 2 weeks in March and April 2006. Upon completion, another email was sent to explain the experiment, with an invitation to view a real (this time) slideshow of more than 300 photos of animals (http://www.ese.u-psud.fr/epc/conservation/pages/explication.html?lang=fr).

Attractiveness of Each Slideshow Type

We measured the visitor's attractiveness to the rare slideshow, based on the proportion of visitors selecting the rare slideshow as their only choice or as their first choice. In the latter case, we distinguished visitors that attempted to view the same slideshow every time and the ones that tried both slideshows (in which case we considered the nature of their first attempt only). We compared statistically the percentages of visitors selecting the rare or the common slideshow by calculating a $\aleph^2$ (between observed vs. expected values).

Patience Awaiting for Each Slideshow

We measured the patience of visitors, based on the relative duration (in time) before cancelation of each slideshow. We firstly focused on the duration before and after 6 min, the time the progress bar was fully filled (i.e., the download was supposed to be complete). We analyzed this data using a generalized linear model with a gamma distribution and a log link function (GLMG) for the dependent variable (time). We included the visitor as a repeated measure, to handle the possible covariance structure given by multiple visits of the same visitor. We also included four more independent variables: the position of the rare species slideshow (right or left), and the sex, age, and education level of the visitor. Before doing so, we re-grouped the six levels of the age categorical variable into four levels only, to homogenize the sample size: extreme data with the smallest sample sizes were grouped with their next level. Similarly we reduced to two the four categories of the education variable: we merged the two lower categories (no degree and general degree) and the two higher categories (bachelor and master degree). We performed a backward stepwise regression, but the main effect (rare or common) was always maintained even when not significant. In a first analysis, we took into account only visits that were canceled before the bar was fully filled (within the first 6 min). In a second analysis, we considered only the attempts that were canceled after that, up to 4 hr. We believe that including periods longer than 4 hr were not realistic measures of visitor persistence or interest in the slideshow.

Secondly, we analyzed the duration of all attempts for either slideshow for each visitor. To do this, we divided visitors that made only one attempt to either the rare or common slideshow, visitors that made more than one attempt to the same slideshow and visitors that made more than one attempt to both slideshows. In the first case, we performed a GLMG with the time duration as the dependent variable and the type of slideshow as the independent variable. In the second case, we performed the same analysis but the dependent variable was the sum of the time duration of all attempts for each visitor. In the third case, we included the visitor as a repeated measure in the model, so that we compared time duration for each slideshow within visitors.

Perseverance for Each Slideshow

We measured the perseverance of visitors, based on the total number of attempts by each visitor to open each slideshow. Similarly to the previous analyses, we firstly analyzed the visitors that made attempts at opening only one slideshow type (either the rare or the common). We performed two GLMG, using the total number of visits as dependent variables and the type of slideshow as the independent variable. This allowed us to compare number of attempts between visitors that only attempted to view the rare or the common slideshow. We secondly analyzed the cases when a visitor visited both slideshows. We performed the same analysis but the visitor was introduced in the model as a repeated measure, so that we compared these values within visitors.

Computations were performed with STATISTICA 6.0 (StatSoft Inc., 2001) and the SAS package (GENMOD, v. 9.1.3., (SAS Institute Inc., 2004)).

DISCUSSION

The experiments performed in this study aimed to validate a key assumption underpinning the concept of the anthropogenic Allee effect; that people value rarity of wildlife. Preference for a rare species could maintain a sufficient demand as to overcome the high exploitation cost for the last individuals, putting it into a vicious circle of overexploitation, and finally leading to its extinction (Courchamp et al., 2006). Here, we have shown that more than half of the 2,560 visitors would have preferred to see the slideshow with photographs of the rare species. Moreover, within the first 6 min waiting to download the slideshow (time the downloading bar took to fill up), people waited longer for the rare species slideshow compared to that of the common species. These results were not affected by their age, sex, or level of education.

Our experiment provided no details of the species supposedly displayed in the slideshows and was based on a comparison between rare or common species, thus rarity is clearly identified as the cause of the preference. This is unusual when searching for relationships between rarity and value (i.e., correlations). For example, it has been shown that caviar price in markets increased as sturgeon (*Acipenser baerii*) abundance decreased (Gault and Meinard, 2008); or fleet size engaged in whale watching increased as killer whale (*Orcinus orca*) abundance decreased (Bain, 2002). In these two examples, as well as in the examples on other anthropogenic Allee effect activities

(Courchamp et al., 2006), it is difficult to separate correlation from causation. Because our experiments were based on two slideshows for which exactly the same (or lack of) information was given, it is actually the comparison between the value of rare and common that we studied. In this regard, any potential bias should logically be similar for the two slideshows, leaving only the rarity attribute as the cause of potential differences. Also, the independence of our results from specific species confers higher generalization to our conclusions.

The value attributed by people to species is generally measured by the price people would, in theory, accept to pay (the willingness to pay). Such metrics have been criticized and the use of non-monetary criteria has been advocated (Martín-López et al., 2007; Ojea and Loureiro, 2007). In this chapter, we propose different metrics to assess the relative value of rarity: the (first or unique) choice of a slideshow to be viewed, the time spent in waiting for the slideshow to appear, and the number of attempts to open the slideshow. Two of these three variables were significantly related to rarity. The main goal of this article was to show that the general public gives more value to rare species relative to common ones. Our results demonstrate that visitors had an increased interest in rare species and we suggest that this interest is potentially linked to an anthropogenic Allee effect. Whether this increased interest could drive a higher economic value should be the focus of future studies.

Within visitors who made a unique choice, more than 60% tried the rare species slideshow, and within visitors who attempted several times to see the same slideshow, almost 70% selected the rare species one. Differences were less important for those who tried to see both slideshows several times; probably at some stage (more than five times), the type of species had become less important to the visitor than the success of seeing any slideshow at all. We assumed that the first choice is a direct indication of the people's value for a species.

Rarity also affected the time spent waiting for the slideshow to begin within the first 6 min. We assumed that time spent waiting is proportional to personal interest, so that here people were more interested in rarity. When we classified visitors by their number of visits to the slideshows, we obtained contrasting results for the time expended waiting for the slideshow. Visitors waited more for the rare slideshow when making more than one attempt, but waited more for the common slideshow when making only one attempt to download a slideshow. This last result could be explained if, when confronted with a choice of two items, people often "leave the best until last." This has been observed in another study of rarity (over commonness) of wildlife-based luxury goods (Gault and Meinard, 2008). When realizing that their second choice also would not download, those visitors would have given up more rapidly. Overall, and because visitors were not aware that their decisions were being monitored, we believe these parameters were not biased and reflected the real relative value visitors attributed to rarity.

We believe our online experiment was original because we were able to obtain a high sample of unbiased people. Assuming that each response from a given IP address came from a single visitor, we obtained a total of 2,560 visitors. Even if a visitor could access the slideshow from different machines or different visitors could log on the same machine, these scenarios should represent a small percentage of the visits and their expected effect should not be very important given the very large sample size we obtained. We tried to diversify the likely recipients of the online slideshow experiment by contacting large newsgroups in random subjects, or by asking recipients to forward their message, but the bulk of the primary email list was the university of Paris XI staff and students. Our online questionnaire requested information on the visitor's education level; even if our final sample was biased in favor of higher education levels, this information was taken into account during the statistical analyses. In summary, we believe these results demonstrate the higher value attributed to rare species by the general public, as opposed to specific wildlife trade users who were not targeted here. Although it is quite likely that different cultural roots, political, and/or social interests could also be biasing them (Torgler and García-Valiñas, 2007), our results should hold for most industrialized countries, and probably beyond. It is also noteworthy that our original, web-based, approach generated a large amount of data: during 2 weeks and with no advertising other than targeted email contact, at least 2,560 different visitors were interested to see online slideshows of photographs of rare/common species, enough to endure through the notoriously painful process of answering three questions before accessing the slideshow page. Given the significant participation in our online experiment, we highlight the potential of the World Wide Web as a tool for conservation actions.

Beside these methodological recommendations, one may extract two main findings from this study. The first one is that rarity by itself is an important trait for the general public when related to animal species, and this should continue to be used as a tool for the conservation of rare and endangered species. The second implication of this study, however, is that as rare species are more valued than common ones, there is a high likelihood of existence of an anthropogenic Allee effect (Courchamp et al., 2006) in diverse wildlife related human activities. The particular threat this effect poses on rare species is sufficiently disturbing for conservationists to use caution when disclosing rarity, as well as to begin a dialogue about the measures that can be adopted to protect rare species from this new threat.

RESULTS

Attractiveness of Photographs of Rare Species

We provided online slideshows of photographs of either rare or common species. Visitors to the website were given the choice between the two slideshows. Upon clicking the link to the selected slideshow, an upload progress bar opened. However, the slideshow never started, and the time passed from starting to cancel the download was automatically recorded. The program also recorded, for each attempt, the time and date, as well as the position (which changed randomly) of the selected slideshow on the web page (rare or common). The IP number of the computer through which access was made was automatically coded and recorded so that we could differentiate attempts from individual computers (= visitors, see Materials and Methods). A total of 4,967 different attempts were recorded in the 2 week duration experiment. Nine events were disregarded as the recording was erroneous due to an unusual system configuration. We also removed data for durations >20 hr and finally obtained a total of 4,941 data that came from 2,560 different visitors.

Almost half (48.4%) of the 1,240 visitors made only one download attempt. Of these, 60.2% made an attempt to see the rare species, while the rest tried the common species ($\aleph^2 = 4.13$, $p = 0.042$, Figure 1a). Within the other half of the visitors, 347 (13.5%) made several attempts to open only one slideshow, and 67.4% of them tried to open the rare species ($\aleph^2 = 12.17$, $p < 0.001$, Figure 1a). The rest of the visitors (N = 973, 38.0%) made several attempts and tried both slideshows at least once. Among them, 50.9% tried the rare first ($\aleph^2 = 0.03$, $p = 0.862$, Figure 1a).

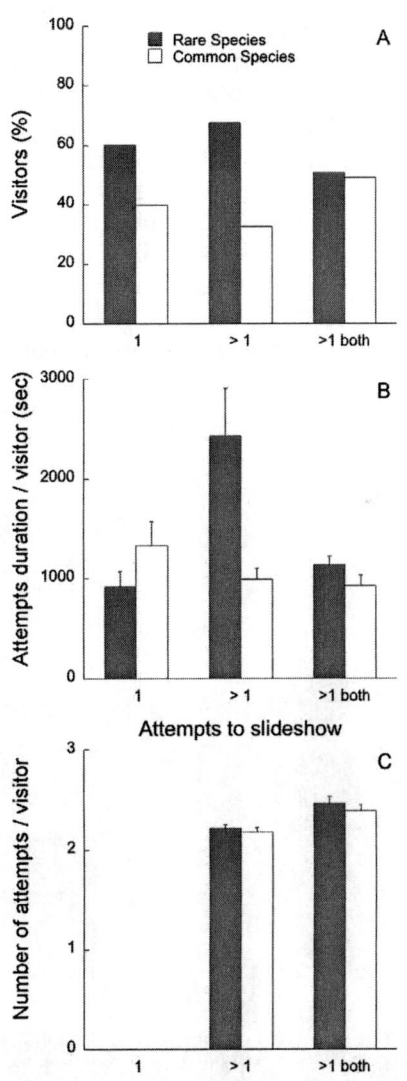

Figure 1. Behavior of visitors having to choose between slideshows of rare or common species. We show (A) attractiveness, (B) patience, and (C) perseverance of visitors. Data comes from visitors who attempted to open only one slideshow type, once (1) or multiple times (>1), or their first choice when they attempted to open both slideshows (>1 both). Error bars indicate standard errors. doi:10.1371/journal.pone.0005215.g001.

Patience Awaiting for the Rare Species Photographs

Visitors remained between 1 sec to more than 20 hr on the page with the progress bar. The time waited (in min) fit a gamma distribution with a peak in the first 2 min. The first 6 min (which corresponded to the time it took for the download bar to be entirely filled) accounted for 3,112 data (63.0% of the total) and the first 4 hr accounted for 4,561 data (92.3% of the total). It was obvious that the longest attempts were made by those of visitors who left the slideshow open in the background while not paying attention to it.

Firstly, we looked at all attempts by classifying them by their duration (shorter or longer than 6 min, the time upon completion of the progress bar). Results regarding the first 6 min showed that only the type of slideshow (rare or common) significantly affected the time spent downloading the slideshow ($\aleph^2 = 9.38$, $p = 0.002$, $N = 3068$ attempts, Figure 2); visitors spent more time waiting for the rare species slideshow to open. Results regarding visitors that canceled the slideshow between 7 min and 4 complete hr showed no relationship with the type of slideshow ($\aleph^2 = 0.0$, $p = 0.982$, $N = 1802$, Figure 2), but visitor's age, sex, and level of studies were significantly related to the time spent: men spent more time waiting for the slideshow to open than women ($\aleph^2 = 4.60$, $p = 0.032$, $N = 1802$ attempts), as did visitors between 26–35 years old ($\aleph^2 = 12.28$, $p = 0.006$; $N = 1802$ attempts) and people of higher level of studies ($\aleph^2 = 4.04$, $p = 0.044$; $N = 1802$ attempts). These variables were recorded before accessing the slideshow web page (see Materials and Methods).

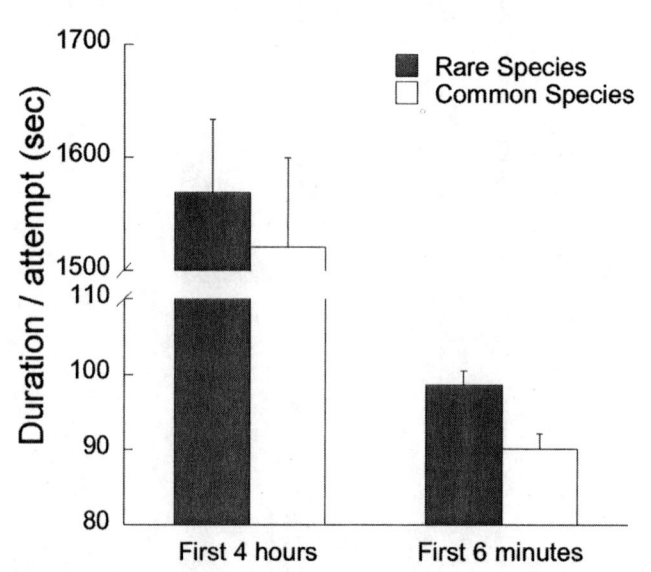

Figure 2. Effect of the slideshow type (rare or common species) on the time spent by visitors. We show data for attempts shorter than 6 min and for attempts between 6 min and 4 complete hr. Error bars indicate standard errors.

Secondly, we focused on the total visit duration per visitor and divided visitors into those attempting to access either slideshow once, those attempting to access the same slideshow more than once and those attempting to access both slideshows more than once. Among the visitors that made only one attempt to the slideshow, the total time spent was higher for the common species ($\aleph^2 = 12.72$; $p < 0.001$; $N = 1240$, Figure 1b). Among the visitors who attempted to access the same slideshow more than once, the total time spent was higher for the rare species ($\aleph^2 = 27.38$; $p < 0.001$; $N = 347$, Figure 1b). Visitors that made more than one visit to the web page and attempted to see both slideshows, spent more time trying to access that of the rare species, although the trend was not significant ($\aleph^2 = 2.76$, $p = 0.097$, $N = 1944$, Figure 1c).

Perseverance to see the Rare Species Photographs
Among the visitors that made more than one attempt, 347 tried the same slideshow every time, and they did so between two and five times. The total number of attempts for each slideshow by visitors attempting to open the rare species slideshow was higher but not significantly different than for the visitors attempting to open the common species slideshow ($\aleph^2 = 0.56$, $p = 0.453$, $N = 347$; Figure 1c). The 973 visitors who tried to see both slideshow types several times, did so between two and 32 different times, with more attempts for the rare species, although not significantly ($\aleph^2 = 2.94$, $p = 0.087$, $N = 1944$, Figure 1c).

KEYWORDS

- **Allee effect**
- **Anthropogenic Allee effect**
- **Gamma distribution and a log link function**

AUTHORS' CONTRIBUTIONS

Conceived and designed the experiments: Franck Courchamp. Performed the experiments: Elena Angulo and Franck Courchamp. Analyzed the data: Elena Angulo. Wrote the chapter: Elena Angulo and Franck Courchamp.

ACKNOWLEDGMENTS

We are very grateful to all people that have participated in the online slideshow experiment and we hope they will not blame us for the time they have lost: we hope its value has been well used with this study. Jean-Paul Briane helped to design the data collection program of the website and S. Gregory edited the text before submission. High motivation and insightful comments were provided by S. Caut, X. Cerdá, A. Gault, S. Gregory, R. Hall, J. Haquet, D. Harris, and O. Marquis.

Chapter 9

Rarity Value and Species Extinction

Franck Courchamp, Elena Angulo, Philippe Rivalan, Richard J. Hall, Laetitia Signoret, Leigh Bull, and Yves Meinard

INTRODUCTION

Standard economic theory predicts that exploitation alone is unlikely to result in species extinction because of the escalating costs of finding the last individuals of a declining species. We argue that the human predisposition to place exaggerated value on rarity fuels disproportionate exploitation of rare species, rendering them even rarer and thus more desirable, ultimately leading them into an extinction vortex. Here, we present a simple mathematical model and various empirical examples to show how the value attributed to rarity in some human activities could precipitate the extinction of rare species—a concept that we term the anthropogenic Allee effect (AAE). The alarming finding that human perception of rarity can precipitate species extinction has serious implications for the conservation of species that are rare or that may become so, be they charismatic and emblematic or simply likely to become fashionable for certain activities.

Overexploitation of living species (i.e., human exploitation exceeding the species' regeneration capacity) is a major threat to biodiversity (Rosser and Mainka, 2002), yet theory predicts that economic extinction (exploitation cessation) will usually precede ecological extinction (population disappearance). As populations become more sparse, it is increasingly costly to exploit them, and exploitation ceases to be beneficial (Clark, 1990). In the absence of natural extinction risks at low population size (e.g., demographic stochasticity), exploitation cessation allows for the species' recovery. However, less-abundant species could suffer disproportionately from exploitation if their rarity makes them systematically more valuable. We postulate that because rarity makes living species attractive, their (over) exploitation can remain profitable, rendering such species even rarer, and driving them to extinction.

This human-generated feedback loop is very similar to the Allee effect (Courchamp et al., 1999; Stephens and Sutherland, 1999), an important process in basic ecology and applied conservation biology. Whereas ecologists have historically focused on negative density dependence, they are increasingly realizing that an ever-growing number of species suffer from positive density dependence at low population density. In many animal and plant species, individual reproduction and survival is diminished in small populations through various mechanisms including mate shortage, failure to optimize the environment, or lack of conspecific cooperation. Populations suffering from Allee effects may exhibit negative growth rates at low densities, which drives them to even lower densities and ultimately to extinction. A typical example is that of obligate cooperative breeding species, which need group members to enable them to raise offspring, survive predators, and/or forage cooperatively, and fail to do so efficiently when their numbers drop (Courchamp and Macdonald, 2001).

Although studies on Allee effects are continuing, it has been generally accepted that the Allee effect is intrinsic to the species concerned, which express it naturally at low density. Therefore, human activities cannot create an Allee effect; at most, they can push species into density ranges where their natural Allee effect will be expressed. On the contrary, we show here that humans can induce a purely artificial Allee effect in rare species through the "paradox of value" (Ekelund and Hebert, 1997). We call it the AAE. Although familiar to economists, the paradox of value also called the "water and diamonds paradox" (water has much value in use but none in exchange, while the opposite is true for diamonds) is absent from ecological theory. Here we will provide a mathematical model to demonstrate how an AAE can, in theory, emerge in wildlife-related trade as soon as rarity acquires value. We then identify a number of human activities where an AAE can occur and use examples to illustrate each of them.

MODEL AND RESULTS THEORETICAL FRAMEWORK

The AAE is founded on two fundamental assumptions: (i) there is a positive correlation between species rarity and its value, and (ii) this correlation fuels sufficient demand to ensure that the market price exceeds the escalating costs of finding and harvesting a declining species. If these simple conditions are met, harvesting reduces the population of the rare species, increasing its rarity and therefore its value, which stimulates further harvesting and drives the species into an extinction vortex.

We added these assumptions as a simple modification to the Gordon–Schaefer model (Gordon, 1954) of resource exploitation to assess their effect on population density equilibrium. The model applies to populations subject to open-access (i.e., unregulated) exploitation (Clark, 1990), and in particular, to the dynamics of rare species subject to poaching (Bulte, 2003). In the absence of harvesting, the population x grows according to the logistic equation with rate r and carrying capacity K. It is harvested at a rate proportional to both the population level x and the hunting effort E. The rate of change of hunting effort is assumed to be proportional to economic rent or profit, which is the difference between the price obtained for the harvest and the total cost of hunting. This can be expressed mathematically as where q is the catchability of the species, α is a measure of how rapidly hunters respond to changes in profit, p is the (constant) price obtained per unit harvest, and c is the cost per unit effort. Provided that one would make a profit when hunting the population at carrying capacity (i.e., pqK > c), this system has a globally stable equilibrium. The population is never hunted to extinction, because cost per unit harvest in unit time, c/qx, becomes very large as x tends to zero (Figure 1A).

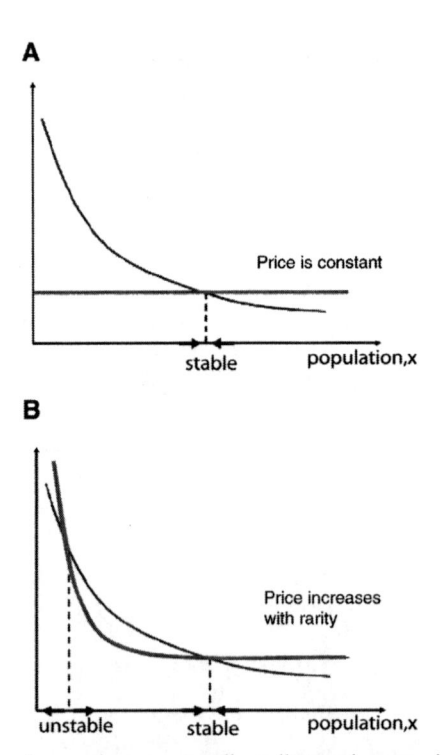

Figure 1. Demonstration of an anthropogenic Allee effect with a simple model of an exploited population. The price (red, thick line) and cost (blue, thin line) per unit harvest in unit time as a function of the population density x when (A) the price is independent of X and (B) the price increases with rarity. The system is in equilibrium whenever the red and blue lines meet, and the bold arrows represent how the population responds when perturbed from equilibrium. In (B), an increased price at low population density induces an Allee Effect.

If, however, the price of a unit harvest is an increasing function of the species rarity (i.e., $p = p(x)$, $dp/dx < 0$) or more precisely, if below some critical population density, someone is always willing to pay enough to offset the costs of finding and hunting the species ($p(x) > c/qx$ for small x) then an unstable equilibrium exists (Figure 1B). Below this equilibrium population density, hunting further reduces the population, which increases the price of a unit harvest, which in turn increases the hunting effort, and the species is driven into an extinction vortex.

These results can also be understood within the framework of supply and demand theory. Clark (1990) showed that the open-access exploitation model can be solved at equilibrium to obtain a relation between yield (qEx) and price, the equilibrium supply curve. That supply curve for an exploited population is backward bending, corresponding to overexploitation when the species is hunted at levels above the maximum sustainable yield. In traditional models, the demand curve is usually elastic (i.e., the quantity purchased is sensitive to changes in price), and hence only intersects the supply curve once. It is this price that determines the equilibrium population size and exploitation effort. However, our assumption that people are willing to pay more for rare species results in a demand curve which becomes increasingly inelastic with rarity, and the supply curve is cut twice, exactly as in Figure 1B: the population is harvested to extinction if its drops below the lower equilibrium.

EMPIRICAL EXAMPLES

Data showing a positive relationship between price and rarity are scarce but do exist for a number of nature-related economic activities (we present some analyses in Figure 2). The second assumption of the AAE, that prices increase with rarity faster than the exploitation costs, may be more difficult to test. In general, one might expect that increasing exploitation costs lead to increasing prices, which in turn results in a drop in demand. However, other factors act to reinforce the demand, for example, when it becomes fashionable to acquire a rare item (see examples below). The second assumption is therefore fulfilled if there are always a few consumers willing to acquire the last individuals at any price. In this case, ecological extinction (the end of the species) will precede economic extinction (cessation of exploitation), contrary to the predictions of classical theory (the simple Gordon–Schaefer model (Gordon, 1954)).

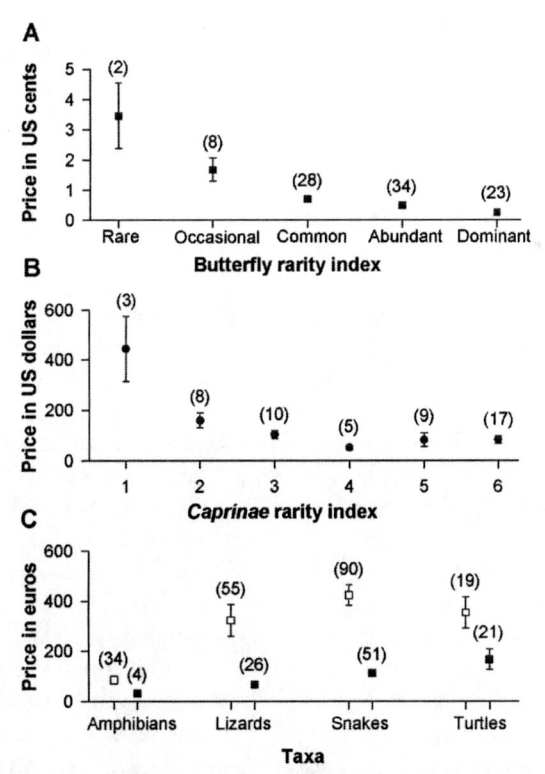

Figure 2. Empirical examples of activities where the price of species is related to rarity or perceived rarity (A) Prices of collectible butterflies in Papua New Guinea (modified from (Slone et al., 1997)). (B) Hunting trophy prices of 57 Caprinae taxa. (C) Selling prices of exotic pet species according to CITES status. Species that have a CITES status (open squares) are more expensive than species with no CITES status (solid squares). Prices were standardized by dividing by (A) male wingspan, (B) trophy size, and (C) adult weight (see text for details). Vertical bars: standard error; sample size in parentheses.

We claim that a number of human activities can create an AAE. Below, we develop some examples that illustrate under what conditions people are willing to pay (or risk) substantial amounts for the satisfaction and/or prestige of acquiring rare species. It is, however, important to stress that correlation does not necessarily prove causation. The only true test of the effect would be to track changes in a particular species' demand curve with rarity, which is not feasible in a dynamic system.

Collections

The most straightforward example of a nature-related activity where rarity is valued is that of hobby collections, where the rarest items are the most valued and thus demand the highest prices. As the value of a rare item increases, more time, effort, or resources may be devoted to trying to acquire it, increasing the pressure on the species as it becomes rarer. The collection of butterflies in Papua New Guinea illustrates this point (Slone et al., 1997), whereby the price of butterflies sold by villagers to insect collectors were correlated with rarity, even when corrected by size (price divided by male wing span; Kendall concordance test for nonparametric data $\tau = -0.39$, $p < 0.0001$) (Figure 2A). Therefore, it is the rarity of the butterflies, not their size, that drives the price of these collection items. Collectors of wildlife items such as other insects, bird eggs, mollusk shells, or orchids often adhere to this rule. For example, the collection of bird eggs threatens many rare species in the UK, and this practice continues despite the threat of financial penalties and/or jail terms (Thomas et al., 2001). When species are protected by local laws and/or by international trade treaties, the high price that the rarest species can fetch on the collection market is a powerful incentive to poachers and smugglers to seek and illegally sell the most expensive (rare) species, constituting a real threat to some of these species.

Scientists have historically been, and in some cases still are, among these enthusiastic collectors of natural specimens. Following the overexploitation of the great auk *Pinguinus impennis* for food and feathers, the species became very rare. As a consequence, these birds became a valuable item for collectors—among them, ornithologists, and museum administrators, who were eager to acquire eggs or skins of the rare and soon to be extinct bird, thereby precipitating its extinction (Fuller, 1999). The great auk provides a possible example of an AAE leading to a species extinction and should serve as a warning for currently threatened species.

Trophy Hunting

Trophy hunting represents another form of collection. For thousands of years, several cultures have valued trophies as a sign of manhood and virility. Species that were difficult to kill symbolized power, because power was required to kill them. However, because sophisticated firearms are now used, the emphasis of hunting has shifted from dangerous to rare animals. Rarer species are harder to find, so greater hunting skill and greater wealth is required, and greater prestige is gained by killing them. We compared the standardized quality of trophies of 57 species and subspecies of Caprinae hunted for their trophies with the average price of the trophy hunting in the 2006 season, as proposed by various hunting tour operators on the Internet. The prices of the hunting trophies were standardized by dividing the average price for each taxon by the current

Safari Club International (SCI) world record for these taxa. The SCI is a standardized measurement method for trophies developed by trophy-hunting societies and is designed to allow interspecific comparisons of trophy quality. Thus, the price of a trophy should depend solely on its SCI value. We then compared this standardized price for species according to their perceived rarity through an index of rarity constructed by attributing points to each species according to their protection status. We accounted for the World Conservation Union (IUCN: critically endangered = 0 point; endangered = 1; vulnerable = 2; others = 3), the Convention on International Trade in Endangered Species of Wild Fauna and Flora (CITES: Appendix I = 0; Appendix II = 1; Appendix III = 2; no Appendix = 3), and local protection (yes = 0; no = 1). Points were added, and the cumulative score was used as an indication of the perceived rarity of the taxon; the lower the score, the rarer the taxon. Once again, our results show that hunting trophy prices are correlated with rarity, regardless of size (Kendall concordance test for nonparametric data $\tau = -0.34$, $p < 0.0001$): the rarer the trophy, the more valuable and expensive it is (Figure 2B). For wild sheep alone, wealthy hunters are willing to pay more than US$400,000 at auctions to shoot a rare animal (Festa-Bianchet, 2003), because few of their peers will be able to do so, and they will gain social prestige in being one of the few who can afford it. Very few hunting permits are delivered for protected species, making the animals even more attractive to trophy collectors and possibly stimulating illegal hunting.

Luxury Items

The consumption of rare species as luxury food items is another way of displaying wealth and/or social status. The rarer the item, the more expensive it is, and the more prestige is gained by its acquisition. When closing deals, wealthy Asian businessmen wishing to display their affluence will pay large amounts of money to eat a plate of lips of a large Napoleon wrasse, *Cheilinus undulatus* (a single pair of lips costs US$250). By the mid 1990s, Napoleon wrasse became the most sought-after reef fish in the world (Donaldson and Sadovy, 2001), and is currently number one on the "top ten most-wanted species" list published by the World Wide Fund for Nature. Populations in South East Asia are now extinct on many reefs, and very few large individuals survive in the remaining fragmented populations (Donaldson and Sadovy, 2001). The caviar obtained from different sturgeon species provides another example for the potential for the feedback loop we describe here. Not only are all sturgeon species currently on the IUCN Red List and CITES Appendices (Pikitch et al., 2005; Raymakers, 2002), but the price of the caviar is correlated with its rarity (Raymakers and Hoover, 2002). Abalones, of which six species suffer from overfishing on the Pacific coast of North America, are another illustration. Considered a delicacy in California, white abalones, the rarest of the six abalone species, have declined by over 99.99% due to increasing overfishing, in part illegal (the fishery was closed in 1996), while at the same time, prices have escalated (California Department of Fish and Game, 2005; Davis et al., 1998; Tegner, 1993). Even taking fishing effort into account, the volume of abalones fished is inversely proportional to the price (power regression model, $F_{40,2} = 139.96$; $p < 0.0001$) (Figure 3). Although white abalones were the first marine invertebrate on the US endangered species list in 2001, this species could become extinct within a decade unless extraordinary recovery measures are implemented (California Department of Fish and Game, 2005). Due to the demand for other types of luxury items, such as exotic woods, furs, turtle shells, or snake and crocodile skins, many other species are likely to be vulnerable to AAEs in this context.

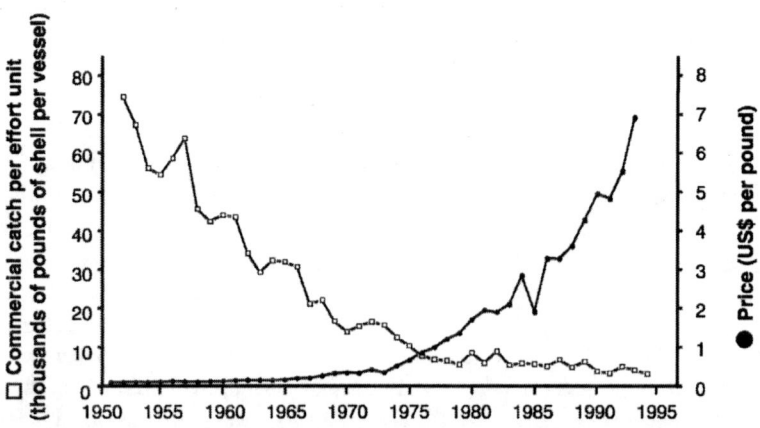

Figure 3. California commercial white abalone haliotis sorenseni landings for 1972–1992.

The price exponentially increased as catch decreased. The catch takes the fishing effort into account, so that decreased catch does not come from a diminishing effort. Results are given as weight in shell divided by the number of ships (open squares) and price (filled circles) (Hobday and Tegner, 2000).

Exotic Pets

Another activity that can lead to an AAE is exotic pet ownership, which is an increasingly important part of the wildlife trade business. Reptile, bird, monkey, and felid pets are becoming ever more fashionable in some parts of the world, with the rarest species being especially sought after. Given that high levels of mortality occur during the capture or transfer of traded species due to inadequacies in care, the massive volumes of live species that are traded are likely to exert considerable pressure on the target populations. Unlike the trophy hunting market, the exotic pet market involves many taxa, including arachnids, mollusks, insects, fish, and other vertebrates. For example, aquarium "hardcore" collectors seek rare items such as the peppermint angelfish Centropyge boylei, which sell for over US$10,000. Even though the trade of many such animals is illegal, smugglers generally face low penalties and therefore continue to deplete endangered populations for large amounts of money.

A recent article reports that immediately after being described in the scientific literature, the turtle *Chelodina mccordi* from the small Indonesian island of Roti and the gecko *Goniurosaurus luii* from southeastern China became recognized as rarities in the international pet trade, and prices in importing countries soared to highs of US$1,500–US$2,000 each (Stuart et al., 2006). They became so heavily hunted that today, *C. mccordi* is nearly extinct in the wild and *G. luii* is extirpated from its type locality (Stuart et al., 2006).

Some individuals in the wildlife trade business believe that the declaration of a species as endangered by a conservation organization provides official proof that the species is rare and therefore more valuable. Hence, paradoxically, declaring a species endangered may make it more desirable and thereby increase the likelihood of exploitation. We compared the selling prices of exotic amphibian and reptile species sold as pets in early 2006 by the largest herpetologist retailer in France (which sells to the other retailers in Europe as well as to the public) according to the CITES status of the species (Figure 2C). When corrected by adult weight, species that have a CITES status were found to be significantly more expensive (analysis of variance (ANOVA); amphibians $p = 0.0024$; lizards $p < 0.0001$; snakes $p < 0.0001$; and turtles $p < 0.0001$) than species with no CITES status, probably as a consequence of them being considered more valuable as a result of their rarity.

To further investigate the effect of CITES status on perceived value of the species, we analyzed the CITES database to assess the effect on illegal trade of a change of status, for species passing from Appendix 2 (species whose survival might be compromised if trade was not restricted) to Appendix 1 (very restricted trade, species threatened with extinction, perceived as the rarest). Of the 133 plant and animal species that have undergone this change over the past 30 years, 44 have never been reported as being traded illegally. Interestingly, classification of some species as highly endangered resulted in an increase in their illegal trade (Figure 4): of the 89 remaining species, 23 (25.8%) have shown a marked peak of illegal trade during the period (±1 year) corresponding to the change in CITES status (because the change is officially proposed 9–15 months before the application, poachers can be informed one full year in advance). This is a compelling illustration of both the increased attractiveness of rarer species and the exacerbated threat this classification may have on species becoming rare if they cannot be properly protected.

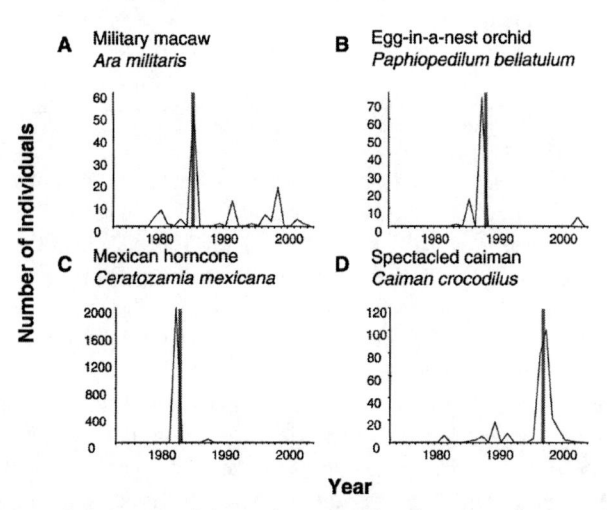

Figure 4. Illustration of the increased demand associated with perceived rarity volumes of illegal trade of four species examples (a bird (A), two plants (B and C), and a reptile (D)), which have undergone a change in CITES status. The year that the change in status took effect is indicated by the red line.

ECOTOURISM

Ecotourism ventures have expanded greatly in recent years, with the public increasingly wanting to experience a closeness to natural ecosystems or species. Such activities often involve encountering and/or observing rare species. Given that some ecotourism activities have been shown to generate disturbances that are detrimental to the fitness of observed species (Bain, 2002; Jacobson and Lopez, 1994; Sekercioglu, 2002), we can assume that rare species, especially those that are charismatic, will be disproportionately impacted upon by ecotourism. Consequently, activities such as observing rare birds, whales, primates, or nesting sea turtles have the potential to generate an AAE, especially when the animals are globally rare but with reliable sightings locally. For example, Bain (2002) studied the relationships between the number of killer whales *Orcinus orca* in the Southern resident population (eastern North Pacific) and the number of boats registered for conducting killer whale watching tours. He found a significant inverse relationship between the number of boats observed in 1 year with the whale population size recorded the subsequent year. Motorized boats are known to cause disturbances to whales and lower their fitness (Bain, 2002). More interestingly, there was also an inverse relationship between the decreasing whale population size recorded during 1 year, and the increasing size of the boat fleet the next year, indicating that contrary to expected economics, the increasing rarity of that population of killer whales did not immediately stop whale watching but may have in fact stimulated it (Bain, 2002). In 2001, the number of boats in the commercial whale watching fleet exceeded the number of killer whales in the population.

The Capercaillie (*Tetrao urogallus*) is a large gamebird that inhabits Scottish forests, where its population has dropped precipitously from 20,000 to 900 birds in the past 30 years (Capercaillie Action Programme, 2006). Mating takes place just a few times each spring at the display grounds, or leks, of the males. Given the rarity of these birds, there is great interest in observing these leks among British birdwatchers, and disturbance of leks is thought to be a serious threat to the survival of the Scottish population.

Traditional Medicine

Traditional medicine uses many rare and endangered species. Although other aspects may influence ingredient choice, rarity certainly plays a role (Sadovy and Cheung, 2003) and may therefore result in an AAE. In western Japan, the red morph of *Geranium thunbergii*, a flower widely used for treating stomach problems and diarrhea, is common, whereas the white morph is rare. The morph frequency is the opposite in eastern Japan, with the white morph being common and the red morph rare. People in western Japan believe that the medicinal efficiency of the "rare" white morph is better, whereas those in eastern Japan consider the "rare" red morph superior (Tetsukazu Yahara, personal communication). This geographic difference in people's beliefs is likely to exert strong selective pressure on flower color and offers a good illustration of the preference for rarity and its perceived medicinal virtues.

The Chinese bahaba (*Bahaba taipingensis*) provides another example of the effect that exploitation for traditional medicine can have on rare populations. Used for the prevention of miscarriages, the swimbladder of this fish is highly valued in Asia; as indicated by the name "soft gold," which was assigned to it by fishers as it became increasingly rare over the last 4 decades (Sadovy and Cheung, 2003). As the exploitation of this fish intensified, its increasing rarity made its value escalate to such a level that despite less than half a dozen fish being caught per year in the 1990s (less than 1% of the amount caught in the 1960s), 100–200 boats continued to target this fish (Sadovy and Cheung, 2003). One large swimbladder was sold in the 1980s for US$64,000 (Sadovy and Cheung, 2003). In 2001, some 70 years after it was first reported in the scientific literature, this species was virtually extinct (Dulvy et al., 2003). At that time, the occasional fish that was caught every few years yielded a swimbladder with a value that on the top retail market, weight for weight, exceeded that of gold by seven times (Sadovy and Cheung, 2003).

CONCLUSION

We have identified six different types of human activities that have the potential to induce an AAE, but there are likely to be others. It is important to realize that an AAE has the potential to target not only the most charismatic and emblematic species, but also the most inconspicuous invertebrate, as long as rarity renders it fashionable to exploit for one reason or another. Furthermore, species that are currently not of concern could very well be in the near future.

Because among the activities presented here, several are primarily stimulated by people interested in nature, it is important that these people are aware of and have an understanding of the potential effect their actions may have on the very species they appreciate. Consequently, informing potential ecotourists, collectors, and pet owners may in part facilitate the process of reducing the likelihood of an AAE and thus the impact on the species that are the targets of these activities. However, activities that relate to prestige or tradition may require more dramatic actions including strengthened regulations and targeted, adapted information to decrease the likelihood of AAEs in the target species.

How the trade of rare species should be regulated is a vast and ongoing debate. The finding that rarity itself could be a criterion for immediate threat to a species because of the psychological and economic value people attach to it is, however, a new and important piece of information in the battle to preserve biodiversity. At the very least, this finding should lead to the realization that declaring a species too rare to be subjected to legal transactions could be dangerous for the species if it cannot be fully protected. At most, it is hoped that such information could change our rationale on the manner in which biodiversity is perceived and exploited.

KEYWORDS

- **Anthropogenic Allee effect**
- **Exotic pet**
- **Safari club international**
- **Trophy hunting**

AUTHORS' CONTRIBUTIONS

Franck Courchamp conceived and designed the experiments. Elena Angulo performed the experiments. Franck Courchamp, Elena Angulo, Philippe Rivalan, Laetitia Signoret, Leigh Bull, and Yves Meinard analyzed the data. Franck Courchamp wrote the chapter. Richard J. Hall constructed and analyzed the mathematical model. Yves Meinard helped construct the mathematical model.

ACKNOWLEDGMENTS

We thank J. Gascoigne, L. Berek, P. Inchausti, D. Couvet, M. Wegnez, and C. Perron for critical reading and Tom Slone and Alistair Hobday for sending data on butterflies and abalones, respectively.

Chapter 10

Parks and Tourism

Ralf Buckley

INTRODUCTION

Why should it matter how many people visit national parks? In a word: politics. Protected areas are not only physical places, reservoirs of biodiversity, and sources of ecosystem services, such as breathable air and drinkable water. They are also human political constructs, and they are under ever-increasing pressures from growing human populations and resource demands. Visitors may bring them the political capital to survive.

Biologists have pointed out for decades that protected areas are not playgrounds, but life-support systems for the planet's population of humans, as well as its other species. Economists estimate that ecosystem services worldwide contribute twice as much to the human economy each year as all forms of human industry combined many trillions of dollars (Balmford et al., 2002; Costanza et al., 1997). At regional scale, ecosystem services from National Wildlife Refuges in the contiguous 48 states of the US have been valued at US$27 billion annually (Ingraham and Foster, 2008). The human economic value of conserving biodiversity is many orders of magnitude higher than the funds invested in it (Balmford et al., 2002, 2003; Buckley, 1994; Carpenter et al., 2009; Ehrlich and Pringle, 2008; James et al., 1999; Pimm et al., 2001). The cost of buying all of the world's biodiversity hotspots outright has been estimated at around US$100 billion less than 5-years' expenditure on soft drinks in the US (Balmford and Whitten, 2003). But the actual funds allocated worldwide each year, a few billion dollars in total, are <5% of minimum requirements for effective conservation (Bruner, 2003). This compares with the trillions of dollars spent in 2009 to prop up financial systems in the US, European Union, and China (Ghazoul, 2009).

Both ecological and economic arguments thus support conservation investment orders of magnitude higher than those currently in place. Public conservation decisions, however, are political, and the currency of politics is power. Votes, money, or force can buy political power in various circumstances, but demonstrating that conservation has a high global ecological or economic value does not generate political capital even in democracies unless voters in marginal electorates will change their voting preferences on this issue above all others. Multi-trillion dollar economic valuations influence political processes only indirectly.

Conservation in the real world (Sinclair, 2000) relies on coupled social ecological systems (Carpenter et al., 2009). Visitors in parks provide an excellent example. Park managers must juggle ecological impacts and political support. Visitors create costs for conservation through ecological impacts (Buckley, 2004a) and by diverting conservation budgets to recreation management. Costs depend on numbers, timing, activities, equipment, and behavior.

Visitors can also provide funds from entry and activity fees, as well as political capital, which buys government budget allocations. That's why parks agencies court recreational visitors through "relationship marketing" (Watson and Borrie, 2003). Government powerbrokers see park visitors as political supporters and regional spenders. More people care about conservation than recreation, but recreation means countable votes in specific electorates, whereas conservation concerns are less localized or vote changing.

The tourism industry is also a powerful political player that sees parks as commercial opportunities scenic attractions, captive clients, and publicly funded infrastructure, interpretation, and marketing. Commercial nature and adventure tourism is indeed growing, but building commercial accommodation inside parks does not increase visitation. Some commercial tourism operations do run profitable private reserves that make net positive contributions to conservation (Buckley, 2008a, 2009), but these are much smaller than public-protected area systems and conservation stewardship schemes (Ferraro and Kiss, 2002; Kleijn and Sutherland, 2003).

Some parks agencies earn up to 80% of total revenue by charging individual visitors directly. Partnerships with tourism developers, however, have incurred high costs, brought few visitors and minimal revenue (<6%), earned no net revenue for conservation, and reduced benefits for private recreational visitors (Varghese, 2008). This approach also brings risks. If individual visitors cause impacts, agencies can restrict access or activities. This is not politically feasible for large private developments. Arguments advanced by commercial tourism interests are not supported by evidence; however, this is lobbying, not logic.

So if fewer people visit parks, it creates political problems for conservation. Historically, park managers worried about crowding, with conflicts and impacts, and about demands from people of different ethnic origins and socioeconomic backgrounds (Eagles, 2002). In the early 2000s, however, US researchers Pergams and Zaradic (2007) argued that US society is experiencing "videophilia," a preference for virtual reality over nature. Their data indicated declines in visitation to national parks in Japan and the US and, to a lesser extent, also other US land tenures since about 1990. The political implications of this led to intense debate (Jacobs and Manfredo, 2008; Kareiva, 2008; Pergams and Zaradic, 2008).

Balmford et al. (2009) obtained visitation data for 280 protected areas in 20 countries worldwide, a much broader dataset geographically than that of Pergams and Zaradic (2007). Balmford et al. report that in most countries, park visitation rates are continuing to rise. In the practical politics of global conservation, these are critically important and timely data. The authors' research also showed, however, that in a few particular parks in the US numbers have remained static. So, the debate will continue, especially given the money at stake for the commercial tourism sector.

There are two key issues. First, few countries have accurate visitor numbers. Reliable counts need continuously staffed access roads with no other entry. Automated counters are expensive and inaccurate. Visitor numbers vary daily by orders of magnitude depending on weather and holiday periods, so comparing single-day snapshot counts means little. Calculating long-term trends needs continuous multi-year time series. These are rare, especially since land management agencies often change the basis for recording visits.

Pergams and Zaradic (2007), for example, also sought data from countries such as Australia. They were sent data from two of eight states, one of which did not actually record visitor numbers the figures were purely estimates. Australian tourism lobbyists quote park visitation estimates derived from very general off-site surveys of people's holiday intentions, carried out by the federal tourism agency. Such surveys are highly unreliable (Pergams and Zaradic, 2007). Even in face-to-face interviews with people who know you have been watching them, many report their own very recent actions inaccurately (Littlefair and Buckley, 2008). On-ground counts show the tourism surveys are inflated by 20–1,000% (Buckley, 2004b). So, it's hard to measure small changes reliably.

Second, if visitation to particular parks has leveled off, this does not mean that parks are unpopular. It means that these parks are full. Their social carrying capacity (Buckley, 1999) has been exceeded. They are so crowded that people go to other parks or other land tenures. Pergams and Zaradic (2007) argued against such substitution within the US, but their data, especially for the US Forest Service, were not entirely convincing. Balmford et al. (2009) propose instead that people have been travelling overseas; international outdoor tourism has been substituting for domestic outdoor recreation. This is supported by tourism research (Buckley, 2009). Crowding is not the only factor. Reduced public funding forces parks agencies to charge higher visitor fees, and increased legal liabilities make them impose more regulations. So people go where they enjoy cheaper and less fettered recreational opportunities.

And why not? It is good policy for people to play where their impact causes less damage, keeping protected areas for conservation and low-impact individual recreation. The former gives the human economy its air, water, and biological resources; the latter gives the human population low-cost improvements in physical and mental health. It's poor policy that in order to maintain budgets, parks agencies should continually increase visitor numbers. Human populations are growing, but the area of parks is not keeping pace. The area of land and water available for conservation outside protected areas is continually shrinking (McDonald-Madden, 2009), so parks themselves are increasingly critical. Parks are assets for tourism, but they are not tourism assets.

The new data from Balmford et al. (2009) show that park visitation rates are still rising. Conservation is a far more valuable use of parks than tourism and recreation, so in theory, parks agency budgets should only reflect conservation management costs, and visitation rates should be irrelevant. In practice, however, since conservation decisions are political rather than economic, these new data are of enormous importance to conservation worldwide.

KEYWORDS

- **Diverting conservation budgets**
- **National Wildlife Refuges**
- **Off-site surveys**
- **Tourism industry**

Chapter 11

The Conservation Business

Henry Nicholls

INTRODUCTION

The language of conservation is changing: protecting biodiversity is no longer just about ethics and aesthetics; the latest buzzwords are commodities and consumers. Traditionally, conservation initiatives have talked up the benefits they will bring to the global community saving species, habitats, ecosystems, and ultimately the planet. But conservation also has its costs, and these are usually borne by local people prevented from exploiting the resources around them in other ways. It is unfair to expect a localized minority to pick up costs that ultimately benefit a dispersed majority, argue conservation biologists. There has to be more money made available by concerned individuals, non-governmental organizations, national governments, and international bodies, and there need to be better ways to spend this money if conservation is to be effective, they say. Biodiversity is a commodity that can be bought and sold. We are consumers and must pay.

COSTS AND BENEFITS

Kenya boasts one of the world's most spectacular networks of national parks and reserves covering around 60,000 km^2 of the country (Figure 1). But devoting such a vast area to conservation has its drawbacks. It has been estimated that were this land developed it would be worth around $270 million to the Kenyan people every year. Similarly, two national parks in Madagascar are estimated to have reduced the annual income of local villagers by around 10%. Of course, protected areas do bring some benefits to neighboring communities, most notably through tourism. But in many cases the rewards are not great, they are rarely distributed evenly among individuals, and do not necessarily outweigh the costs.

Figure 1. The Masai Mara National Park in Kenya.

"The costs of conservation fall disproportionately on local people, whereas the benefits are dispersed," says Andrew Balmford, a conservation biologist at the University of Cambridge in the UK. National and global communities stand to benefit from conservation of tropical biodiversity, but they must pay if they want to realize that benefit, he says. Conservation expenditure in the developed world is only about a third of what is needed for effective protection of 15% of the earth's terrestrial habitats, an area just large enough to preserve a representative sample of species, habitats, and ecosystems in the medium to long-term (Balmford et al., 2003). The developed world must make up this funding shortfall, argues Balmford. What's more, there need to be smarter ways to spend the money that's available, he says.

CONSERVATION BY DISTRACTION

In recent years, many funding bodies have taken an indirect approach to conservation, investing in projects that encourage people to take up alternative practices that are compatible with conservation rather than investing in conservation itself. Perhaps the best example of this "conservation by distraction" is plowing money into community-based ecotourism projects. Such initiatives aim to bring the benefits of tourism to local people, thereby encouraging them to preserve the biodiversity they have.

It's an attractive idea. In the mid 1990s, the United States Agency for International Development was investing more than $2 billion a year in 105 conservation projects with an ecotourism component. Similarly, between 1988 and 2003, the World Bank funded 55 development projects that supported protected areas in Africa, 32 of which placed an emphasis on ecotourism.

However, an absence of quantitative data and analysis has made it hard to judge whether these projects actually achieve their dual purpose of preserving biodiversity and simultaneously reducing rural poverty. "Much of the information about community-based ecotourism is anecdotal and subjective," says Agnes Kiss of the Environment and Social Development Unit at the World Bank. The real contribution of these initiatives to biodiversity conservation is debatable, she says. "Many community-based ecotourism projects cited as success stories actually involve little change in existing local land- and resource-use practices, provide only modest supplement to local livelihoods, and remain dependent on external support for long periods, if not indefinitely." (Kiss, 2004)

For example, communities involved in the Infierno Community Ecotourism Project in Peru have received nearly $120,000 from their share in a tourist lodge and wages for providing services to visitors. This may have increased the income for a minority that are lodge employees, but only one family, whose adult members were all employed by the lodge, could afford to live solely on tourism. In the community as a whole, the average annual income from tourism was only $735 compared with nearly $2,000 earned elsewhere. Most of the community was still heavily dependent on other activities, and most of those activities are somewhat disruptive of conservation goals, says Kiss.

Johan du Toit of the Mammal Research Institute at the University of Pretoria in South Africa is also critical of this kind of indirect approach to conservation. At the heart of the argument for community-based ecotourism is the idea of the "ecologically noble savage," he says the notion that those living closest to nature will know what's best for it. "It's a wonderful idea, but it just doesn't work. Nowhere in the history of evolution has sustainability ever been naturally selected for," says du Toit. "The AK47 automatic assault rifle has replaced the bow and arrow. Every individual in a rural community that's out hunting will shoot what he sees when he sees it, because if he doesn't somebody else will." (du Toit et al.,2004)

Nowhere is this problem more evident than in the ecotourist paradise of the Galápagos Islands (Figure 2), where a small minority of fishermen is coming into conflict with conservation aims with increasing regularity (Figure 3). "Things are going down very quickly," says one Galápagos guide. "The iceberg is starting to tip over, and we are going to lose everything." If it still pays locals to exploit the environment rather than take part in one of the world's most buoyant ecotourism industries, it is clear that ecotourism alone cannot solve the world's conservation problems. Many think that "direct payment" could be a useful tool. "Direct payment, very boldly speaking, is paying people in rural areas not to bugger up their environment," says du Toit. "It's just like if we want exclusive artworks to be looked after in the Louvre Gallery in Paris. Somebody's got to pay for it," he says. "You can't expect the Parisians who live in that arrondissement to cover the costs."

Figure 2. Ecotourist paradise in the Galópagos.

Figure 3. The prized Galópagos Sea Cucumber, Stichopus fuscus.

YOU GET WHAT YOU PAY FOR—YOU SHOULD PAY FOR WHAT YOU WANT TO GET

For people living in developing countries, where most of the world's biodiversity exists, the short-term rewards of exploiting these natural resources are significant. Replacing indirect conservation measures, such as community-based ecotourism, with payments directly into the pockets of local people could turn out to be a much more effective way to stem this exploitation, argues Paul Ferraro, an economist at Georgia State University in Atlanta (Ferraro and Kiss, 2002). It could also bring far greater development benefits than indirect financial support, he says (Figure 4). An additional spin-off is that direct payments force conservation biologists to quantify and hence clarify their objectives, says John Hough, principal technical advisor on biodiversity for the United Nations Development Program. "We know what we don't want," he says, "but we're not very good at saying what we do want."

Figure 4. Forest protected by Costa Rica's PSA.

A hypothetical model simulating how Madagascar should distribute an annual conservation budget of $4 million reveals that direct payments would have protected some 80% of original forest compared with only 12% protected through a system of indirect incentives. What's more, the annual income of rural residents would have been twice that generated through indirect investment (Conrad and Ferraro, 2001).

For Ferraro, the logic of direct payment is simple. He draws an analogy with a car journey from A to B. There are two routes that will bring you to B, one circuitous and the other direct. If you only have a single tank of fuel, opting for the direct route improves the likelihood you will arrive at your destination. An indirect approach to conservation is like taking the circuitous route, he says, and the chances are that you will run out of fuel. But if it's that simple, why are governments, non-governmental organizations, private bodies, and international organizations not jumping at the chance to experiment with this approach?

PAYING IN PERPETUITY

There are those that have reservations about direct payments. The distinction between indirect and direct interventions is artificial, says Thomas Lovejoy, president of the Heinz Center, a nonprofit institution dedicated to improving the scientific and economic foundation for environmental policy. "In some cases, direct payment is the only way conservation can happen," he says. "In others, the indirect is important to reinforce a situation where there already is conservation. In yet others both are needed."

Sjaak Swart of the Section of Science and Society at Groningen University in The Netherlands argues that if conservation is to succeed, it must be rooted in the hearts and minds of those involved. Direct payments create a vision of nature dominated by calculable, monetary concerns, he says. This approach can only work in the short-term, he argues, and indirect tools like debate and education are needed to involve communities in the long-term. "You need the commitment of the local people to save the biodiversity of our world," he says.

Marine biologist Steve Trott agrees. He is project coordinator for the Local Ocean Trust, a charity-based conservation organization operating in the Watamu and Malindi Marine Parks and Reserve in Kenya (http://www.watamuturtles.com), and is using direct payments to help reduce the slaughter of turtles by local fishermen. The Watamu Turtle Watch Program is currently paying fishermen just over $3 a turtle to release the animals from their nets rather than kill them. Before the scheme started in 2000, only around 50 turtles were being released from nets each year. By 2003, more than 500 a year were making it back into the sea. Elsewhere along the Kenyan coast, where fishermen do not get these payments, turtles continue to be killed, says Trott. However, the financial incentives are only part of a grander program of education and support to sensitive people to the conservation message, he says. Eventually, the plan is to stop payments altogether. "Payment will be reduced as education and awareness is increased to the point where it's phased out," he says.

Reducing or stopping the payment could work, says Ferraro, but it is more likely that the turtles will begin to suffer once more. "If I had to wager, I'd bet people would go back to their old patterns eventually." This means that direct payments require an ongoing financial commitment, and many people don't like this idea, he says.

TO THE TEST

The idea of direct payments needs empirical testing before it can be embraced with confidence, admits Ferraro. Funding bodies should demand experimental and control data to allow the success of an intervention to be gauged. Conservation biologists must therefore be trained in the skills needed to collect and evaluate these data. "Without adequate data and controls you're only going to be left with guesses and vague anecdotes about the effects of a program intervention," he says. Decision makers should begin to design controlled experiments from which they can make inferences about the effectiveness of these different interventions, he suggests.

There are other drawbacks of direct payments. One concern is that they might just shift the pressure from one site to another that was not previously being exploited. Furthermore, in developing countries, land tenure is often ambiguous, which can make investment an unattractive prospect for funding agencies they want to be sure they know where their money is going. But, notes Ferraro, such objections also apply to indirect interventions. "I don't necessarily believe that conservation payments will be successful," he says. "It's more I believe that of all the ideas out there for protecting biodiversity, this is the least bad."

All this talk of cost, benefit, and efficiency is creeping into conservation speak. For some, these cold and calculating terms are an odd way to describe the world's wonderfully unpredictable wildlife. But, increasingly, there are calls for conservation biology to cast aside its sentimental demons: biodiversity is a commodity that can be bought and sold; conservation is business.

KEYWORDS

- **Biodiversity**
- **Community-based ecotourism**
- **Conservation by distraction**
- **Direct payment**

Chapter 12

Ecological Sports Tourism Resources and Its Industry

Pengfei Zhu

INTRODUCTION

Through the analysis of ecological sports tourism resources and its characteristics, we investigated the key ecological sports tourism resources from the angle of regional planning, industrialization programming, design, and so on in the present chapter and put forward novel countermeasure for sustainable development.

Modern Chinese physical education is the combination of western and traditional Chinese sports. From the angel of historical development, whether western or Chinese sports deriving from natural sports, are all the products of human production and survival development. Modern sports civilization is the human civilization of industrial revolution and cultural development, and similar to the environmental issues imposed by industrial revolution, also bring many new issues. Along with the enhancing cognition and investigation level of human being on resources and environment, the combination of ecological and social science make people consider the return of modern sports to nature and the construction of new sports ecological environment. Therefore, sports ecology has been a new research area promptly developing in and out of China at present. Research directions developed currently mainly includes: composition of sports ecological system, basic characteristics and development law, sports and environment, green Olympics, leisure sports and so on. All these fail to form a systematic and complete theory and method system for sports ecology. Some research areas on sports ecological resources, such as systematic investigation, scientific analysis, sustainable development utilization, and so on, have not attracted great attention, and especially, research on sustainable development utilization have not been systematically and comprehensively developed.

With abundant ecological resources, protection and utilization of ecological resources have been paid more and more attention during the process of ecology construction by Chinese government. In china, resource base is profound for the investigation and development of multi-ethnic ecological sports, ecological tourism is required by more and more people of the whole society and attention have been paid to investment and development of high-grade ecological tourism industry. All these resource dominance afford a wider development space for ecological sports tourism industrialization. Spontaneous mass sports activities have always been developed well, which offers an excellent mass basis for the investigation of sports ecology and industrialization construction. On such condition of resources, environment and market demand, by using theory and technology of ecology, in combination with industrial development requirement, investigation and study of ecological sports tourism resources is systematically undertaken in order to seek countermeasures for sustainable development of ecological sports tourism industry, offer novel insight into sports development, pave a new space for the comprehensive development of society and economy in China and protection and utilization of ecological environment, and promote coordinated development of society, economy, and ecology. Therefore, ecological sports tourism industry will bring favorable benefits of society, economy and ecology (Zhu, 2001, pp. 13–15).

RESOURCE ANALYSIS OF ECOLOGICAL SPORTS TOURISM INDUSTRY

Ecological sports tourism industry resources mainly include: ecological sports tourism resources, ecological tourism resources, and tourism industry resources.

Ecological sports tourism resources are ecological sports items resources which meet with the demand of increasing healthy consumption of human society with respect to sports, including traditional, ethnic sports items, and so on, and historical and traditional culture resources covered by those items, with obvious ethnic characteristics and personality (Wang, 2005, pp. 29–31). Chinese traditional and ethnic sports items, with distinctive characteristics, are the non-negligible high quality historical and cultural heritage in the inheritance of Chinese history and culture. Cross-synthesis of subjects, such as ethnology, sports science, tourism science, ecology, and so on, are essential for understanding the values of its resources. Through investigation on such resources and combination with Chinese reality, characteristic resource evaluation and development system of Chinese history and culture could be developed, followed by product or production of industrialization (Zheng, 2005, pp. 43–46).

Ecological tourism resources are the general designation of all resources with respect to natural ecological environment in tourism resources, and the natural environment and its historical cultural background tourists learn, taste, and enjoy, namely natural ecological, social, and historical cultural resources. All these resources possess natural attributes, such as distinctive regionality, seasonality, and so on, and social culture attribute. Such resources could be independently developed into ecological resource industry, but in combination with ecological tourism resources could get mutual benefits and form a novel industrial feature.

Tourism industry resources are summation of industrialization resource, tourism and item management with respect to tourism. Different from the two resources mentioned above, it could not only rely on the basis of natural ecological, ecological sports, tourism resources, and so on, but also be independent on those resources. It is a kind of soft management and industrialization resource, implementation security of socialization, economization and ecology for tourism items, products and industry, and hence possesses indispensable values similar to the above-mentioned resources.

REGIONAL PLANNING OF ECOLOGICAL SPORTS TOURISM KEY RESOURCES

Scientific comprehensive investigation and study on ecological sports resources has not been undertaken at present. The question how to recognize and understand scientifically and comprehensively the characteristics and dominance of regional ecological sports resources, appears to be a mainly obstacle to industrialization development of ecological sports resources. Through the application of modern technological means of 3S (Remote sensing, geography information systems and global positioning systems) and mathematical statistics, in combination with requirement survey of ecological sports tourism resources, environmental capacity, carrying capacity, etc., sorts, quantity, scale, characteristic, and so on of regional key resources was ascertained. Based on this, further in combination with theory and method of regional planning, advisable regional planning was undertaken in order to offer scientific basis for the development of ecological sports tourism industry and government decision making, which could not only guarantee the scientific development of ecological sports, but also avoid the waste and destruction of ecological sports resources during the process of development, gradually pave a sustainable way for ecological sports industry and thus promote harmonious development of regional society, economy, culture, and ecology and bring forward good social, economic, and ecological benefits (Zhao, 2006, pp. 90–94).

In order to implement sustainable development of ecological sports tourism industry, latest achievements in subjects, such as ecological science, sports science, tourism management science, and so on, should be applied in this area, and an investigation system including resource investigation, resource evaluation and analysis, resource utilization planning, and resource management should be established. Based on this, resource dominance of industrial management should be exerted well to achieve the values of resources under performance of integration and actualization. Due to vast territory, lots of nationalities and abundant historical cultural heritage in China, it is tough to ascertain the policy and strategies for sustainable development. In the first stage, a comprehensive survey should be undertaken about Chinese ecological sports tourism resources. On the basis of the survey, basic and key resources of regional ecological sports tourism were ascertained through scientific analysis, and regional industrial development planning should be undertaken on such resources (Song, 2005, pp. 75–78).

Regional development planning of ecological sports tourism industry mainly includes:

1. Basic constitutes, distribution charts, protection and utilization general planning of basic resources;
2. Characteristics, distribution charts, and regional planning of key resources;
3. General planning of industrialization development; and
4. Design and planning of regional industrialization item.

Establishing supporting industrial policy according to the requirement of resources and planning, is essential for ensuring healthy sustainable development of industry. Industrial policy includes:

1. Protection and utilization policy of basic resources;
2. Protection, utilization, and special management policy of key resources;

3. Supporting and preferential policy of industrialization sustainable development; and
4. Strengthening the cognition of resource value, science popularization and correlated policy of resource management.

PLANNING AND DESIGN OF ECOLOGICAL SPORTS TOURISM INDUSTRY

Any industrialization developments all carry out through specific project design and implementation, and hence scientific and normative industrialization project design and implementation management become important content and guarantee for sustainable development. Because industrial development require strong and powerful economic guarantee, industrialization planning and design sometimes have many contradictions. Actually, relationship among economic, ecological, and social benefits is complementary to each other. Scientific planning and design could attenuate such contradictions. Therefore, it becomes paramount for the prospective of planning and design, science of project planning and design and concrete embodiment of technical progress achievement. Studies on subjects, such as ecological science, sports science, tourism management science, industrial economics, and so on, should be successfully undertaken to realize its sustainability by planning and its enforceability and validity by planning and design.

Principles of planning and design: Economic benefits priority, unification of economic, and social benefits; adaption to local conditions; protection and reasonable exploitation of resource; unified planning, highlighting key points and implementing step by step.

Objective and index system: Objective is to establish an ecological sports tourism item with good economic benefits, meanwhile pay attention to ecological and social benefits; corresponding index system includes economic indices (ratio of output to input, progressive increment capability of economic benefits, and so on); ecological indices (green cover percentage, ecological recovery ability, suitable degree of resource protection and utilization, environmental quality, pollution control rate, and so on); social indices (healthy tour and healthy body and mind, public environmental awareness and resource consciousness, universal education of ecological environment protection science, and so on).

Objective feasibility analysis: Such analysis is kind of technical feasibility assess in terms of planning and design of ecological sports tourism item industrialization development, including environmental evaluation, population evolution law analysis, ecological recovery ability, resource optimization, item optimization setup and construction, and so on, and offer technical support and guarantee for industrial planning and design.

Item functional planning and design: According to the investigation, analysis, and evaluation of ecological sports tourism resources, all kinds of resources are undertaken conceptual and functional planning with function optimization in light of the requirement of tourism item development, with attempts to enhance resource protection, decrease resource destruction, sufficiently exert resource values and offer insight into the subsequent specific item design.

Item design: According to functional planning, industrialization specific items are designed, including item design of key ecological sports tourism resources, optimal combination design of basic resource item, tourism function guarantee design, special item design for health, tour and leisure, novel item design such as science popularization, environmental protection education, and so on. All these items become industrial chain and cluster after integrated development.

Guarantee measures for industrial development and item construction: It mainly includes establishing and perfecting management system guaranteed for industrial development and item construction; industrial planning brought into social economy development planning and yearly development plan by local government, accomplishing fund input for supporting early construction, widening capital channels, inducing further input of social fund, guarantee input of development fund, taking macro-control; strengthening environmental protection and unified supervision; exerting effects of media and education to promote awareness of public participation; relying on scientific and technological progress, protecting, and guaranteeing for industrial development; drawing supporting policies and regulations, management regulations and detailed rules for implementation for the practice of ecological sports tourism industry in terms of national law, regulations and rules; intensifying international exchange and cooperation, and so on.

COUNTERMEASURE FOR SUSTAINABLE DEVELOPMENT OF ECOLOGICAL SPORTS TOURISM INDUSTRY

Sustainable development theory and method system have been developed for many years, and formed into certain mode. Such mode promotes social development, but at the same time, not always satisfies the development requirement of specific industry and item. Therefore, novel insight into sustainable development of ecological sports tourism industry is essential, and this update embodies specific innovated thinking and countermeasure in development countermeasure. Previous studies conformed that, and hence the following several key innovations are used as main content of sustainable development countermeasure to construct and develop.

Novel protection and utilization of ecological sports tourism resources is essential according to the characteristics of ecological sports tourism industry. Innovation in this area is based on the investigation, analysis, and evaluation of ecological sports tourism industry, facilitates understanding the heterogeneity and value generality of natural ecological resources, sports ecological resources, tourism resources and historical cultural resources, and constituting measures of resource protection and strategy of resource exploitation and utilization (Liu, 2005, pp. 17–19).

Ecological sports tourism industry contains subjects, such as ecology, sports, tourism, sociology, culture, and so on, and refers to ecological industry, sports industry, tourism industry, and so on. Due to segmentation of trap and block resulted from professional research and industrial development, it is tough to form a systematic research and development, which becomes a limiting factor significantly affecting sustainable development of this industry. Consequently, sustainable development of the industry should break traditional limitations, under the guidance of local government, organize and develop cooperation of trans-subject and industry units and talent, integrate multi-subjects theory and technology application achievement to guarantee smooth progress of industrialization.

The formation and development of an industry relies on the progress of science and technology. In light of the requirement of industrial development, ecological sports tourism science and its related frontier and interdisciplinary subjects should be established and developed. Only in this case, innovative development has its stamina.

Due to vast territory, irregular distribution of resources, notable discrepancy in economy between eastern and western regions, as well as main ecological sports tourism resources distributed in central and western regions and minority areas where development of economy, science and technology is relatively backward, and talent resources is scarce, diversification of developing modes should be mainly adapt to the requirement of industrial development, and moreover, government, investors, talents, and so on should be provided with novel idea and sustainable development notion, and cooperate with innovation planning and science construction to achieve sustainable development.

Taken together, ecological sports tourism industry already possesses a qualification for healthy industrial development. During the period of industrial development, it can be anticipated that it could result in the progress of science and technology and grandness of excellent professional talent team, and based on those, promote economy development, social progress and human ecological civilization, and exhibit a profound prospect for the industrial sustainable development.

KEYWORDS

- **Ecological sports tourism**
- **Sustainable development**
- **Tourism industry**

Chapter 13

Ecotourism in the Northern Piedmont in the Qinling Mountains

Hongmei Dong

INTRODUCTION

Tourism resources in the Northern Piedmont in the Qinling Mountains (NPQM) are quite abundant and play an important role in the development of the tourist industry in Shaanxi Province. Based on reviewing the status quo of ecotourism in the NPQM and existing issues, this chapter puts forward countermeasures and recommendations for sustainable development of ecotourism in the NPQM. Firstly, a systemic tourism resources investigation should be conducted; secondly, a comprehensive assessment should be made on tourism resources; thirdly, suitable and reasonable principles of protective development should be established, considering to facilitate organic unification of ecological environmental protection and exploitation of tourism. All steps are helpful to realize scientific and sustainable development of ecological economy and tourism zone in the NPQM.

Qinling Mountains is not only a climatic boundary between North and South in China, but also one of areas with abundant biological diversity, acknowledged as "Kingdom of Animals and Plants" and "Chinese Medicinal Herb Storehouse." In recent years, the surrounding tourism roads and highways have been constructed in the NPQM and Shaanxi Province and Xi'an city governments have published series favorable polices and promoted the infrastructure investment, tourism industry has rapidly developed at the NPQM. However, extravagant exploitation and negligence of protective construction have led to ecological crisis, such as, random development of tourism resources, vegetation deterioration, valley and water interception, environmental pollution, aggravation of water loss and soil erosion, and shortage of water resources, and so on. On the basis of analyzing the status quo of ecotourism in the NPQM and existing problems, this chapter puts forward countermeasures and recommendations for sustainable development of ecotourism in the NPQM.

GENERAL CONDITION OF NPQM AND ECOTOURISM RESOURCES

The NPQM is located between Qinling watershed and South Rim of Kuan-Chung Plain, with important ecological functions, and is the ecological protective screen and water source reserve in the Central Shaanxi area. Its west is to Gansu, its east is to Henan, its north extends to villages and towns along mountainous highway, and its south is to the major ridge of Qinling Mountains. It presents a zonate form from west to east. It is approximately 450 km long, with an area of about 9,290 km^2, among which the area of scenic spot and forest park is 1,116 km^2, accounting for 12% of the total area. Administratively, it is attached to the three cities of Xi'an, Baoji, and Weinan with well developed transportation. Qinling Mountains possess different climate features because of complicated topography, have various rare animals and plants, which are favorable to develop ecotourism. Its main tourism resources are as follows:

Natural Ecotourism Resources
There are abundant natural tourism resources in the NPQM, with grotesque peaks and steep mountains, suspending spring and waterfall on the upper reaches of rivers and rivulets, hot springs distributed along the piedmont, relatively obvious vertical zoning of mountainous region, complicated geological structure, abundant geothermal resources, diversified forest covers and animal types within the area, typical remains of fossil glacier, unique magic of physiographic sight, hydrologic sight, and climatic and biological sight of landslide physionomy and karst landform. Its major scenic spots include the six national natural reserves. There are 11 state-level forest parks, such as Zhongnanshan and Taibai Mountain, three state-level scenic spots of Hua Shan, Lishan and Tiantai Mountain, and four provincial level scenic spots, and wetland ecotourism resources. In addition, the National Botanical Garden of Qinling Mountains is under construction. Biological resources in Qinling Mountains are extremely rich, such as, 3,446 species of seed plants, 144 species of beasts, 399 species of birds, more than 5,000 species of insects. There are 28 kinds of plants with key state protection, such as, *Kingdonia uniflora*, yew, and 56 species of wild animals with key state protection, such as, giant panda, golden monkey, nipponia nippon, and takin. Hence, Qinling Mountains will not only become the base of bio-diversity conservation, research and popularization of science, but will also become a brand-new ecotourism garden plot in Shaanxi Province, and even all over the country.

Humanistic Ecotourism Resources
The 800-li Qinchuan (plain) at the NPQM is the birthplace of Chinese nation, and is the capital city for 13 emperors of the five dynasties of Zhou, Qin, Han, Sui, and Tang; its humanistic ecotourism resources spread over the NPQM. The Holy Land of the Taoism of Lantian Man ruins (a history of 1.1 million years), and Terra-cotta Warriors (the Eight Wonders of the World), and the holy place of Buddhism of Caotang Temple are located in the plain.

Rural Ecotourism Resources
There are numerous rivers at the NPQM, especially along the circle line of mountainous tourism, with green mountains, fresh air, clear water, and hot springs, and it is a good choice for vacation tourism. With further development of tourism industry in the NPQM, vacation mountain villa, summer villa, place of entertainment, and happy farmhouse are rapidly development.

STATUS QUO AND PROBLEMS OF DEVELOPMENT OF ECOTOURISM

In recent years, with implementation of the policy of Western Development, rapid development of economy and general improvement of people's living standards, tourism industry in Shaanxi Province has experienced a fast development. At the time of reconstructing former scenic spots, new tourist attractions have continued to bring out in the NPQM. Declaration for the World Geological Park of Zhongnanshan in Qinling Mountains gained success in August 2009, and the Central National Park that is under declaration promotes rapid development of regional ecotourism industry to a great extent. Statistically, the tourist population in only 45 major scenic spots in Xi'an and Baoji in 2007 attained 10.876 million and they earned 513.097 million Yuan. The 39 scenic spots in Xi'an had a tourist population of 10.385 million in 2007, accounting for 96% of the total tourist population, and their annual gate receipts reached 497.807 million Yuan, accounting for 97% of the total gate receipts. The four scenic spots in Lintong in Xi'an had an annual tourist population of 6.2 million and their annual gate receipts reached 382.028 million Yuan, respectively accounting for 60% of the total annual tourist population in Xi'an and for 77% of the total gate receipts in Xi'an. The five scenic spots in Baoji had an annual tourist population of 0.49 million and their annual gate receipts attained 15.3 million Yuan. In 2009, the Municipal Party Committee and Government of Xi'an is considering to establish the tourism base in the NPQM, and an area of 6,000 Mou of tourism ecological region will be constructed in the NPQM. In August 2009, Shaanxi Travel Bureau formally issued "Tourism Development Project in Qinling Mountains", and attempted to establish Qinling into a demonstration base of international ecotourism. However, there still exist the following problems at the time of tourism development.

Ecotourism Resources of Geological Landform is Damaged
Damage of geological landform resources is mainly embodied in that of mountains shapes, ecology, landscape, and environment, which is mostly caused by such economic activities as exploitation of real estate, mineral exploration, construction and highways, cables and hotels, and so on. In the NPQM, some projects of exploitation of real estate, exploitation of mineral resources and scenic spots go to construction without any approval or assessment of environmental impact. Besides, the phenomena of construction getting out of line are serious. Thus, such geologic hazards as serious water loss and soil erosion and mountain landslide happen. In June 2002, Dabagou Forest Park and Fengyu Manor suffered from flood disaster as a result of occupying riverways, and caused heavy losses. In 2007, construction projects of NPQM merely within Chang'an District were as many as 50, but there were only eight projects with authentic procedures. With villa projects in the NPQM being called to a stop and villa exploitation in the guise of tourism project again "seeking for new life," the degree of damage to geological landform resources were not under effective control.

Ecotourism Resources of Water Body and Biology are Polluted
There are 28 branches of Weihe River in the Kuan-chung Plain from Baoji and to Tongguan along the NPQM, there are 16 branches are polluted in some extent. In recent years, many vacation mountain villas, hotels, guesthouse, and agritainment have been constructed in the surrounding of mountain passes of such rivers as Fengyukou in Qinling Mountains. However, because environmental protection facilities are lacking in urban and rural areas, household garbage and waste residue in these units have

had no fixed storage occasion, and are concentratively land filled by local towns and villages at present. However, formal measures to prevent and control pollution are lacking in landfill occasions, and there exists indiscriminate discharge without any treatment, and even some units discharge a great deal of household garbage and sewage into valleys and river ways without any treatment. A large majority of industrial enterprises are short of sewage treatment facilities or are unable to run normally, and their industrial waste water is discharged without reaching standards, which causes environmental pollution and endangers security of water source. Therefore, the Xi'an Municipal Government planned to invest an amount of 0.5 billion Yuan in 2009 to concentratively treat with the problems of garbage and pollution in exploitation of ecotourism in the NPQM. At the same time, devastation of forests for arable land, ore exploitation, excessive cutting of forest, and excavation of medicinal materials, and so on, result in serious damage to forest cover, and frequently poaching for rare animals. Animals protected in some of happy farmhouses along Qinling Mountains become a specialty. Ecological environment of Tourism is seriously damaged.

Relatively Laggard Project, Disordered Management, Serious Duplication of Similar Projects, and Low Level of Tourism Resources Exploitation
Quite a large number of scenic spots are short of a unified management and coordination institution and a long-term plan, with blind and disordered construction, and a large majority of forest parks and holiday resorts simply go on their own way, following the same pattern, without any individual characteristics. The phenomena of construction by several units and management by several departments exist, without a unified standard and requirement, outstanding phenomenon of disordered management and insufficient coordination of management system, which has a direct influence on investment and construction, and constrains exploitation of tourism resources and development of tourism industry. By the year 2008, there had already 1,130 projects of sightseeing tour and agritainment in the NPQM merely within the urban district of Xi'an, including Shangwang Village and Tangyu Town, and so on. There are also a large number of tourism development projects and all sorts of happy farmhouses that are not approved and registered in the government. Exploitation of tourism resources in a large majority of scenic spots are in an initial state, with low levels and monotonous activities of tourism, and their tourism functions are similar, merely focusing on the aspect of sightseeing, with bad comprehensive tourism benefits.

Shortage of Talents and Inefficient Management
Ecotourism industry is an industry with high scientific content, which calls for professional talents with high quality. However, the relatively laggard local education, under-emphasis on talents of tourism, and unsound training mechanism, together with intensification of talents mobility, shortage of talents in ecotourism becomes more serious. Such shortage of talents is not only embodied in shortage of talents in high-level project and management, but also in low level of their managerial and administrative expertise and their shortage of experiences, so they cannot adapt to the needs of tourism development. Shortage of managerial and operational talents and corresponding scientific knowledge and skills causes low management efficiency of ecotourism

within the district. Besides, randomness of decision making and the fact that everyone goes his own way result in chaos of the ecotourism market, inferiority of service quality, and difficult development of real ecotourism.

COUNTERMEASURES AND SUGGESTIONS OF SUSTAINABLE DEVELOPMENT OF ECOTOURISM IN THE NPQM

Ecotourism is a form of tourism that involves traveling to tranquil and unpolluted natural areas. According to the definition and principles of ecotourism established by The International Ecotourism Society (TIES) in 1990, ecotourism is "Responsible travel to natural areas that conserves the environment and improves the well being of local people." Connotation of ecotourism attaches more importance to protection on natural tourism resources, and refers to tourism with sustainable development. Ecotourism should not only harmonize with the nature at the cost of sacrificing the environment. On the contrary, ecotourism should qualify contemporary human beings with equal opportunities to share the natural landscape and human landscape of tourism with the later generation. A tourist should share vivid and concrete ecological education in the whole process of ecotourism. In order to bring advantages of tourism resources in the NPQM into play, and to realize rational utilization and rational distribution of tourism resources, the author puts forward the path for tourism resources exploitation in the NPQM in the future. First of all, an investigation is necessary to find out the foundation, and a comprehensive assessment should be conducted on tourism resources to establish the principle of protective exploitation; a medium and long-term project should be strengthened to highlight characteristics of ecotourism in Qinling Mountains; the strategy of sustainable development should be carried forward to promote the organic integration of ecological environmental protection and tourism exploitation; characteristics and individuality of each district should be emphasized, and investment should be strengthened to develop rural ecotourism and ecological agriculture; quality of practitioners and level of managerial personnel should be improved so as to realize the scientific and sustainable development of ecological and economic tourism zones in the NPQM.

In Order to Provide Potent Scientific Support for Exploitation of Ecotourism, a Comprehensive Survey and Assessment Should be Conducted on Ecotourism Resources in the NPQM

Scientific experts and experts from universities and colleges are organized to conduct a detailed survey and assessment on ecotourism resources in the NPQM, determining ecological environment capacity of each ecotourism scenic spot, controlling carrying capacity of ecological environment and confirming critical capacity of tourists in sightseeing districts at different periods. At the same time, we should analyze existing issues in development of ecotourism from the perspective of sustainable development of tourism industry, and provide scientific evidence for the government to formulate medium and long-term tourism projects.

To Establish the Principle of Protective Development, Strengthen Medium Term Project, and to Highlight Characteristics of Ecotourism in Qinling Mountains

Development of ecotourism in the NPQM should be undertaken appropriately on the precondition of protecting ecological environment. Development and construction of ecotourism should not be undertaken at the cost of sacrificing ecological environment. Thus, when preparing to construct tourism facilities and travelling routes, we should pay special attention to those fragile and sensitive ecological districts, and when conflicts happen between economic interest and ecological environment, we should lay more importance to protecting the ecological environment. The project should follow the standard of advanced level in the world, designed in a long-range vision and persisting in the strategy of sustainable development. Hence, Shaanxi Province is going to formulate a series of standards about tourism development in Qinling Mountains, and especially stationing of newly developed tourist attractions and happy farmhouses should be conducted according to formally issued standards. High standards should be carried out, such as, environmental protection standard, environmental capacity standard, happy farmhouse construction standard, standard of tourist receipts capacity, and sanitary standard, and so on. A medium and long-term project should be drawn up, in which standards will be implemented one by one in batches, and those areas with mature conditions will be taken into consideration with priority and those projects that cannot meet standards or are not in accordance with the project should be refused. In August 2006, Shaanxi Province passed "Environmental Protection Project in the NPQM in Shaanxi." This project makes an analysis and assessment on the status quo and existing issues of ecological environment in the NPQM, and has directive significance to coordinating relationship between ecological environmental protection and development of tourism in the NPQM.

Strengthening the Prevention of Water Loss and Soil Erosion and Ecological Environmental Protection

In the NPQM, forest cover suffers unprecedented damage, together with clouded rivers, high drop of rivers, frequent rainstorms, and frequent geologic hazards of landslide and debris flow, so water loss and soil erosion is extremely serious. Therefore, we should strengthen comprehensive prevention by combination with establishment of forest for water and soil conservation, returning land for farming to forestry, natural forest protection and river training works, so as to guarantee security of people's lives and properties. We should extensively publicize and deeply carry out " Act of Ecological Environmental Protection in Qinling Mountains", and come to realize that ecological environmental protection is not only obligation of leaders at all levels and relevant departments of the government, but is also responsibility and obligation of the great masses and tourists. We should intensify management of protection on waterhead areas centered with reservoirs, especially reservoirs of Heihe and Stonebrook, and so on. We should prohibit or restrict some exploitation activities so as to improve water quality and guarantee drinking water security of people and animals. We should insist on the strategies we have always been following to protect biological diversification.

To Strengthen Development for Poverty Relief and Capital Investment, to Development Vigorously Rural Ecotourism and Ecological Agriculture, and to Realize Regional Sustainable Development

We should enlarge capital investment in tourism, green industries and development for poverty relief, and strengthen investment force by means of governmental investment, attraction of investment, utilization of foreign investment and social financing, and so on. We should support all projects of exploitation and construction, and vigorously development rural ecotourism economy and such new types of ecological agriculture as vegetables, flowers, fruits, and forest, and sightseeing tour, and so on, to promote overall coordination of regional tourism and social economy, to realize sustainable development and to establish a harmonious society.

To Improve Quality of Practitioners in Tourism and Relevant Industries and the Level of Managerial Personnel, and to Build up an Ecological Atmosphere in the Scenic Spots

Protection of ecological environment is one of the central connotation of ecotourism, which requires ecotourism managerial personnel to change the traditional development scheme of tourism, and to place ecological environmental protection in the first place. It is not allowed to take ecotourism as a "label" to attract tourists and to concentrate merely on economic interest, regardless of damage to tourism resources and environmental protection. Thus, we should strengthen training, cultivate professional ecotourism talents, and establish a scientific management concept. For the time being, most practitioners in relevant industries in the NPQM come from local rural areas, who have no professional learning and training experiences, with low professional quality, management level and inferior service quality. At the time of improving tourism infrastructure, we should continue to improve quality of practitioners, and their service quality. We should adopt various means to conduct ecological education on tourists and to improve their self-consciousness to protect ecological environment. At the time of making a sightseeing tour, tourists should protect every tree and bush within the conservation district. We should attempt to make our tourists come to comprehend the environmental protection idea of "taking only photos, leaving only footprints."

KEYWORDS

- **Countermeasures**
- **Ecotourism industry**
- **North Piedmont of Qinling Mountains**
- **Sustainable development**

Chapter 14

Heritage Ecotourism in Micronesia

Dirk H. R. Spennemann, David W. Look, and Kristy Graham

INTRODUCTION

Cultural heritage tourism is on the increase worldwide, focusing on sites, sights, museums, and cultural experiences such as festivals and traditional communities. At the same time, various decision makers see cultural heritage places as an asset and studies have been undertaken to assess the feasibility of using such sites as attractions. The development of ecotourism opportunities in the heritage arena has created increased visitor demand, with Micronesia the last largely unassessed region. If heritage ecotourism is to succeed, coordination and planning are required. This begs the question: What are the attitudes of Micronesian government officials toward ecotourism and toward cultural heritage sites?

A recent symposium organized from February 28 to March 3, 2000, by the mayor of Rota, the Commonwealth of the Northern Mariana Islands (CNMI) Historic Preservation Office, and the US National Park Service provided the opportunity to poll participant decision makers. Attended by approximately 100 participants from the CNMI, Guam, Republic of Palau, Republic of the Marshall Islands, Federated States of Micronesia, and Hawaii, the symposium was intended to make a substantial contribution to the management of cultural and natural resources in Micronesia while encouraging ways to develop heritage ecotourism that is responsible and sustainable.

A questionnaire was administered to each participant (except presenters) at the beginning of the symposium. It contained demographic and attitudinal questions (using a seven-point Lickert scale from "strongly agree," to "strongly disagree"). The overall response rate was 52.2%. Some results of the survey are presented below.

The breakdown of the nature of employment of the respondents is important. All too often, symposia such as this are only attended by a specialized, self-nominating minority. At the Rota Heritage Ecotourism Symposium the key stakeholders of heritage managers, parks and wildlife staff, and people involved in the tourism businesses (both government and private enterprise) made up 56%, with 34% of the attendees coming from other government agencies (Finance, Public Works, and so on). The remaining 10% were students and others.

WHO ARE THE EXPECTED VISITORS?

An integral aspect of any heritage ecotourism development is the ability to identify the potential market. By ascertaining who the perceived visitors are expected to be, it is possible to understand the various attitudes of the government parties involved in the survey. Clearly, ecotourism is seen as a privilege of the middle-aged wealthy. The demographics of the eco-tourist were perceived to be adults predominantly between the ages of 36 and 50 (63.2%) with a substantial income in excess of $50,000 dollars (US) per annum (33%). Although all age groups should be considered clientele, it is intriguing that the age profile of the expected eco-tourist roughly resembles that of the respondents.

PROFILING HERITAGE ECOTOURISM

The heritage ecotourism industry does not benefit from a standardized definition. The conceptual definition of sustainability, environmental awareness, economic benefits to local communities, education through interpretation, and social and cultural sensitivity, can be somewhat different to the operational situation.

Do the Micronesian decision makers understand the concept of heritage ecotourism? Only 1% of the respondents stated that they did not possess an understanding of the concept of heritage ecotourism. On face value this could be regarded as a positive sign, as one might assume that the participants were well prepared for the symposium. On the other hand, it could be interpreted as misplaced confidence.

The questionnaire posited that heritage ecotourism does not exist as a bona fide industry, but rather it is just a small segment of the overall tourism industry. Almost 64% of respondents agreed with this statement. The opinion was more polarized with respect to the assertion that heritage ecotourism is just a fashionable term for general tourism, which capitalizes on natural and cultural heritage. In that case 43.8% agreed and 56.2% disagreed, with no one undecided on the matter. All forms of tourism capitalize on the natural and cultural resource base of a destination; they are two integral factors in formulating a place, into a primary destination. The concept of heritage ecotourism is to go beyond this and inspire an appreciation and to educate people about its value. If the participants truly understood the conceptual description of heritage ecotourism—as their responses to a previous assertion would have us believe—the response should have been decidedly more toward disagreement. As it stands, the responses to this assertion demonstrate the symposium participants' propensity to overstate their prior knowledge.

Although heritage ecotourism was not perceived to be a bona fide industry, the overwhelming majority of respondents (91.6%) agreed with the assertion that heritage ecotourism is not a short lived phenomenon, indicating that they believe heritage ecotourism is more than just a trend and will continue to have a future.

THE IMPACTS OF HERITAGE ECOTOURISM

Heritage ecotourism is often perceived as "softer" on both the natural and the cultural environment than mainstream tourism. Heritage eco-tourists are often attracted to those sites of particular rarity and of cultural and natural significance. Hence, the threat of impacts to these sites may be greater due to the fragility or significance of such sites. Even if we do pull back from heritage ecotourism, some impact may not be able to be mitigated and reversed. If left unmanaged, however, the potential severity of these impacts could increase. The survey demonstrated that a large majority of respondents (71%) disagreed with the assertion that we can pull back from heritage ecotourism development if environmental problems occur and that nature will not heal itself. What could not be assessed is participants' knowledge to what extent re-vegetation of environments could mitigate some or all of the impact.

On the question whether "damage done by tourists to cultural heritage places can be repaired without detriment to our heritage," 86% of the respondents disagreed. If we combine the responses to the two questions it becomes clear that the symposium participants had some idea about the fragility of the natural and cultural environment and the lasting effects of any damage done.

Given this, the question has to be posed how that can be achieved. The use of a sacrificial area is one of the common strategies. When assessing the attitudes toward the fragility of sites, it was found that 52% agreed that it is better to have more tourists in a less fragile area than fewer tourists in a fragile area thereby indicating that it is better to sacrifice a resource of lesser fragility in order to ensure the conservation of those more fragile areas. However, 43% of respondents disagreed with this statement, demonstrating that opinions were well divided, possibly due to lack of information on the matter.

RANKING OPPORTUNITIES

Heritage ecotourism opportunities arise in many aspects of the natural and cultural environment. By assessing the responses, it is possible to identify the perceptions and values of various heritage ecotourism opportunities. In keeping with the training opportunities of the symposium 10 options were chosen. Participants were asked to rank these, according to their perceived potential (one being the most important and 10 being the least important).

From the 10 options provided, the most prominent response in ranking was archeological sites closely followed by natural landscapes. Both responses could be expected given the theme of the symposium. This is an interesting result when we consider that heritage managers constituted 22% and parks and wildlife staff only 17%. The second cluster comprises local bird life and local plants. The means for both responses were very close together. This ranking is possibly biased by the high percentage of participants from Rota. The fact that local bird life outranks local plants has most likely come about because the symbol of Rota is the Marianas fruit dove, which is also the national bird of the Mariana Islands and features predominantly in a local environmental education campaign.

The third conceptual cluster comprises the social aspects of island life, preferring traditional skills, and traditional fishing. The mean of the two are over one ranking unit apart, and the standard deviations are quite large. The transition from traditional fishing to shipwrecks and diving opportunities (part of the next cluster) is not that clear cut.

The fourth cluster comprises the non-indigenous heritage locations. These ranked poorly, with an average rank of 6.5 and less. Of these, World War II sites ranked the poorest, a full rank value lower than the others.

Overall, the rankings indicated that indigenous past was seen as the most important aspect of heritage ecotourism followed by the local environment. Traditional cultural values are then much less important, while the tangible heritage places associated with colonial administration ranked last. The fact that non-indigenous heritage sites, and in particular WWII sites ranked so poor may be due to the negative perception of the war by the local population.

PRIORITIES FOR HERITAGE ECOTOURISM

Asked to rank various priorities for heritage ecotourism, cultural issues ranked highly, with the options "Preserve cultural heritage sites," "Ability to showcase my own culture," and "Preserve local plants and animals" taking the top three spots. Although the survey previously identified that it was the perception of the participants that heritage ecotourism has the potential to increase visitor numbers without increasing the problems they pose, large visitor numbers were not a priority and ranked lowest.

DISCUSSION

The questionnaire provided a good insight into the attitudes of Micronesian decision makers. The lack of opportunity to pretest the questionnaire resulted in two questions returning ambiguous answers.

The responses to a number of attitudinal questions showed that the decision makers attending the symposium had a limited understanding of the concepts of ecotourism, despite their initial claim that they did. The opinions were divided whether ecotourism was a bona fide industry, or whether it was simply general tourism focusing on the natural and cultural heritage. Overwhelming agreement existed on the assertion that ecotourism was not a short-lived phenomenon. Overall, ecotourism was perceived to have fewer negative impacts than mainstream tourism. The respondents expressed awareness that the development of ecotourism may have impacts on the natural and cultural environment, as well as social impacts on the community, that may not be easily mitigated—if at all.

Yet at the same time the participants expressed the opinion that there was much potential to increase the number of visitors without increasing the problem they pose and that other island communities would be receptive to the development of heritage ecotourism. The respondents saw archeological and natural landscapes as the main ecotourism opportunity, while attractions related to the colonial periods were perceived to be much less significant.

While the symposium was successful in raising awareness and the overall state of knowledge on the matter, further training in the form of country-specific case studies is required if the expectations for the economic return inherent in heritage ecotourism opportunities are to be fulfilled.

KEYWORDS

- **Cultural heritage tourism**
- **Ecotourism**
- **Ranking opportunities**

Chapter 15

Economic Value of Ecotourism in the Nigerian Rainforest Zone

Eugene E. Ezebilo, Leif Mattsson, and Carolyn A. Afolami

INTRODUCTION

This study estimates community willingness to contribute for an ecotourism improvement project and its determinants in the Okwangwo Division of the Cross River National Park, Nigeria. Personal interviews were conducted with 150 households in three communities located in the proximity of the park. The study showed that the respondents were willing to contribute an average of about 1% of their mean annual income per year. Determinants of the respondents' willingness to contribute amount was estimated with the aid of the ordinary least squares (OLSs) and Tobit models. The results showed that willingness to contribute were influenced by factors such as income, distance of respondents' residence to the park, post-high school education, occupation, and membership of an environmental conservation group. The results generated from this study will contribute to the knowledge of sustainable management of ecotourism projects. The increase in human population and preferences for leisure activities often leads to an increase in demand for recreational use of public lands in many parts of the world (Bowler et al., 1999; Foot, 1990, 2004; Nickerson, 2000). Ecotourism, travel to natural areas that conserves the environment and improves the well being of local people (TIES, 1990), is a fast growing industry. Research shows that there are more than 5 million eco-tourists and most of them are from North America, Europe, and Australia (Kamauro, 1996). Ecotourism accounts for a large share of some countries' gross domestic product, and so contributes to livelihoods of many people, as in Kenya, Madagascar, Nepal, Thailand, and Malaysia (Isaacs, 2000). Benefits of protected areas often accrue to the national and global economy, but the costs are usually borne by local communities. Therefore integrating nature conservation and ecotourism has become a popular way to motivate local communities to support nature conservation projects (Abbot et al., 2001). When ecotourism is supported in protected areas, it is often argued that economic benefits will accrue to local communities (Marsh, 2000). Some of the economic benefits which local communities can derive from ecotourism are employment opportunities, development associated with infrastructure (e.g., better road network and water) and ecotourism businesses (Hall, 2006a; Marsh, 2000; Weiler and Scidl, 2004).

Benefits from recreational use of public lands, for example ecotourism, are typically estimated by means of non-market valuation methods (Loomis, 1993; Mitchell and Carson, 1989). The contingent valuation method is widely applied in estimating the economic value of non-marketed goods (Carson, 2004; Champ et al., 2003; Garrod and Willis, 1999; Majid et al., 1983). It uses survey questions to elicit people's preferences for non-marketed goods by asking them how much they would be willing to pay for specified improvements or to avoid decrements in them (Mitchell and Carson, 1989). Most contingent valuation studies (Lindsey et al., 2005; Maharana et al., 2000; Nuva and Shamsudin, 2009; Yacob et al., 2009) on ecotourism have focused on values which eco-tourists attach to ecotourism. Values of ecotourism development to local communities are rarely studied and it is often claimed that ecotourism promotes conservation of natural and cultural heritage of an area and may improve the standard of living of local residents (Boo, 1990; Eraqi, 2008; Lindberg and Hawkins, 1993). Advocates of national parks often claim that income from ecotourism will supplement the livelihoods of individuals who reside in the vicinity of a park. The support of local communities is often required for sustainable development of ecotourism. Therefore, it is important to have knowledge about the value which local communities attach to ecotourism development projects. This will help policy makers with regards to decisions concerning how to package an ecotourism project to benefit more individuals in local communities. The aim of this study is therefore to estimate, using the contingent valuation method, how much local communities would be willing to contribute to support an ecotourism project and also the determinants of these values. The location of the study is the communities in the vicinity of the Okwangwo Division of the Cross River National Park.

MATERIALS AND METHODS

Study Site

The Okwangwo Division (OD) of the Cross River National Park is located in the Cross River State in southeastern Nigeria and covers an area of 1,000 km^2. The elevation of the OD ranges from 1,000 to 1,700 meters above sea level. The vegetation of the park comprises lowland rainforest at lower elevations and montane grasslands along the ridges in the higher elevations. The OD plays an important role in protection of fisheries, watersheds and climatic stability, ecotourism, and preservation of genetic resources (Coldecott et al., 1990). Wildlife found in the park includes antelopes, chimpanzees, high forest monkeys, buffaloes, high forest elephants, manatees, wild pigs, baboon, leopards, and gorillas. The area is a center of endemism for frogs, birds, and four primates, including the endangered Cross River Gorilla—*Gorilla gorilla diehli* (Oates et al., 1990; White, 1990). Over 280 bird species have been recorded including *Picathartes oreas* and *Calyptocichla serina* (BirdLife International, 2009). The park harbors 950 species of butterflies (Cross River State Government, 2008). Apart from seeing diverse plant species and mammals the OD also offers eco-tourists opportunities for hiking, bird watching, sport fishing, and boat cruising. The park is surrounded by 66 villages with a total population of 36,000 people (Ite, 2004). The economy of these communities is characterized by subsistence agriculture. The crops cultivated include banana, plantain, cocoa, oil palm, cassava, and yam, while livestock reared include poultry, cattle, sheep, and goats. Some individuals in the communities engage in hunting and gathering of non-timber forest products such as game animals, bush mangos, wild vegetables, mushrooms, and medicinal plants. Some people already engage in ecotourism businesses such as guided tours, transportation of tourists and catering.

If quality of services in the ecotourism sector of the economy is improved, more individuals in the local communities may participate in and benefit from ecotourism.

Data Collection

The data collection involved standardized face-to-face interviews that were designed, and tested in a community outside the study area. Pre-test interviews were conducted in November 2007 covering 20 randomly selected individuals. Findings from the pre-test interviews motivated several changes in the questionnaire for example the wording of the hypothetical market scenario and the payment vehicle. The major survey was conducted during the months of April and May 2008. Two interviewers were recruited and trained for 2 days. Three villages from the 66 villages located within the proximity of the OD were randomly selected for the survey. The villages were Bukalom, Butatong, and Wula in the Boki Local Government Area of Cross River State. Every other house along the street was visited in each of the villages. If a house was not occupied, then it was omitted and the next house was visited. The interviewees alternated between the eldest male and the eldest female in each selected household. If the gender of the eldest in a household did not coincide with the interviewee selection method, then a member of the opposite gender was interviewed and the respondent's gender was alternated again from there on. Interviews were conducted in the Boki language. A total of 150 respondents were interviewed in the study area (50 respondents in each village).

The study was described to the respondents and then they were asked series of demographic questions such as their occupation, annual income, and whether they have passed through primary, high, and post-high school education.

Furthermore, they were asked about the distance of their residence to the OD and also whether they belonged to an environmental conservation group.

Contingent Valuation Format

The hypothetical market scenario was developed to describe improvement in the quality of services in ecotourism in order to attract more eco-tourists to the OD. This would give more individuals in the local community the opportunity to derive income from ecotourism. It will also help to improve infrastructure such as better road network. The people in this study area often contribute to the provision of infrastructure such as community school classrooms. This kind of contribution is known as development levy. Therefore the payment vehicle—annual contribution to a community development fund—was not new to the respondents. Individuals in the study area often bargain the price of anything they wish to buy. This is the tradition of the people thus the bidding game elicitation technique may not be new to the respondents.

The hypothetical market scenario and payment vehicle was described to the respondents. They were asked if they were willing to contribute anything at all for improving the quality of services in ecotourism. If the answer was "no," which was the case for only a small fraction (6%) of the respondents, the respondent was asked to give the reason. If the answer was "yes," the second step was to determine the maximum amount the respondent was willing to contribute. The interviewer started the bidding game by an initial bid of 100 Nigeria Naira (NGN). If the respondent said "yes" to that amount, which a large majority of the respondents did, the interviewer raised the amount sequentially by five times (NGN 500), 10 times (NGN 1,000), 15 times (NGN 1,500), 20 times (NGN 2,000), 30 times (NGN 3,000), 40 times (NGN 4,000), 50 times (NGN 5,000), and 60 times (NGN 6,000), until the respondent's answer was "no." No respondent answered "yes" to the highest bid of NGN 6,000. The amount which the respondent said "no" to was then reduced by 12.5%, 25%, and 50% respectively, until the respondent's answer was "yes." If the respondent said "no" already to the initial bid of NGN 100, the interviewer reduced the amount by 12.5%, 25%, and 50%, respectively, until the respondent's answer was "yes." No respondent who said "no" to the amount equivalent to 50% of the initial bid that is NGN 50.

THEORETICAL FRAMEWORK AND STATISTICAL ANALYSIS

The OD serves as site for nature conservation. The park also attracts eco-tourists and some local residents in the periphery of the park benefit from income from ecotourism. However, it is considered that if quality of services in ecotourism is improved it will attract more eco-tourists to the park and more of the residents may derive income from ecotourism. Suppose that improvement in quality of services in ecotourism is proposed. Before the improvement in quality is implemented, we would like to know the residents' preferences for the improvement. The utility function can be written as:

$$U = U(J, Q) \tag{1}$$

where, J denotes a vector of goods consumed and Q denotes quality of services in ecotourism. The status quo of the quality of services is Q_0, and it is proposed to improve the quality to the level Q. The individual's willingness to contribute (WTC_i) for improvement in quality from Q to Q is given by:

$$WTC_i = e(p, U_i, Q_{1i}; S_i) - e(p, U_i, Q_{0i}; S_i) + \varepsilon_{1i} - \varepsilon_{0i} \tag{2}$$

where, p is a price vector for goods consumed J, e (.) is an expenditure function and S_i is vector of personal characteristics of the individual i. The individual expenditure function is assumed to be known to the individual, but is known with a margin of error ε_i to investigators. The WTC_i can be expressed as:

$$WTC_i = X_i \beta + \varepsilon_i \tag{3}$$
$$\varepsilon_i \sim N(0, \sigma^2)$$

where, X_i is vector of explanatory variables thought to influence the valuation process, β is the set of unknown parameters which reflect the effect of changes in a given explanatory variable on WTC_i, and ε_i is a random error term which reflect factors affecting utility that the researcher is unable to observe. The parameter ε_i is assumed to be normally distributed with zero mean and constant variance.

Valuation functions using WTC estimates, which result from open-ended contingent valuation studies, can be examined with (OLSs and Tobit models, respectively. However, there is often debate among contingent valuation researchers as to whether it is more appropriate to use censored regression (Tobit) models or linear models using OLS. Proponents of the Tobit models argue that it addresses the censoring, that is large number of zeros typically found in contingent valuation surveys, but linear models ignore this censoring. The OLS model fail to account for qualitative differences between zero and positive WTC values (Greene, 2003). This may result in a biased estimate of the parameters of interest. This has led to widespread use of Tobit models especially among economists (Floro and Miles, 2003; Kimmel and Connelly, 2007). The linear models we estimate using OLS are of the form:

$$y_i = X_i \beta + \varepsilon_i \qquad (4)$$

where, y_i is the observed individual i WTC value which is greater than 0, X_i is the vector of the individual i personal characteristics, β is vector of parameter to be estimated and ε_i is the error term which is normally distributed with mean zero and variance σ^2.

For the censored Tobit, model the dependent variable is observed only if it is above or below some cut off level. The Tobit model (Tobin, 1958) combines the elements from OLSs with a normal probit equation, that is the size of the bid and the probability of bidding a positive amount. In this study the WTC values were censored at zero, that is all reported WTC values are larger or equal to zero since it is not possible to bid negative amounts. The formulation of the Tobit model is:

$$y_i^* = X_i \beta + \varepsilon^i \qquad (5)$$

where, $\varepsilon_i \sim N(0, \sigma^2)$. y_i^* is a latent variable that is observed for WTC values greater than zero and censored otherwise. The observed y_i is defined by:

$$y_i = y_i^*, \text{ if } y_i^* > 0 \qquad (6)$$
$$y_i = 0, \text{ if } y_i^* \leq 0$$

The log likelihood function for the Tobit model is:

$$\log L = \sum_{y_i > 0} -\frac{1}{2}\left[\log(2\pi) + \log \sigma^2 + \frac{(y_i - \beta X_i)^2}{\sigma^2}\right] + \sum_{y_i = 0} \log\left[1 - F\left(\frac{\beta X_i}{\sigma}\right)\right] \qquad (7)$$

These models were estimated using the LIMDEP NLOGIT version 4.0.1 statistical package (Table 3). In this study we have examined the impacts of the respondents' characteristics on WTC using the OLS and the Tobit model, respectively. The OLS was used to analyze the influence of the respondents' characteristics on WTC > 0, and WTC $\geq$ 0 for the Tobit model, respectively.

The principles for consistency in the bidding game means that a point estimate of the individual respondent's maximum WTC was not determined. Instead, the respondent's true maximum WTC lies in the interval between the highest amount that the respondent said "yes" to, and the lowest amount with a "no" answer from the respondent. Mean WTC (MWTC) was thus estimated as:

$$MWTC = \frac{1}{n}\sum_{i=1}^{n}\frac{B_{ij+}B_{ik}}{2} \qquad (8)$$

where, n is the sample size, B_{ij} is the highest amount with a "yes" answer from the respondent and Bik is the lowest amount with a "no" answer from the respondent. A description of variables that were used in the analysis is presented in Table 1.

Table 1. Definition of variables.

Variable	Description
WTC	Willingness to contribute for the improvement in the quality of services in ecotourism (NGN per individual per year).
INCO	Annual disposable income (NGN per individual per year)
DIST	Distance (Kilometre) between the respondent's residence and the OD
P_SC	Respondent has passed through primary school (Yes = 1, No = 0)
H_SC	Respondent has passed through high school (Yes = 1, No = 0)
PH_SC	Respondent has passed through post-high school (Yes = 1, No = 0)
OCCU	Occupation of the respondent (1 = traditional, 0 = non-traditional)
GENDER	Gender of the respondent (Male = 1, Female = 0)
MEG	Member of environmental conservation group (Yes = 1, No = 0)

We expect the following impacts of the explanatory variables on the WTC:

Annual Disposable Income

Individuals who have more money are often willing to pay more for public goods (Boman et al., 2008; Hökby and Söderqvist, 2003). They are often less risk averse and may be more willing to invest in new projects. Hence, we expect a positive influence of income on WTC.

The Distance of the Respondent's Residence to the Okwangwo Division

Ecotourism activities often take place in the national park therefore individuals (respondents) who live closer to the park will expect to derive more net benefit from an ecotourism project (Pate and Loomis, 1997). Therefore we expect a negative effect of distance of the respondent's residence to the park on WTC.

Respondents Who Have Passed Through Primary, High, and Post-high School Education

Education often gives individuals the opportunity to access information about benefits of new projects (Baral et al., 2008; Brander et al., 2006). We expect a positive influence of the coefficients associated with the respondents who have passed through primary, high, and post-high school on WTC, respectively.

Occupation

Individuals who engage in formal (non-traditional) employment such as teaching and nursing often have more education thus may have greater tendency to infer the importance of developmental projects. Hence, we expect the coefficient associated with the respondents' occupation to have a negative influence on WTC.

Gender

In Nigeria, men are often "bread-winners" of the household. Ecotourism projects would give them the opportunity to diversify their livelihood and earn more income. It is expected therefore that gender will have a positive influence on WTC.

Membership of an Environmental Conservation Group

Environmental conservation groups comprise individuals who have positive views about protection of nature. Ecotourism project is an incentive for local communities to support environmental conservation. Therefore we expect the coefficient associated with membership of environmental conservation group to have positive influence on WTC. The results of the impacts of the above variables on respondents' WTC are presented in Table 3.

RESULTS AND DISCUSSION

Description of the Sample and WTC Estimate

Ninety-four percent of the respondents were willing to contribute to the improvement in quality of services in ecotourism and of these 47% were female and 53% male. Of the respondents who were not willing to contribute anything at all for ecotourism 78% (7) were male and 22% (2) female. The mean annual disposable income for the female and male respondents was NGN 123 672 ($US 824.48) and NGN 185 508 ($US 1,236.72), respectively. Seven percent of the respondents belonged to an environmental group. Descriptive statistics for the respondents' characteristics are presented in Table 2.

Table 2. Descriptive statistics for respondents.

Variable	Mean	Std. Dev.
INCO	158,554.000	88,191.800
DIST	4.763	3.099
PR_SC	0.840	0.368
H_SC	0.707	0.457
PH_SC	0.353	0.479
OCCU	0.483	0.501
GENDER	0.553	0.499
MEG	0.0733	0.262

I $US = NGN 150

Fifty-five percent of the respondents were male as shown in Table 2. Eighty-four percent of the respondents passed through the primary school education, about 71% passed through the high school education and 35% passed through the post-high school education.

The MWTC of the respondents was NGN 1 047. The mean willingness to contribute for the female and male respondents was NGN 885 and NGN 1 215, respectively. A possible reason may be that the male respondents earned more income than the female. The mean annual income of the male respondents (NGN 185,508) was 33% more than that of the female (NGN 123,672).

The adult population (≥20 years) in the Cross River State is estimated to be 35% as reported by the Cross River State Government (2008). Since the human population in the periphery of the OD is 36,000, the adult population there should be 12,600. Aggregating the MWTC over the relevant population of 12,600, the total perceived welfare benefit for the improvement in quality of services in ecotourism to residents at the periphery of the OD is estimated to be NGN 13,192,200 (US$ 87,948) each year.

Impacts of the Respondents' Characteristics on Willingness to Contribute

We now examine whether support for the improvement in quality of services in ecotourism cuts across all, or just some groups of the respondents, and so whether some common factors might have influenced the elicited WTC amount. This analysis is shown in Table 3, which is based on OLS and Tobit models estimates. The dependent variable was respondents' WTC amount for the improvement in quality of services in ecotourism.

Table 3. The OLS and Tobit models results for determinants of respondents' WTC.

Variable	OLS Coefficient	Tobit Coefficient
Constant	283.002 (254.003)	210.825 (275.623)
INCO	0.002* (0.001)	0.002* (0.001)
DIST	-59.844** (25.676)	-72.963** (29.400)
PR_SC	23.209 (269.867)	318.672 (287.042)
H_SC	112.248 (245.128)	157.026 (257.7!4)
PH_SC	453.973** (181.440)	423.235** (189.456)
OCCU	355.316**' (159.853)	358.429** (168.201)
GENDER	21.291 (164.150)	-31.447 (172.657)
MEG	545.548** (263.374)	545.466** (275.260)
R^2	0.263	0.243*
Adjusted R^2	0.208	
Log likelihood	-942.255	-872.290
Chi-sq	35.660****	
LM slatistic for tobit		35.742

Figures in parenthesis and standard errors.
' represents pseudo R^2
*, **, ***, **** represents 0.10, 0.05, 0.01, and 0.001 levels of statistically significance, respectively.

The Tobit and OLS estimates showed similar effects. For these models, coefficients associated with the respondents' income, post-high school education, distance of residence to the OD, occupation, and membership of environmental conservation group were statistically significant. A possible reason may be that the data used in this study contains only a few observations (6%) that were censored at zero. There are some sizable differences between OLS coefficients and that of Tobit. In general Tobit coefficients are larger than that of the OLS.

The coefficient associated with the respondents' annual disposable income has a positive and statistically significant impact on WTC for the improvement in quality of services in ecotourism. This suggests that an increase in the respondents' annual disposable income increases the WTC. A possible reason may be that respondents who earn more income may expect to derive more benefit from the improvement of quality in services perhaps because they often have more access to resources for investment. For example, respondents who earn more income may have higher propensity to save money thus giving them more opportunity to invest in more alternatives to increase livelihood.

As expected, the coefficient associated with the distance between the respondent's residence and the OD had a negative and statistically significant effect on WTC, that is, the farther the respondent's residence is from the park the lower would the WTC be. A possible reason may be that the respondents who live farther from the OD may not expect to derive much benefit, in the form of an increase in income from the improvement in the services in ecotourism, because most of the ecotourism activities take place in areas closer to the OD. The distance between the respondent's residence and the park is also likely to influence the amount of information that the respondent may have about the improvement in quality of services, that is the longer the distance the less the information about the park would be. Respondents who have more information about the quality of services in ecotourism may be willing to contribute more.

The coefficient associated with the respondents who have post-high school education has a positive and statistically significant effects on WTC, that is, the respondents who have post-high school education were more likely to contribute to the ecotourism project. Respondents who have post-high school education are more likely to be employed in the formal sector of the economy and may earn more income and thus may have more money to support the improvement in quality of services project. Another reason may be that post-high school education helps to comprehend the news about for example future benefits of an improvement in quality of services in ecotourism.

Unexpectedly, the coefficient associated with the respondents' occupation has a positive and statistically significant effect on WTC, that is, respondents who engaged in traditional employment such as farming and gathering of non-timber forest products were more willing to contribute for the improvement in quality of services in ecotourism. A reason may be that respondents who are occupied with traditional income generating activities may expect to benefit more from the improvement in quality of services because it may provide them the opportunity to diversify in their livelihood activities. This may reduce the risk associated with farming activities and thus improve their opportunity to have a sustainable livelihood. Furthermore, income from farming activities is often seasonal therefore improvement in quality of services in ecotourism may give the respondents whose livelihood are associated with farming an opportunity to earn more income to supplement their present income.

As expected, the coefficient associated with the membership of an environmental conservation group has a positive and statistically significant effect on WTC. This indicates that respondents who were member of an environmental conservation group were more willing to contribute for the improvement in quality of services in ecotourism. A possible reason may be that members of environmental conservation groups are often individuals who support environmental friendly activities. Ecotourism is often seen as an activity which has the potential to promote sustainable development of nature conservation, that is contribute to the livelihood of local communities and also maintain nature conservation. This is often the goal of environmental conservation group thus respondents who belonged to this group may be willing to contribute more for ecotourism project to indicate their interest for the environmental group.

The coefficient associated with the respondents' gender has the expected sign however it was not statistically significant. The coefficients associated with the respondents who have primary school, and high school education, respectively were not statistically significant.

Respondents Who Were not Willing to Contribute

As with any type of economic development, ecotourism development could create changes that threaten the quality of life. Social and cultural changes that ecotourism may introduce to host societies include changes in value systems, traditional life styles, family relationships, individual behavior, or community structure (Ratz, 2002). Six percent of the respondents did not support the improvement in the quality of services in ecotourism, and all of these were farmers and most (78%) were male. The most important reason was that they thought that the project will decimate their land and thus dissipate their source of livelihood. Another important reason was that they raised doubt about the capacity of the park authority to successfully implement the quality improvement project, and they also raised concerns regarding the sustainability of the project. They thought that successful implementation of the quality improvement project will attract more people to the area and could increase the demand for land for commercial activities such as market places and guest houses, which could reduce the land available for farming and collection of non-timber forest products.

The portion of respondents who did not support the project appears to be small, but the concerns raised indicate the presence of lapses in communication between the OD authority and the local residents, especially farmers. It suggests that sensitive issues, such as the impacts of ecotourism on the traditions of the people, need to be addressed.

CONCLUSION

Local communities often support projects which they believe will contribute to their livelihood. If they do not expect to derive benefit from a project they may not cooperate with the managers of the project. This study has been conducted in a developing country to examine the value which local communities attach to an ecotourism project and factors which may influence this value. The study showed that most of the respondents were willing to support the project. The study revealed that respondents who earn more income, reside closer to the OD, are occupied in traditional income generating activities, have post-high school education and belonged to an environmental conservation group may benefit more from the ecotourism project. There was no difference in the qualitative results for our models regardless of whether we used OLS or Tobit model. The study indicated that annual contribution to a community development fund can be used as payment vehicle for contingent valuation studies in developing countries. The study suggests that when planning an ecotourism project there may be a need to involve the local communities. This may give them more access to information about the project and may influence more of the local people to support the ecotourism project. Further research is needed in areas such as estimation of costs of a proposed improvement in quality of services in ecotourism and factors which could engender more local support for protected areas.

ACKNOWLEDGMENTS

We would like to extend our appreciation to Mattias Boman, Swedish University of Agricultural Sciences (SLU), for his useful advice regarding the statistical analysis. We thank Jack Sinden, School of Business, Economics and Public Policy, University of New England, Australia for his useful comments regarding the econometric model and for editing the manuscript. We also thank Franz-Michael Rundquist, Lund University for his useful advice regarding the survey design.

KEYWORDS

- **Contingent valuation**
- **Cross River National Park**
- **Ecotourism**
- **Willingness-to-contribute**

Chapter 16

Visitor Access to Cumberland Island National Seashore, Georgia

Ryan L. Sharp and Craig A. Miller

INTRODUCTION

Cumberland Island National Seashore (CUIS), located off the coast of Georgia, was created in 1972 to preserve the island's ecosystem and primitive character. The CUIS management staff has recently been charged with developing a Transportation Management Plan (TMP) to provide better access to the northern portion of the island, where several sites of historical significance are located. This assignment has created a conflict between providing transportation and preserving the island's naturalness. Proposals include providing transportation by passenger vehicles, trams, horseback, and even a horse and carriage. A total of 2,227 public comments on the proposals were received from individuals and organizations and have been analyzed to help guide the decision-making process. Eighty-one percent of the comments expressed opposition to or offered only conditional support for the proposed TMP. Hence, CUIS is facing a delicate state of transition and will need to further consider the balance between preservation and use of the island.

The CUIS was created in 1972 to preserve the island's primitive character and natural processes. The CUIS managers are further charged with preserving the area's natural, cultural, and historical aspects, while offering visitors a feeling of isolation and wonder. These ideals, set against the backdrop of the National Park Service's (NPS) mission of protecting the natural character of the park while accommodating the recreation needs of visitors, cause some conflicts of interest (NPS, 2007). The island has been inhabited for approximately 4,000 years and had been home to wealthy industrialists since the late 19th century. Human impacts on the island are obvious, but Cumberland has recovered from years of grazing and farming to such an extent that almost half of the island is now a federally designated "wilderness." Imposing a low limit on daily visitors to CUIS over the past 30 years (a maximum of 300 people per day) has helped the island recover even further, resulting in a mostly pristine environment.

Although Cumberland Island has remained relatively unchanged throughout the tenure of the NPS, CUIS now faces some significant changes. The original "wilderness" designation meant that a portion of the main road that runs the length of the island is off-limits to vehicular traffic in accordance with the Wilderness Act of 1964. New legislation requires CUIS staff to provide better access for visitors to the northern portion of the island, where several sites of historical significance are located. To allow this access, the island's wilderness designation had to be changed since the only access to the north end of the island is a dirt road that runs directly through the wilderness.

The CUIS management staff now has been charged with developing a TMP to provide access to the northern portion of the island.

This chapter provides a brief background of CUIS to enhance understanding of how the current situation developed. The TMP and related issues will then be discussed. Visitor perceptions of the proposed TMP will also be examined, along with issues related to the future of transportation on the island.

THE HISTORY AND MANAGEMENT OF CUIS

Cumberland Island Ecology

Cumberland is a barrier island off the southern coast of Georgia near the border with Florida. It is one of the largest, most pristine, undeveloped barrier islands on the East Coast. The island is composed of second-growth maritime forests, inland salt marsh, grassy dunes, and miles of pristine beaches. The island has had time to recover from early settlers' extensive farming and grazing, but the current incarnation of Cumberland Island is different from when the Europeans found it. Large stands of live oak and pine once covered the island, and undergrowth of such species as saw palmettos was less prevalent. The felling of the original large tree stands opened the door for more groundcover to develop, which resulted in its present-day look.

The mild climate, with temperatures in the 1960s in the winter and mid-1980s in the summer, makes Cumberland Island an ideal place for both humans and animals. This ecosystem is home to a wide variety of native and exotic wildlife, including bobcats, feral hogs, wild horses, armadillos, and deer. Federally protected loggerhead sea turtles use the many miles of beaches to lay their eggs.

Cumberland Island Cultural History

Cumberland Island has a long and storied history of human inhabitance stretching back 4,000 years. For most of this time the indigenous people, the Timucuan Indians, cultivated the land. They manipulated the local ecology by burning tracts of land to develop it for agriculture and encourage grazing by desirable animals such as the white-tailed deer (Dilsaver, 2004). By the time Spanish explorers arrived in 1562, the island had visible signs of human impact. In fact, European settlers later adopted the trail system established by the Timucuans and today many of the trails are remnants of these ancient byways (Dilsaver, 2004).

In 1783, Revolutionary War General Nathaniel Greene was awarded land on the island in recognition of his heroic role in the war. Greene built what would become one of the lasting images of the island, the original Dungeness Estate. Dungeness was the residence of the Greene family until it burned down. It remained in ruins until 1881 when the most famous residents of the island, the Carnegie family, razed the ruins and built their own Dungeness.

The Carnegies were the primary landowners on Cumberland for close to 100 years and they established several sites around the island. In 1972, after years of deliberation and negotiations, the Carnegies and other minor landholders sold their land to the NPS. Some families still reside on the island today as the result of agreements they have with the NPS, although many of these titles will revert to the NPS in 2010. Despite these few remnant in-holdings, the majority of the land on Cumberland Island is now owned and managed by the NPS.

NPS Involvement on Cumberland Island

On October 23, 1972, Public Law 92-536 was signed by President Nixon to establish Cumberland Island as a 40,500-acre National Seashore, making it one of the largest, mostly undeveloped, barrier island preserves in the world. The NPS decided early on that this island was a unique treasure to preserve and that preservation was made easier by its detachment from the mainland. The NPS subsequently set a visitor limit of 300 people per day to the island to limit visitor impacts on the ecological and recreational resources. A ferry runs twice daily to and from the island, taking up to 150 people per trip. It is not well understood how this visitor limit was established; the 300 people per day limit is generally accepted as an arbitrary number imposed by the NPS that lacks validation through scientific study. However, without imposing such restrictive limits, it is possible that social and ecological impacts would increase (Freimund and Cole, 2001). A University of Georgia study in 1970 calculated that the island had a daily carrying capacity of more than 14,400 visitors (Ike and Richardson, 1975). However, Ike and Richardson (1975) suggested that the NPS set the maximum at 10,000 and monitor visitor impacts to determine a more appropriate number. Research on crowding at wilderness areas by Dawson and Watson (2000) found that visitor satisfaction often remains high despite the perception of crowding.

From the outset, NPS managers considered designating a portion of the island as wilderness. This discussion came to fruition in 1982 when the northern part of the island (roughly 9,986 acres) was established as a wilderness to be managed by the NPS as part of the National Wilderness Preservation System. In accordance with the Wilderness Act of 1964, this new designation prohibited vehicular traffic on a portion of the main road that runs the length of the island. The NPS staff members could use only primitive tools to maintain the trails in the wilderness area and they were encouraged to use the water as their primary means of travel to the north end. Individuals who retained private property on the island were still allowed to use the main road with the agreement that when their use rights ended (most during 2010), the area would become a more "proper" wilderness (Dilsaver, 2004).

As time went on, it became apparent to many users and the park management staff that the north end of the island was inaccessible to many visitors due to lack of transportation. This realization led to new legislation requiring NPS to provide access to the environmental and historical sites at the north end of the island. Passed in 2004, Public Law 108-447 removed the main road's wilderness designation, once again allowing vehicular traffic access to the north end of the island. The legislation also required the NPS to develop a TMP to accommodate no less than five and no more than eight tours a day to the north end of the island.

THE TRANSPORTATION MANAGEMENT PLAN

As an agency, the NPS believes that resource conservation should take precedence over visitor recreation (NPS, 2007). In 1981, researchers Bonnicksen and Robinson noted that the NPS is often hesitant to expand recreational development within national seashores because of its commitment to preservation. The NPS mission states that CUIS is to provide for public outdoor recreation use and enjoyment of significant shoreline, lands, and water and to preserve related scenic, scientific, and historical values (NPS, 1984). The CUIS is mandated to preserve the island's natural environment as well as its cultural heritage, and this is where the TMP comes into play.

Currently, the island is divided into two well defined areas: the north and south end. The south end of the island is where the majority of visitor activity takes place. This is the location of the two ferry drop-offs, Sea Camp, and Dungeness Mansion, as well as easy access to the beach. The north end is primarily a designated wilderness and the only access is by foot or bicycle (private holdings are an exception; individuals are allowed to drive their private vehicles to the north end). The north end is the site of a 100-year old Carnegie Mansion (Plum Orchard), and the settlement where the First African Baptist Church resides. Plum Orchard is undergoing a multi-million dollar renovation and will be a big attraction for tourists. The first African Baptist Church and the settlement are of great cultural significance in African–American history and heritage. The issue is how visitors will get to these historical and cultural sites.

The first issue to be addressed is how visitors will reach the north end of the island; specifically, what type of vehicle will be used to transport visitors around the island. Several ideas have been proposed, such as passenger vehicles (vans or SUVs), trams, horseback, and even a horse and carriage (Hartrampf, Inc. and Jordan, Jones, and Goulding Inc., 2006). The idea getting the most attention is the vehicle proposal, but it faces several obstacles that must be overcome if it is to succeed. For instance, will the vehicles be gas-powered or possibly electric? Environmentalists argue that gas is not an option. With five to eight tours a day running to the north end of the island, gasoline-fueled vehicles will have a detrimental effect on the natural environment. Electric vehicles, however, come with their own problems. The overall trip to the north end and back (as the road currently exists, and allowing for touring the sites) takes approximately 3–4 hr. The electric car may be more environmentally friendly, but would the vehicle have enough of a charge to make the return trip? If the answer is no, then a charging station may have to be built on the north end of the island, which would further impact the area and possibly be an expensive endeavor. Furthermore, these vehicles, electric, or gas-powered, will need a hub from which to operate. This option would require the construction of a costly transportation center where the vehicles could be stored and maintained, and may be perceived as an intrusion in the natural environment.

Discussion has also included bidding the tours of the north end out to a private concessionaire. However, the public has made it clear that bidding is not an option, nor is it in the best interest of CUIS (Georgia Conservancy, n.d.). The concerns range from turning CUIS into an amusement park to prioritizing profit over protection to adding yet another burden to the already overworked NPS staff (Hartrampf, Inc. and Jordan, Jones, and Goulding Inc., 2006).

Another factor to consider when discussing shuttling people back and forth to the north end of the island is the condition and maintenance of the road. The current road is primitive and is not maintained on a regular basis. The road is also narrow, treacherous, and riddled with washboard striations. In its present state, it would not be feasible to take five to eight tours a day, comfortably, to the north end of the island. Therefore, along with determining the mode of transportation, the road itself would most likely need modification to accommodate tours. Modification probably would include grading the road to provide a smoother and more comfortable ride. Vegetation encroaching on the road includes saw palmettos, pines, and live oaks, which would need to be pruned or removed altogether to accommodate the increased traffic safely. These adjustments to the natural environment go against the mission of the NPS and CUIS, and thus present a major challenge for park management.

Before vehicle type is chosen or new facilities are built, however, the main access point for the north end needs to be determined. There are currently two main access points to the island via the ferry: Sea Camp and Dungeness Dock. A third access point is being considered at Plum Orchard (Jerry Brumbelow, personal communication, 2007). The existing wharf at Plum Orchard could not accommodate the ferry, and a substantial monetary investment by the NPS would be needed to build a new dock. Plum Orchard, however, may be an ideal place for the hub of the tours to and from the north end.

Plum Orchard is the approximate mid-point of the island and could be an ideal place for incoming visitors to experience the historical, cultural, and natural wonders of CUIS. Renovations to the existing wharf at Plum Orchard would enable visitors to be ferried directly from Sea Camp or Dungeness Dock, thus alleviating the need for added vehicle traffic on the Main Road. Plum Orchard is also a good spot for the hub of the proposed transportation system. There is an existing facility on site, which with renovations would suit the needs of housing and maintaining the vehicles. Plum Orchard is a destination that visitors could enjoy in and of itself, with tours to the north end being an added value. This alternative is only one of the options at this point, but nevertheless one of the stronger options.

In light of the mandate to offer five to eight tours of the north end of the island to the visiting public, this chapter, so far, has primarily discussed how visitors would reach the north end of the island but has neglected the possibly more important question of why visitors should be shuttled there. One major attraction at the north end of CUIS is Plum Orchard. With the possibility of offering ferry service to this location, the TMP is not necessary. However, sites such as the settlement and the first African Baptist Church are not easily reached by foot or bike, nor are there suitable water depths for ferry service at the northern end. The TMP is necessary to access these destinations.

Another consideration is: What will be the interpretive value of the experience? The CUIS will need to provide drivers (if a private concessionaire is not involved), who will require interpretive training for the tour. The NPS-trained drivers may be a good option considering work done by Miller and Wright (1999), who found that the quality of visitors' experiences in Denali National Park in Alaska is largely affected by the courtesy and knowledge of tour bus drivers. These are subjective questions open for interpretation but are important to ask nonetheless because the NPS still has a no-action clause. It is unlikely that this alternative will be chosen, but at this stage of TMP development, all options must be weighed.

The Decision-making Process

As of this writing, CUIS managers and NPS regional and national managers are making decisions about the final form of the TMP. Decisions will be based on NPS and CUIS policy and the missions of the agency. Public comments have been collected and analyzed to help guide the decision-making process. In the upcoming months, intercept surveys will be conducted on the island to get a better understanding of visitors' perceptions and desires regarding the TMP. A mail survey also will be conducted to help better understand visitor preferences and desired experiences regarding CUIS and the TMP.

Public Scoping Summary

Between August 1 and September 15, 2006 the NPS held an open comment period on proposals for the TMP. A total of 2,227 comments were received from individuals and organizations. About 86% of the comments were sent via email and the remaining 14% were sent by mail, fax, or in person at public meetings. Content analysis showed that 81% of the respondents opposed or offered only conditional support for the proposed TMP. Approximately 14% of the comments were in support of the TMP; about 5% of the respondents were uncommitted (Hartrampf, Inc. and Jordan, Jones, and Goulding Inc., 2006) (see Table 1).

Table 1. Summary of public comments on Cumberland Island National Seashore transportation management plan received in August and September 2006.

Category	Concerns
Tours	Privatization, Fee, Number of trips, Guided vs. Non-guided
Route	Beach Driving, Ferry Routes and Docks, Use of Main Road
Mode	Fuel Type, Non-Motorized Options
Support Facilities	Type/Use of Facility, Paving
Miscellaneous	Limit on Number of Visitors

(Modified from Hartrampf, Inc. and Jordan, Jones, and Goulding, Inc. 2006).

Specific public comments reflected a range of concerns and interests regarding the TMP. A few examples of pro-TMP comments are: "The Island should be more accessible to the general public…the tax payers;" "a means of having transportation for the disabled would be most beneficial;" and "The beauty of the island should be shared by all." The comments of those opposed to the TMP generally have a more resentful tone: "Georgia's last pristine wilderness… tourists are … ruinous to the environment;" "no changes to Cumberland Island;" and "our family goes there for peace and quiet and lack of people…this plan will undo that." One comment in particular sums up much of this discussion: "Leave the park in its natural state and preserve the environment, the purpose of the NPS."

Moving Toward the Future

Fitzsimmons (1976) noted, "Society has generally viewed the national parks as places for relaxed nature appreciation with largely unspoiled, scenic, natural landscapes, as opposed to commercial playgrounds amid scenic beauty." Over the next few years, CUIS will be in a delicate state of transition and management will need to further consider the balance between preservation and recreation, a common theme for the NPS. Sax (1980) raises the concern that national parks may be turning into Disneyland, where people are there simply to be entertained on vacation. Perhaps the best way to educate visitors is to provide as much information as possible about the wide range of opportunities available within any given park. Educating the public would allow visitors to choose an experience that best meets their expectations (Shelby, 1980).

The NPS is increasingly beginning to focus on alternative transportation systems in the national parks (White, 2007). It will be important to understand the meanings that visitors construct about different transportation systems within the parks. White (2007) also states that very little research has been done on how visitors perceive transportation systems and how these transportation systems impact visitors' experiences. Studies of existing NPS transportations systems (Mace et al., 2006; Miller and Wright, 1999) have shown that visitors perceive such systems as a satisfying experience. In White's (2007) study on a proposed transportation plan in Yosemite National Park (California), most people responded they would be in favor of a shuttle service to reduce emissions and traffic problems within the park. The situation at CUIS is unique. Unlike Yosemite and Zion National Park (Utah), where TMPs were used to reduce traffic and the impact of too many visitors, the TMP at CUIS has the potential to increase the number of visitors to the park.

Much remains to be decided at CUIS in the upcoming years. Developing a realistic carrying capacity for the island requires further research. Other national parks that are working through similar problems have decided to restrict access in hopes of decreasing congestion. Acadia (Maine), Grand Canyon, Yellowstone, and Zion National Parks have all instituted various shuttle systems to alleviate traffic congestion during peak visitation times of the year (Sims et al., 2005). The CUIS, however, is not concerned about further restricting access to the island, which is the major focus of many previous studies. Interviews and surveys along with public meetings need to be implemented to obtain a better understanding of what the best options for the TMP may be. This is the beginning of a long process for CUIS. We hope that when the TMP has been fully implemented and evaluated, it will provide a model for other parks facing similar situations.

KEYWORDS

- **Cumberland Island National Seashore**
- **National Park Service**
- **Transportation systems**

Chapter 17

Sustainable Development of China's Ecotourism

Wei Chen and Wenpu Wang

INTRODUCTION

The sustainable development of ecotourism is the inevitable choice and developing direction for China's tourist industry. Based on profoundly analyzing the actuality and problems of the sustainable development of China's ecotourism, according to the developing directions of economy, society, science and technology, culture, and tourist industry, this chapter brings forward the concrete strategies to perfect the sustainable development of China's ecotourism. Ecotourism is the flushest industry with the quickest developing speed and new tourist economic growth point in the world, which naissance has a close relation with the universal recognitions of human society to the quality of environment, the objective requirements of sustainable development of tourist industry and theoretical research of ecology (Song, 2003, pp. 5559). The idea of sustainable development is brought forward under the people's self-examinations to such problems as population, energy, resources and environment, and so on, which final goal is to realize the sustaining and stable development of society, economy, resources, and environment. Therefore, the development of ecotourism and the implementation of sustainable development strategy have common springboard, and both optimal combination is to realize the sustainable development of ecotourism.

Instructed by the ecology theory, the sustainable development of ecotourism is a tourist activity which is responsible for environment and to develop tourist resources reasonably, orderly, and scientifically (Lu and Wang, 2001, p. 213). Based on the uniform benefits of economy, society, and environmental ecology, its core idea is to fulfill people's requirements of tourist, protect tourist resources and tourist environment, ensure later generations share coequal opportunities and rights of tourist development, and realize harmonious development of tourist industry together with society, resources, and environment.

At the beginning of 1990s, ecotourism began to rise and took on well developing situation in China. But because of its short history of naissance and development, the relative establishment of legal system, theoretical research, managing system and people's cognitions and concepts relatively dropped behind, and there appeared some serious problems and negative influences. Therefore, from the view of social and historical development, it has very important practical meanings to deeply study and establish the sustainable development strategies of ecotourism.

THE ACTUALITY AND PROBLEMS OF THE SUSTAINABLE DEVELOPMENT OF CHINA'S ECOTOURISM

Though China's ecotourism starts late than some countries with developed tourist industry in the world, its developing tendency is very swift, that mainly profits from the existing good conditions such as abundant ecotourism resources, tremendous consumer market, sustaining increase of requirements on ecotourism, and recognitions of all levels governments. At present, the building engineering of the sample area of national ecotourism has been completely started, and many ecotourism zones such as forest park, natural ecotourism resources, landscape and famous scenery, nature reserve, and natural wetland reserves have been opened. Besides, the forms of ecotourism have been developed from original natural sights to half-artificial ecological sights, the tourist objects include ocean, hilly country, desert, grassland, glacier, nature reserve, and country field landscape, and so on, and the diversification situation of tourist forms has come into being which includes visiting, viewing, scientific investigation, exploration, hunting, fishing, field picking, and topic activity of eco-agriculture, and so on (Liang, 2006, pp. 7274).

But as a whole, because of the short period of exploitation the tourist industry in China, China's tourist industry still rest on the elementary level of tourist exploitation mode in developing nations at the present stage, and people are short of scientific understanding to the relation of tourist and environment. The development of ecotourism still rest on the elementary stage and many problems exist in the process of the sustainable development of ecotourism.

Lacking in the Right Comprehension to the Sustainable Development of Ecotourism

Decision-makers, layout designers, and managers of ecotourism always do not pay enough attention to the integrative consideration and serious thinking of ecology and environment protection. Many tourists are short of the understandings to ecological and environmental knowledge, the good consciousnesses of environment protection in the process of ecotourism, which take ecotourism be equal to traditional tour or natural tour. In fact, the real ecotourism is to take ecological protection as precondition, take the popularization of environmental education and natural knowledge as core contents, and make more people further aroused their nice feelings of loving nature, enhance their consciousnesses of environment protection when they enjoy and experience glory and graceful natural scenes and taste returning to nature (Chen, 2006, p. 84). Just because of the inapplicable concepts and inadequate cognitions, the meanings and functions of the sustainable development of ecotourism has not fully been embodied.

Blindly Developing and Utilizing Resources and Lacking in the Uniform Programming

When many local governments develop ecotourism resources, they always lack in deep investigations and full-scale scientific demonstrations, assessments and layouts, or though they establish the tour layouts, but the layouts are not performed well in the practice. And to blindly develop, to be eager for quick success and instant benefit, to emphasize development and to despise protection in the exploitation all induce damages and wastes of many irreproducible and precious tour resources (Zhao, 2006). In addition, some layouts in some areas are established by investors who always start from the authorized rights or the benefits of their own departments or enterprises and do not organically combine the environmental, social, and economic profits to perform the layout.

Tourists are Seriously Superfluous and Overstep the Ecological Enduring Capability of the Landscape

The idea of emphasizing development but despising protection always makes the development businessmen establish the economical targets and restrict the amounts of the tourist without thinking about the ecological enduring capability. It induces the direct threats to the ecological environment of landscape. These threats include seriously superfluous tourists in nature reserve and landscape and famous scenery, and so on in the midseason of tour, and solid wastes, water pollution, air influences, and noise brought by tourists. This not only influences the tour quality, but also seriously destroys the brittle ecological environment of precious reserve. When a great deal tourists swarm into the reserve, the excessive tramples and leaving around various garbage such as plastic bottles, plastic bags, and pop cans, and so on, and the living sewages let by the tourist industry, all induce the interferences and damages to the environment of tour zone and wildlife.

Legal System is Unsound and the Management is not Normative

There is still not a special law about ecotourism in China, though in practice, it can refer to some items in the relative laws but which always are short of pertinence and veracity, and strict bylaws and effective supervising mechanism in the microcosmic management. The managing level of many ecotourism areas is very low, the relations among rights, responsibility, and benefit are not treated well in many charging departments, and the phenomenon of multi-ply management is serious. At the same time, in the managing group of ecotourism, many personnel without systematic trainings of professional knowledge only depend on the method of general administration management to manage ecotourism. When this tour resource is developed in many areas, many wild animals suffer abuse catch and killing because of unsound management and weak law enforcement. Adding the drive of economic benefits, this managing mechanism make the uniform layout and management become difficult and cannot ensure the sustainable development of ecotourism from the system.

Serious Pollution and Damage of Environment in Tour Areas

According to the investigation, the water quality, air, soil, and vegetation of vast majority of tour landscapes in China have been polluted and damaged to some different extent, noise and soot have also exceed the stated standards, and over standard of harmful substance and acid rain in the atmosphere are prevalent at present. At the same time, some tourists' bad living habits work the tremendous increase of living sewage, garbage, waste residue, and rubbish in the landscape (Liang, 2006, pp. 7274). These reasons all induce the decline of environmental quality and tour value in the tour areas.

To pursue unilateral economic benefits, some tour areas build many artificial houses and architectures in the interior of the landscape and damage the integrated and harmonious characteristics of the landscape. At last, the flooding of artificial landscape and establishment and the sameness of landscape become very serious. Simultaneously, the environmental pollution and the invading of exotic species also threaten the diversity of the biology in the ecological area and induce the local rare species are in severe danger. And the commercial development and exterior people and cultures will all bring large impacts to the special culture and traditional custom in the tour areas.

THE MAIN STRATEGIES OF THE SUSTAINABLE DEVELOPMENT OF CHINA'S ECOTOURISM

Essential Premise: Perfecting the Relative Legal System of Ecotourism

The actual China laws including "Regulations for Nature Reserves," "Environmental Protection Law of the People's Republic of China," "Forest Law of the People's Republic of China," and so on. cannot fulfill the requirements of rapid development in ecotourism industry (Song, 2003, pp. 5559). To realize the sustainable development of ecotourism, it must establish the law system and standards of ecotourism. It should combine the domestic actuality, take foreign experiences as references, and quicken to establish relative laws such as "Law of Ecotourism" and its relative detailed rules about implementing, "Quality Grade Standard of Ecotourism Area" and its implementing detailed rules, "General Rules of Layout in Ecotourism Area," "Byelaw of Resources management," "Behavior Criterion and Standard of Ecotourism," and so on. At the same time, it should synthetically consider the ownership, management right, development using right of ecotourism resources, establish the system of using with compensation, synthetically using, constitute special tour enforcement organization, and enforcement contingent which charge in the drumbeating of legal system and enforcement check to ecotourism, and thereby make the decision-making, layout, design, development, using, and tour behavior in ecotourism have laws to go by and have regulations to abide by.

Important Guarantee: Establishing the Management System of Ecotourism

The healthy management system of ecotourism is the important guarantee to the sustainable development of ecotourism. Therefore, it firstly should adjust the present management system, tidy up relations among administration management, industry management, and ecology management and setup harmony organization and comprehensive management organization of ecotourism sustainable development in term of the principles of reasonable setting and scientific management. Secondly, it should constitute supervising management mechanism, definitely delimit the responsibility and purview of resources managing department, environmental protection department and tour administration department, in particular, it should strengthen the relations and cooperation among different departments (Luo, 2002, pp. 78). At last, the governing department should seriously perform the functions of order management to ecotourism and resources protection, strictly examine and approve the construction of ecotourism item in the nature reserves and special culture and society areas, quicken the structure adjustment and reasonable development of tourist industry, and try to ensure the capital sources of the sustainable development of ecotourism through multiform financing methods such as domestic and foreign loans, foreign investment, project financing, international donation, and personal investment and so on.

Necessary Foundation: Establishing Scientific Building Layout of Ecotourism

The scientific building layout of ecotourism can avoid the blind exploitation and unrestricted development, and it is the necessary foundation for the sustainable development of ecotourism. Therefore, firstly, when we workout the general layout of tour area, we must seriously investigate various resources which come down to the environmental quality such as geological resources and biological resources (Zhao, 2006), scientifically measure the ecological and environmental bearing capability of tour area, develop tourist industry in the permissive frame of ecological bearing capability (Zhou and Wang, 2007, p. 51), and confirm the boundary of ecotourism area and the limiting range of the ecotourism activities. Secondly, according to the layout, we should confirm the object and scale of development, development position, space conformation, basic establishment, tour lines, consumer flow and capability, and time and fashion of tourism, and so on. At last, to ensure the high quality of ecotourism environment, the relative construction in tour area must develop moderately, orderly and from different layer, and every project must evaluate its environmental influences, and strictly control the scale, amount, material, sculpt, and style of the service establishment from the view of ecology.

Objective Requirement: Strengthen the Ecological Consciousness and Ecological Protection Education

At present, the sustainable development of ecotourism has not completely been cogitated and understood by peoples. Therefore, firstly, we should perform drumbeating and education to tour developers and managers, and make them realize the essence of ecotourism in deed and establish the concepts of ecotourism. Secondly, the ecological education and ecological moral education should be brought into the national education plan (Liang, 2006, pp. 7274). Some ecological education should be often developed in the whole society through the methods such as press drumbeating and subject lecture. In tour area, it can propagandize natural scientific knowledge through such activities as launching hobbledehoy green camp, providing garbage bags and organizing citizens foster viewing trees to enhance the tourists' consciousnesses of environmental protection (Tu et al., 2002, p. 40), and finally make maintaining the sustainable development of ecology become people's conscious behaviors and ethics. Thirdly, it should actively foster and introduce a great deal of professionals in the ecotourism aspect, strengthen the researches about the ecotourism theory and layout, for offering talents guarantee to realize the sustainable development of tourism. At last, the ecotourism area should enrich the cicerones' ecological knowledge and make them become the active propagandists of ecological protection who can perform vivid and vigorous environmental educations to tourists in the process of tour.

Persistent Impetus: Ensuring the Reasonable Economic Benefits of Relative Principle Parts

When protecting natural environment, the sustainable development of ecotourism must attach importance to the reasonable economic benefits and promoting the economic development in the local communities, especially enhancing the local income level and increasing protection capitals (Luo, 2002, p. 78), which is the persistent impetus to realize the sustainable development of ecotourism. Therefore, every project of ecotourism must perform investment analysis of feasibility, which includes not only the propulsive and negative influences to natural environment and social cultures, but also the development cost and marketable foreground of the ecotourism project, and measure the economical, social, and environmental benefits possibly brought by the project of ecotourism. At the same time, it must establish reasonable distribution mechanism of benefits to make the enterprises which develop ecotourism obtain corresponding returns, think much of the benefits distribution of local communities and the increase of the protection capitals, especially bring along the development of local economy and increase the denizens' income through developing ecotourism, consequently offer persistent impetus for the sustainable development of ecotourism.

Eternal Pledge: Establishing the Sustainable Development Culture of Ecotourism

Ecological consciousness is the comprehensive reflection of the values and moral outlook in the period of ecological civilization. The sustainable development of ecotourism should depend on the tourists and managers to transit their traditional tour concepts, establish brand-new values, world outlook, philosophy, and scientific tour outlook, which all has relate to some cultural backgrounds. Only under the supports of proper culture and philosophy backgrounds, the sustainable development can become people's self-conscious behavior fashion. To implement the sustainable development strategies of ecotourism, the all-important thing is to change traditional culture and establish the idea of the sustainable development to offer theoretic support and practice for the sustainable development of ecotourism, and make ecological conscience, ecological justice and ecological obligation become people's self-conscious behaviors and ethics, effectively depress the destroying actions to zoology and ensure the sustainable exploitation and development of ecotourism.

Important Measure: Enhancing the Scientific Content of Sustainable Development of Ecotourism

Now the scientific foundation of ecotourism is instable in China, in the mass which is still in the development mode with high speed but low quality. To implement the sustainable development, firstly, it must possess the concepts of scientific innovation, carry out the strategies of scientific innovation to various layers of the development of ecotourism in deed, and increase the investment of science and technology to ecotourism. Secondly, it should spread mature advanced technologies such as the technology of electronic information, the technology of cleanness, the technology of repair, and the technology of assessment, and so on, and strengthen the cooperation with domestic and foreign units of science and technology to perform theoretic and applicable researches aiming at some important problems such as the sustainable using and development to the present ecotourism resources. At last, it should establish the assistant system with expert layout and instruction of ecotourism, strengthen the associations between ecotourism area and research organization of ecotourism and between management department of ecotourism and research organization, and promote the technological and management innovation of ecotourism.

CONCLUSIONS

Nowadays, the sustainable development has become the important strategy to harmonize the relations among population, resources, environment, and economy for every country in the world. The sustainable development of ecotourism is the outcome of this idea, which core is to harmonize the relations among ecological environment of tour area, community, and denizens of tour area and tourists, realize the stabilization, harmoniousness, sustainable development for tourist industry and unisonous development of environment and human-beings.

Based on the actual situation and international direction, China selects and implements the sustainable development strategy of ecotourism. At present, we should adequately recognize the situation, positively discover problems, and adopt accurate replying measures. Through a series of effective measures such as highly noticing, positively participating, perfecting system, reasonable layout and strengthening management, and so on in the whole society, the sustainable development of ecotourism must be realized in deed.

KEYWORDS

- **Ecotourism**
- **Environment protection**
- **Strategy**
- **Sustainable development**
- **Tourist industry**

Chapter 18

Ecotourism in Protected Areas in Cross River State, Nigeria

Jeffrey J. Brooks, John Neary, and Blessing E. Asuquo

INTRODUCTION

Nigeria has abundant natural resources, and the nation, working with its partners over the years, has made large strides toward conservation of this natural wealth, but the future of Nigeria's natural resources remains uncertain.

In 1962, George Petrides recommended a national park system for Nigeria based on his extensive travels in country where he observed hunting of wildlife for local consumption and trade in bushmeat (Oates, 1999). Several locations were recommended for park status, including the Oban Hills and Obudu Plateau of southeastern Nigeria in present day Cross River State (CRS). Implementing the vision to preserve the globally significant rainforests and endemic wildlife in CRS was stalled for decades because of civil war, political restructuring, and economic instability (Oates, 1999).

Since Petrides, the ongoing conservation efforts of Nigerians and their outside partners have progressed. For example, Cross River National Park (CRNP) was established in 1991 by decree of the Federal Government of Nigeria (FGN) and is administered by the Nigerian National Park Service (NNPS) (Ite and Adams, 2000). This federally managed national park is located near the Cameroon border and comprises the core of a network of protected areas, including forest reserves, managed by the Cross River State Forestry Commission (CRSFC), and communally owned forests and agricultural lands, partially controlled by communities. Many people live in this network of forests and protected areas surrounding CRNP. The northern division of CRNP, for example, is surrounded by more than 60 communities (Ite, 1996) whose livelihoods largely depend on agriculture, and to a lesser extent, non-timber forest products, timber, and bushmeat (CRE, 2006; Meludu, 2004).

The Cross River State Government (CRSG), the NNPS/CRNP, and their partners from non-governmental organizations (NGOs) continue to face challenges. Throughout the 1990s and into this century, evidence has been documented of agricultural encroachment, illegal logging, and commercial hunting for bushmeat in protected areas, and government officials have few committed programs to adequately regulate or control exploitation (ARD BIOFOR Consortium, 2004; Oates, 1999). Indiscriminate logging practices have led to the suspension of the state's timber concessions (Chris Agbor, personal communication). Recently, there was an unconfirmed report that hunters had allegedly killed two Cross River gorillas (*Gorilla gorilla diehli*) (Wildlife Conservation Society, 2006). Cross River gorillas are a critically endangered subspecies (Oates et al., 2003; Sarmiento and Oates, 2000). These small fragmented gorilla populations hold tremendous scientific value in the form of endemic biodiversity and ecotourism potential.

Economic development and stability are priorities for the CRSG, and intensive tourism development is the current thrust. This is evident in the newly created CRS Tourism Bureau (CRSTB) and the ongoing construction of TINAPA, a large-scale, integrated business and leisure resort, situated next to the free trade zone on the Calabar River (Nigerian Business Info, 2005). The TINAPA resort is expected to bring domestic and foreign visitors to CRS, some of whom are expected to travel to the interior to visit places such as Afi Nature Reserve, Obudu Plateau, and CRNP in search of smaller-scale cultural and ecotourism experiences (Tony Bassey and Stephen Haruna, personal communication). The CRSTB and its partners recognize a need to balance business-driven tourism projects like TINAPA with smaller, community-based ecotourism operations, which, if properly planned and operated, can help to achieve social, economic, and ecological objectives for CRS (Hochachka and Liu, 2005).

Expectations for economic development are being raised on promises of tourism, but it is uncertain how increased tourism will affect long-term community development, protected area management, and biodiversity conservation. A successful ecotourism industry in CRS will depend on supportive and healthy host communities, protection of remaining natural assets, and preservation of rich cultural diversity (Wearing, 2001). However, the integration of conservation and economic development through alternative livelihoods has failed to meet expectations of CRS communities in the past (Ite and Adams, 2000; Oates, 1999). Moreover, it has been documented that most protected areas in CRS lack clearly demarcated, legally enforceable boundaries and management plans.

The CRSG, NNPS, and partnering NGOs recognize a need to collaboratively formulate policies and plans to reduce threats to forest communities, protected areas and wildlife, and the broader landscape while beginning to realize ecotourism potentials. Recently, the Wildlife Conservation Society (WCS) has obtained funds from the US Fish and Wildlife Service to support the development of a comprehensive management plan for CRNP (Andrew Dunn, personal communication). The CRSG has also partnered with the United States Government (USG) to preliminarily plan and implement ecotourism operations that have linkages with the state's important protected areas and forest communities. This report details the results of the initial USG assessment mission sponsored CRSG.

Purpose, Objectives, and Activities of the Mission

In the role of international partner, the US Forest Service Department of Agriculture, International Programs Office (USFS/IP) was consulted by the CRSG to conduct an assessment of needs focused on collaborative ecotourism development in and near forest communities and protected areas in CRS. Providing assistance in this role is consistent with the vision of USFS/IP for its work with West African nations:

> Facilitation of transparent and sustainable forest management to promote economic development and regional stability via empowered communities and strengthened institutions.

A technical assistance mission to CRS was organized (Appendices I and II). The USFS/IP team (We) consisted of three individuals with experience working in Africa and knowledge of and skills in protected area management, community development, collaboration, and principles of ecotourism. The overall purpose of this assessment was to develop specific, short-term work plans to address site planning, ecotourism, and collaboration with communities and partners at Afi Nature Reserve at Buanchor and the Obudu Plateau while giving secondary consideration to longer-term initiatives at other CRS protected areas and forest reserves, including CRNP. The specific objectives were to (1) conduct a participatory rapid assessment of related needs for ecotourism developers, protected area managers, and their partners and (2) provide a written report of observations, findings, recommendations, and proposed plans for guiding implementation and moving forward.

Guided by principles of participatory action research (Stringer, 1999), we used informal methods such as site visits, unstructured interviews, field observations, field notes, and review of available documents to gain a preliminary qualitative understanding of the situation in CRS (Beebe, 1995). We asked questions; listened to presentations; and discussed past, present, and future issues. Available resources such as maps, aerial photographs, and satellite images were studied to learn local geography and to identify priority areas for ecotourism development in and around CRS protected areas. During mission activities, we primarily interacted with key individuals within CRSTB, CRSFC, and CRNP. Representatives from these Nigerian agencies accompanied our team during formal meetings and site visits and played a large role in steering the assessment and structuring the report.

We formally and informally met and spoke with other people and partners (Appendices III and IV). We were in Nigeria 15 days, and adequate time was not allocated to thoroughly interact with all government agencies, local NGOs, and community leaders who have a stake in the complex problems surrounding ecotourism development and protected area management in CRS. We consider this to be an unfortunate limitation of this particular assessment, but key partners in CRS, both in and outside of government, have reviewed and commented on the report, and their input is reflected herein.

With our Nigerian counterparts, we made site visits to:

- Boki Birds Protection Foundation at Bashu, a community-based ecotourism initiative centered around conservation of the Grey Necked Picathartes;
- Drill Ranch primate rehabilitation center, operated by Pandrillus Foundation, at Afi Nature Reserve at Buanchor in Boki Local Government Area;
- The canopy walkway at Afi Nature Reserve, Buanchor;
- The Oban Hills Division of CRNP near the Kwa River;
- The community of Butatong and the Bemi River;
- Afi Mountain Wildlife Sanctuary and Swallow City at Ebakken near Boje;
- Becheve Nature Reserve and canopy walkway at Obudu Plateau;
- The resort, dairy, and cable cars at Obudu Plateau;
- The water park at Bottom Hill, Obudu Plateau;

- The future site of the Olongo Safari Hotel and Bebi Airstrip; and
- The TINAPA construction site, near Calabar.

With our Nigerian counterparts, we spoke with area and project managers, guides, rangers, and other agency representatives, NGO staff, and residents and leaders from communities at these sites. We observed, photographed, and discussed unique community, forestry, conservation, and ecotourism attributes, issues, and potentials and considered specific locations and facilities for ecotourism planning and development. As an international collaborator (Western, 2003), the USFS/IP desires to build relationships that support existing partnerships in CRS and elsewhere. The intention of this study is to complement the work of others by documenting and reformulating many of their previous findings. The intention is to build on existing projects, programs, facilities, and policies already set in progress by the CRSTB, CRSFC, NNPS/CRNP, and a number of NGOs.

We also learned of three community-centered projects in CRS: (1) Centre for Education, Research and Conservation of Primates and Nature (CERCOPAN); (2) Ekuri community forest management initiative (Dunn and Otu, 1996); and (3) Sustainable Practices in Agriculture for Critical Environments Project (SPACE). Although not formally responsible for ecotourism development or protected area management, these projects used methods of community involvement and engagement that can be used as models for the inclusive collaboration that will be needed to address the highly complex problems and critical needs identified in this study. Community successes and lessons learned from these collaborative initiatives should be considered when planning and operating ecotourism sites in CRS.

METHOD OF ASSESSMENT

The USFS/IP technical assistance team dialogued with representatives from Nigerian natural resource and tourism management agencies and their key partners working in CRS. The Nigerian counterparts directly participated in the assessment to inform the reporting. Informal methods were used such as site visits; unstructured interviews; field observations and notes; and review of available documents, photos, and maps to gain a preliminary understanding of the issues, local geography, and critical needs of ecotourism developers and protected area managers.

ECOTOURISM FOR NATIONAL AND INTERNATIONAL VISITORS

There is potential for successful ecotourism development in CRS. However, depending on the forces that drive ecotourism, it can have both positive and negative effects on society, economic stability, and ecology in CRS.

The concept of ecotourism in a Nigerian context may diverge, to some extent, from internationally recognized standards. Current levels of development at some sites in CRS are primarily business-driven tourism ventures that do not meet internationally recognized principles of ecotourism. Caution is suggested because business-driven approaches to ecotourism planning often alienate, rather than benefit, local communities. There is a need in CRS to balance the business model of tourism with a community-driven model of ecotourism which begins with the needs, values, and well-being of host communities.

Ecotourism site planners in CRS need better guidelines. Developing comprehensive plans for ecotourism will allow managers to more completely identify and address the specific social and economic needs of forest communities and the ecological requirements of habitats. Future ecotourism planning in CRS could become substantially more efficient in the long-term if guided by government regulated impact assessments, policies, and laws that reflect international conventions but are flexible enough to incorporate the unique social, economic, and ecological needs of CRS and her people. Blanket policies for ecotourism solely designed to meet international conventions may fail in Nigeria.

NEEDS OF THE CROSS RIVER STATE TOURISM BUREAU

The CRSTB is a relatively new agency, established in 2003 by the CRSG, with substantial organizational needs. Building institutional capacity, strengthening human resources, and streamlining management of the CRSTB are top priorities. It is recommended that the CRSTB collaborate with outside and internal partners to conduct an assessment of its management structure and operating systems. Another short-term need is to improve the standards and quality of ecotourism sites, products, interpretive services, facilities, experiences, and community participation on a sustainable basis to meet current and future needs.

KEY FINDINGS AND RECOMMENDATIONS FOR USFS SHORT-TERM TECHNICAL ASSISTANCE IN TWO ECOTOURISM SITES

Visitors and tourists are discovering the new canopy walkway and nearby Drill Ranch facilities at Afi Nature Reserve, but they are confused about how to use the area. An overall visitor experience package does not exist for the entirety of Afi Nature Reserve and the surrounding communities. Based on findings and recommendations, the USFS intends to provide short-term technical assistance to CRSTB and its partners on site planning, interpretive themes, and training of tour-guides at Afi Nature Reserve and Obudu Plateau. The objectives are (1) design simple primitive trails to integrate the tropical moist rainforest experience with visitor facilities, (2) link the trails and canopy walkway with the preliminary design for a visitor reception center and parking area, (3) develop interpretive themes and messages for visitor center displays, brochures, and other materials, and (4) hire and train people from neighboring communities as tour guides, rangers, and interpreters.

At Obudu Plateau, the new Cultural and Natural History Center is under construction without a site plan to integrate the Center with the Becheve Nature Reserve or aspects of the neighboring communities such as their roles in tourism or their cultural heritage and ancestral history in the Obudu Plateau area. Better access is needed to the nearby Okwangwo Division of CRNP to provide opportunities for visitors to experience local culture, art, and traditions in addition to the ecological assets of the place. It is recommended that the CRSTB and its partners work with the USFS/IP to complete a site plan for the new Cultural and Natural History Center at Obudu Plateau. The objectives are to (1) link opportunities to visit Becheve Nature Reserve and experience the culture of local communities with visitor center displays and interpretive materials and (2) in collaboration with the Nigerian Federal Government, plan to locate and construct a trail, or improve the existing trail, leading into CRNP Okwangwo Division.

CRITICAL NEEDS FOR CROSS RIVER STATE PROTECTED AREAS

The boundaries of CRS Forest Reserves were mapped, marked, and legally described prior to independence but are now difficult to locate. The legal location of boundaries is confused for CRS protected areas, and the agencies and partners do not agree on the legal descriptions of boundaries shown on existing maps. In some cases, individuals, communities, or businesses have taken advantage of the lack of enforceable boundaries to conduct illegal activities within protected areas.

Boundaries for the CRNP were created more recently using the original forest reserve descriptions. National park boundaries were supposed to have been surveyed within 2 years of enacted legislation in the Federal National Park Service Act of 1999, but the boundaries have not been surveyed. Representatives from the NNPS that participated in this assessment indicated that boundary location and enforcement present ongoing and long-term problems, but resources and full support from all CRNP partners are not yet available to start the long-term processes involved with legal demarcation.

The follow-up USFS/IP proposed missions in 2007 will not provide direct technical assistance, resources, or other support to address legal boundary demarcation for protected areas in CRS, but we consider determining and enforcing legal boundaries for CRS protected areas to be a critical need and priority that will require a longer-term, inclusive, and open collaborative process to resolve.

It is recommended that the CRSG continue to support the Afi Partnership in their ongoing efforts and newly funded project involving Flora and Fauna International (FFI) to set agreed upon goals and objectives for legal boundary demarcation and area management planning at Afi Mountain Wildlife Sanctuary.

If funding and stakeholder agreement can be obtained, the NNPS and its partners such as WCS are strongly encouraged to continue their efforts to locate and delineate legal boundaries for both divisions of CRNP.

Although the NNPS Decree no. 46 of May, 1999 directs the formation of management committees (Section 21) and completion of management plans (Section 28), neither management committees or working management plans exist for CRNP. In addition, there are no protected area plans for wildlife sanctuaries. As a result, decisions about where to build facilities or where and how to alter habitat are made without clear goals and objectives.

The WCS, working with NNPS and other partners such as NCF, has obtained funds from US Fish and Wildlife Service to complete a management plan for CRNP. It is recommended that these ongoing efforts be fully supported by the CRSG.

It is recommended that the CRSG and its partners support and work to inform the efforts of FFI and NCF with the new project entitled "Community Management Planning for Sustainable Forest Livelihoods and Biodiversity Conservation at Afi Forest Complex, Cross River State, Nigeria." Developing a management plan for the Afi Mountain Wildlife Sanctuary should be considered as an objective for this important project.

CRITICAL NEEDS OF THE CROSS RIVER STATE FORESTRY COMMISSION

Delineation and maintenance of forest reserve boundaries on the ground using the 1949 Reserve Settlement Orders remains of high priority for CRSFC. In view of current and past population and community expansion, some portions of forest reserve boundaries need to be readjusted to meet current realities.

Building the capacity of CRSFC staff to conduct inventory and stock surveys for selected forest reserves remains high priority.

There is a need to develop a comprehensive ecotourism plan for Afi Mountain Wildlife Sanctuary on the part of CRSFC, CRSTB, NGOs, and leaders from local governments and neighboring communities. One of the key issues is how to address the numerous farms that now exist inside forest reserves while maintaining trust, community support, and cordial working relationships. It is critical that planning efforts seek to balance conservation objectives with the livelihood needs of the rural people because striking this balance remains the only means for sustaining community interest and collaboration.

ENHANCING CAPACITY FOR COLLABORATIVE APPROACHES IN CROSS RIVER STATE

Although long established partnerships such as the Afi Partnership do exist and have made remarkable progress in CRS, the degree of inclusive communication and consensus that is needed to collectively address social, economic, and ecological objectives for sustainable ecotourism development, protected area management, and natural resources conservation is substantially lacking among partners. The diverse stakeholder groups working in these areas face a number of highly complex problems, and the challenging question of how collaboration will best work to address these situations in CRS has not been adequately addressed. The government agencies, their partnering NGOs, and the other stakeholders such as forest community leaders need help in reaching consensus.

It is recommended that an inclusive group of stakeholders meet in CRS in order to (1) solidify a collaborative partnership by building new and rekindling old relationships based on trust and commitment for the long-term, (2) collectively produce a number of short-term and long-term goals and objectives on which the group can agree to implement, and (3) develop shared definitions and mutual understandings of concepts and words used to talk about ecotourism, conservation, and protected areas management, so everyone at the table understands the objectives that are emerging. This would allow the CRS partners to develop a common language to use throughout the collaborative process.

WHAT SHOULD GUIDE ECOTOURISM IN CROSS RIVER STATE?

Ecotourism for National and International Visitors

Ecotourism has become an important economic activity in and near protected areas around the world (Drumm et al., 2004). A recent case study on ecotourism in CRS conducted by the Cross River Environmental Capacity Development Coalition (CRE) reported (2006):

> Ecotourism holds immense potential for CRS as a viable economic alternative and a strategy to protect its globally significant rainforests ... a promising sustainable development initiative that would positively impact rural villages, the CRSG and the flora and fauna of CRS. (Hochachka and Liu, 2005)

Finding 1

In the assessment, we observed potential for successful ecotourism development in CRS. It is important that we restate that ecotourism is not a Panacea, however. Depending on the forces that drive ecotourism, it can have both positive and negative effects on society, economic stability, and ecology in Nigeria and elsewhere (Buckley, 2001; Hochachka and Liu, 2005; Lindberg and Hawkins, 1993; Scheyvens, 1999; Wearing, 2001).

The concept of ecotourism in a Nigerian context may diverge, to some extent, from internationally recognized standards. We observed that current levels of development at the Obudu Plateau, for example, are primarily business-driven tourism ventures that do not meet internationally recognized principles of ecotourism. Similar observations have been reported by the CRE Project. Implementing the recommendations described below for site planning at the Obudu Plateau would add smaller-scale cultural and ecological components that are more characteristic of ecotourism.

The CRSG considers large-scale tourism developments to be legitimate avenues for economic development in CRS. The CRSTB has expressed a desire to offer tourists a diversity, or spectrum, of opportunities. We encourage providing a range of tourism experiences as a preferable development strategy in CRS. Projects such as TINAPA and Obudu Resort are best positioned at the large-scale, business end of this spectrum and require adequate planning, regulation, and evaluation that will differ in many respects from the planning required for smaller-scale ecotourism projects at the opposite end of the spectrum that are community-driven. The Boki Birds operation at Bashu, for example, provides a different experience from Obudu Resort, and, therefore, it requires different planning and monitoring strategies than Obudu Resort.

Nigerian culture, in general, is business oriented, so it is easy to see how business could become the main driving force behind ecotourism in CRS, but caution is suggested because business-driven approaches to ecotourism planning often alienate, rather than incorporate and benefit, local communities (Scheyvens, 1999). There is a need within the CRSTB to balance the business model of tourism with a community-driven model of ecotourism which begins with the needs, values, and well-being of host communities.

Internationally recognized principles of ecotourism can be used as guides for achieving balance in development, and, perhaps, for defining what ecotourism means for Nigerians in a Nigerian context. The International Union for the Conservation of Nature (IUCN) has adopted the following definition to guide ecotourism planners and operators:

> Environmentally responsible travel and visitation to relatively undisturbed natural areas (and any accompanying cultural features) in order to enjoy and appreciate nature, that promotes conservation, has low negative visitor impact, and provides for beneficially active socio-economic involvement of local peoples. (Ceballos-Lascurain, 2006)

The CRE Project cited this definition as a guide for ecotourism development in CRS, recommending that, prior to developing sites for ecotourism, socio-economic, and environmental impact assessments be completed with specific directions for how to reduce negative impacts. The Environmental Impact Assessment Decree (No. 86) was enacted in 1992 by the FGN, and ecotourism developers are required by law to complete these assessments (Pandrillus Foundation, personal communication). The decree describes mandatory conditions for environmental impact assessments pertaining to resort and recreational development, including within National Parks, which most likely encompasses ecotourism development. Planners of ecotourism in CRS are strongly encouraged to develop a process for complying with this existing legislation.

The CRE Project also recommended that the CRSG, in collaboration with key partners, develop and implement a long-term ecotourism strategy modeled after internationally recognized ecotourism standards (Edom et al., 2006). During the assessment, we confirmed that site planners do require better guidelines for ecotourism at places such as Afi Nature Reserve, Obudu Plateau, and AfiMountain Wildlife Sanctuary. Developing comprehensive plans for ecotourism at these sites would allow managers to more completely identify and address the specific social and economic needs of neighboring communities and the ecological requirements of habitats. Future ecotourism planning in CRS could become substantially more efficient in the long-term if guided by government regulated impact assessments, policies, and laws that reflect international conventions but that are designed to meet specific situations in CRS.

Recommendation 1a
As a starting point, the CRSTB, CRSFC, and NNPS/CRNP are encouraged to revisit the general recommendations outlined on pages 18–20 of the CRE ecotourism case study (Hochachka and Liu, 2005) to gain basic insights about international conventions for ecotourism. Where appropriate, some of these insights might be adapted to specific conditions at Afi Nature Reserve and Obudu Plateau, for example, before and during business and site planning. Challenges can be expected at sites where visitor facilities and tourists already exist, but changes can, and should be made to current operations, existing plans, and future plans as conditions at these places change and new information is learned through an adaptive and collaborative decision-making process involving CRSTB and its partners such as CRE, CRSFC, Pandrillus Foundation, and USFS/IP.

Recommendation 1b

We encourage the federal and state government agencies in CRS to consider developing additional strategies, policies, and laws for ecotourism that are modeled after international standards where appropriate. Above all, ecotourism policies, plans, and laws must include flexibility to incorporate the unique social, economic, and ecological needs of CRS and her people (Western, 2003). Flexible plans and policies better allow changes over time than do rigid planning strategies. Blanket policies for ecotourism designed to strictly meet international conventions may fail in a Nigerian context.

Prerequisite Needs of the Cross River State Tourism Bureau

Finding 2

The CRSTB is a relatively new agency, established in 2003 by the CRSG, with substantial organizational needs. At present, there is no ecotourism specialist employed, for example. Building institutional capacity, strengthening human resources, and streamlining management of the CRSTB are top priorities. Recognizing basic needs for organizational capacity, the CRSTB has formulated and shared with us two short-term objectives (Tony Bassey, personal communication).

- Organizational development of the CRSTB is a priority objective. It is critical that the CRSTB receives adequate technical assistance to carry out its role as the driver of tourism growth in CRS.
- A second objective is to re-engineer the organization to fulfill its mandate as a service provider and sector manager through targeted service, vocational training, and skills development in both the private sector and within CRSTB.

In addition, the CRSTB requested direct technical assistance and support from USFS/IP to address a number of related areas. However, more time, expertise, and research would be needed to fully address this entire suite of issues and priorities. We do consider documenting their needs to be an important first step for the CRSTB in achieving and sustaining ecotourism development. In this section, we attempt to reformulate and prioritize some of the short-term needs of the CRSTB.

Recommendation 2

We suggest that the first priority action for meeting these two objectives would be to conduct an assessment study of the management structure and operating systems of the CRSTB. Collaboration with outside partners to conduct this assessment will be required. Professionals from Opportunities Industrialization Centers International (OICI), Citizens Development Corps (CDC)/JOBS NIGERIA, REFORM, and/or World Bank or others, with experience in developing organizational capacity for tourism agencies and business organizations in West Africa, should be consulted to help the CRSTB employees to:

- Identify strengths and weaknesses in how CRSTB currently operates;
- Identify other governmental agencies with which to partner;
- Identify private sector organizations and clients with which to partner;

- Reformulate specific needs for technical assistance, and then identify and contact potential sources to provide the technical assistance needed;
- Determine and better understand what policies and laws enable and empower CRSTB so that these can be applied to the design and improvement of budgets, operating directives, policies, and so on. (If current legislation and policies are found to be inadequate, propose new policies, and amendments to current laws.);
- Assess operational/business sectors within CRSTB for redundancy (e.g., is it necessary to hire an ecotourism/conservation specialist, or can this position be staffed by a current employee who receives additional training?);
- Assess operational/business sectors for needs and inadequacies;
- Inventory skills and credentials of current staff and better match these skill sets to business sectors such as ecotourism, conservation, planning, marketing, budgeting, and so on;
- Determine training needs for supervisors and staff, leading to a training curriculum, and training sessions;
- Identify potential sources of internal funding or revenue (and outside donors) to support training, equipping, and furthering the education of staff;
- Identify and consult with outside partners who are capable of developing and conducting training sessions for CRSTB staff;
- Locate and target sources of skilled professionals in CRS and Nigeria such as universities and vocational schools for technical assistance and recruitment of staff as needed; and
- Reformulate and draft new vision and mission statements and priority objectives based on the results of these assessments, if determined necessary.

Finding 3
The CRSTB has another short-term objective, which is to improve the standards and quality of ecotourism sites, products, interpretive services, facilities, experiences, and community participation on a sustainable basis to meet current and future needs (Tony Bassey, personal communication).

Recommendation 3a
We suggest the following actions for moving forward:

- Work with partners such as CRSFC and Pandrillus Foundation to identify current needs by directly asking tourists at Afi Nature Reserve canopy walkway and Drill Ranch, Obudu Plateau, and Bashu what they think should be added or removed so as to improve visitor experience and facilities. Short survey post cards can be developed and handed to tourists by the local guides and rangers to be collected on site and/or mailed back to CRSTB in Calabar (Knudson et al., 2003);
- At these sites, advertise and make available a website address, an email address, and/or comment cards so that the CRSTB staff responsible for marketing

research can receive feedback from visitors. Inform visitors that the agency is seeking their comments and suggestions about existing programs and facilities. Keep record of the responses and periodically tabulate results.
- Project future needs for visitor products, experiences, and facilities by comparing the current situation to estimated future tourism demand and the changing needs of visitors; additional long-term research, monitoring, and evaluation at tourism and ecotourism sites will be required;
- Determine who will support and conduct this evaluation research: CRSTB staff, local community staff, and/or outside consultants closely working with and training CRSTB local staff;
- Identify consulting partners who can support and conduct training of staff in determining schedules, guidelines, and timelines for needs assessments, marketing research, monitoring, evaluation, and regulation of ecotourism operations;
- Follow similar assessment procedures to identify the current and future needs for communities that neighbor ecotourism developments; for example, conduct an assessment of the needs, skills, and resources of key communities such as Buanchor and Bebi to determine how and to what extent community members can participate in tourism at Afi Nature Reserve canopy walkway and the Bebi airstrip at Obudu Plateau, respectively. An opportunity may exist to work with the Afi Partnership and local cocoa farmers near Afi Mountain Wildlife Sanctuary to develop opportunities for tourists to the Boje area to learn about cocoa bean production, farming traditions, and Nigerian culture in addition to the forests and wildlife of the area;
- Do the same to determine the needs and skills of local guides and rangers who are employed at ecotourism sites before designing new trainings (These employees may not require training in the interpretation of local culture or identification and usage of non-timber forest products if they are local people who have lived near the site for years, but they may need training in basic first aid and ecological interpretation to develop skills, e.g.); and
- Conduct similar assessment procedures to determine site specific needs for conservation and visitor education materials such as posters, booklets, brochures, maps, trail signs and learning kiosks, displays, and education programs in visitor centers and cultural centers at existing sites. This information can be used by CRSTB planners and their partners for developing visitor interpretation at current and future tourism and ecotourism sites.

Recommendation 3b
We suggest that at least one employee of the CRSTB be rededicated to identifying and prioritizing specific ecotourism development initiatives and future sites within CRS. This employee would also be responsible for identifying and partnering with private sector businesses and development and conservation organizations such as JOBS NIGERIA and NCF to support the work with matching grants between CRSTB and outside partners.

Key Findings, Recommendations, and Short-term Technical Assistance

This section describes a proposal for two additional USFS/IP missions to CRS. The missions will be short-term and will provide technical assistance and training. Details for implementation are described. The intent is to start incrementally by working out a template for addressing the most critical and basic needs related to site planning and interpretation at two sites where underdeveloped ecotourism attractions and facilities currently exist but are in need of further planning. Once tested and refined at these specific places, the plans may be adapted and applied to other ecotourism developments linked to other protected areas managed by the CRSG and NNPS.

Findings and recommendations from the assessment activities are outlined and described in two sub sections, one for each proposed USFS/IP mission, including (1) short-term priority needs for ecotourism planning and site design at Afi Nature Reserve and enhancement of existing tourism facilities at Obudu Plateau and (2) development of interpretive materials and training of local tour guides and rangers at these sites.

Recommendations for Afi Nature Reserve and Obudu Plateau are outlined together because these will be implemented simultaneously due to constraints of time, resources, and staff for CRSTB and the USFS/IP.

Ecotourism Development and Site Planning for Afi Nature Reserve and Tourism Enhancement at Obudu Plateau

Findings 4 and 5

4) Visitors and tourists are discovering the new canopy walkway and nearby Drill Ranch facilities at Afi Nature Reserve, but they are confused about how to use the area. An overall visitor experience package does not exist for the entirety of Afi Nature Reserve and surrounding communities. There is no visitor reception center, identification and roles of local guides and rangers are unclear, fees are not collected, existing trails do not have signs, and future opportunities for new trails in the area to view the river and access visitor facilities are under discussion but the planning process has not been initiated. The roles and participation of neighboring communities are not well understood or defined.

5) At Obudu Plateau, the new Cultural and Natural History Center is under construction without a site plan to integrate with the Becheve Nature Reserve or aspects of the neighboring communities such as their roles in tourism or their cultural heritage and ancestral history in the Obudu Plateau. In addition, better access is needed to the nearby Okwangwo Division of CRNP, which could offer additional opportunities for visitors to experience local culture, art, and traditions in addition to ecological assets.

Recommendations 4 and 5

4) Complete a site plan for Afi Nature Reserve canopy walkway area. Design simple trails to integrate the tropical moist rainforest experience with visitor facilities. Link the trails and canopy walkway with the preliminary design for a visitor reception center and parking area near the road. Discuss planning for interpretive themes and messages for visitor center displays and for brochures and materials and hire and train locals as tour guides, rangers, and environmental/cultural interpreters (see Finding 6).

5) Complete a site plan for the new Cultural and Natural History Center at Obudu Plateau, linking opportunities to visit Becheve Nature Reserve and experience the culture of local communities with visitor center displays and interpretive materials. Preliminary planning should be completed to locate and construct a trail, or improve the existing trail, leading into CRNP Okwangwo Division. Since this action involves the CRNP, formal permission is required and must be obtained from the NNPS in Abuja prior to planning and implementation. Also, ecotourism developments that link Becheve Nature Reserve and CRNP should be completed within the context of the ongoing efforts of CRNP, WCS, and other partners to develop a management plan for CRNP Okwangwo Division.

Objective

Provide immediate design support to CRSTB and its associated partners for ecotourism development at Afi Nature Reserve and canopy walkway at Buanchor and tourism enhancement at the Obudu Plateau Cultural and Natural History Center.

Methods

A landscape architect with USFS/IP will provide the technical assistance and will work directly with key employees of the CRSTB and other stakeholders such as Pandrillus Foundation to inform appropriate design goals for the site plans. The landscape architect should bring a laptop computer (and extra battery components) with appropriate software for designing site plans. One possibility for base maps is digital orthophotos (scale 1:10,000) available from the Ministry of Lands, Surveys, and Housing in CRS (Department of Surveys), although no contours are available. Other base maps may be available from design work previously completed by Greenheart Conservation Company for the Afi Nature Reserve canopy walkway, or contractors at Obudu Plateau for the Cultural and Natural History Center.

The USFS/IP West Africa Programs Manger, in collaboration with CRSTB and partners, will write a concise scope of work for the landscape architect and the CRSTB liaisons for this mission. The scope of work should closely follow the recommendations, objectives, and methods outlined in this study to keep the mission on track. As a matter of protocol, the USFS/IP mission team will begin in Calabar by briefly meeting with the CRSTB director and other key partners, but it is essential that the bulk of the time be spent at the Afi Nature Reserve canopy walkway and Obudu Plateau.

Participants

The USFS/IP will organize and cost-share with CRSTB a technical assistance mission to CRS in late February or early March 2007. A landscape architect will provide technical assistance with site planning. The CRSTB will provide liaisons to work with the landscape architect to coordinate key contacts with other stakeholders such as Pandrillus Foundation and traditional rulers from Buanchor community and local government authorities from the area.

The architect contractor, who developed the visitor center design plans for the Afi Nature Reserve will work with the landscape architect to integrate site planning with facility design.

Other stakeholders such as Pandrillus Foundation, NCF, and CRSFC should be strongly encouraged to appoint liaisons to consult with the landscape architect at Afi Nature Reserve.

The CRSTB will appoint a second liaison to work with the landscape architect at the Obudu Plateau.

At both Afi Nature Reserve and Obudu Plateau, local communities must play key roles in planning, decision making, and, eventually, operation. Local tour guides and rangers are currently working at both sites, which will be continued. The CRSTB will contact traditional community leaders at both Afi Nature Reserve and Obudu Plateau and strongly encourage them to appoint community liaisons to work with the USFS/IP landscape architect and the CRSTB liaisons in discussing the extent and methods of involving local communities at these sites early on in the site planning phase. Guides and rangers from the local area may best serve in the role of liaison.

Each site will also require a specific business plan that would ideally be developed before or during site planning by a partnering organization to be determined. The CRSTB should pursue the opportunity to work with a tourism planning specialist to complete the business plans. The extent and methods of community involvement should be explicitly written into these business plans to institutionalize local participation, income generation, alternative livelihoods, and other benefits and to facilitate a sense of local pride and self-sufficiency for neighboring communities rather than resentment toward the CRSG.

Timeline
This is a tentative schedule subject to changes.

February–March 2007
- Complete site planning for Afi Nature Reserve canopy walkway area in approximately 7–10 days.
- Complete facility plan for the Cultural and Natural History Center at Obudu Plateau in approximately 5–7 days.

Constraints
Andersen (1993) recommended that developers of ecotourism facilities first asses the existing infrastructure, physical resources, and human capabilities of an area prior to constructing visitor facilities. Although facilities exist and some visitors have begun to arrive at Afi Nature Reserve and Obudu Plateau, these sites are far from completion, and it remains necessary to identify and address constraints related to roads and transportation as well as constraints on water supply and sustainable power sources. For example, roads conditions between Calabar and these two sites need improvement. The Bebi airstrip, which services the Obudu Plateau, may need to be expanded, and the villagers near the Bebi airport have no current social or economic connection with the tourists who arrive to visit Obudu Plateau. The water supply at the Obudu site should be assessed to determine if it will meet projected growth in tourism.

The USFS/IP technical assistants and their CRS liaisons should recognize that the Afi Nature Reserve has been called Drill Ranch for over a decade, and Pandrillus

Foundation originally negotiated with the community of Buanchor to lease this land from 1993–2005 (Pandrillus Foundation, personal communication). The CRSG has now secured it for the purposes of Pandrillus Foundation and the operation of the canopy walkway facilities by the CRSTB. All Pandrillus project facilities are on this land, and Pandrillus has expressed plans for the area, such as rehabilitation and tree planting, now that community farms are abandoned and farmers have received compensation from the CRSG. The site was strategically selected for the Pandrillus project to preserve a habitat corridor from Afi Mountain down to the lowland forest reserve, extending east towards the Mbe Mountains where there is a sub-population of endangered gorillas (Pandrillus Foundation, personal communication). For this reason, ecotourism developments on this land must be carefully planned to restore and preserve as much forest as possible to maintain this habitat corridor. There should be inclusive participation in planning for this small but strategic area, especially with Pandrillus Foundation and Buanchor Community who have substantial stake and long-term investment there, but also with their Afi partners (CRSFC, FFI, NCF, and WCS), who are collectively concerned with the habitat corridor and have been working together as a focused group in the area for several years (Pandrillus Foundation, personal communication).

The USFS/IP landscape architect may be distracted by, or unintentionally drawn into, larger issues at Afi Nature Reserve and Obudu Plateau unless the landscape architect and the CRS liaisons closely follow a concise scope of work for the short period of time allotted to complete this mission. Both sites have noticeable needs for design beyond what will be contained in the USFS/IP scope of work for this proposed mission. There is a risk that the landscape architect involved with site planning will begin negotiations with community members that spiral into many issues that he or she does not have proper time or expertise to address.

Support for software needs does not exist in CRS outside Calabar.

Office space at Afi Nature Reserve is minimal and may be unavailable. The Drill Ranch primate rehabilitation and ecotourism facility operated by Pandrillus Foundation may be the best partner to provide office support to the USFS/IP team members, but discussions and coordination with the management staff at Pandrillus will be necessary to find out if appropriate facilities are available at Drill Ranch for the work of this mission.

Each of these constraints and others that are not yet identified will need to be carefully considered and addressed before and during site planning at Afi Nature Reserve, Obudu Plateau, and similar sites designated for future ecotourism development in CRS.

Development of Interpretation and Training of Tour Guides

Finding 6
Closely related to business and site planning is planning for interpretation. The overall goal of an interpretive plan is to convey to visitors the primary story of an ecotourism site, the value of the site, and what it means for the visitor and the neighboring communities (Knudson et al., 2003). A short-term need exists to plan for and develop interpretive

themes, concepts, and visitor materials for Afi Nature Reserve and the Cultural and Natural History Center/Becheve Nature Reserve at Obudu Plateau.

In addition, there is an immediate need to develop curriculum, programs, and training workshops for local tour guides and interpretive rangers at both sites. The CRSTB has the ability to train tour guides and rangers about work ethics such as showing up on time, remaining at post, wearing a crisp uniform, smiling, being courteous, answering inquiries politely, and other "good host" training. The CRSTB most likely requires some short-term assistance in training tour guides and rangers about creating interpretive themes and messages from those themes, methods of delivering effective interpretive messages, and work duties to fill the time between interpretive programs or walks when visitors are not present at their duty sites.

Recommendation 6

Develop visitor education materials such as posters, booklets, brochures, maps, trail signs and learning kiosks, displays, and education programs in visitor centers and cultural centers at Afi Nature Reserve and Obudu Plateau. The materials should focus on the ecological and cultural attributes of each site and how preservation of these areas is intertwined with the livelihoods and well-being of surrounding communities and populations of endemic plants and wildlife.

Develop, organize, and conduct trainings for the tour guides and interpretive rangers working at each location.

Objectives

Provide short-term design, development, and training support to CRSTB and its associated partners for ecological and cultural interpretation and visitor education at Afi Nature Reserve canopy walkway at Buanchor and the Obudu Plateau Cultural and Natural History Center/Becheve Nature Reserve.

Methods

The USFS/IP team will provide technical assistance and will work directly with key employees of the CRSTB and other partners such as CRSFC, Pandrillus Foundation, and those at Obudu Plateau. The interpretive specialist and trainer should bring a laptop computer (with extra battery components) and appropriate computer software for conducting training presentations and simulations and designing educational materials.

The USFS/IP West Africa Programs Manger, in collaboration with CRSTB and partners, will write a concise scope of work for the interpretive and training specialists and the CRSTB liaisons, which should closely follow the recommendations, objectives, and methods outlined in this study to keep the mission on track. The USFS/IP mission team will begin in Calabar by briefly meeting with the CRSTB director and other key partners as needed, but it is essential that the bulk of the time be spent with local tour guides and rangers at Afi Nature Reserve and Obudu Plateau and at a central meeting place to conduct the training workshop.

The primary themes for the content of the training course curriculum should generally include, but not be limited to (see Drumm et al., 2004):

- Natural history of the sites and surrounding areas including the major species of plants and animals (i.e., communities and ecosystems), how these ecological components interact, and the conservation status of each;
- Cultural attractions including history, archaeology, and traditional activities and foods, and the relationships between culture and ecology at the sites;
- The conservation priorities and activities of those who manage the sites;
- Guides and interpretive rangers need to be aware of the rules and regulations governing visitor use of the sites and facilities, including how ecotourism is defined and how it is applied at the sites;
- Guides and interpretive rangers need to learn how to best manage groups of visitors that have disparate attention spans, knowledge levels, expectations, and reasons for visiting the sites; and
- Basic interpretive and communication techniques and strategies.

We recommend using, and bringing to CRS, two comprehensive manuals designed for training tour guides and interpretive rangers.
- RARE Center for Tropical Conservation (2001). Interpreting for conservation: A manual for training local nature guides. Arlington, Virginia: RARE Center for Tropical Conservation.
- Ham, S. (1992). Environmental interpretation: A practical guide for people with big ideas and small budgets. Golden, Colorado: North American Press.

Participants

A second USFS/IP mission to CRS will be organized to implement these recommendations and will be funded by a cost share agreement between CRSTB and USFS/IP. The USFS/IP team will consist of an ecological and cultural interpretive planner/specialist and a tour-guide/interpretive trainer both with experience working in rural Africa.

At Afi Nature Reserve, the USFS/IP team should work closely with liaisons from CRSTB, Buanchor Community and Pandrillus Foundation. Representatives from CRSFC can be consulted as technical specialists in flora and fauna identification and natural history. Members of the neighboring forest communities can be consulted as technical specialists in identification and use of non-timber forest products and to explain key cultural aspects of their people.

At Obudu Plateau, the USFS/IP team should work closely with liaisons from CRSTB, Becheve Nature Reserve, and NNPS/CRNP Okwangwo Division.

Timeline

This is a temporary schedule subject to changes.

March–April 2007
- Conduct an assessment of training needs to determine the skill base of current tour guides and interpretive rangers in approximately 5–7 days.
- Consult with partners at CRSTB, Pandrillus Foundation, Obudu Plateau, and community leaders about which interpretive themes and messages are most appropriate for each site in approximately 5–7 days.

- Conduct a workshop to teach interpretive planning and skills that are most lacking and the themes for interpretation that are most appropriate in approximately 5–7 days.

Constraints

It is critical that a substantial number of the tour guides and interpretive rangers to be hired and trained come from neighboring communities. When tour guides and interpreters are from local communities, they can serve an important role in improving communication between the administrators of the site and the neighboring communities, especially when misunderstandings between the two occur (Drumm, 2004). If the CRSTB primarily hires guides that originate in Calabar or regions of Nigeria far from Afiand Obudu, business relations with local communities cannot be expected to prosper.

The USFS/IP technical assistants should recognize that there is a relatively long and varied history of relations between Pandrillus Foundation and the community of Buanchor and an inclusive approach to interpretive planning will be necessary. Both groups have valid needs and desires that should be taken into account during the decision-making process.

Training of tour guides and interpretive rangers should not be a one-time event (Drumm et al., 2004). Courses and curriculum will need to be continually developed and updated, and employees at each site will need to receive additional trainings as conditions and visitors change over time.

It is recommended that the CRSTB and other site administrators make an effort to hire some female guides and interpreters from the local communities as well as hiring and training young men, which are currently the majority at these sites. Many of the visitors to these sites will be females who will appreciate learning from and meeting female residents of CRS. Older, well-respected community members should also be hired and trained to work at the sites (Drumm et al., 2004).

ADDITIONAL FINDINGS AND RECOMMENDATIONS

We present additional findings and recommendations based on our assessment activities. The USFS/IP will not be directly involved in implementing these general recommendations in the foreseeable future, but these are worth noting in the report because these issues could substantially impact current and future activities in CRS protected areas and the success of ecotourism. The USFS/IP considers documenting these observations to be an important prerequisite for achieving and sustaining successful ecotourism, conservation, community development, and protected area management.

Critical Needs for Cross River State Protected Areas
Finding 7

The boundaries of CRS Forest Reserves were mapped, marked, and legally described prior to independence but are now difficult to discern. Survey pillars were installed at various locations in 1949, but most are now missing, difficult to locate, or clearly see. The legal location of boundaries is confused for CRNP and other protected areas

(ARD BIOFOR Consortium, 2004), and the agencies and partners working in CRS do not agree on the legal descriptions of boundaries shown on existing maps. In some cases, individuals, communities, or businesses have taken advantage of the confusion and lack of enforcement to conduct illegal activities within protected areas such as agricultural plantations, construction for community expansion, poaching, and commercial tree plantations.

Boundaries for the CRNP were created more recently using the original forest reserve descriptions. National park boundaries were supposed to have been surveyed within 2 years of enacted legislation in the Federal National Park Service Act of 1999 (National Park Service, 1999), but the boundaries have not been surveyed. Representatives from the NNPS/CRNP that participated in this assessment indicated that boundary location and enforcement present ongoing and long-term problems, but resources and full support from all CRNP partners are not yet available to resolve the complex issues surrounding legal demarcation and community negotiations.

Recommendation 7
Locate and delineate the legal boundaries of high priority CRS protected areas. It has been suggested that the 1949 Reserve Settlement Orders can serve as an official guide. Boundaries indicated by green line on the 1994 vegetation map (1:250,000 scale) appear to be the most accurate indication of legal boundaries, however, agreement on which maps actually reflect the law and the situation on the ground is lacking among key stakeholders.

The follow-up USFS/IP proposed missions in 2007 will not provide direct technical assistance, resources, or other support to address legal boundary demarcation for Afi Nature Reserve or Obudu Plateau or any other protected areas in CRS. The USFS/IP considers determining and enforcing legal boundaries for CRS protected areas to be a critical need and priority that will require a longer-term, inclusive, and open collaborative process to resolve. The USFS/IP will not have adequate time and funds to directly address boundary demarcation in the immediate future.

The Afi Partnership and other stakeholders should continue to be supported by the CRSG in their ongoing efforts and new project involving FFI to set agreed upon goals and objectives for legal boundary demarcation and area management planning at Afi Mountain Wildlife Sanctuary.

If funding and stakeholder agreement can be obtained, the NNPS and its partners such as WCS are encouraged to continue their efforts to locate and delineate legal boundaries for both divisions of CRNP.

Since there is at present no formal plan or funded project to demarcate CRS protected areas (with the possible exception of Afi Forest Complex), we provide further planning details to inform future efforts.

Objectives
Map, locate, and mark clear boundary lines that allow enforcement of regulations in CRS. Strive to allow communities to fulfill their needs and maintain well-being while protecting the long-term interests of the protected areas. This will require three general steps:

1. Temporarily mark the original, legal boundaries of the national park and forest reserves with teams of trained employees from CRNP and CRSFC such as guards and rangers, especially those who reside in or come from local communities.
2. Negotiate with communities and other stakeholders the locations of boundaries that no longer make sense. The aim should be to balance fulfilling the purposes of the national park and forest reserves in the long-term with stakeholder trust building and compromise in decision making that meets community livelihoods and protected area objectives.
3. Mark and describe the new boundaries permanently.

Methods

Legal descriptions of the 1949 Reserve Settlement Orders and maps of these descriptions should be digitized to create electronic files. The electronic data should be loaded into field GPS receivers for teams of rangers to accurately locate boundaries. Reserve Settlement Orders should also be followed, where appropriate, by field teams for meets-and-bounds type legal descriptions.

As boundaries are located in the field, these should be clearly marked with temporary flagging, survey stakes, or similar devices.

Community and stakeholder negotiations should follow in areas where controversy exists or where legal boundaries have been encroached upon by settlements, plantations, or other means. Tradeoffs that meet social, economic, and ecological objectives should be agreed upon in a collaborative approach that includes discussions among all stakeholders.

Participants

The lead agency for demarcating forest reserves should be the CRSFC and NNPS for demarcating CRNP. Guards and rangers from local communities should be hired and trained to implement the field work for boundary surveys and their supervisors should be involved with negotiating boundary locations with traditional community rulers and local government authorities. The Ministry of Lands, Surveys, and Housing in CRS (Department of Surveys) could serve as the supporting agency to help digitize maps, train staff in GPS methods, and support Arc-GIS processing. Department of Surveys could also serve as the lead agency for conducting surveys at Obudu Plateau.

Technical assistance should be provided by a GIS specialist working in CRS. Project personnel should have skills in use of GIS hardware and software, and field experience in use of portable GPS surveys, and, experience working in CRS.

Constraints

It is critical that government agencies and their partners working in CRS protected areas determine, and agree to, what maps and other legal documents to use in official boundary demarcation.

Some CRS communities feel that their problematic relationships with CRNP are related to poorly demarcated boundaries, and these communities are in favor of renegotiating boundaries and laws to redefine community rights and access, clarify community roles in park management and enforcement, and implement alternative livelihood programs (CRE, 2006).

Before formal activities begin to implement demarcation of boundaries for CRNP, the NNPS personnel and their partners, who propose boundary demarcation, will be required to obtain permission from the NNPS headquarters in Abuja. Local government authorities and community chiefs in CRS should also be informed prior to the start of any formal procedures on the ground that concern communities neighboring protected areas.

Digitizing maps may have to be done by private contractor if the Department of Surveys cannot complete the work. Area Maps Inc., in Calabar, may be used as a contractor to digitize and run the required Arc-GIS computer software.

Skills in downloading digitized map information to GPS receivers may not be available unless Department of Surveys is available, or a private contractor is used.

Department of Surveys largely works with urban and suburban projects in Calabar. Knowledge of Arc-GIS software may be limited to the Department of Surveys, but these civil servants do not normally survey remote protected areas, so lack of experience in rural CRS, low priority, and time constraints may exist.

Field work must be conducted during the dry season of January to April, while negotiations with communities and office work can be conducted at any time. However, meeting with communities during the rainy season may be constrained by wet and muddy road conditions and peak agricultural activities.

Desktop or laptop computer(s) are not available to run Arc-GIS software, except at the Department of Surveys, which is normally busy with other work.

Some GPS receivers are available, but the number is undetermined.

Final boundary marking requires completion of long-term negotiations with an inclusive group of community leaders, representatives, and other stakeholders. This could result in substantial lack of permanent boundary markers in areas where these are most needed, especially in CRNP.

Community and stakeholder negotiations will take considerable time for controversial and contested areas or places where significant changes in boundary location are anticipated. Substantial time and discussion will be required to establish trust and develop shared goals for boundary demarcation and enforcement. This is especially the case where expectations of communities were raised, but remain unfulfilled, due to undelivered promises that they believe were made to them when CRNP was originally established (CRE, 2006; Ite and Adams, 2000; Oates 1999).

Government agencies, communities, and other partners must make honest and open assessments of what communities can expect to gain from enforcement of protected area boundaries given the constraints faced by the CRSG and NNPS. Community expectations should not be raised to unrealistic levels regarding land tenure or alternative livelihoods. The CRSG and NNPS must find ways to fairly share power in decision making with neighboring community leaders and local government authorities if they wish to minimize conflicts and meet objectives for both conservation and economic development (Adams and Hulme, 2001).

Other Sites
After refining procedures and training staff at the CRSFC, the NNPS, and local community members and leaders, boundary demarcation and community negotiation should be planned, applied, and enforced at other CRS forest reserves and protected areas including, but not limited to, Cross River North Forest Reserve, Cross River South Forest Reserve, Agoi Forest Reserve, and Ukpon Forest Reserve.

Finding 8
Although the NNPS Decree no. 46 of May, 1999 directs the formation of management committees (Section 21) and completion of management plans (Section 28), neither management committees or working management plans exist for CRNP. In addition, there are no protected area plans for wildlife sanctuaries such as AfiMountain Wildlife Sanctuary. As a result, decisions about where to build facilities or where and how to alter habitat are made without clear goals and objectives.

It is important to note that development plans were published by World Wide Fund for Nature (WWF) (referred to as "project plans") for both divisions of the CRNP in 1990. Some implementing partners (i.e., Pandrillus Foundation) do not necessarily support all the activities in the ambitious plans developed by WWF (Pandrillus Foundation, personal communication). The WWF plans should be reviewed as a stating point for ongoing and future efforts.

In addition, the WCS, working with NNPS and other partners such as NCF, has obtained funds from US Fish and Wildlife Service to complete a management plan for CRNP.

Recommendation 8
Support the ongoing efforts of WCS and NNPS to complete a management plan for CRNP. One strategy would be to form a NNPS collaborative management committee as outlined in the May 26, 1999 decree Section 21 and prepare the plan in accordance with Section 28 of the decree to oversee park planning (National Park Service, 1999). Establishing collaborative management committees should be given careful consideration so that committees can focus on actual park management issues rather than political agendas (Pandrillus Foundation, personal communication).

Support the efforts of FFI and NCF with the new project entitled "Community Management Planning for Sustainable Forest Livelihoods and Biodiversity Conservation at Afi Forest Complex, Cross River State, Nigeria." Developing a management plan for the Afi Mountain Wildlife Sanctuary should be considered as an objective of this recently funded and important project.

Critical Needs of the Cross River State Forestry Commission
Finding 9
Delineation and maintenance of the forest reserve boundaries on the ground using the 1949 Reserve Settlement Orders is a critical priority for the CRSFC (Chris Agbor, personal communication). In view of current and past population and community expansion, some portions of forest reserve boundaries need to be readjusted to meet current realities for neighboring forest communities.

Building the capacity of CRSFC staff to conduct inventory and timber surveys for selected forest reserves remains a priority. These surveys would be guided by previously developed forest management plans.

There is a need to develop a comprehensive ecotourism plan for AfiMountain Wildlife Sanctuary. This planning process should involve CRSFC, CRSTB, NGO partners, and leaders from neighboring communities. The planning process should clearly define community roles in and benefits from ecotourism.

One of the key issues that is likely to attract much attention and require substantial time in protected area management will be addressing the numerous farms that now exist inside forest reserves while maintaining trust, community support, and cordial working relationships. It is critical that future planning efforts seek to balance conservation objectives with the livelihood needs of the rural people because striking this balance remains the only means for sustaining community interest and participation.

ENHANCING CAPACITY FOR COLLABORATIVE APPROACHES IN CROSS RIVER STATE

During the assessment, review of documents, and report writing, we observed a broad overarching challenge faced by the agencies and partners working in CRS. There is a need to build the capacity of stakeholders to engage in productive collaboration.

The USFS/IP cannot provide short-term assistance in addressing the overarching need for better collaboration among partners in CRS. But, we do consider documenting and addressing these observations to be an important prerequisite for achieving and sustaining successful ecotourism development, biodiversity conservation, community development, and protected area management in CRS. We elaborate on the need for better collaboration and provide details to be considered by the Nigerian agencies and other stakeholders during their ongoing efforts.

Characteristics of Successful Collaboration

Research on stakeholder processes has identified several key factors necessary for successful, balanced, and integrated collaboration. These include sound development and planning of collaborative initiatives early in the process; open, interactive, and free exchange and sharing of information; solid organizational support to keep the process on track; effective communication that encourages listening, understanding, discussing, and decision-making; building relationships and partnerships based on trust, honesty, and respect; and prioritizing accomplishments and outcomes such as report writing, follow-up action on key issues, evaluation, and monitoring of the process (Schuett et al., 2001).

Power sharing, on the part of government agencies, is critical for successful collaboration directed toward meeting social, economic, and ecological objectives (Adams and Hulme, 2001). In most cases, the CRSG and the NNPS are ultimately and legally responsible for ecotourism and protected areas management, and therefore have tremendous power in decision-making. Relinquishing formal decision-making authority is not required for government agencies to participate in long-term collaborative efforts; what is important is sharing the decision-making space with stakeholders so that collaborative efforts have a real impact on plans and decisions (Keough and Blahna, 2006). Stakeholders in CRS, including the agencies, must be made to feel that they have been heard and that they play a meaningful role in the collaborative process regardless of whether their agendas are fully met—they need to know that their voices count.

Several questions then arise: do the partners working in CRS support this type of collaborative process to drive decision-making; is it a priority? Which, if any, of these factors of success are relevant in a Nigerian context? Which of these can be achieved? What level of capacity exists in CRS for successful collaboration? Who will take the lead in initiating collaboration with these goals in mind? What groups will be invited to participate? Based on what we have learned from the assessment activities, we hope to provide some insights and suggestions for addressing these questions and strengthening capacity to collaborate in CRS.

Finding 10

Although long established partnerships (e.g., the Afi Partnership with CRSFC, FFI, Pandrillus Foundation, NCF, and WCS or the partnering between CRNP and several NGOs) do exist and have made remarkable progress in CRS, the degree of inclusive communication and consensus that is needed to collectively address social, economic, and ecological objectives for sustainable ecotourism development, protected area management, and natural resources conservation is substantially lacking among partners. The diverse stakeholder groups working in these areas face a number of highly complex problems, and the challenging question of how collaboration will best work to address these situations in CRS has not been adequately addressed. The government agencies, their partnering NGOs, and the other stakeholders such as forest community leaders need help in reaching consensus.

Recommendation 10

Set a priority to create a new reality, a new way of doing business in CRS, by genuinely talking and listening to one another, setting past agendas and differences aside, and building new collective goals and relationships for the future. This coming together can facilitate collective action whereby stakeholders make decisions and implement plans as a whole. Acting collectively is necessary to resolve tough problems related to ecotourism, protected areas management, and natural resources conservation.

Brainstorm to identify representatives from as many stakeholder interest groups as possible in CRS and Nigeria, including, but not limited to, the CRSTB, CRSFC, NNPS/CRNP, the NGOs, local government authorities, and forest community leaders. Inviting representatives from all possible groups to the decision-making table would be ideal, but this may not be realistically feasible. At a minimum, we suggest that it is necessary to identify and invite a partial list of key stakeholders in order to achieve integrated collaborative decisions and planning (Keough and Blahna, 2006). A transparent and accurate assessment of the social, ecological, and economic impacts and conflicts for each ecotourism site and protected area is needed to understand which key stakeholders to include and for which areas (Endter-Wada et al., 1998.) Such assessments can be used to carefully identify and invite the key stakeholders into the process for each specific area and situation.

Employing an outside neutral facilitator may be required to help stakeholders in CRS learn how to create mutual resolutions for the tough problems that they face (Generon Consulting, 2001; Kahane, 2004). Ideally, the group and the facilitator would meet for multiple days at a neutral quiet place with few distractions. With the assistance of the facilitator, the participants would talk and listen to each other about their concerns and roles in collaboration. Participants would make an effort to talk about past, present, and future issues in order to become reacquainted and discover common ground, shared values, mutual desires and needs, and their roles regarding ecotourism development, protected areas management, and natural resources conservation.

Initial Outcomes

We suggest the following goals for these meetings:
- Solidify a collaborative partnership by building new and rekindling old relationships based on trust and commitment for the long-term.
- Collectively produce a number of short-term and long-term goals and objectives on which the group can agree to implement.
- Develop shared definitions and mutual understandings of concepts and words used to talk about ecotourism, conservation, and protected areas management, so everyone at the table understands the objectives that are emerging. This allows the group to develop a common language for the partnership to use throughout the collaborative process.

Caveat

We describe a model for understanding collaboration and achieving collective action in order to provide more detailed information and citations to support this recommendation. We admit that we lack a complete understanding of the situation in CRS, and sources of support and funding have not been identified, but moving forward by building new relationships should be considered by the partners in CRS. We have observed that something to this effect is needed to achieve integrated and effective collaboration.

CONCLUSION

The primary purpose of this US Forest Service Department of Agriculture International Programs Office (USFS/IP) mission was to assist government agency employees to refine and implement their vision for sustainable ecotourism development and related management issues linked to various protected areas in CRS, Nigeria. The objectives of the mission were to (1) conduct a participatory preliminary assessment of the needs of ecotourism developers and protected area managers and (2) provide a written report of observations, findings, recommendations, and implementation plans.

This assessment report is the result of international collaboration and provides insights for moving forward in CRS to develop ecotourism potentials that depend on forest communities and conservation of the state's remaining natural assets. General recommendations for addressing a number of complex challenges facing partners in CRS were identified. We outlined specific findings and short-term recommendations for implementing site planning and developing interpretive training programs at Afi Nature Reserve and Obudu Plateau. Other findings from the assessment were described that represent longer-term issues at other protected areas in CRS. The CRS partners are encouraged to immediately consider how they can come together in a collaborative process to address these major challenges.

The CRSTB, CRSFC, NNPS, the NGOs working in CRS, and leaders from forest communities each have their own needs, directives, and missions, but these partners share common ground with regard to the well-being, economic stability, and capacity of the people living in CRS; the unique and highly important natural resources of the state; biodiversity conservation; and sustainable ecotourism development. This common ground must be recognized as the foundation for improved understanding, cooperation, and communication in planning, management, and development of sustainable ecotourism linked to CRS protected areas and neighboring communities.

A common vision for CRS seems to be re-emerging that is focused on balancing economic development and livelihoods with sustainable ecotourism development, protected area management, and conservation, but a comprehensive plan, or road map, is lacking for achieving the vision. Nigeria and CRS must continue to work with existing partners and identify new partners, both within and outside its borders, to form a network of stakeholders. Such a partnership will be based on long-term relationships, trust, and a common vision for achieving social, economic, and ecological goals in CRS. This newly integrated CRS partnership can achieve success if it works incrementally and prioritizes inclusive and fair stakeholder participation in a Nigerian context.

This assessment report is the result of international collaboration and provides insights for moving forward in CRS to develop ecotourism potentials that depend on forest communities and conservation of the state's remaining natural assets. General recommendations for addressing a number of complex challenges facing partners in CRS were identified. We outlined specific findings and short-term recommendations for implementing site planning and developing interpretive training programs at Afi Nature Reserve and Obudu Plateau. Other findings from the assessment that represent longer-term issues at other protected areas in CRS were briefly described. The CRS partners are encouraged to immediately consider how they can come together in a collaborative process to address these long-term challenges.

Balancing economically viable tourism and small-scale sustainable ecotourism with community needs, conservation objectives, and protected area management presents a long-term challenge for CRS and Nigeria as a whole. The USFS/IP team recognizes and respects the complex challenges faced by our Nigerian counterparts and their partners, and we hope that this report provides insights and recommendations that can be adapted and used to meet some of their critical short-term needs and longer-term priorities. Ultimately, Nigeria and her people living in CRS hold the final decision for making changes that best fit her diverse needs and challenges, which, unfortunately, are not easily or quickly understood by outside partners.

APPENDIX 1

Initial Scope of Work and Team Credentials

Title: US Forest Service International Programs/Department of Agriculture Technical Mission (USFS/IP) to Cross River State (CRS), Nigeria: Assessments and recommendations exercise for planning and management of CRS protected areas and forest reserves and development of sustainable ecotourism.

Introduction

On Tuesday, April 25, 2006, the US Forest Service met with the Governor of CRS, Donald Duke, and Mr. Gabe Onah, managing director of Cross River State Tourism Bureau (CRSTB). Prior to the meeting, Governor Duke met with the US Department of State Regional Environmental Officer for West and Central Africa, Matthew Cassetta, to discuss the possibility of receiving technical assistance from the US for proposed ecotourism activities and improve protected area management. The CRSTB seeks to develop a circuit of tourist attractions. Ecotourism sites of priority include the Afi mountain wildlife sanctuary, the Mbe mountains, and the CRNP (Oban and Okwangwo Divisions).

Mission Objective

The objective of this technical assistance mission is to assess the current situation and management structure of a sample of CRS protected areas and make recommendations to improve protected area management, conservation, sustainable local resource management, and the well-being and economic stability of communities living in and around the protected areas. The team will propose methodologies for the development of sustainable ecotourism.

Background

Loss of Forest Habitat and Biodiversity

Threats to wildlife resulting from the bushmeat and pet trades are apparent in CRS protected areas. Recent reports included the alleged killing of two Cross River gorillas. In addition, indiscriminate logging practices (legal and illegal) have led to the suspension of the state's only active logging operation. Consequently, the deforestation is causing sedimentation of streams and rivers. Calabar river, where both TINAPA and the Calabar free trade zone are situated, is undergoing damage to aquatic life and reduced navigability. In an effort to reduce these threats to broader landscape and biodiversity, the CRSG requests assistance to resurvey and demarcate protected area boundaries and possibly prepare area management plans to begin to address conservation needs.

Participatory Forest Management

The livelihoods of communities in and around the CRS protected areas depend on agricultural production. How local communities see linkages between protection of forest resources and agricultural production is not clearly understood and little community participation exists in the overall management of the protected areas. The CRSG is in need of assistance in developing and implementing sustainable agriculture and alternative livelihood options for communities that neighbor protected areas.

Sustainable Tourism

The CRSTB has taken extensive measures to expand its tourism industry, as shown by the construction of a canopy walkway at Buanchor and Obudu Plateau. The historically popular resort, Obudu Cattle Ranch, has seen an increase in both domestic and international visitors. It is estimated that the annual number of tourist visits to CRS is 100,000. The CRS is ready to enhance its tourism industry, expressing an urgent need for assistance in several areas related to ecotourism development at protected areas.

Other Considerations

Additional support was requested by the CRSTB in several key areas. Addressing this list in total requires more time than the 2-weeks allocated for this specific mission and the realistic capabilities and expertise of the USFS/IP team. Of the 2-weeks, only 5 days were spent in the field visiting actual tourism sites in the state, and we had one meeting where we indirectly discussed the operation and management of the Tourism Bureau and its staff.

1. Improving the standard and quality of ecotourism products and services on a sustainable basis to meet current and future needs.
   - Assist with conducting training workshop on tour guiding skills and basic first aid techniques for maintenance staff and tour guides at Buanchor and Obudu Plateau.
   - Support training of tour guides on identification techniques for key taxa at Buanchor and Obudu Plateau, tree phenology, nature walk interpretive techniques, basic ethno-botany, non-timber forest product identification and usage.
   - Contribute to the production of quality conservation and visitor experience material (posters, booklets, worksheets, brochures, maps, signage, etc) for Visitors Reception Centre at the Afi Nature Reserve and Obudu Plateau ecological areas.
2. Develop capacity for improved monitoring and evaluation.
   - Support in the development of a monitoring and evaluation plan at Afi Nature Reserve and Obudu Plateau facilities.
   - Assist to carry out studies to identify weaknesses in service delivery and product quality at ecotourism facilities.
   - Contribute to the development of a training curriculum based on results of needs assessment.
   - Support the conducting of training based on results of needs assessment.
   - Support the training and equipping of Tourism Bureau tour guides and facility maintenance staff at the canopy walkway sites.
   - Support the review of checklists currently used for monitoring and inspections of ecotourism operations.
   - Support the review of guidelines and schedules currently used to regulate ecotourism sector operators.
3. Assessment of management structure and systems of the CRSTB.

Activities

The technical assistant team will meet and dialog with key partners in the management of CRS protected areas. These partners may include, but are not limited to, CRSFS, Cross River Forestry Commission, Nigeria National Park Service, the director of CRNP, USAID/Nigeria, US Embassy/Abuja, USDA/FAS, ARD, and WCS. The team will visit the Afi Nature Reserve, the AfiMountain Wildlife Sanctuary, Obudu Plateau, and CRNP. In collaboration with the CRS Forestry Commission, CRS Tourism Bureau, and NNPS the mission team will conduct an assessment of the CRS protected areas using rapid participatory methods. In addition, available resources such as aerial photos and satellite images will be used for the identification of critical areas and perhaps facilitate the analyses for viable visitor centers within these selected protected areas. The team will build on available information from the USAID-funded Sustainable Practices in SPACE Program. The team will also visit other specific sites to determine their suitability for proposed ecotourism projects.

Description of Team Members' Roles and Credentials

- Mr. John Neary, B.Sc.: Protected area management and planning specialist; US Forest Service, Alaska; Parks and Wildlife Volunteer, US Peace Corps Rwanda; advisor to Wilderness Advisory Group, South Africa; US Peace Corps training advisor, Uganda.
- Jeffrey J. Brooks, Ph.D.: Community collaboration, outdoor recreation/tourism and social science research specialist; US Peace Corps Benin (1990–1992), rural health education and extension
- Ms. Blessing E. Asuquo, B.Sc.: Mission Team Leader, US Forest Service International Programs Office, West Africa Program Manager; US Peace Corps Guinea (2001–2003), agro-forestry; mission logistics coordinator.

Deliverables

The mission team will produce a report of observations and findings from the assessment mission, including short-term recommendations to improve and enhance the development of sustainable ecotourism at selected sites in CRS administered by the Tourism Bureau. The report will include a short-term action plan for Afi Nature Reserve and Obudu Plateau with a description of partners and stakeholders, which is intended to lead to formal area, site, and business planning facilitated by future USFS/IP assistance missions in collaboration with both governmental and NGO partners in CRS.

Secondarily, the report should also include, to a lesser extent, some discussion of the longer-term needs for work plans and management plans at protected areas administered by the CRS Forestry Commission and the NNPS, specifically, CRNP, including their partners such as NCF and WCS.

Timing

Mission dates: October 20—November 5, 2006 the first draft report is to be submitted to the Nigerian counterparts and their partners in November 2006 with a revised final report based on their comments to follow in January 2007.

Funding

All costs incurred (international and domestic travel, domestic transportation, and lodging) during this detail will be covered by the CRSTB except the daily per diem rate and a 2-week salary for each of the three members of the mission team which will be covered by US Forest Service.

Logistics

All logistics will be coordinated by the USFS/IP West Africa Program Manager and the CRSTB team.

APPENDIX II

Model of Collaboration and Collective Action in Addressing Complex Problems

The opposite of collective action for addressing problems is stalemate and paralyzing conflict (Innes and Booher, 2003). Highly complex tough problems tend to get stuck or solved by force, which is a closed approach, leading to further problems (Kahane, 2004). This appendix describes three broad, interrelated, long-term social processes that are important for avoiding stalemate and collectively improving problem situations in ecotourism and protected area management (Figure 1):

- Building relationships and the capacity of partnerships to develop a shared vision.
- Problem definition—Developing shared definitions and understandings of concepts and words used to talk about ecotourism, conservation, and protected areas management. This allows partnerships to develop a common language for communicating during the collaborative process.
- Mutual trust—Positive public relations; respect; and inclusive and interactive communication.

Community capacity has been defined as the interaction of human capital, social capital, and the physical resources existing within a given community that can be leveraged to collectively solve problems and improve or maintain community well-being (Chaskin, 2001; Kaplan 2000). From an organizational perspective, collaborative capacity means having a clear vision and strategy to enable relationship building, collective thinking, adaptive planning, and implementation beyond the tangible elements of money, skilled personnel, and equipment—although these too are important for successful collaboration (Kaplan, 2000). A collaborative entity, or partnership, with a common vision, self-organization, an attitude of confidence, and a coherent frame of reference may have the capacity to collectively act in ways that improve problem situations related to ecotourism development and protected area management.

Problem definition involves the different ways that stakeholders frame, or view, the problem and the terminology and concepts related to it, such as community involvement and sustainability. Problem definition accounts for stakeholders' multiple understandings of a complex situation—their various frames of reference. Different frames of reference allow stakeholders to see what they want to see, or what they are guided to see, but stakeholders tend to have trouble seeing the same problem situation, or reality, from another group's frame of reference (Spicer, 1997). The existence of many different frames of reference for the same problem highlights a need to develop common goals and a common language.

Long-term committed partnerships that communicate using a common language tend to have mutual trust between members and outside stakeholders. Mutual trust leads to positive public relations and respect and tolerance for different frames of reference. Mutual trust is developed over time through fair, inclusive, interactive communication, and co-learning processes, rather than one-way persuasion strategies (Schusler et al., 2003; Toman et al., 2006).

When and where these processes are integrated, collective action may be achieved through long-term partnerships that have common goals and use a common language (Figure 1). The integration of capacity to collaborate and mutual trust can allow for partnerships that are characterized by long-term relationships. Partnerships with capacity are sustained by a guiding vision, strong leadership, and a sense of collective identity (Moore and Lee, 1999). The integration of collaborative capacity and problem framing can allow for common goals, including shared understandings of future desired conditions, acceptable development and management practices, and successful outcomes sustained over time. The integration of mutual trust and problem definition can allow for a common language, including shared definitions of ecotourism, protected area management, conservation, ecological conditions, social conditions, economic conditions, and successful outcomes of collaboration.

Common Goals
Shared understandings and a guiding vision for:
- Future desired conditions
- Acceptable development and management practices
- Successful outcomes

Common Language—Framing
Shared definitions of:
- Planning
- Management
- Sustainable development
- Ecotourism
- Community involvement and well-being
- Evaluation
- Success

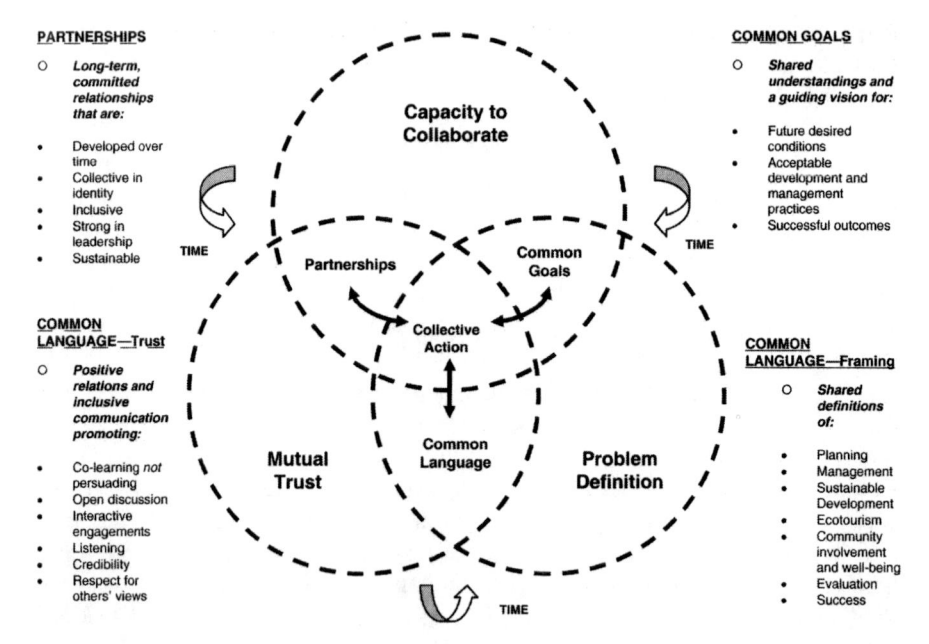

Figure 1. An open framework for collective action and collaboration in addressing complex problem situations (Brooks et al., 2006).

APPENDIX III—LIST OF ACRONYMS AND ABBREVIATIONS

ARD—Associates for Rural Development

CERCOPAN—Centre for Education, Research and Conservation of Primates and Nature

CRE—Cross River Environmental Capacity Development Coalition

CRNP—Cross River National Park

CRS—Cross River State, Nigeria

CRSFC—Cross River State Forestry Commission

CRSG—Cross River State Government

CRSTB—Cross River State Tourism Bureau Department of Surveys—Ministry of Lands, Surveys, and Housing in Calabar

DIN—Development in Nigeria

FFI—Flora and Fauna International

FGN—Federal Government of Nigeria

IUCN—International Union for the Conservation of Nature

CDC JOBS NIGERIA—Citizens Development Corps Jobs Nigeria

NCF—Nigerian Conservation Foundation

NGO—Non Governmental Organization

NNPS—Nigerian National Park Service

OICI—Opportunities Industrialization Centers International

REFORM—Nigeria Restructured Economic Framework for Openness, Reform and Macroeconomic Stability Project
SPACE—Sustainable Practices in Agriculture for Critical Environments Project
USFS/IP—United States Forest Service Department of Agriculture, International Programs Office
USG—United States Government
WCS—Wildlife Conservation Society
WWF—World Wide Fund for Nature

APPENDIX IV—ACKNOWLEDGMENTS

The USFS/IP mission team would like thank their Nigerian hosts and counterparts in Calabar and throughout Cross River State (CRS), Abuja, and Lagos. True West African hospitality was displayed by essentially everyone we met. For all those with whom we worked, thank you; this report would not have been possible without your dedication, hard work, and long hours, especially during the Ramadan Holiday. In particular, we appreciated the companionship, leadership, and chauffeuring of the Cross River State Tourism Bureau and Forestry Commission as well as the CRNP. Mr. Sunday in Lagos, Tony Bassey, Lisa Badru, Gabe Onah, Chris Agbor, Stephen Haruna, and Mr. Abong, you were wonderful hosts and members of the assessment team! We also thank the hotel operators in Ikom who fed us and washed the rainforest sweat, rain, blood, tears, and mud from our clothing at two in the morning. We loved the food and the drinks of CRS, especially the pounded yam and palm wine!

We would like to thank Shaun Mann for his advice and council. We also thank Andrew Dunn, Allen Turner, Peter Jenkins, Elizabeth Gadsby, Adeniyi Egbetade, Zoe Parr, Nicky Pulman, Kelly Chapman, Ubi Sam, Ranger Sylvester, Chief Edwin Ogar, Joel Frank, Matthew Cassetta, Wayne Frank, and John Haid for sharing insightful advice and documents.

We thank all the local rangers and guides who helped us about in the bush, testing their skills by leading us out of the bush (when mysteriously turned around), for guiding us across streams on wobbly bamboo bridges, and for keeping us on those crazy canopy walkways. We acknowledge the village representatives who we met at their homes in forest communities near protected areas for their welcoming spirit, hospitality, tours of local attractions and facilities, straight forward questions, and insightful answers. We regret that we did not have more time with you and your leaders. Conservation ultimately depends on you folks.

The CRS government is acknowledged for their contribution to the cost-share mission. We thank the Honorable Governor Duke for receiving us in Calabar and for supporting our recommendations. We thank the NNPS, USAID, and the US State Department for receiving us at their headquarters in Abuja. We are grateful for the important support that we received from our US Forest Service home offices in Alaska and Colorado, and we appreciate the thoughtful reviews and comments on the report provided by the CRSTB, WCS, Pandrillus Foundation, and CRSFC.

We greatly appreciated the opportunity to serve this unique and challenging mission of international collaboration to Nigeria, which was made possible by an agreement between the US Forest Service International Programs Office in Washington, DC and the CRSG. Finally, we thank Ms. Blessing Asuquo, West Africa Program Manager with USFS/IP, for coordinating a wonderful, authentic African adventure and learning experience; thank you for sharing your knowledge of West African history and politics.

KEYWORDS

- **Cross River National Park**
- **Cross River State Tourism Bureau**
- **Nigerian National Park Service**
- **Wildlife Conservation Society**

Chapter 19

Kilim River Mangrove Forest Ecotourism Services

Mohammad Zaki Ayob, Fatimah Mohd Saman, Zaliha Hj Hussin, and Kamaruzaman Jusoff

INTRODUCTION

Ecotourism is a revenue generator for many countries, especially those endowed with natural attractions. In order to sustain industry growth, its players are looking for essential factors contributing towards tourists' satisfaction. This chapter presents findings of a micro study on Langkawi mangrove forest ecotourism site along the Kilim River estuary. Four theoretical models were constructed and analyzed using Structural Equations Modeling (SEM). The baseline comparisons, parsimony adjusted measures, and the RMSEA were used to evaluate good model fit and Model 3 was found to fulfill that fit. The overall tourist satisfaction index was found to be 79.1 of a possible 100 points. Significant contributing factors towards tourists' satisfaction consist of marketing practices (42.1%), business ethics (23.9%), environmental management (14.5%), and business management/operational systems (7.8%).

Ecotourism, one of the fastest growing segments within the travel and tourism industry, comprises about 20% of all tourist arrivals. This rapid global growth in ecotourism illustrates an increasing interest in nature and the environment. According to Arlen (1995), ecotourism grossed over $335 billion a year worldwide, and attracted millions of interested tourists. In Malaysia, ecotourism is also a major revenue earner and had benefited the country, its natural areas, and local communities.

One of Malaysia's well-known eco-sites is Langkawi. Now a duty free geopark, it was listed by UNESCO as one of the Global Network of Geoparks on June 1, 2007. This serves as an impetus for it to develop further as an eco paradise. The forests and waters of Langkawi mangroves are home to species of monkeys, reptiles, birds, and even dolphins. Langkawi provides ecotourism experiences such as nature walks, bird watching, jungle-tracking, and mangrove tours in motorized boats. The eagle-feeding sessions at the mangrove swamps of the Kilim River have become one of the main tourist attractions.

This study seeks to gauge tourists' feedback on Langkawi's Kilim mangrove forests ecotourism tour services and to discover the contributing factors and their related elements leading to tourists' satisfaction. The four hypothesized factors having probable influence on tourists' satisfaction are business ethics, environmental management, marketing practices, and business management and operational systems.

METHODOLOGY

The data collected during the study relates to tourists' assessment and ratings on Langkawi mangrove forest ecotourism services. The basic information sought consists of dimensions related to business management systems, ethics, marketing, environmental management, and overall impact of ecotourism services.

The target population comprises tourists having recent experiences with Langkawi mangrove forest ecotourism ranging from December 2007 to January 2008. The sample subjects selected are tourists having prior engagement with the mangrove ecotourism service. Subjects were conveniently sampled at mangrove forest jetty points immediately after disembarking their chartered tours. Survey questionnaires were distributed to consenting tourists for immediate response. Sample subjects consisted of 454 males and 456 females with ages ranging from 20 to 50 years. Eighty-seven percent were Malaysians.

Data collection process covered a period of 2 months beginning early December 2007 and ended late January 2008. Responses regarding product, service, and their satisfaction level were measured using the Likert scales of 1–10. Tourists' responses on all the 34 statements made regarding respective independent and dependent variables were measured on the scale that range from 1 (strongly disagree) to 10 (strongly agree). The mean scores of each item of "1–10" are simultaneously converted to a scale of "0–100" to determine the index scores for the items based on the formula stated in Table 1.

Table 1. Variables in environmental management.

	BUSINESS MANAGEMENT & OPERATIONAL SYSTEMS		
Q1	Product maintenance	64.3	
Q2	Customer service	66.6	
Q3	Safety measures	65.3	77
Q4	Operational procedures observed	66.0	
Q5	Operational procedures effective	66.2	
	BUSINESS ETHICS		
Q7	Meet reasonable expectations of all customers	66.9	
Q8	Treat all customers equally	66.5	
Q9	Deliver activities exactly as advertised	67.7	
Q10	Provide receipts for monies received	67.4	
Q11	Attend to customers' queries	68.1	
Q13	Address customers' safety effectively	67.7	79
Q14	Address customers' comfort effectively	68.2	
Q15	Ensure product in good working order	67.5	
Q16	Address travel ethics relating to minimal impact	67.7	
Q17	Equipment, clothing, supplies are suitable	68.4	
	MARKETING PRACTICES		
Q18	Adequate transportation	64.7	
Q19	Provide relevant facilities	67.9	
Q20	Provide sufficient equipment	66.1	

Table 1. *(Continued)*

Q21	Provide tips for maximum enjoyment	67.1	
Q22	Spent 75% of activities within the natural area	67.3	78
Q23	Helped to experience nature	68.4	
ENVIRONMENTAL MANAGEMENT			
Q24	Garbage management	66.3	
Q25	Waste management	67.1	
Q26	Minimal disturbance to wildlife	66.3	78
Q27	Prevent irreversible danger to nature	66.6	
Q28	Prevent damage to environment	66.6	
CUSTOMER SATISFACTION			
Q29	Overall ecotourism service	66.6	
Q30	Service is worth money paid	67.9	
Q31	Would certainly recommend to friends	67.5	79
Q32	Service exceed normal expectations	68.1	
Q33	Service much better than competitors	67.7	
Q34	Overall satisfaction	69.3	

Data analysis to test the overall fit of models to the data was done using the SEM. The procedure follows Mulaik and Millsap (2000) four-step approach to modeling and deriving the best estimates for regression equations, squared multiple correlations (R^2), and path coefficients. The models used for testing are as in Figure 1, 2, 3, and 4. Step 1 involves performing factor analysis to establish the number of latent factors or components. The latent variables in SEM are similar to factors in factor analysis, and the indicator variables likewise have loadings on their respective latent variables. These coefficients are the ones associated with the arrows from latent variables to their respective indicator variables. By convention, the indicators should have loadings of 0.7 or higher on the latent variable. The loadings were used to impute labels to the latent variables, though the logic of SEM is to start with theory, including labeled constructs, and then test for model fit in confirmatory factor analysis. Step 2 involves performing confirmatory factor analysis to confirm the measurement model. This research tested the measurement model first, and only then tested the structural model by comparing its fit. Step 3 involves testing the structural model and Step 4 relates to testing nested models to get the most parsimonious one. The goodness of fit tests determines whether a model will be rejected or accepted. Only upon acceptance will path coefficients of the model be analyzed and interpreted. In SEM, we want to prove that the null hypothesis should be accepted (we fail to reject the model) and is indicated by having the probability value equal or above 0.05. If the probability value (P) is below 0.05, the model is rejected. In situations where the chi-square test of absolute fit displays a probability value lesser than 0.05, the tests of relative fit will be used to assess model fit. The AMOS output produced several model fit statistics designed to test or describe overall model fit. The indicators for relative fit of these fit statistics vary. The RFI coefficient should be close to 1 to indicate good model fit. In terms of IFI or delta2, the acceptable fit should range from 0.9 to 1.0. Values above 0.90 are considered acceptable fit. For Tucker-Lewis Index (TLI) or rho2, any value close to 1 indicates good model fit despite suggestions by Hu and Bentler (1999) that the value should be higher than 0.95. For comparative fit index (CFI) values above 0.90 are considered acceptable fit. For parsimony ratio (PRATIO), the closer the coefficient to 1.0, the stronger and more parsimonious the model fit. In terms of the root mean square of approximation (RMSEA), the general rule of thumb is that RMSEA should be below 0.05 or 0.06. The standardized regression weights of variables (measured and latent) in AMOS output will indicate variables having relatively high influence.

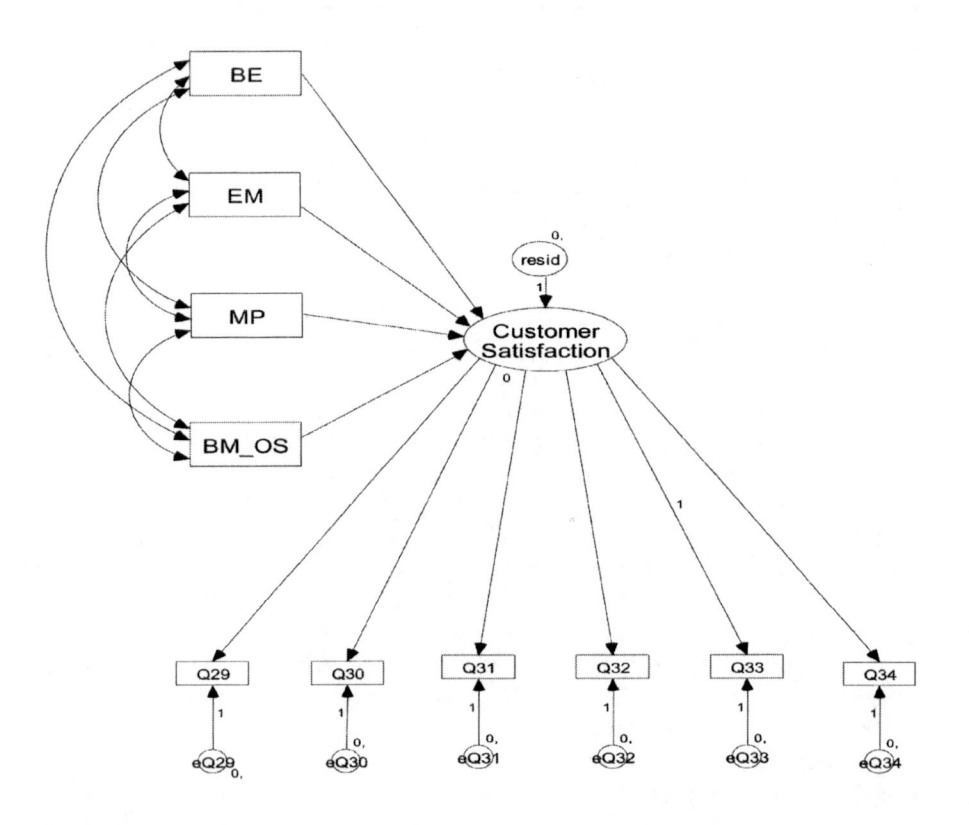

Figure 1. Conceptual model 1.

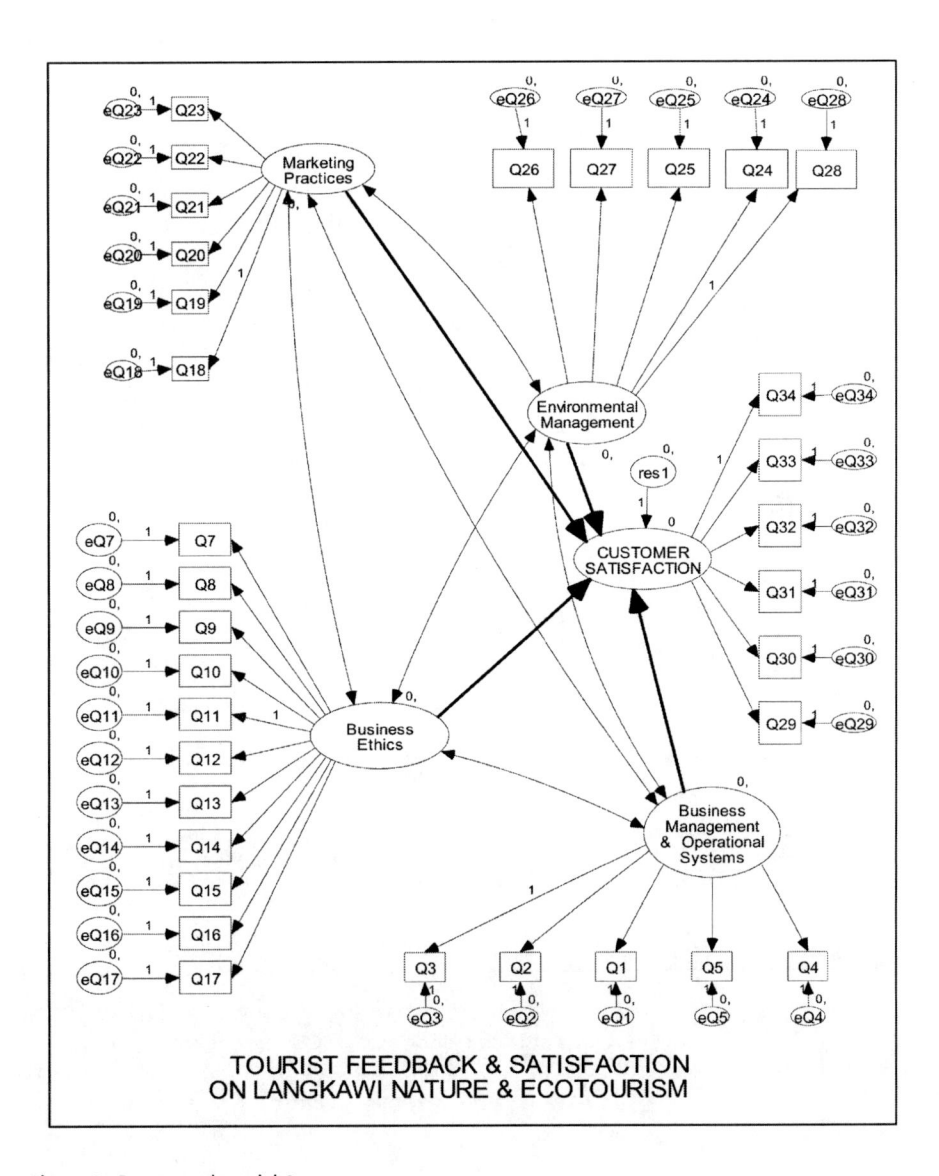

Figure 2. Conceptual model 2.

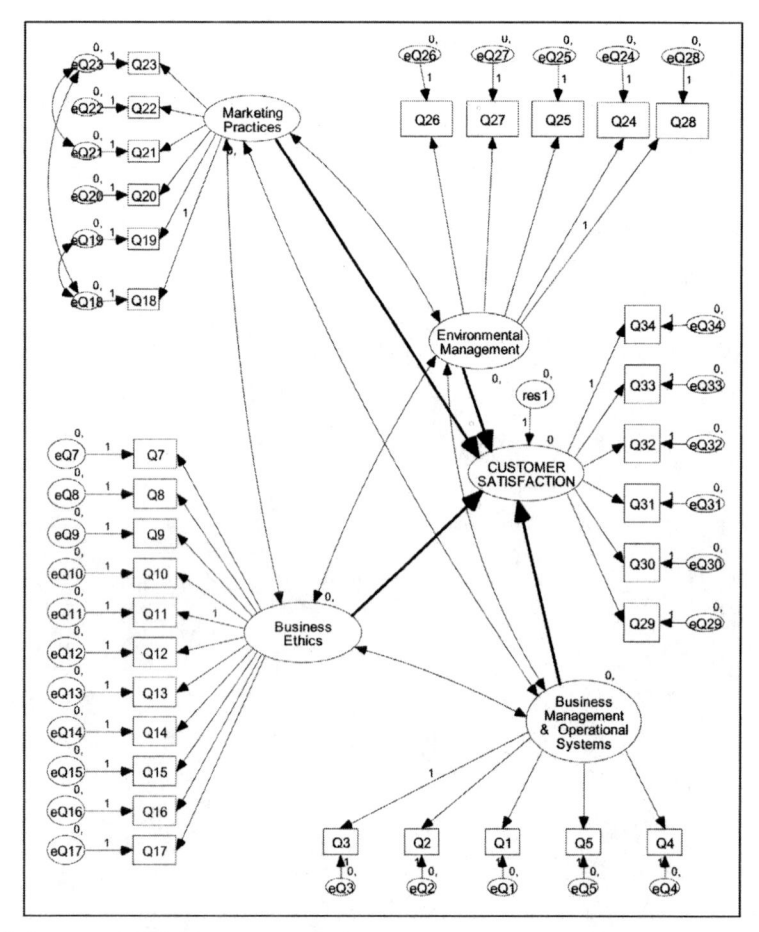

Figure 3. Conceptual model 3.

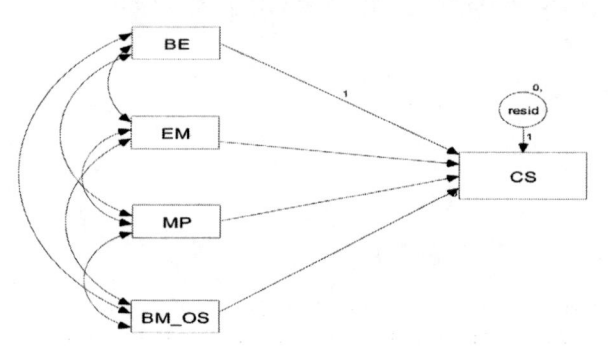

Figure 4. Conceptual model 4.

DISCUSSIONS AND RESULTS

Based on the AMOS output, minimum identification for all four models was achieved. This implies adequate fit for collected data and "Minimum was achieved" message was evident in the output. Based on the rules of thumb on assessing model fit statistics, Model 3 fulfilled the baseline comparisons (rho1, delta2, rho2), the PRATIO, and the RMSEA. Model 1 fulfilled all model fit statistics except the parsimony adjusted measures (the PRATIO, PNFI, PCFI) and the RMSEA. Model 2 is the third choice since its RFI is a bit away from 1. Model 4 does not fulfill the RFI, IFI, TLI, CFI, and the PRATIO. Its RMSEA however, is below 0.6.

Tourists' overall satisfaction index (Table 1) was found to be 79.1 of a possible 100. This implies that tourists' rating on Kilim River mangrove forest ecotourism service is basically good. Specific strategies requiring improvements include enhancing overall service delivery, making service worth the money tourists paid, raising tourists' satisfaction level, ensuring ecotourism services exceeding tourists' expectations, and striving to be above the competitors.

Table 2. Index.

	Standardized Total Effects (Group number 1 -Default model)				
	Environmental_ Management	Business_Management & Operational_Systems	Marketing_ Practices	Business_ Ethics	CUSTOMER_SATISFACTION
CUSTOMER SATISFACTION	.145	.078	.421	.239	.000
Q17	.000	.000	.000	.714	.000
Q16	.000	.000	.000	.745	.000

Based on AMOS Output (Table 2), marketing practices was found to influence 42.1% towards customer satisfaction. Hence, an increase of one standard unit of marketing practices index is expected to help increase tourists' satisfaction by 42.1 standard units. This was followed in descending order by Business Ethics (23.9%), and Environmental Management (14.5%). Business management and operational systems influence only 7.8% towards customer satisfaction. The estimated influence of these four factors towards tourists' satisfaction is 65.3%.

CONCLUSIONS

Based on the above results, we infer that tourists are least concerned on how tour operators internally manage their services. This is evidenced in Table 2 whereby the business management and operational systems factor only influence 7.8% towards tourists' satisfaction.

Business ethics (Table 3) is relatively more important to tourists. It influences about 23.9% of tourists' satisfaction. Specific variables having significant contributions include effectiveness in addressing customers' safety (Q13) and providing services the best possible way (Q12). Variables requiring improvement include attending to customers' queries (Q11), providing receipts for money received (Q10), delivering activities exactly as advertised (Q9), treating all customers equally (Q8), meeting reasonable expectations of all customers (Q7), effectively addressing customers' comfort (Q14), ensuring products are in good working order (Q15), addressing travel ethics relating to minimal impact behavior for natural areas (Q16), and providing equipment, clothing, supplies that are suitable for areas being visited (Q17). These variables, if improved, will probably make more tourists remember and recommend Kilim mangrove ecotourism to others.

Table 3. Variables in business ethics.

Q11	<---	Business Ethics	.767
Q10	<---	Business Ethics	.751
Q9	<---	Business Ethics	.770
Q8	<---	Business Ethics	.723
Q7	<---	Business Ethics	.725
Q12	<---	Business Ethics	.787
Q13	<---	Business Ethics	.791
Q14	<---	Business Ethics	.777
Q15	<---	Business Ethics	.784
Q16	<---	Business Ethics	.745
Q17	<---	Business Ethics	.714

Marketing practices (Table 4) is another very important factor to tourists. It was found to influence 42.1% towards tourists' satisfaction. An increase of one standard unit of marketing practices will help to increase tourists' satisfaction by 42.1 standard units. Specific variables that provide significant contribution towards marketing practices include providing sufficient equipment (Q20), providing tips to tourists for their maximum enjoyment (Q21), and spending at least 75% of ecotourism activities within the natural areas (Q22). Specific areas requiring improvement include upgrading facilities (Q19), providing adequate transport (Q18), and increased personalized assistance in experiencing nature (Q23).

Table 4. Standardized Total Effects.

Q23	<---	Marketing_ Practices	.797
Q22	<---	Marketing_ Practices	.809
Q21	<---	Marketing_ Practices	.820
Q20	<---	Marketing_ Practices	.835
Q19	<---	Marketing_ Practices	.761
Q18	<---	Marketing_ Practices	.777

Table 5. Variables in marketing.

Q28	<---	Environmental_ Management	.781
Q24	<---	Environmental_ Management	.764
Q25	<---	Environmental_ Management	.786
Q27	<---	Environmental_ Management	.811
Q26	<---	Environmental_ Management	.845

The environmental management factor (Table 5) contributed about 14.5% towards tourists' satisfaction. Specific variables providing high impact to this factor include measures undertaken to prevent irreversible danger to nature (Q27) and also provision for minimal disturbances towards wildlife (Q26). Variables requiring further improvement include efforts to prevent damage to the environment (Q28), garbage management (Q24), and waste management (Q25).

KEYWORDS

- **Ecotourism services**
- **Mangrove forest**
- **Structural equations modeling**
- **Tourist**

Chapter 20

Wilderness Stewardship in the Kruger National Park, South Africa

F. J. (Freek) Venter

INTRODUCTION

The Kruger National Park (KNP) faces greatly amplified problems than was the case in the early 1900s when the KNP was established. Areas surrounding the park have experienced a human population explosion with a rapid expansion of farming areas and rural settlements. In the 1970s the KNP was fenced. Ecologically the KNP became an island and previous regional animal movements were restricted to within its boundaries. A network of management roads was established and the KNP worked to keep the poaching onslaught at bay. However, the KNP may have succeeded in conserving its animal populations, but it has also paid a heavy price in the process—a loss of wilderness qualities.

Protected area managers and scientists in the KNP, with its 2 million ha (4,942,108 acres) of bush-clad savannah, face greatly amplified challenges than was the case in the early 1900s when the KNP was established. The areas surrounding the KNP experienced a human population explosion during the past three decades, causing a rapid expansion of farming areas and rural settlements, and subsequently land uses that are largely conflicting with protected area management.

In the 1970s the boundary of KNP was fenced to control wildlife diseases and to protect the neighboring areas from damage-causing animals, as well as to prevent animal movement into the war-ridden Mozambique. Ecologically the KNP became an island and previous regional animal movements were restricted to within its boundaries. A network of management roads was established and artificial water was subsequently provided through boreholes and dams to supplement sources no longer available to animals.

Commercial poaching, especially for bushmeat, ivory, and rhino horn, increased to such an extent that wildlife populations in many protected areas in Africa were nearly decimated. The KNP managed to keep the poaching onslaught at bay largely due to its effective and well-trained ranger contingent, extensive network of management roads, and its capacity to use intelligence to track organized poachers. The network of roads was created to be able to manage fires and also to provide access for management purposes.

To make the KNP available to the public and to help finance its conservation mandate, 16 rest camps containing approximately 5,000 beds and a well-maintained set of tourist roads have been developed. Numbers of tourists to the KNP grew to more than 1.2 million in 2004.

The KNP may have succeeded in its tourism endeavors and conserving its animal populations from the poaching onslaught, but it has also paid a price in the process. The price it paid was diminished wilderness qualities. This chapter describes the process and thinking followed to regain some of those wilderness qualities.

NEW LEGISLATION AND NEW OPPORTUNITIES

Wilderness protection has recently been included in the new Protected Areas Act (Act 57 of 2003) of South Africa. This provides the first opportunity for national parks to legally protect wilderness areas within national parks. Wilderness in the act is defined as. " ... an area designated ... for the purpose of retaining an intrinsically wild appearance and character, or capable of being restored to such and which is undeveloped and roadless, without permanent improvements or human habitation."

The purpose of designating wilderness status to an area is described as follows in the act:

1. to protect and maintain the natural character of the environment, biodiversity, associated natural and cultural resources and the provision of environmental goods and services;
2. to provide outstanding opportunities for solitude; and
3. to control access which, if allowed, may only be by non-mechanized means.

The restoration option that is stated in the act presented a challenge to take a 100- to 200-year vision and consolidate wilderness in the KNP by closing down management roads, but still maintain the ability to combat the increasing poaching onslaught and maintain the integrity of the area.

METHODS

A rezoning process was initiated to consolidate existing wilderness areas in the KNP, reduce management roads to the absolute minimum, and officially proclaim wilderness areas under the new legislation. This formed part of a wider process whereby a generic zoning system (Conservation Development Framework) for use in all national parks has been developed (Briton, et al., 2004, internal report on file at SANParks, Pretoria, South Africa).

The existing Geographic Information System (GIS) infrastructure data of the KNP (including camps, roads, and concession areas) were used (MacFadyen et al., 2004, internal report on file at KNP) in a Distance Analysis (ArcView 3.2a with Spatial Analyst 2.0). Using previous zoning systems (Braack 1997, internal report on file at KNP; Venter et al., 1997, internal report on file at KNP.) the KNP's management road network was revised according to the area integrity management requirements of each region or ranger section. The process included workshops with rangers of the different sections in the KNP. Roads were subsequently classified according to the level of associated disturbance and assigned an appropriate buffer distance to ensure the integrity of surrounding natural areas.

The following buffers were applied on both sides of roads:
- Tarred tourist roads, 2 km (1.24 miles)
- Graveled tourist roads, 1 km (0.62 miles)
- Graveled management roads, 500 m (1,640 ft)
- Tourist track, 200 m (656 ft)
- Management patrol track, 100 m (328 ft)

As the poaching problem is a constant one and will probably be with us forever, the aim of this exercise was to close down and rehabilitate as many roads as possible and downgrade others from annually graded firebreaks to tracks for patrol purposes only, but to still retain the necessary anti-poaching and general management maneuverability.

DISCUSSION

In the past, the existing and projected future levels of ecotourism and other development was not seen to pose a real threat to the conservation goals of the park. This belief was based on the fact that less than 4% of the surface area of the KNP was physically disturbed by developments. The assumption was made that impacts related to such developments were limited to the immediate vicinity of the developments. The present study, however, indicates that there are indeed also significant aesthetic impacts associated with these kinds of developments.

Freitag-Ronaldson et al., (2003) presented a list of tourism and management related biophysical and aesthetic impacts experienced in the KNP. Although these impacts are usually considered to be limited and localized and not presenting a real threat to the KNP ecosystem as a whole, they are the cause of a feeling that the KNP is trammeled.

A clear distinction is made in the KNP between "wilderness areas or zones" and "wilderness qualities" in an effort to overcome the problem of different perceptions of wilderness as expressed by different people. Wilderness zones refer to specific designated areas that are set aside for special protection according to the new legislation and that comply with the definition described above. Wilderness qualities refer to the experience that one will be subjected to in any zone or area in the KNP, including but not exclusive to wilderness zones. This experience will vary from one person to the next. Wilderness zones will normally offer the best quality wilderness experience, whereas rest camps and roads do so at a lesser extent but much better than developed areas outside the KNP. The following description may enlighten the different interpretations of the two terms as used in the KNP.

RESULTS

The fragmentation of Kruger before the exercise is considerable (MacFadyen et al., 2004, internal report on file at KNP) and the consolidation process was found to significantly alter the situation:
- Fifty-nine percent of the KNP was closer than 1 km (0.62 miles) from infrastructure (including rest camps, power lines, tourist roads, and management roads).

- As a result of the road system, Kruger was divided into 481 blocks.
- Patches with wilderness potential, (e.g., patches further than 1 km (0.62 miles) from a road), had an average size of 5,728 ha (14,154 acres).
- Two hundred ninety of these patches were smaller than 1,000 ha (2,471 acres) and only 5 were bigger than 10,000 ha (24,711 acres).
- During the consolidation process 1,523 km (946 miles) of management roads were earmarked for closure.
- After the consolidation process, the number of blocks decreased from 481 to 162.
- The average size of blocks increased from 5,728 (14,154 acres) to 15,200 ha (37,560 acres).
- Only 5 of these blocks are now smaller than 1,000 ha (2,471 acres) and 39 are bigger than 10,000 ha (24,711 acres).

WILDERNESS ZONES

There was a time when the whole world was wilderness, according to our present definition, with a few pockets of human habitation (forming an integral part of the wilderness). Today this situation has changed and it is the other way round. Very few pockets of true wilderness areas remain in a sea of development and they are shrinking by the day as technology increases. At first it was a challenge to conquer wilderness—now it has become an obligation to protect it. A few decades ago some people that lived in the most remote areas possible would not even understand the notion of wilderness—it was part of their everyday lives.

Thus, there is a trend, especially in developed countries to set aside and legalize wilderness zones, areas deemed to have an intrinsic right to existence and conservation with no or limited disturbance by humans. In the KNP such areas are set aside for the following reasons:

- To satisfy the need of an increasing number of people wishing to experience truly pristine, unaffected wilderness where for a while they can consciously immerse themselves in a sense of remoteness and a return to basic essentials. Some measure of the need for such opportunities is the considerable sums of money many people are willing to pay to have access to such wilderness zones. The very high and growing popularity of tourism products in the KNP that offer this kind of experience is proof that it is indeed a growing need.
- To keep options open for future generations of people. Once an area has been trammeled and scarred by development, it blots out other options, or use that is wilderness dependent. The irreversibility of permanent developments means that mistakes made during the development also become largely irreversible.

Such pristine wilderness areas have therefore been included in the spectrum of zones proposed for use in South African national parks (Briton et al., 2004). Whereas these "minimum-impact" zones are motivated essentially by biodiversity conservation and recreational opportunity it affords to a segment of society (especially the "back-to-basics" or "return-to-roots" nature lovers), the ethical/moral justification for at least some such areas should not be forgotten (bequest to future generations).

WILDERNESS QUALITIES OR WILDNESS

People do not visit conservation areas simply to see wildlife, which could be viewed at less cost in smaller nature reserves and zoological and botanical gardens. Although often not consciously realized, in the case of the KNP it is the intangible attributes associated with this conservation area, which attracts and appeals to so many people. These attributes include solitude, remoteness, wildness, serenity, peace, harmony, opportunity for reflection and self-appraisal, and a host of others that for convenience sake can be termed "wilderness qualities."

Wilderness qualities or wildness is therefore based on human perception. The range of perceptions about wilderness is about as wide as the wide range of humans in the human race. For one person it is an incredible wilderness experience to enter the KNP on a road without fences flanking it and sleeping over in one of the restcamps. For the more experienced protected area visitor this kind of activity is far too sophisticated and they prefer to "get away from it all."

Even within the confines of a restcamp, for example, certain wilderness qualities can be achieved by sensitive and appropriate landscaping, building material and building styles, noise management, and a variety of other means, all amplified by the proximity of undisturbed natural bush and wildlife adjoining such a camp. Some people, again, would shun relatively sophisticated camps in favor of rugged and primitive tented camps and walking trails.

Wilderness qualities are the intangible spiritual and experiential aspects associated with protection areas that are the primary attractants for people visiting the KNP, and these qualities should therefore be maximized and managed. A range of differing intensities of such wilderness qualities can be offered to satisfy the needs of different people, and this can be achieved through managing different zones in different ways to achieve differing degrees of wilderness experience.

As a national park, the KNP has a responsibility to provide for this wide range of needs as well as it possibly can. The challenge therefore lies in providing appropriate opportunities and satisfying as wide a range of public needs along this continuum of undiluted to diluted wilderness qualities.

The impacts of mass tourism on biodiversity and wilderness qualities are still not well understood in the context of the KNP, and research in this regard is seriously needed.

KEYWORDS

- **Commercial poaching**
- **Kruger National Park**
- **Wilderness protection**

Chapter 21

Sustainable Tourism Development in Cross River State, Nigeria

Eugene J. Aniah, Judith E. Otu, and M. A. Ushie

INTRODUCTION

Today, Obudu Ranch Resort is one of the tourism havens in the world, which has attracted great number of visitors to Nigeria and Cross River State in particular. This resort has not only aided the development of existing tourism potentials but has equally transformed the livelihood of most communities in Cross River State through income generation, employment, and also provision of basic social amenities such as electricity, water supply, road network among others in the area. This chapter critically examines the level of domestic and international patronage of Obudu Ranch Resort between 2001 and 2008, tourist preference of the resort, major attraction, and facilities in the resort, population threshold of the enclave communities within the study area and the purpose of tourists visit to the Ranch Resort. Chi-square was used in testing the stated hypothesis as regards to the amount expended by the tourist as fare to the ranch. In spite of the tremendous facilities available in the Ranch Resort much is still needed to be done in other to boast the image of the resort and also to attract high patronage of domestic and international tourists. Therefore, the hope of the masses and development of the Ranch Resort is rested on the government and the private sector.

Tourism could be related to the Biblical story of the visit of the queen of Shebba to King Solomon. Tourism is seen as a leisure activity, which is international in character. Eboka (1999) described tourism as the movement of people to destinations outside their usual abode or residence on short-term bases. In the same vein, tourism is seen as a visit as well as the services industries created to satisfy the needs arising from movement within or across international boundaries temporary. In recent times, Ecotourism has attracted increasing attention in recent years not only as an alternative to mass tourism, but as a means of economic development and environmental conservation (Campbell, 2002).

Ormsby and Mannle (2006) opened that ecotourism venture have sustained the economy of most nations for example east African countries like Kenya, Tanzania, and part of West Africa like Senegal. Ecotourism is mainly the interaction between the physical environmental features for leisure purposes. It is in this light the several thousand of people live their usual residencies to areas with friendly climate, coastal regions for hiking and trekking, surfing and swimming, and the enjoyment of friendly ambience. Cross River State is endowed with great ecotourism potentials such as Obudu Ranch Resort, waterfalls, warm spring among others which have attracted both local and international tourists patronage.

In Cross River State, the green vegetation, the rising sun, escorting many people from the capital city of Calabar, through the mangrove swamps to the tropical virgin forests to Akamkpa, Ikom, and Boki, then to the mountain savannah of Ogoja and Obudu. This great eco-tourism potentials has afford several tourists and visitors a unique opportunity to see the beauty of the physical features of an enticing bride called Cross River State. Today the overwhelmed, beautiful landscapes, colorful folks, and overwhelming serenity and the agreeable climate has made Obudu Ranch Resort a natural paradise. However, this chapter critically assesses the level of the patronage of Obudu Ranch Resort particularly as regards to domestic and international tourist patronage of the resort between 2001 and 2008, tourism facilities and attraction in Ranch Resort, reason for tourists preference of the ranch, population threshold of the area and purpose for their visit to the Ranch (Table 1). To achieve the above stated research findings, two hypotheses were put forward thus:

H_0: There is no significant difference between the number of tourists visiting Obudu Ranch Resort and the distance between Obudu and the tourist home.

H_1: There is significant difference between the number of tourists visiting Obudu Ranch Resort and the distance between Obudu and the tourist home.

Table 1. Population threshold of communities in Obudu Ranch Resort.

Purpose of visit	No of respondents	Percentage
Business	79	25.2
Leisure	53	16.9
Holiday	108	34.4
Research	33	10.5
Conference	27	8.6
Any other (specify)	14	4.5
Total	**314**	**100**

Source: Development in Nigeria, 2003 + Quash Bully and Associates, 2008. The data collected also reveals that 10.5% of the tourists are researchers, 25.2% are for Business, 8.5% visit the ranch for the purpose of attending conferences.

STUDY AREA

Obudu Ranch Resort is located at an altitude of 1,575 meters above sea level, and a unique temperature climate and vegetation with temperature ranging between 70–150c all year round. It is a gold mine, anxiously wanting to be fully exploited. It is bounded to the north by Benue State, to the South by Ogoja local government area, and the East by the Republic of Cameroon (Figure 1).

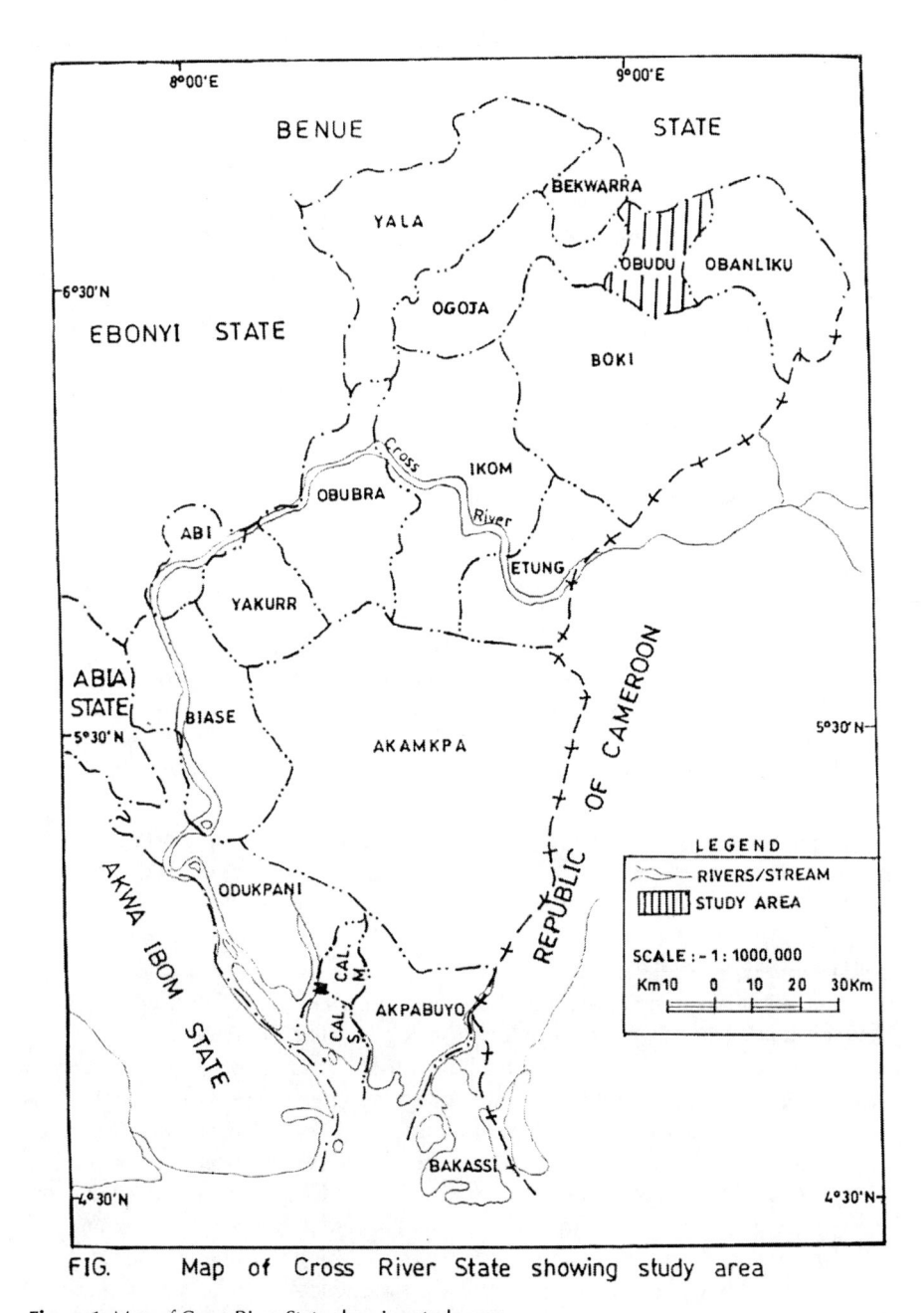

Figure 1. Map of Cross River State showing study area.

METHODOLOGY

This chapter focuses on patronage of an ecotourism resort for sustainable tourism development in Cross River State using Obudu Ranch Resort as a case study. Data were collected in the field using Participatory Research Method (PRM), questionnaires, interview, field observation, and library materials.

Three hundred and forty copies of questionnaires were administered to different tourists. While the management of the ranch resort were interview to ascertain the level of domestic and international of patronage of the ranch resort. However, PRM was adopted to help familiarize and also to have a focal group discussion with the different administrative cadre or staff in the ranch resort. Information concerning population threshold of the adjourning communities were collected from National Population Commission, Cross River State. However, the stated hypothesis was tested using chi-square to confirm the validity of the data collected in the field. The chi-square formula is stated as:

$$x^2 = \frac{(f_0 - f_e)^2}{f^2}.$$

The chi-square was used to examine the variables in the sample population.

LITERATURE REVIEW

Tourism in Theory and Practice

Tourism in Nigeria today is not a new phenomenon. It is also considered as one of the most profitable industries with perhaps one of the lowest possible investment. The tourist industry in Nigeria is still fairly developed when compared to those found in other countries of both the developed and developing world.

Tourism has become a powerful vehicle of economic growth which has contributed to the socio-economic development of most countries of the world especially countries like Switzerland, Brazil, Thailand among others where tourism is the main stay of her economy. (Goswami, 1979). An instance could be cited from Spain with 2–6 million dollars from foreign tourism in 1992, this figure represents two thirds of its invisible export for that year.

Ukpana (2005) has contended that "domestic tourism in developing countries is a phenomenon that has so far been under estimated in scientific literature." This statement applies to Nigeria almost more than any other country in view of the dearth of literature on this subject in the country. Among the few studies so far done on this topic with particular reference to Nigeria is one by (Ojo, 1976) in which he traced the historical development of tourism and recreation in Nigeria from the pre-colonial through colonial to the post colonial eras of the country. He also delved deeply into the present state of the industry in the country. Ojo concluded his study with an analysis of the attitude of Nigerians to tourism and recreation using Illorin as a case study. He concluded that there is a relationship between the individual's educational background and his desire to participate in tourism. Another important variable is the individual's level of awareness of the existence of a tourist resort. It is true that a tourist will be motivated to go to any particular resort only when he is attracted and the facilities of his choice are available in such a place. Broadly speaking, the hall mark of Obudu Cattle Ranch include:

1. Good weather/climate
2. Scenery
3. Amenities and accommodation
4. Historical and cultural features
5. Accessibility
6. Natural resources such as (the hill, fertile, land, different animal species, etc).

Fine weather is one of the most important attractions of a tourist center. Good weather is important in tourism that it has been capitalized upon by such places that are blessed with a unique and peculiar kind of climate. It should be stressed that in the tropics, any area with a mild or temperature climate is preferred to areas with strictly tropical climate. The development of Obudu Cattle Ranch as a holiday resort can be explained mainly by its fine and exhilarating climate, which is all year round.

A report of the cognizance survey of Obudu Cattle Ranch the cultural heritage of the people describes the place as "The best site in the world to constitute a game reserve…" (UNESCO, 1979). Beautiful and unique national scenery have also continued to be a great fascination to tourists all over the world. To be able to attract tourist in appreciable numbers, sceneries like mountains, waterfall, moorland, and so on should combine both age and physical splendor. The important of scenery in tourism has also emphasized by Coppock and Duffied (1980) in observing the "scenery is the principle resource in formal outdoor recreation and that the appearance and perception and landscape are very important denominator in public enjoyment and country side. For tourists to visit any centers, the must be available facilities for lodging, swimming, recreation, amusement, games, and spoils, viewing etc." This then brings out the importance of the third element of tourism. Increasingly, the holiday maker has demanded entertainment and recreational facilities in larger measures. What has come to be known as "development" has preoccupied the resort management.

Robinson (2006) went further to say that, putting green and bathing pools, theatres, cinemas, fun palace, chair lift, and so on are some of the amenities is the provision of lodging and food, loosely called accommodation. The importance of accommodation lies in the fact that most tourists visit particular sport simply because there is first class accommodation where food, sleep, and other things could be obtained. Features of historical and or of culture interest also exert a strong pulling force for many tourists.

However, the incomparable Egyptian pyramid, cathedrals, temple, art galleries, musical festivals, long historical, and cultural significance cities like Carro, Paris, London, and other attract most tourists to this great areas. In planning spatial behavior (Lynch, 1975) state that "the likelihood of the person going to the particular place is a function of its attributes (resources) modified by the person's knowledge and attitude towards the attribute (perception) and further qualified by the availability of access to the place (accessibility)." By this, it implies that no matter the quality of a place, the person going there must first know that such a place exists. The physical relationship of any tourist center and the problem inadequate transport facilities which can clearly, affect the development of tourism for example, a resort can posses a much attraction and amenities that could have naturally attracted tourist, but because of accessibility, tourists will become rare bird in such a center.

Hall (2003) in his study of the impact of tourism discovered that tourism has become a significant source of foreign exchange revenue for many countries of the world. According to him, tourism activities in Maldives contributed 66.6% of the country's Gross Domestic Product (GDP) and accounted for 65.9% of its exports. According to Hall analyses, tourism industry in Vanuatu has contributed 47.0% of the country's GDP and 73.7% of its total export earnings. They went further to emphasize that 13 developed countries in Asia (Cambodia, Lao people's democratic Republic, and Neps). Tourism accounted for more than 15% of export earnings.

They further stress that tourism alone contributed 43.5% of the export earnings of Fiji and one third of its GDP. Other small Islands such as Tonga and Vanuatu are dependent on tourism for half or more of their export earnings. Prentice (2007) in his study opines that tourism in China has provided a substantial contribution to its GDP, amounting to 13.7% in 2006. Taking full advantage of the potential of their natural and cultural tourist resources, countries in the greater Mekong sub-region are benefiting from the tourism industry. He went further to stress that in 2006, tourism in Cambodia and the Lao people's Democratic Republic accounted respectively for 22.3 and 21.4% of their total export earnings and contributed 19.6 and 9.3% respectively of the GDP.

RESEARCH FINDINGS

Domestic and International Patronage of Obudu Ranch Resort

The data obtained was base on domestic and international patronage of Obudu Ranch Resort. The data collected indicate that the total number of Nigerian visitors who visit the Ranch supersede that of foreign visitors as shown in Table 2. Table 3 also reveals that there is a progressive increase of tourist patronage of the resort from 2001 to 2008, this could be due to improvement in infrastructural development in the Ranch Resort. The data collected also indicate that 2008 recorded the highest domestic patronage of the Ranch Resort with a value 16.843 compared to international patronage, which had 6,727 as present in Table 2.

Table 2. Purpose of tourist visit to the Ranch.

Year	Number of Visitors Nigerian	% of Total	Number of Visitors	% of Total
2001	1,231	1.88	253	1.39
2002	1,613	2.47	373	2.05
2003	3,074	4.70	536	2.95
2004	6,307	9.65	921	5.07
2005	9,715	14.87	1312	7.22
2006	12,091	18.50	3117	17.16
2007	14,467	21.14	4922	27.10
2008	16,843	25.77	6727	37.04
TOTAL	65,341		18,161	

Source: Field Work, 2008.

Data were also collected to show the amount expended by tourist as fare to the ranch as indicate in Table 3. Table 3 reveals that the choice of the site tends to be base on the cost as indicated by the number of respondents.

Table 3. Patronage of domestic and international tourist between 20012008 in Obudu Ranch Resort.

Amount (N)	Response Frequency	% of Sample
Below 5,000.00	106	41.9
5,000.00- 14,000.00	63	25.82
15,000.00-25,000.00	36	14.75
25,000.00-34,000.00	28	9.24
35,000.00 and above	81	12.71
	314	

Source: Resort Management, 2008.

To confirm the validity of the stated hypothesis using the amount expended by the tourist as fare to the ranch, the result indicates a high significance level as the computed value was 82.31 while table value at 0.5 was 3.38. Therefore, the null hypothesis (H_0) was rejected in favor of the alternatives hypothesis. Table 4 shows basic tourism attractions and facilities in Obudu Ranch Resort. These potentials are of great important to tourists, as they offer the best satisfaction to different categories of tourist that visit the ranch resort.

Major Tourism Attractions and Facilities in Obudu Ranch Resort

The ranch resort affords many people a unique opportunity to see the beauty of the physical features of an enticing "bride" called Cross River State. The overwhelming beautiful landscapes, colorful folks, agreeable climate, and vegetation welcome visitors to the highland of the race. However, there are different facilities provided for tourist at the ranch resort. However, these facilities range from conference center, education center, main restaurant, cable car, traditional huts, fire station, honeymoon, warehouse, new reception zone among others. Most of these facilities also provide other sub units such as library/research, shop, storage convenience, tea rooms, changing rooms for male, and female among others. The provision of all these facilities by the government and private sector is in a bid to boost the image of the ranch and also to create an enabling environment for visitors wishing to patronage the resort.

Table 4 indicates reasons why tourists preferred visiting the Ranch Resort. The data collected reveals that most people are attracted to the climatic condition of the Ranch Resort as it had a value 35.6% follow by the facilities in the Resort with 24.8%. Although other factors such as scenery with a value 21.7%, popularity of the resort 10.8% are also responsible for why people visit the Ranch. However, the data collected in Table 5 reveals that almost everybody visits the Ranch due to climatic and weather condition and scenery of the environment. Other factors such as availability of facilities with 24.8%, popularity of the resort 10.8% and others were also responsible why certain persons visit the ranch.

Table 4. Amount suspended by tourist as fare to the Ranch.

S/N	Reasons for preference Obudu Ranch Resort	No of Respondent	Percentage
1	Climate/weather	112	35.6
2	Scenery	68	21.7
3	Availability of facilities	78	24.8
4	Popularity of the resort	34	10.8
5	Others	22	7.0
	TOTAL	314	

Source: Fieldwork, 2008.

The ranch, which has a temperate weather condition, is very unique and has different characteristic of this part of the world. Table 5 shows the population threshold of the various communities within the study area. The population of the various communities was obtained from development in Nigeria 2003 and the Quash Bully and Association 2008. The population indices obtained reveals a fluctuation in population of the different communities such as Anape, Okpazawge, Kogol, Keji-Ukwu, Okwamu, and Apeh-Ajil respectively as shown in the Table 5.

Table 5. Tourist's preference of Obudu Ranch Resort.

			2003 *		2004 +	
S/n	Village	Population	Average Household size	Population	Average Household size
1	Anape	336	8	958	22
2	Okpazawge	225	9	693	19
3	Kegol	286	13	770	20
4	Keji-Ukwu	221	13	678	24
5	Okwamu	112	8	444	18
6	Apeh-Ajili	165	15	567	28
		1,345	11	4,110	22

Source: Field Work, 2008.

CONCLUSION

Tourism development in Cross River State is a phenomenon which has impacted significantly to the livelihood of most Nigerian in general and Cross River State in particular through income generation, employment, and has also transform most of the enclave (rural) communities endowed with these laudable potentials into a natural paradise through the provision of basic amenities and infrastructures such as road network, electricity, pipe borne water among others. Today Obudu Cattle Ranch is a distributive hub in West Africa and has attracted domestic and international tourists and visitors all over the world into Nigeria in general and Cross River State in particular hence making Cross River State a holiday town. However, the sustainability (future used) of the Ranch Resort lies in the hands of all the stakeholders such as private individual, the government and the local people whose livelihood depend solely on the environment of this great industry and potentials. Therefore, the private individual and government must advocate programs and policies that will enhance the livelihood of these local communities within these areas so as to salvage environmental problems such as unemployment, poverty, theft among others capable of disorganizing the entire ecosystem and the ranch resort in particular.

KEYWORDS

- **Ecotourism**
- **Patronage**
- **Sustainable**
- **Tourism**

Chapter 22

Conserving Biodiversity on Mongolian Rangelands

Richard P. Reading, Donald J. Bedunah, and Sukhiin Amgalanbaatar

INTRODUCTION

Mongolia is a sparsely populated country with over 80% of its land used by pastoralists for extensive livestock grazing. Mongolia's wildlife and pastoralists have faced dramatic challenges with the recent rapid socioeconomic changes. Livestock numbers increased dramatically in the 1990s following the transition from communism to democracy and capitalism. Yet, limited industrialization and cultivation and relatively low rates of natural resources exploitation leave geographically large areas of the nation with few adverse impacts. In addition, the nation's heritage is strongly conservation oriented. As a result, Mongolia's protected areas system has been growing rapidly and its grasslands support the largest populations of several globally important species. Alternatively, several challenges exist, including growing pressure to exploit the nation's vast mineral reserves, the potential for conflict between pastoralist and conservation objectives, and insufficient conservation capacity to manage and protect natural resources. Arguably, a unique opportunity exists in Mongolia to develop economically while maintaining healthy and productive grasslands that support large populations of native flora and fauna. We suggest that doing so will require strengthening protected areas management; increasing ecotourism; instituting socially acceptable grazing reform; beginning to manage wildlife throughout the entire nation; and finding ways to integrate solutions for both sustainable pastoralism and conservation while minimizing unproductive conflict.

Mongolia is a vast (>156 million ha), sparsely populated, central Asian nation of about 2.5 million people (NSO-Mongolia, 2004). Over 80% of the country, or about 126 million ha, are used by pastoralists for extensive livestock grazing (MNE, 2001; Sheehy, 1996), and these extensive grazing lands represent the largest remaining contiguous area of common grazing in the world (World Bank, 2003). Mongolia has been grazed by livestock for millennia and livestock numbers were estimated at 1.97 million horses, 1.79 million cows and yaks, 0.26 million camels, 10.76 million sheep, and 10.65 million goats in 2003 (NSO-Mongolia, 2004). Limited industrialization and cultivation and relatively low rates of natural resources exploitation leave geographically large areas of the nation with little adverse anthropogenic impacts. As such, Mongolia represents an opportunity to realize positive and significant conservation objectives. However, several important challenges also exist, especially as Mongolia embraces a free market system and pressures, both internal and external, to utilize and develop the nation's vast mineral reserves increase without the development of sound environmental laws and regulations. Whether or not Mongolia can balance economic development with nature conservation remains to be seen, but arguably a unique opportunity exists in Mongolia to develop economically while maintaining healthy and productive grasslands that support large populations of native flora and fauna.

THE CONTEXT OF RANGELAND CONSERVATION

Adequately conserving Mongolia's rangelands requires a sound understanding of the ecological, social, and cultural context and values of these rangelands. Henwood (1998a; 1998b) stressed the low levels of protection for temperate grasslands. He stated that the world's temperate grasslands were the most beleaguered biome, as only 0.7% of the world's temperate grasslands fall within the global system of protected areas. Mongolia represents an opportunity to conserve and protect the biodiversity of its grasslands and provides an opportunity to increase the World's protected grasslands. We briefly discuss Mongolia's biodiversity, protected area systems, current and historical use of rangelands, important cultural considerations, the history of conservation efforts in the country, and threats.

Biodiversity

Mongolia retains a substantial amount of its "natural" biodiversity and although biodiversity values are not as great as in many tropical systems, they are still considered high. Two of the world's most biologically outstanding ecoregions, the Daurian Steppes, and the Altai-Sayan Mountains, lie partly within Mongolia (World Wildlife Fund, 2000). More than 2,823 species of plants inhabit Mongolia (Gunin et al., 1998) and indeed, the Mongolian steppe represents one of the largest contiguous unaltered grasslands in the world (WWF, 2000). As a result, some species persist in impressive numbers, such as the millions of Mongolian gazelle (*Procapra gutturosa*) that still roam the eastern steppes, and other wild species persist in relatively healthy population in Mongolia; starkly contrasting neighboring regions (Lhagvasuren et al., 1999; Reading et al., 2000, 2002). The ability of Mongolia to maintain its natural biodiversity largely stems from its long history of pastoralism, low human population (per-capita land area is the largest in the world; World Bank, 2003) and lack of industry and crop agriculture. Mongolia also boasts a long history of protecting special areas and a strong cultural tie to the land. Both flora and fauna have benefited from the small amount of land area transformed by cultivation and from only limited introduction of exotic plants.

Grazing lands dominate Mongolia's land area, with over 80% of the land area categorized as rangeland. Forests represent the next largest land type, with about 10% of the area categorized as forest. Arable lands, urban areas, and water each comprise about 1% of the land area (Bedunah and Miller, 1995; World Bank, 2003). Mongolia's vegetation zones based on geography and climate include the High Mountain Belt, the Mountain Taiga Belt, the Mountain Forest Steppe, the Steppe, the Desert Steppe, and Desert (Hilbig, 1995; Johnson et al. this proceedings). For more detailed vegetation descriptions see Hilbig (1995) and Gunin et al. (1999). Livestock graze all of these vegetation zones, with areas grazed by several of the "five types" of Mongolian livestock (camels, horses, sheep, goats, and cattle, including yak).

The vegetation zones result from (1) a severe continental climate characterized by very cold winter temperatures (as low as −52°C) and high summer temperatures of >40°C in the Gobi; (2) elevation changes that range from about 4,400m on the western border in the Altai Mountains to 500 m in the eastern steppes; and (3) short growing seasons, especially in the high mountains and northern part of the country. A low precipitation regime (100–400 mm) extends over about 82% of the country. For most of the nation, the precipitation is relatively variable, both spatially and temporally, resulting in a "non-equilibrium ecological system. Scoones (1999) provides an overview of non-equilibrium dynamics and how this new paradigm offers opportunities for interactions between social and natural sciences. In these systems, plant-herbivore interactions are weakly coupled and environmental degradation from livestock grazing is often wrongly blamed for "natural" conditions (Behnke and Scoones, 1993; Ellis and Swift, 1988). However, ecological systems are complex and exhibit a continuum between equilibrium and non-equilibrium characteristics, and livestock can significantly impact vegetation attributes even in areas considered to be dominated by "non-equilibrium dynamics" (Fernandez-Gimenez and Allen-Diaz, 1999).

Mongolia's fauna, like its vegetation, represents a mixture of species from the northern taiga of Siberia, the steppe, and the deserts of Central Asia. The fauna of the country includes at least 136 species of mammals, 436 birds, eight amphibians, 22 reptiles, 75 fish, and numerous invertebrates (http://www.un-mongolia.mn/archives/wildher/biodiv.htm). Animal species inhabiting Mongolia's rangelands exist relatively intact, especially compared to other grassland ecosystems worldwide. People have extirpated few species from Mongolia's grasslands and one species that went extinct in the wild, the Przewalski's horse (*Equus przewalski*), has been successfully reintroduced into two regions. Today, of the species known to previously inhabit Mongolia in historic times (the past 1,000 years), only the dhole (*Cuon alpinus*) remains absent from Mongolia's rangelands, although the nominate subspecies of saiga (*Saigatatarica tatarica*) has also disappeared.

Several additional species are considered threatened or endangered in Mongolia, but even many of these persist in much larger populations than in surrounding nations. For example, Mongolia boasts the world's largest populations of many ungulates, including Mongolian gazelle, goitered gazelle (*Gazella subgutturosa*), khulan or Asian wild ass (*Equus hemionus*), Mongolian saiga (*S. t. mongolica*), argali (*Ovis ammon*), and wild Bactrian camel (*Camelus bactrianus ferus*) (Amgalanbaatar et al., 2002; Mix et al., 1995, 2002; Reading et al., 2001). Similarly, small carnivores, such as Pallas' cats (*Otocolobus manul*) and corsac foxes (*Vulpes corsac*), appear to exist in relatively large populations. Large carnivores, such as snow leopards (*Uncia uncia*), are faring less well; however, relatively large populations of wolves (*Canis lupus*) are common across much of Mongolian rangelands.

The situation is similar with the country's avifauna, although many species of birds are declining due primarily to mortality outside of Mongolia. Birdlife International (2003) lists four species of grasslands birds that inhabit Mongolia as vulnerable: the imperial eagle (*Aquila heliaca*), lesser kestrel (*Falco naumanni*), great bustard (*Otis tarda*), and white-throated bushchat (*Saxicola insignis*). The latter may only retain a breeding population in Mongolia. Mongolia's grasslands support relatively large populations of most of those species, as well as cinereous vultures (*Aegypius monachus*) and saker falcons (*Falco cherrug*), especially compared with surrounding areas. Henderson's ground jays (*Podices hendersoni*) and Houbara's bustards (*Chlamydotis undulata*) survive in the more arid desert and desert steppe communities.

Riparian and wetland systems embedded within Mongolian rangelands are home to globally significant populations of waterfowl and wading birds, including several species of cranes. Birdlife International (2003) lists seven globally important bird areas in the steppe wetlands of Mongolia. The only breeding population of the conservation-dependent Dalmatian pelican (*Pelicanus crispus*) in East Asia, nests in Airag Nuur in western Mongolia (Birdlife International, 2003). In addition, these wetlands are particularly important for breeding populations of several globally vulnerable or endangered species, such as swan geese (*Anser cygnoides*), white-naped cranes (*Grus vipio*), relict gulls (*Larus relictus*), white-headed ducks (*Oxyura leucocephala*), and non-breeding populations of the critically endangered Siberian crane (*G. leucogeranus*) and vulnerable hooded crane (*G. monacha*) (Birdlife International, 2003). A wide variety of less threatened species of water birds also depend on Mongolia's steppe wetlands.

The status of Mongolia's herptifauna, invertebrates, fishes, and smaller mammals remains less studied and therefore more poorly understood. In all probability, most of these species are thriving or at least faring better in Mongolia than in surrounding nations because of the small number of dams and other hydrological projects and the previously mentioned low levels of industrialization, cultivation, and exotic species introductions in Mongolia.

Protected Areas

Mongolia boasts a centuries old tradition of nature conservation using protected areas (Johnstad and Reading, 2003). Chinggis Khan created Mongolia's first protected area to protect game species nearly 800 years ago and Bogdkhan Mountain Strictly Protected Area, first established in 1778, represents one of the world's oldest continuously protected areas (Chimed-Ochir, 1997; Enebish and Myagmasuren, 2000). Nevertheless, creation of a comprehensive system of protected areas developed slowly until the 1990s. Following the political and economic transformation of 1991, Mongolia has shown a strong commitment to establishing a modern network of protected areas based upon principles of landscape ecology (Enebish and Myagmasuren, 2000; Reading and et al., 1999). In 1992, the Mongolian Parliament or "Ikh Khural" adopted a goal of placing 30% of the nation in some form of protected status (Chimed-Ochir, 1997). Enebish and Myagmarsuren (2000) also provide a time frame and list potential areas for protected designations that will meet the goal of 30% of the total area of Mongolia protected by 2030. Since 1992, Mongolia has rapidly increased the number and area of protected areas (Figure 1) and in 1994, the Mongolian Parliament passed a new "Protected Areas Law" (Wingard and Odgerel, 2001). This law, which went into effect in 1995, recognizes four primary categories of protected areas in Mongolia: strictly protected areas, national parks, nature reserves, and national monuments (Table 1).

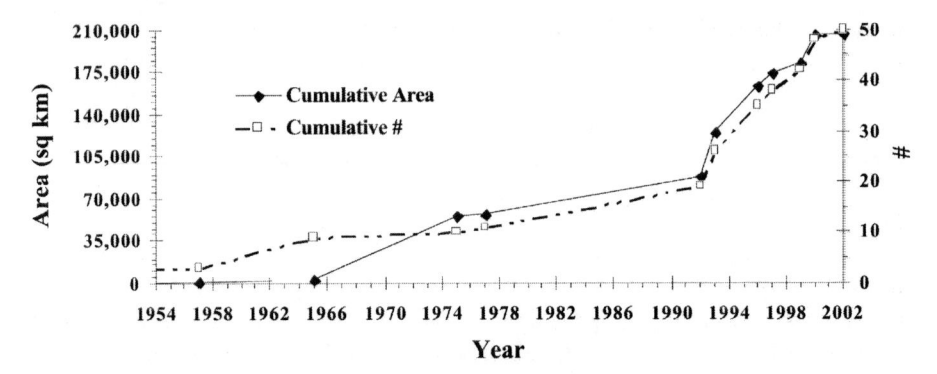

Figure 1. Increase in the area and number of protected areas in Mongolia (1954–2002). Note the rapid increase in both number and area of protected areas from 1992 to 2002.

Table 1. Mongolian protected area designations.

Designation	Definition
Strictly Protected Areas	Areas whose natural conditions are very well preserved; represent areas of natural and scientific importance; and are protected to ensure environmental balance. Human use is severely restricted.
National Conservation Parks	Areas whose natural conditions are relatively well preserved, and which have historical, cultural, scientific, educational, and ecological importance.
Nature Reserves	Areas protected for conservation, preservation, and restoration of natural features, resources, and wealth. Reserves are designated as Ecological, Biological, Paleontological or Geological.
National Monuments	Areas protected to preserve the natural heritage of unique formations and historical and cultural sites. Areas are designated as Natural Monuments or Historical and Cultural Monuments.

As of 2002, Mongolia's 50 protected areas covered more than 20.68 million hectares—over 13% of the country (Figure 1). The network includes strictly protected areas (50.7% of the total area protected in Mongolia), national parks (40.1%), nature reserves (8.8%), and monuments (0.4%) (Johnstad and Reading, 2003). As of 2003, there were also 552 relatively small provincial protected areas scattered throughout the nation, covering 3.1 million ha (Anonymous, 2003).

Rangelands remain under-represented in the Mongolian protected areas system, with only 1.97% of steppe, 2.73% of forest-steppe, and 3.41% of desert-steppe ecosystems protected (Enebish and Myagmarsuren, 2000; Johnstad and Reading, 2003). As is common with most nations, protected areas dominate in regions little utilized by people, such as high mountains, desert, and border regions. Still, the inequity in the distribution of protected areas by biome has been recognized by Mongolian conservationists and many conservationists advocate rectifying this situation with new protected areas proposals (e.g., Enebish and Myagmarsuren, 2000).

According to the Protected Areas Law, Mongolian strictly protected areas and national parks should be divided into zones with different management regimes (Wingard and Odgerel, 2001). Using the biosphere reserve model, strictly protected areas, and national parks are managed with zones that ideally lead to increasing nature protection toward the center of the protected area. Under the law, protected area zonation includes pristine, conservation, and limited use zones for strictly protected areas and special, travel, and tourism, and limited use zones for national parks. The level of protection afforded to natural features, flora, and fauna varies by zone, differing even between limited use zones in strictly protected areas and national parks. In addition, the 1997 Mongolian Law on Buffer Zones permits the creation of multiple use zones around protected areas that permits even greater development and use of natural resources than do the internal zones of protected areas (Wingard and Odgerel, 2001). Thus far, buffer zones have only been established for strictly protected areas and national parks.

With the significant land area placed in protected area status and the potential for a much larger area to be placed in protected status, there is a need to understand how well protected areas in Mongolia conserver sources and how they may impact historical communal land use. Management plans and actions within protected areas remain rudimentary for most protected areas in Mongolia (Johnstad and Reading, 2003; Reading et al., 1999). Notable exceptions do occur where international aid organizations have invested resources (e.g., Khustain Nuruu and Gobi Gurvan Saikhan National Parks) (Reading et al., 1999). For example, although most, if not all, protected areas have established management zones where pertinent, these zones have meant little in terms of actual management to date (Bedunah and Schmidt, 2004; Johnstad and Reading, 2003; Maroney, this proceedings). As we discuss below, most protected areas receive insufficient resources and lack the expertise to even develop management plans, let alone implement management actions that vary by zones. Nevertheless, there is evidence of progress toward improved management and establishment of a system of protected areas is a good first step for protecting and conserving natural resources (Reading et al., 1999; Schmidt, this proceedings) and may help pastoralists to maintain their livelihoods (Bedunah and Schmidt, 2004).

Pastoralism—Pre-1990s
Pastoralism has been the dominant land use in Mongolia for millennia, and at first appearance, Mongolian's maintain livestock in much of the same ways as their ancestors. Grazing systems are transhumant with winter bases for protection of livestock from severe winter conditions. Traditionally, herders moved their livestock to make the best use of available forage and water on their allotted spring, summer, autumn, and winter pastures, and they required skill to ensure that livestock were sufficiently fat going into winter to reduce winter losses. However, changes during the 20th century altered pastoral systems with ramifications for sustainable use of grazing lands. We briefly describe some of the historical aspects of the pastoral system, recent changes, and ramifications for sustainable use of rangelands. For detailed reviews of pastoral social economic units, historical land tenure, and pastoral systems see Bazargur et al. (1993), Fernandez-Gimenez (1999), Germeraad and Enebish (1996), Humphrey (1978), and Jagchid and Hyer (1979), Muller and Bold (1996), and Sneath (1999).

For several centuries prior to the communist era (pre-1921), land tenure was feudal and stock management transhumant with family groups as units. Livestock were herded using seasonal migrations and a rotation of moves, often fairly rapidly, over an area. Each herder owned a winter camp that usually included a corral and at least a small amount of shelter. In years of poor forage, herders traveled further to find adequate pasture. The distance herders moved their livestock or camps depended on the ecological characteristics of their grazing lands; herders in less productive zones, for example, the Gobi, moved livestock greater distances and were "more nomadic" than herders in the steppe. Also, herders with many livestock would move more often and over greater distances because the number of livestock necessitated more moves. Feudal officials allotted grazing areas on the principle that a person with many herds should have more and better land (Humphrey, 1978). Grazing was allowed only within the circuit of common lands (khoshuun) held by the feudal lord and migration outside would bring some kind of punishment for the herder and possibly his prince.

With Mongolia's independence from China in 1921, and a move toward Soviet communism, the feudal system was abolished, religion strictly suppressed, and administrative units altered from the larger khoshuun to the smaller sum districts. In general, little formal regulation occurred during this period, migrations of livestock were reduced, but some customary rights remained within administrative units and traditional neighborhood groups worked together (Fernanedez-Gimenez, 1999). The first attempt to form herding collectives was in 1928. However, the majority of the herders refused collectivization and the policy of compulsory enforcement was abandoned. In the 1950s, the government gave existing collectives massive aid and strongly encouraged people to join. Private herders were heavily taxed, but at this time, joining a collective permitted some ownership of private stock. By 1960, the government enacted a compulsory law that required all herders to join a collective. The goal of collectivization was to create a surplus of livestock products to feed urban populations, both in and out of Mongolia. These herding collectives, called "negdels," occupied territories the size of a sum, a subdivision of a province. The government assigned each collective herds and a territory. It further subdivided each territory into land assigned to herding brigades to carry out the main work. Brigades were specialized to manage only certain kinds of herds and further divided into units called "suur," which generally consisted of three or four households. Suur were further specialized to manage one area, perhaps only castrated rams, or 1- and 2-year-old lambs, or rams and male goats, or cross-bred sheep, or goat kids separated in autumn.

During collectivization several livestock and range management problems were reported. Separating goats and sheep in winter apparently caused heavy winter losses of goats in some areas because the sheep kept the goats warm in winter. Large, specialized herds also concentrated grazing use and changed forage use patterns. Herders preferred to remain close to the services provided by sum centers, threatening to overuse nearby pastures, but apparently the brigade councils sent suurs out to distant pastures (Humphrey, 1978). Livestock movement was strongly regulated, but the long distance movements possible in earlier times were much more restricted.

By the early 1990s, livestock collectives collapsed with the dismantling of the command economy. The collectives distributed their property in two phases in 1991 and 1992, with a large share of the herds distributed among members (Bruun, 1996). New herding households attained an almost unlimited and unprecedented freedom of choice with respect to lifestyle, livestock management, and economic activities

(Brunn, 1996), with little or no formal regulatory structures to control livestock grazing. This "new freedom" also moved risk from the collective to the individual household. In many areas, and likely all of Mongolia, the lack of strong formal or informal institutions to regulate livestock movement led to declining mobility and increasing out-of-season grazing and trespassing and associated conflicts (Agriteam Canada, 1997; Fernandez-Gimenez, 1999; Swift and Mearns, 1993).

Livestock Numbers
Total animal numbers did not fluctuate greatly as Mongolia moved into collectivization (Figure 2). In fact, animal numbers were somewhat higher in the 1930s and early 1940s compared to collective period (1960s–1990s). This is somewhat surprising because collectivization led to increased inputs, such as veterinary support, greater mechanization in hay production, increased livestock movement, and development of water sources, and because a push for more production accompanied the command economy. However, Mongolian rangelands were apparently close to being "fully stocked" by the 1930s. Sheehy (1996) estimated that there are approximately 60 million sheep forage units available in Mongolia and in 1940 livestock sheep units were about 56 million. Collectivization also introduced changes in the proportion of types of livestock raised in different ecological zones and other management changes that reduced the efficiency of livestock production. For example, during collective times birth rates for private livestock exceeded those for collective livestock (Bedunah and Miller, 1995).

After the central government relinquished control over livestock production in the early 1990s, livestock numbers increased rapidly from about 25.2 million head in 1993 to over 33.5 million head in 1999 (Byambatseren, 2004; NSO-Mongolia, 2004). Livestock numbers reached an all time high in 1999, as calculated as total numbers or on an animal equivalent basis (Sheep Forage Units) (Figures 2 and 3). Numbers of goats increased most dramatically, rising 215% from 1990–1999 (Figures 2 and 3), resulting in a growing preponderance of goats in Mongolia overall (Figure 4). Horses and cattle numbers also increased dramatically, rising 140 and 135%, respectively (Figures 2 and 3). It difficult to assess the accuracy of historic livestock numbers, but during the communist era (pre 1992) it is likely that livestock estimates were accurate. During the late 1990s, it became more difficult to evaluate accuracy and Kennett (2000) reported that estimates were often 25% lower than actual numbers, as herders under-reported their holdings to reduce taxes paid on livestock.

The increased livestock herds in the 1990s were undoubtedly related to greater numbers of herding families (Figure 5) and increases in numbers of livestock for many herders (Figure 6). The increase in the number of herders possibly resulted from Mongolia's "culture of pastoralism." Many Mongolians consider pastoralism to be an ideal lifestyle and thus returned to their "roots" as herders because they were now free to do so and because they retained the knowledge of, or at least were not too far removed from, herding and pastoralism. However, for some people herding became a necessity as they lost their jobs and other livelihood opportunities disappeared with the collapse of the command economy. The degree to which these individuals retained herding as part of their past likely influenced their ability to transition into this occupation;

while most apparently succeeded, others failed and the number of herders decreased each year between 2000 and 2003 (Figure 5). From 1992 to 1999 the number of "small herds" decreased, medium sized herds was generally stable, and large herds increased (Figure 6). Increasing mean herd sizes reflects a general increase in wealth. Despite growing pastoral wealth, a large percentage of herders maintained small herds (<100 animals), while only a few herders owned very large herds. This disparity in wealth is a recent phenomenon on the rangelands of Mongolia, not seen since the feudal lords controlled livestock wealth.

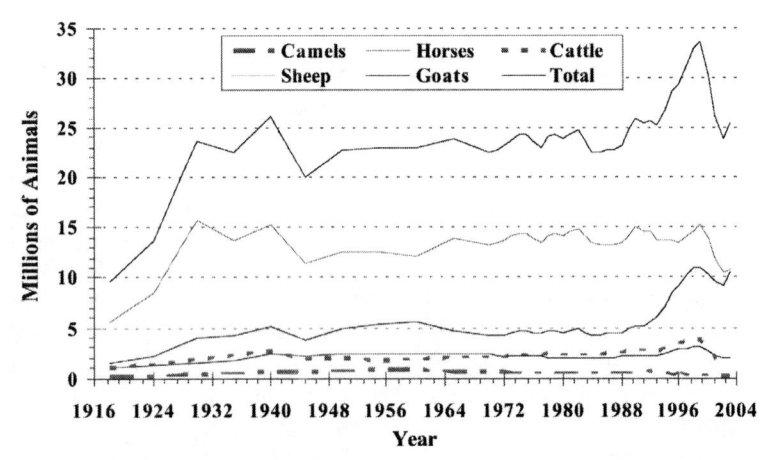

Figure 2. Livestock trends in Mongolia, 1918–2004.
Source: Mongolian National Statistical Office.

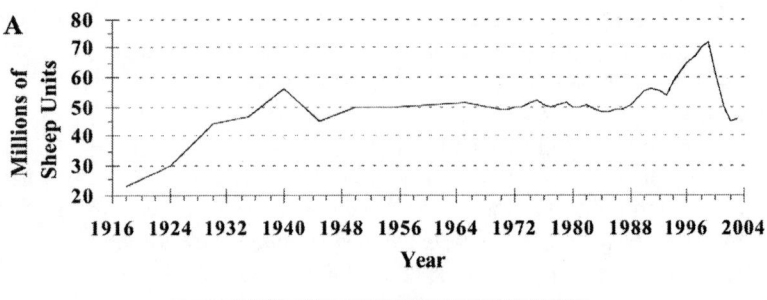

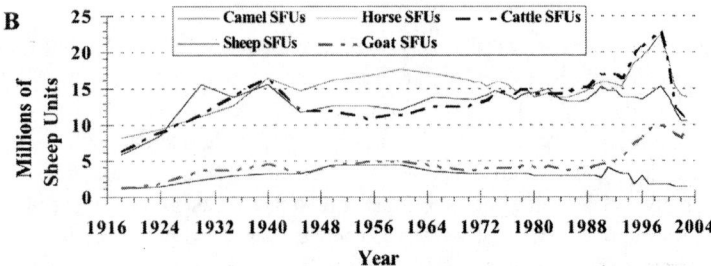

Figure 3. Livestock trends in Mongolia using Sheep Forage Units, 1918–2002. (A) All species combined.

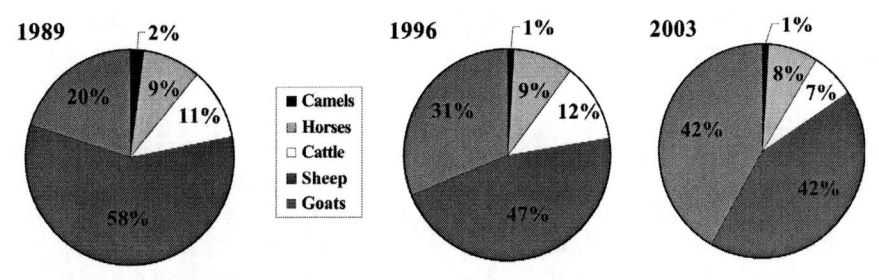

Conserving Biodiversity on Mongolian Rangelands 221

Data Source: Mongolian National Statistical Office (Byambatseren 2004, NSO-Mongolia 2004).
Figure 4. Change in the percentage of each type of livestock in Mongolia, 1989–2003.

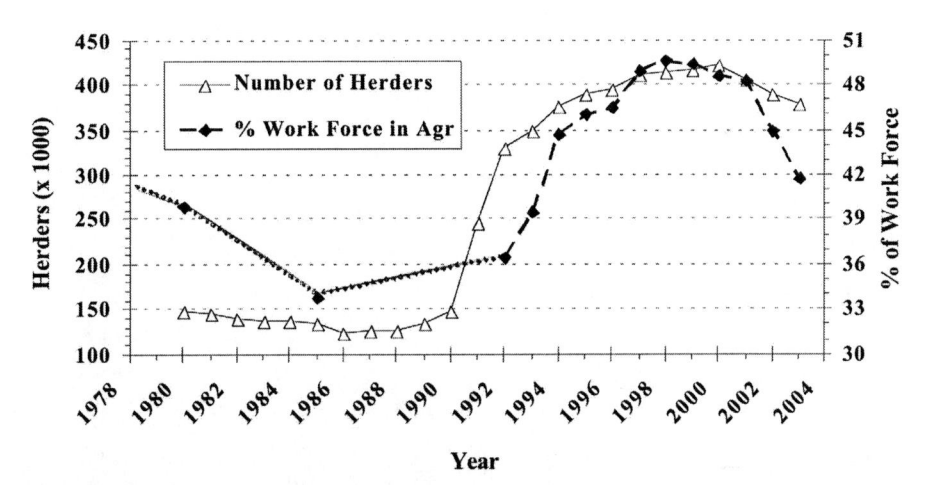

Figure 5. Change in the number of herders in Mongolia and the percentage of the Mongolian workforce engaged in agriculture (the vast majority of whom are herders).

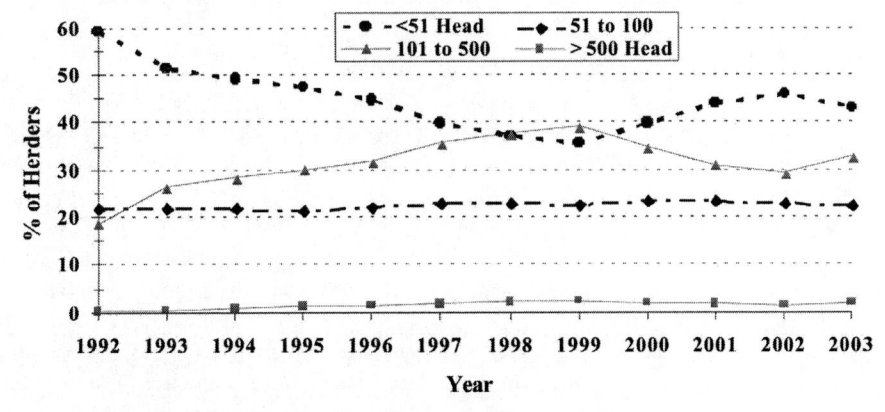

Figure 6. Change in distribution of herd sizes over time in Mongolia.
Source: Mongolian National Statistical Office (Byambatseren, 2004; NSO-Mongolia, 2004).

In the winter of 1999–2000, and again in 2000–2001, dzuds (a general Mongolian term for various winter conditions during which livestock cannot forage) struck much of Mongolia causing severe livestock losses (Table 2) and a reduction in average herd sizes (Figures 3 and 6). Summer droughts undoubtedly made the impacts of winter dzuds more severe, but determining the extent to which overstocked ranges increased drought severity is difficult to quantify. The large losses of livestock during this period exceeded any since the 1944–1945 dzud (Table 2). These losses not only impacted pastoral livelihoods, but the national economy; the overall Mongolian economy grew a mere 1% in 2001 and 3.9% in 2002 (Mearns, 2004). The Government of Mongolia (2003, from Mearns, 2004) estimated that without the dzud impacts, economic growth from 1999 to 2002 would have been on the order of 8%.

Table 2. Livestock losses in Mongolia through drought and dzud over the last 60 years.

Years	Type of Disaster	Losses (# of Head) Adult Stock	Young Stock
1944-45	Drought + dzud	8,100,000	1,100,000
1954-55	Dzud	1,900,000	300,000
1956-57	Dzud	1,500,000	900,000
1967-68	Drought + dzud	2,700,000	1,700,000
1976-77	Dzud	2,000,000	1,600,000
1986-87	Dzud	800,000	900,000
1993	Dzud	1,600,000	1,200,000
1996-97	Dzud	600,000	500,000
1999-00	Drought + dzud	3,000,000	1,200,000
2000-01	Drought + dzud	3,400,000	?

Source: http://www.un-mongolia.mn/archives/disaster/

Since the mid-1990s, indices of Mongolian herder wealth have increased as the percentage of pastoralists owning jeeps or trucks, motorcycles, or televisions, and with access to electricity (usually through solar panels or wind mills) continues to rise (Figure 7) (Byambatseren, 2004; NSO-Mongolia, 2004). However, as with livestock figures, these statistics belie the fact that most herders remain poor. The Mongolian government considers a herd size of about 150 animals as the minimum necessary to maintain a household's livelihood (World Bank, 2003). In 2002, about 75% of herding families retained herds smaller than this threshold (Figure 6) (World Bank, 2003). Of course, many of these families obtain additional income from other sources. Indeed, herding represents supplementary income for many people whose incomes are too low to sustain themselves and their families. Thus, overgrazing increasingly degrades areas around towns and cities (Ferguson, 2003).

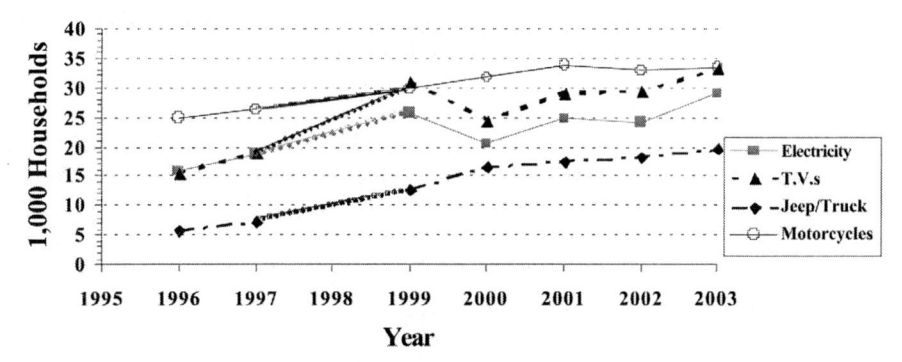

Figure 7. Changes in indices of Mongolian herder wealth over time.
Note: No data for 1998.
Source: Mongolian National Statistical Office (Byambatseren, 2004; NSO-Mongolia, 2004).

We suggest that stabilizing and improving the health of the nation's livestock herd is crucial to the long-term stability of the nation, especially given the importance of livestock production to such a large proportion of the population. Mearns (2004) stressed the neglect of the livestock sector in development priorities and thus the decline in agricultural productivity. In the past, Mongolians stressed the need for creating reserve pastures and forage reserves (hay and other supplements) for times of shortages and for providing ways of protecting animals from unfavorable conditions (Minjigdorj, 1995). Although the level of hay production that occurred during the highly subsidized Soviet period is impractical today, we argue that historic practices of using reserve pastures and native hay production are necessary to avoid dramatic livestock losses and ensure food security. This requires a more moderate or conservative level of stocking to ensure better animal condition and less pasture degradation. Potential causes of pasture degradation can be complex and are often ultimately attributable to complex institutional changes. However, ultimately animal numbers that are not in balance with forage resources will impact rangelands and the animals (both livestock and wildlife) that use these grasslands. Ward and Ngairorue (2000) discuss the extremely long-term nature of declining productivity or desertification brought about by heavy grazing in arid habitats. For in-depth discussions of issues and concerns regarding desertification and identification of desertification see Leach and Mearns (1996) and Swift (1996). We believe there is a strong need for research to better understand grazing impacts to ecological systems in Mongolia. For example, the much greater numbers and percentage of goats (Figures 2 and 4) have no doubt impacted shrub communities by increasing browse use. Thus, researchers need to quantify long-term impacts or changes that may negatively impact natural resources.

Mongolian Culture and Conservation

"Mongolians have a deep reverence for their environment and a close symbiotic relationship with the natural world (UNDP, 2000, p. 34)." The roots of Mongolian culture stretch back thousands of years and emanate from animistic beliefs that still strongly influence thoughts and practices in the country, especially among some minority groups (Finch, 1996; Germeraad and Enebish, 1996). Tibetan style Buddhism arrived in Mongolia in the 1500s and quickly and profoundly affected the culture of the nation (Gilberg and Svantesson, 1996). Although ruthlessly repressed by the communist government in the 1930s, the influence of Buddhism remains powerful today and is experiencing a marked resurgence (Bruun and Odgaard, 1996). Buddhism teaches love and respect for nature that usually translates into strong support for conservation (Germeraad and Enebish, 1996; World Bank, 2003).

After a brief period as a Buddhist theocracy, Mongolia became the world's second communist nation in 1921. Yet, even under communism the country's policies maintained support for conserving and protecting the wildlife and natural resources of the nation. With the shift from communism to democracy and capitalism in the early 1990s, the government made an initial, strong drive for conservation, reflecting the desires of most of the populace (UNDP, 2000). Yet that same shift to a free market economy hastened economic growth and has more recently resulted in policies directed at natural resources exploitation (Ferguson, 2003). Given the vast, untapped mineral wealth, rapidly changing policies regarding resource development, and low standard of living affecting most Mongolians, it is perhaps not too surprising that the last few administrations have faced numerous corruption scandals, with several officials convicted and sent to prison. Unfortunately, modern approaches to conservation have not kept pace with this altered political and economic landscape.

Today, most Mongolians still embrace nature conservation, at least in word (UNDP, 2000). This attitude appears particularly prevalent in rural areas, including pastoralists. For example, when the government removed a portion of a National Conservation Park in the Gobi, the local people rallied and petitioned for its return (unsuccessfully). Similarly, many pastoralists lobby for the creation of new protected areas (Reading et al., 1999). Most protected areas in Mongolia allow grazing by domestic livestock, and even areas that prohibit livestock by law remain largely unmonitored and pastoralists continue to use most of these areas at least periodically. As these parks begin to grapple with issues of grazing management, including restricting livestock numbers and creating zones of livestock exclusion it will be interesting to see how pastoralists react (Reading et al., 1999).

A romanticized view of nomadic pastoralism and nature conservation continue to pervade the psyche of most Mongolians (Germeraad and Enebish, 1996; Reading et al., 1999). Yet, increasing desires to "westernize" and improve standards of living challenge these traditional values. Cultural changes in urban Mongolia appear meteoric to us and are increasingly affecting rural Mongolia as well. Balancing tradition with change affects all nations, of course, but in Mongolia that change comes coupled with the disruptive transition from communism and a command economy to democracy and a free market. And in Mongolia, pastoral nomadism arguably defines their traditional culture more than in most other nations with a relatively large pastoral component. Pastoralism certainly comprises a larger portion of Mongolia's economy (15.9% in 2003) than most other nations (NSO-Mongolia, 2004). So, effectively conserving Mongolia's rangelands would not only help ensure a sustainable rural economy, but also help preserve the nation's cultural and natural heritage (Reading et al., 1999).

The new constitution and variety of new laws passed since 1991 codify the strong conservation values of most Mongolians. The constitution guarantees every citizen the right to a healthy environment. In keeping with this mandate, the Mongolian parliament, or Ikh Khural, passed a number of new environmental laws since the early 1990s (Wingard and Odgerel, 2001). While these laws and subsequent regulations represent an important first step, their effectiveness is limited by a serious lack of implementation and enforcement (e.g., see Amgalanbaatar et al., 2002). Similarly, as we noted above, Mongolia has rapidly expanded its protected areas network in recent years, but that expansion has not enjoyed a commiserate increase in the capacity of the Mongolian Protected Areas Bureau to manage the new reserves (Johnstad and Reading, 2003; Reading et al., 1999). To help address this short-coming, several international aid organizations (such as the United Nations Development Programme, German Technical Advisory Cooperation or GTZ, the Ministry for International Cooperation of the Netherlands, the US Agency for International Development or USAID); non-governmental conservation and environmental organizations (such as the World Wide Fund for Nature-Mongolia, Mongolian Association for the Conservation of Nature and Environment, Denver Zoological Foundation, Philadelphia Academy of Natural Sciences, International Crane Foundation, Wildlife Conservation Society); and universities (e.g. University of Montana, Columbia University, Colorado State University) have developed and begun implementing programs to train protected areas staff, develop management plans, involved local people, and provide much needed funding (Johnstad and Reading, 2003).

The end of communism also led to a rapid increase in the number of non-governmental organizations (NGOs) focused on the environment and nature conservation, and by 2003 there were several environmental NGOs registered with the government (Anonymous, 2003). Indeed, Mongolian conservationists recognized the need to increase the effectiveness of the growing number of small environmental NGOs by creating an umbrella organization, the Union of Mongolian Environmental, Non-governmental Organizations (UMENGO) in 2000 (Mooza, 2003). The NGOs are becoming increasingly involved in conservation initiatives, but lack of resources and professional capacity limit the effectiveness of most of them (Anonymous, 2003). Still, the overall capacity of Mongolian environmental NGOs grows yearly and enthusiasm among members remains high, boding well for the future (Mooza, 2003).

THREATS AND CHALLENGES TO RANGELAND CONSERVATION

Mongolia's rangelands persist largely unfragmented and only minimally degraded (UNDP, 2000). Still, threats and challenges to maintaining this situation are growing, primarily in the form of increased natural resources exploitation, growing conflicts between pastoralism and conservation, and a lack of conservation capacity to address these issues.

Natural Resources Exploitation

Mongolia harbors vast reserves of many natural resources that have largely gone untapped until recently. The country's mineral wealth includes vast deposits of gold, copper, uranium, fluorspar, and molybdenum (MNE, 2001; Sanders, 1996). Additionally important minerals include iron, silver, tin, tungsten, zinc, lead, phosphates, and nickel (MNE, 2001). Vast coal deposits and more modest oil and gas reserves also exist throughout large portions of the nation. Since the transition to a free market economy, mining activity has increased dramatically (Brooke, 2003; Ferguson, 2003; UNDP, 2000). For example, gold production increased by over 11 times (1,100%) from 1993 to 2000 as the number of mines increased to 150 (MNE, 2001). In addition, numerous wildcat mines illegally excavate gold throughout the country. By 2004, companies already licensed 29.9% of Mongolia's territory for exploration and mining and over 6,000 significant deposits of 80 minerals have been found (Mineral Resources Authority of Mongolia, 2004).

Because minerals represent 15–20% of the nation's GNP and 57% of its exports (MNE, 2001; Mongolian National Mining Association, 2004), the mining industry exerts tremendous influence on environmental management in Mongolia. As the Mineral Resources Authority of Mongolia (2004, p. 6) states, "[Mining] opportunities are facilitated by a supportive government attitude and alluring foreign investment business environment." Although mining companies are required to prepare environmental impact assessments, undertake reclamation activities, and place 50% of their environmental protection budget in a government account prior to beginning work (Wingard and Odgerel, 2001), the Mongolian Ministry for Nature and Environment states that "none of these laws are enforced" (MNE, 2001, p. 17). As mining continues in the absence of law enforcement, companies have simply ignored environmental mitigation and restoration requirements (Brooke, 2003; Ferguson, 2003).

Pressure for increased mining activity continues to mount and Farrington (2005) suggests the largest threat to the protected-area system from mining has come from within the government itself. In June 2002, the Ministry of Nature and the Environment proposed deprotecting 434,000 ha of land in 10 protected areas and at the same time, the Mineral Resources Authority of Mongolia proposed deprotecting an additional 1.5 million ha of land in eight protected areas (Farrington, 2005). These motions were later rejected by the Mongolian parliament, but a new proposal in December 2003 proposed deprotecting 3.1 million ha or approximately 15% of Mongolia's protected-areas system, in four different protected areas so that the areas could be opened to mining (Brooke, 2003; Farington, 2005).The Mongolian conservation community has strenuously opposed such actions, as have most local people (Anonymous, 2004; Brooke, 2003; Johnstad and Reading, 2003). Nevertheless, the precedent was set in the early 1990s when the government deprotected a portion of Three Beauties of the Gobi National Conservation Park to permit the establishment of a gold mine. In addition to resource extraction, talks are underway to de-protect portions of border parks to allow the construction of transportation corridors (raillines and paved roads) to facilitate the exportation of natural resources to Russia and especially China (Anonymous, 2004; Birdlife International, 2003).

Despite the increasing extraction of minerals from Mongolia, the nation's refining industry has not developed (Wingard and Odgerel, 2001). As a result, a source of economic development is being lost. Similarly, mining and taxation laws generous to extractors permit companies to exploit natural resources, while paying modest taxes and royalties to the government (Anonymous, 2004; Brooke, 2003). For example under the Minerals Law of Mongolia, passed in 1997 and amended in 2001, exploration fees are US$0.05/ha for the 1st year, US$0.10/ha for the 2nd and 3rd year, and then rises to US1.50/ha by the 7th year (Ariuna and Mashbat, 2002). Mining fees are US$5.00/ha for years 1–3, US$7.50/ha for years 4–5, and US$10.00/ha thereafter (Ariuna and Mashbat, 2002). There are no customs fees or limits on repatriated money earned from mining (Wingard and Odgerel, 2001). Mining royalties are set at 2.5% for all minerals, except gold (7.5%) (Ariuna and Mashbat, 2002). In addition, the government is not required to approve business or operational plans; foreigners can work for extraction companies; and firms can export raw materials (Mineral Resources Authority of Mongolia, 2004). Given this situation, the benefits to Mongolia seem meager.

Conflicts Between Pastoralism and Conservation
Pastoralists remain among the staunchest supporters of conservation initiatives in Mongolia, including the creation of new protected areas, yet their knowledge of the meaning of terms like "biodiversity" and of Mongolian environmental laws and conservation activities remains low (Anonymous, 2003). Still, conflicts between pastoralism and conservation do arise and require attention. For example, Agriteam Canada (1997) raised concerns over additional constraints placed on herders by the establishment of large protected areas. They reported that in Khustain Nuruu Nature Reserve, established for the reintroduction of Przewalskii horse, a reduction in total area available for herders in Altanbulag sum created conflicts associated with a loss of traditional winter and spring camps. Establishment of the Gobi B Ecological Reserve also reportedly reduced winter grazing areas for local herders (Agriteam Canada, 2003). We found no information on conflicts associated with removing domestic livestock from protected areas established before the 1990s; however, O'Gara (1988), in describing the success of the Khokh Serkhi Strictly Protected Area for conserving wildlife, reported that within 5 years of its establishment in 1977, all pastoralists and their livestock had been removed. We do not know how the removal of pastoralists was achieved or the impacts on those pastoralists, but we assume that displacement of pastoralists did impact their lives. A more recent study reported that the creation of Gobi Gurvan Saikhan National Park was a positive influence on some communities of pastoralists living in the park, largely because of planning and support by GTZ (Bedunah and Schmidt, 2004). Bedunah and Schmidt (2004) reported that the pastoral issues identified in Gobi Gurvan Saikhan National Park were not associated with the park, but were issues faced by the entire country associated with the lack of land-use controls for addressing livestock grazing. This situation has arisen during the transition from the command economy to free-market system because of a lack of institutional controls and thus a deterioration to more or less free access of grazing lands (see Fernandez-Gimenez, 1999; Mearns, 2004).

Just after the transition to democracy, Sheehy (1996) suggested that most of the grazing land in Mongolia remained in good or excellent condition, and that degraded pastures responded favorably to reduced grazing pressure. At the time range scientists considered only about 11 million ha, or 7% of Mongolia's land area, of pasture land as degraded. However, livestock numbers rose markedly during the 1990s (Figures 2 and 3), resulting in greater degradation and increased desertification, especially in the more marginal desert steppe and desert regions (Amgalanbaatar et al., 2002). By 2001, government officials reported that over 70% of total pastureland was degraded and 7% was heavily degraded (MNE, 2001; UNDP, 2000); although, a recent World Bank report (2003) disputes these figures as likely being too high and not based on valid studies.

The increased degradation of pasturelands in Mongolia, whatever the current level, has been attributed to global climate change, vehicular damage, and especially over-grazing of relatively fragile rangelands (MNE, 2001; UNDP, 2000). Over-grazing resulted from an increase in the national livestock herd, drought, and poor management of livestock (e.g., reduced livestock movement by many pastoralists) associated with a loss of land use controls or institutional development for ensuring sustainable grazing management. The rapid increase in livestock, from 24.7 million in 1989 to about 33.6 million in 1999 (Byambatseren, 2004; NSO-Mongolia, 2004) (Figure 2), has been attributed to (1) reduced livestock prices that encouraged herders to maintain live animals rather than selling them for slaughter and (2) an increasing number of pastoralists as many urban residents turned to pastoralism as a way of life following the collapse of communism and a loss of other livelihood opportunities (MNE, 2001; Sheehy, 1996; UNDP, 2000; World Bank, 2003). Following two severe winters coupled with large expanses of drastically over-grazed pastures, the national herd size dropped dramatically to 23.9 million head by 2002 (Byambatseren, 2004) (Figure 2). Persistent droughts undoubtedly exacerbated overgrazing in some areas, but herders did not reduce animal numbers to balance animals with forage resource when conditions called for such actions. Reportedly, over 7 million head of livestock died (World Bank, 2003). Of course, wildlife also suffered from these impacts. At our argali research site in Ikh Nartiin Chuluu Nature Reserve, we witnessed the starvation deaths of dozens of argali and ibex as little forage remained following heavy livestock grazing.

The increased numbers of nomadic herders and livestock also meant increased displacement of wildlife from traditional pastures. For example, in western Mongolia, pastoralists are pushing higher and further into the mountains, increasing the stress on the ever more fragmented and declining argali populations that remain (Amgalanbaatar and Reading, 2000; Amgalanbaatar et al., 2002; Mallon et al., 1997; Schuerholz, 2001). We also recently discovered that domestic guard dogs predate on argali sheep (Reading et al., 2003). Indeed, domestic dogs represent one of the major sources of mortality for argali at our study site.

Pastoralists also displace wildlife by poaching (Pratt et al., 2004). Although the extent of poaching remains largely unstudied (but see Zahler et al., 2004), we have observed poachers throughout Mongolia at all times of the year while conducting our research, suggesting that it represents a significant source of mortality for ungulates. Pratt et al., (2004) examined reasons for rising poaching in Mongolia. Much of the increase occurs because of the rising market value of game animals in Asian markets and for meat, coupled with declining standard of living many people are facing during this difficult transition to a market economy. Pastoralists also readily admit to poaching wolves and snow leopards out of concern for livestock depredation. Although both species are faring relatively well in Mongolia, they remain heavily persecuted. Mongolian pastoralists do not actively herd or guard large livestock species, such as horses, cows, yaks, and camels. Instead, they permit these animals to roam relatively freely until required for slaughter, to provide products (e.g., milk, wool), or to serve as beasts of burden. As such, many depredations undoubtedly go undetected. Alternatively, many pastoralists blame large carnivores, especially wolves, for most large livestock losses that occur, despite the fact that disease, malnutrition, and other factors (theft and poisonous plants) probably represent the majority of missing animals.

An additional cause of mortality to wildlife, and a continued threat, is indiscriminate use of rodenticides. For example, the Mongolia Agricultural Ministry initiated massive Brandt's voles (*Microtus brandtii*) poisoning programs because of the perception that the voles compete with livestock. The poisons, zinc phosphate, and bromadiolone, were applied to grains and broadcast across vast expanses of steppe (Birdlife International, 2003; Natsagdorj and Batbayar, 2002). The pesticides kill far more than voles and other rodents, however, and massive dieoffs of several species of birds, small mammal carnivores, and even livestock have been reported (Birdlife International, 2003; Natsagdorj and Batbayar, 2002; Zahler et al., 2004). Ironically, the reason for the increased vole populations is likely associated with overgrazing and the subsequent shorter vegetation. Short vegetation enables voles populations to expand due to increased ability to detect predators (Birdlife International, 2003; Natsagdorj and Batbayar, 2002). The loss of vole predators will exacerbate the problem by facilitating future population irruptions at shorter time intervals (because there are fewer predators, whose slower population growth means they require more time to recover from the mass poisoning campaigns), to help stem the growth of vole populations.

Despite the generally high level of support that most pastoralists express for conservation, conflicts do arise with some conservation initiatives. Perhaps the most of important of these are the loss of traditional grazing rights and restricted rangeland access that come with the establishment of new protected areas. This source of conflict has the potential to increase dramatically, as protected areas become increasingly better and more actively managed. Although most protected areas permit some level of continued grazing by domestic animals, most also include or permit establishing special zones where grazing is restricted or prohibited for the benefit of wildlife (Wingard and Odgerel, 2001). In addition, many protected areas will require more active grazing management to sustain the unique plant and animal communities they were established to protect. As park managers remove pastoralists from protected areas, limit the number of livestock they graze, or restrict the seasonality of grazing, the potential for conflict rises.

Lack of Conservation Capacity
Arguably the greatest challenge to successfully conserving Mongolia's rangelands is the lack of conservation capacity that currently exists in the nation. A joint government-independent assessment found that Mongolia lacked adequate conservation capacity to conduct effective conservation actions (Anonymous, 2003). Luckily,

however, this challenge is probably the most easily addressed. The national assessment of conservation capacity found that problems stemmed primarily from too few staff, inadequate, or inappropriate professional training of staff, lack of experience among conservation professionals, and insufficient resources, both for field and office work (Anonymous, 2003).

Poor environmental monitoring and law enforcement well illustrate the lack of conservation capacity in Mongolia. Currently, monitoring and law enforcement are almost nonexistent. The government itself readily admits this problem (MNE, 2001). Lack of monitoring and enforcement stems from several factors, including lack of resources to monitor, lack of political will to prosecute, corruption, lack of adequate training, and the vast size of the nation (especially, relative to available resources) (Anonymous, 2003).

Mongolia remains a very poor nation (NSO-Mongolia, 2004). The nation's sparse resources mean that environmental monitoring usually receives inadequate funding. Mongolia invests only US$2 per km^2 in protected area management, well below the global mean of US$893 per km^2 or even the mean among developing nations of US$125 per km^2 (Anonymous, 2003). A mere 194 rangers patrol the nation's 20.7 million ha of protected areas and only one ranger per sum patrols the rest of the nation (Anonymous, 2003). And although every sum (like a county) employs an environmental ranger, most lack the resources necessary to permit the ranger to actually leave the sum center to monitor natural resources exploitation activities, patrol against poaching, and collect data on the state of the environment. To a lesser extent, the same is true for rangers of protected areas (sums are actually responsible for managing nature reserves, but most go unmanaged). As such, most natural resources exploitation occurs without any governmental oversight, especially for small operations (Anonymous, 2003). Natural resources exploitation will likely continue unless political will to counter this exploitation is generated.

Similarly, most rangers possess little to no equipment or training (Anonymous, 2003). Some rangers have benefited from limited training and equipment provisioning by international aid organizations, conservation organizations, and universities. Yet, generally such equipment and training remain insufficient, especially relative to the size of the enforcement task. Even when rangers are able to monitor their territories, they must confront poachers unarmed; they lack the means to determine whether or not mining activities are negatively impacting the environment; they generally do not have the capacity to collect evidence for effective prosecution; and so on. As such, even when monitoring occurs, it is usually ineffective (Anonymous, 2003). As a result, most pastoralists, resources extractors, and others are able to operate with little regard to the law or their impacts to the environment.

Lack of conservation capacity is not restricted to government agencies. Mongolian environmental NGOs face many of the same constraints as the nation's agencies of the 120 environmental NGOs, only 37 actively engage in activities; most remain simply organizations on paper (Anonymous, 2003). Even the 37 most active environmental NGOs struggle—80% of these lack stable finances, 60% have no permanent office space, and 25% are without paid staff (Anonymous, 2003). Only 20 environmental

NGOs employ >1 staff members and only four employ >10 (Anonymous, 2003). Finally, most environmental NGOs suffer from the same lack of resources and training as do the government agencies, seriously constraining their effectiveness.

IMPROVING PROSPECTS FOR CONSERVATION

Opportunities for successful conservation of Mongolia's rangelands in a manner that sustains both the pastoralist traditions of the nation and the wildlife of the steppes remain within our grasp. Yes, Mongolia is changing rapidly and threats are growing; but, Mongolian pastoralists are among the greatest allies of conservationists in that country. Better cooperation and integration of government agencies, Mongolian environmental NGOs, international donor and conservation NGOs, and local people arguably offers the best path toward more holistic and sustainable conservation of Mongolian rangelands.

Strengthening Protected Area Management

Mongolia's protected area system is currently under attack from natural resources extraction interests (Johnstad and Reading, 2003). The government largely supports the industry's initiatives, and many people believe that some change is likely. Not only does natural resource extraction threaten wildlife and scenic values, but it also may threaten customary grazing lands. We suggest that those opposed to the deprotection process need to engage those favoring the process in a constructive dialog to ensure wildlife and cultural values are considered and valued.

Although establishing new protected areas or expanding existing ones may be difficult given efforts to reduce the current system, many areas deserve protection to preserve important wildlife habitats and should be pursued. For example, some of the crucial breeding grounds of Mongolian gazelle remain unprotected and thus subject to development or degradation. As the wildlife of Mongolia is increasingly better studied, additionally vital habitats undoubtedly will be discovered and delineated. Biologists should work quickly to determine where these areas lie and conservationists should then move rapidly to protect them. In addition, most protected areas remain too small and isolated to protect viable populations of dependent wildlife species (Johnstad and Reading, 2003). Conservationists should determine the size and location of habitats required to conserve focal species. In many cases, protecting some form of linkage (e.g., corridors or small "stepping stone" reserves) may be easier and more effective than expanding reserves.

Finally, but perhaps most importantly, the capacity of Mongolia's protected areas agency requires serious improvement. A report issued by the Mongolian government and independent evaluators recommends improving conservation capacity through increased training; more and better equipment; better fund raising; improved and more frequent collaboration and cooperation with Mongolian and international environmental NGOs and donors; and better public awareness and education program, including training and empowering local people to assist with conservation through grassroots community groups (Anonymous, 2003). Such recommendations hold outside of protected areas as well. Conservationists should work with local people to determine areas that remain vital to wildlife, but cause minimal conflict with pastoralists. Community-based management then should be developed to manage these areas (Johnstad and Reading, 2003). Such community-based systems may provide a method of improving management at lower costs, while simultaneously reducing conflict.

Tourism
Many conservationists advocate nature-based tourism as an alternative to natural resources exploitation. In Mongolia, such ecotourism is unlikely to provide benefits to offset losses from foregoing exploitation. Although generally increasing, few tourists visit Mongolia each year. Officially, 50,835 tourists visited Mongolia in 2002 (Byambatseren, 2004). Because of the Severe Avian Respiratory Syndrome (SARS) scare, tourism dropped to 21,890 visitors in 2003; although some portion of the 180,558 people that visited Mongolia for "private purposes" were probably also tourists. (NSO-Mongolia, 2004). Of tourists that visited Mongolia in 2003, 78.9% came from East Asia and the Pacific and 17.6% came from Europe (NSO-Mongolia, 2004). In addition, the majority of these tourists likely came for cultural-based tourism, not ecotourism. Although cultural tourism in Mongolia requires conservation of rangelands, a small proportion of the nation's territory can accommodate the vast majority of that tourism. Therefore, while locally important, tourism will likely not facilitate efforts to conserve Mongolia's rangelands.

Still, nature-based tourism in Mongolia potentially represents a much larger source of additional revenue for conservation than is currently being realized. Protected areas in Mongolia generated about 30% of their budget from tourism (primarily), international aid, and collection of fines, which could be much higher if all fines issued were collected (Anonymous, 2003).

Ecotourism is increasing in Mongolia (Johnstad and Reading, 2003). Further increasing ecotourism and associated revenue requires additional capacity building in this sector as well, including improved infrastructure (accommodations, travel, etc.); better trained more knowledgeable guides; and more aggressive marketing. Most high end ecotourism to date has focused on fishing and trophy hunting, but we believe could be expanded, especially if improvements in law enforcement led to more and better wildlife viewing opportunities. However, tourism comes with its own ecological and socioeconomic impacts that largely remain unaddressed in Mongolia (Johnstad and Reading, 2003). As such, conservationists must strengthen their capacity to develop and manage ecotourism in a socially and ecologically sustainable manner.

Grazing Reform
Perhaps the greatest opportunity for improving rangeland conservation in Mongolia lies with grazing reform. Currently, the absence of any functioning formal structure for managing rangelands precludes effective conservation. Instead, grazing management lies in the hands of thousands of independent, semi-nomadic pastoralists, often with differing skill levels and goals. After several years of livestock declines and continually degrading rangelands, most pastoralists and government officials realize that a problem exists and livestock controls are necessary. Most are open to, if not actively

searching for, solutions. Schmidt (this proceeding) suggests that community organizations of herders are improving this situation and indeed, the process has begun with a conflict-laden land reform process currently underway.

Obviously, to succeed, any grazing reform requires the involvement of pastoralists during its development and implementation from the beginning. Yet, we also believe that wildlife biologists and conservationists should be included in discussions directed at grazing and rangeland management reform in Mongolia. Thus far, these interests have been excluded from active involvement in the grazing reform process. We believe it is crucial. In the US, public lands are to be managed for multiple-use. In Mongolia, there is appreciation of land for watersheds, aesthetic, and biodiversity values, as well as a lack of monitoring and management for ensuring these values. In fact, there seems to be a prevalent attitude by many Mongolians that livestock are a part of the natural system and thus are unlikely to degrade or negatively impact other values.

How best to manage grasslands to protect and conserve biodiversity and cultural diversity will depend on a number of variables. However, it seems logical that where grazing is practiced best management practices (BMPs) and resource management plans should be developed for the particular area. In some ways it may seem unnecessary to recommend BMPs for Mongolian herders who have a long history of herding; however, with the changes in the 20th century and a generation of "new herders" we strongly believe that development agencies should help Mongolia develop an extension service that can develop and demonstrate grazing practices that will protect biodiversity and conserve rangelands under the changing social and economic conditions impacting pastoralists. The BMPs could be developed in a general way for regions, but for each particular protected area the BMPs should be based on the goals of that protected area. For example, in protected areas where argali are the major species of concern and their primary use is during the winter, park plans should reduce livestock grazing, especially sheep and goat grazing because of the high dietary overlap on argali winter range. Restrictions would vary, but in this example it may be best to completely restrict livestock grazing with the knowledge that some transient horse, camel, yak, and cattle grazing will likely occur as these animals are not herded. Resource management plans would provide the means for herders and park officials to develop plans cooperatively and to understand each other's objectives. Multiple-use planning with communities of pastoralists using protected areas, based on grazing association use of public lands in the US may provide a model to meet a number of resource objectives in many of the protected areas used by pastoralists.

Wildlife Management

Mongolia lacks a wildlife management agency. All wildlife outside of protected areas remains largely unmonitored and almost completely unmanaged (other than limited monitoring by sum rangers). Yet, obviously, most of Mongolia's wildlife persists outside of protected areas, suggesting the need to expand management throughout the nation. We suggest that wildlife species could be managed as indicators of rangeland health and well-managed pastures should support large populations of native wildlife, especially ungulates.

A wildlife management agency, perhaps based on a Western wildlife agency could be created and funded via institution of a permit hunting system. Additional funds could be garnered from tourism taxes. Game species, including non-trophy species such as marmots, require active management if populations are to remain viable (Zahler et al., 2004). Given the prevalence of hunting in Mongolia, such a program should generate substantial revenues.

Integrated Solutions and Conflict Reduction

Finally, our ability to develop sustainable pastoralism and nature conservation on Mongolia's steppe will require that we develop integrated solutions and avoid unproductive conflict. This, in turn, depends on effectively employing interdisciplinary approaches and working with the full complement of stakeholders. We firmly believe that sustainable pastoralism and conservation of Mongolian rangelands are fundamentally linked. As such, both should proceed in tandem. Conservationists should work closely with herders to develop management plans that consider and address both issues. In the case of protected areas, protected areas staff should involve herders at levels of the planning and implementing processes (Pimbert and Pretty, 1995). Outside of protected areas, herders may well be the ones to initiate range management changes. It is less clear which government agencies and officials should work in unprotected landscapes. The Ministries of Agriculture, Mining, and Nature and Environment all can appropriately participate, as can local aimag and sum governments. In some cases (e.g., border areas), the Defense Ministry may also be included.

Herders must recognize that legislation requires government officials to follow certain regulations and officials should make herders aware of pertinent laws and recognize the constraints that herders face in trying to make a living on Mongolia's rangelands. Even with increased understanding and respect, conflicts will inevitably arise. Not all conflict is bad, as well-managed conflict can lead to better ideas, creativity, and innovation. Community-based approaches to conservation offer a variety of methods to help local people and conservationists avoid and manage conflict (Ghimire and Pimbert, 1997; Western and Wright 1994). An in-depth discussion of such approaches goes beyond the scope of this chapter. We support such initiatives; however, we stress that they must go well beyond traditional sustainable development approaches that often have focused on development while giving short shrift to conservation (Brandon et al., 1998a; Frazier, 1997). Similarly, a variety of environmental dispute resolution methods exist to help avoid and manage conflict (Wollondeck et al., 1994; Wondolleck and Yaffee, 2000). Such methods should be employed before conflicts become intractable and the people involved become so distrustful they are unable to work together.

CONCLUSIONS

Proper management of Mongolia's rangelands is critical for ensuring a productive livestock industry, maintaining livelihood options of pastoral cultures using these rangelands, and supporting the natural diversity of flora and fauna. Vast expanses of rangelands extend unfragmented and largely unaltered by crop agriculture or industry throughout the nation. In general, rangelands retain their natural potential although degradation caused by livestock grazing is a critical problem, especially near towns and watercourses. Few introduced exotics have established and much of the historic flora and fauna survive, often in relatively large, apparently healthy populations. Yet, since the end of communism and command-control economy in the early 1990s, Mongolia has been changing rapidly. Several challenges have emerged and now face conservationists interested in preserving sustainable pastoralism and wildlife populations on the steppe. We propose developing a variety of interdisciplinary approaches that link conservation biology, range management, and the social sciences to address these threats and increase the chances for effective rangeland management that is sustainable and enjoys enduring public support. This requires a concerted effort by state and local government as well as support at the local or user level. The international conservation community is committed to helping Mongolia, but success in conservation requires acceptance by and planning with those most dependent on the rangelands. Others have stressed that livestock overgrazing has been greatly exacerbated by a loss of institutional capacity (loss of control by government or community control), a loss of historic norms in cooperation and management, and so on. Protected areas that restrict livestock grazing may have some future, detrimental impacts on individual households; however, in general grazing in protected areas should allow modest additional development with pastoralists by combining efforts to preserve flora and fauna and pastoral cultures. We propose that protected areas work with pastoral communities to develop conservation plans, including grazing management plans, monitoring, and BMPs, that permit adaptive management of grazing lands. This requires that the government agencies enter into cooperative agreements with each other (e.g., the Ministries of Agriculture and Nature and Environment) and with local people to ensure the conservation of Mongolian rangelands and native species, as well as sustainable pastoralism for local people grazing those lands.

KEYWORDS

- **Argali**
- **Ecotourism**
- **Endangered species**
- **Nature reserves**
- **Snow leopard**
- **Wildlife**

ACKNOWLEDGMENTS

This manuscript benefited from conversations and helpful comments of a number of people, including A. Bräunlich, Chimgee, C. Finch, T. Galbaatar, Galbadrakh, B. Lhagvasuren, H. Mix, S. Severinghaus, T. Tuya, G. Wingard, and J. Wingard. Support of much of our work in Mongolia has been provided by the Denver Zoological Foundation, University of Montana, Mongolian Academy of Sciences, Mongolian Conservation Coalition, and GTZ (German Technical Cooperation).

Chapter 23

Predictors of Sustainable Tourism in Holland and China

Stuart Cottrell, Jerry J. Vaske, and Fujun Shen

INTRODUCTION

Construct validity of four dimensions of sustainability on local residents' satisfaction with tourism is examined. Data came from communities bordering Hoge Veluwe National Park (HVNP) in Holland (n = 142) and Chongdugou Village in China (n = 400). As suggested by prior research, we hypothesized that economic, socio-cultural, ecological, and institutional dimensions of sustainable tourism would influence resident satisfaction with tourism. Dimensions were based on three to six survey items with reliability coefficients ranging from 0.55 to 0.75. Perceived satisfaction, a dichotomous variable, measured resident satisfaction with tourism in their area. From a logistic regression, two dimensions were statistically significant for HVNP and all four for Chongdugou. The HVNP model correctly classified 81% of respondents and 70% for Chongdugou. The socio-cultural component was the strongest predictor for HVNP and the institutional for Chongdugou. The results supported the hypotheses that the four dimensions can contribute to resident satisfaction with sustainable tourism, however, the relative contribution of each varies depending on the site context. We argue for improving the measurement of sustainable tourism indicators and the developing standards associated with each indicator.

"Sustainable development meets the needs of the present without compromising the ability of future generations to meet their own needs" (WCED, 1987). Sustainable tourism can play an important role in community development, especially in areas abundant in natural capital, yet lacking financial resources or ability to pursue other avenues of growth. Any tourism promotional effort, however, can have positive and negative ecological, economic, and socio-cultural consequences. Achieving a balance among these three classic dimensions of sustainable tourism is difficult to realize, however, without an institutional perspective to manage, mediate and facilitate growth (Eden et al., 2000; Spangenberg, 2002; Spangenberg and Valentin, 1999). This fourth institutional dimension emphasizes participatory decision-making processes such as public participation and involvement. The German Wuppertal Institute combined these four dimensions into a single framework called the "prism of sustainability" (Figure 1) with clearly defined links among the dimensions (Spangenberg and Valentin, 1999). This study examined the construct validity of these four indicators of sustainability on local residents' satisfaction with tourism in communities bordering HVNP in Holland and Chongdugou Village in China.

```
                    INSTITUTIONAL
              justice         democracy
                        care
                 burden sharing
ECONOMIC   ◄■■■■■■■■■■■■■■■■■■■■■►   SOCIAL
              eco-efficiency    access
                   ENVIRONMENTAL
```

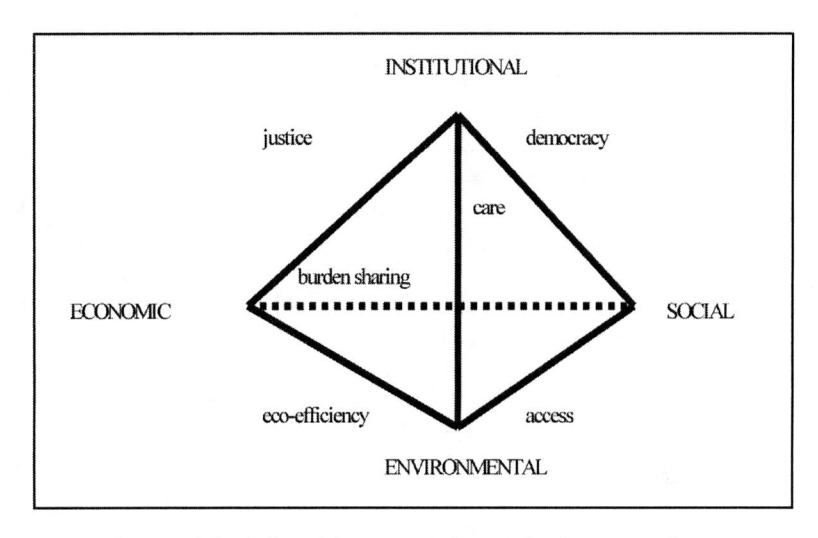

Figure 1. Prism of sustainability (adapted from Spangenberg and Valentin, 1999).

The ecological dimension emphasizes the need to reduce pressure on the physical environment. The environment is considered the sum of all bio-geological processes and their elements. The economic dimension considers human needs for material welfare (e.g., employment) in a framework that is competitive and stable at the macroeconomic scale. An economic system is environmentally sustainable only as long as the amount of resources utilized to generate welfare is restricted to a size and quality that does not deplete its sources for future use. The social dimension refers to individuals' skills, dedication, experiences, and resulting behavior. Societal interaction and associated social norms are necessary preconditions for economic activities (Spangenberg, 2002). Institutions represent organizations within a system of rules governing interaction among members. The institutional dimension calls for strengthening people's participation in political governance. As acceptance of and identification with political decisions become broader, public participation is strengthened. Valentine and Spangenberg (2000) imply that the four dimensions can be linked to indicators for local communities to monitor and evaluate sustainable development.

Indicators of Sustainable Tourism

Agenda 21, the document outlining principles for sustainable development adopted during the 1992 "Earth Summit" in Rio de Janeiro (Twining-Ward and Butler, 2002), called for coordinated efforts to develop sustainable development indicators at local, regional, national, and global levels. In response, the United Nations Commission on Sustainable Development (CSD) launched a program to develop indicators of sustainable development in 1995. Five years later, highly aggregated indicators were completed and applied in many countries. These indicators, however, primarily concentrated on regional, national, and global levels and focused on the physical environment. The World Tourism Organization (WTO in Dymond, 1997), for example, identified 11 core indicators for sustainable tourism categorized as ecological, social, economic, and planning. Nine of the 11 were physical indicators (e.g., site protection, development control, waste management planning process). Only two core indicators were psychological (e.g., local satisfaction with tourism) (Dymond, 1997).

Although the WTO effort provided a useful starting point, it failed to justify the choice of indicators, lacked clear stakeholder participation, did not consider local level indicators, and did not offer a monitoring framework for translating indicator information into management action (Twining-Ward and Butler 2002). In response, research has focused on developing practical sustainable tourism indicators, emphasizing the importance of local community involvement during sustainable indicator creation (Sirakaya et al., 2001; Spangenberg, 2002; Valentin and Spangenberg, 2000). Yuan, James, Hodgson, Hutchinson, and Shi (2003), for example, examined local indicator development in a case study of Chongming County, Shanghai, China. Similar work has been conducted by others (Dymond, 1997; Hughes, 2002; Innes and Booher, 2000; Miller, 2001). Not all indicators, however, are relevant to every community (Valentin and Spangenberg, 2000). Each community should develop an individual set of indicators within a common structure (Spangenberg, 2002).

This approach (common structure, different indicators) allows for community comparisons without ignoring their specific needs and situations. If the four dimensions of sustainable tourism (ecological, economic, socio-cultural, and institutional) are generalizable as suggested by prior research (Berg et al., 2004; Coccossis et al., 2001; Cottrell, et al., 2004; Cutumisu, 2003; Spangenberg, 2002; Spangenberg, and Valentin, 1999), all four predictors should influence local residents' satisfaction with tourism. This chapter examined the relative contribution of the four indicators to explaining satisfaction with tourism development in two study locations (i.e., a Dutch National Park and a Chinese tourism village).

Study Settings
The HVNP, established in 1935, is one of the largest national parks (5,500 hectares) in the Netherlands. The area was fenced in the early 1900s to serve as a hunting area with animals brought from abroad. The Hoge Veluwe remained a family estate of Kröller-Müller's until 1935 when they donated their land to the Dutch government as a national foundation due to financial problems. The founding philosophy and principles of Kröller-Müller, however, remained to preserve the park as a nature reserve combining art and culture with nature. The Kröller-Müller Art Museum and Sculpture Garden located in the center of the park houses fine works of art attracting international tourists while the park itself attracts mostly Dutch visitors. Visitors must enter the park to access the art museum. There are three entrances to the park, each adjacent to a small village representing three sample sites for the HVNP study.

Chongdugou is a small mountain village in the Henan province, China, located in the confluence of two rivers and the Shuilian palace historical site. Chongdugou village includes four sub-villages (Chongdujie, Xigou, Nangou, and Xiagou) with 340 families (1,300 residents). Local people have traditionally relied on mining, bamboo and timber harvest, each of which contributed to environmental degradation. In 1996, the local government began developing Chongdugou tourism as an economic alternative. Local residents turned spare rooms into guest rooms for home stays. A local government sponsored tourism company manages the Chongdugou happy-in-farmhouse tourism project characterized by experiencing life on the farm. After 4 years of development, residents participating in the project have had substantial increases in yearly income (Yuan et al., 2003).

PURPOSE

This study examined the construct validity of the four sustainability indicators on local residents' satisfaction with tourism in their location. The following empirical questions were examined:

1. What is the relationship between the four dimensions of sustainable tourism (economical, socio-cultural, ecological, and institutional) and resident satisfaction with tourism development?
2. Which sustainability dimension is the strongest predictor of resident satisfaction with tourism development?
   - The prism of sustainability provided the framework for comparing the settings (Berg and Bree, 2003; Berg et al., 2004). Given the inherent cultural differences between the two study locations, the indicators of sustainable tourism were adapted to each study context.
   - If the constructs are valid, each of the four dimensions of sustainability should influence resident satisfaction with tourism. The following conceptual question was examined:
3. To what extent is the prism of sustainability a useful framework for monitoring sustainable tourism development?

METHODS

Data were obtained from on-site surveys at three communities bordering HVNP in Holland (n = 142) and four communities of Chongdugou Village, an agri-tourism destination in China (n = 400). For HVNP, the study population included local people 16 years or older in the villages of Hoenderloo (N = 1400), Otterloo (N = 2360), and Schaarsbergen (N = 864). Interviewer completed surveys were conducted in shops and bakeries during June 2003. There were 142 respondents (response rate = 46%). For Chongdugou Village, multi-stage random sampling was used to proportionately represent households in the four sub-villages (Fujun, 2004): Chongdujie (N = 492, n = 156), Xigou (N = 450, n = 143), Nangou (N = 200, n = 63), and Xiagou (N = 121, n = 38).

Variables Measured

Drawn from previous research (Ankersmid and Kelder, 2000; Cottrell and Duim 2003; Dymond, 1997), four to eight items were used per study to measure each dimension of sustainable tourism. Perceived satisfaction was operationalized as a single dichotomous variable that asked respondents to indicate whether or not they were satisfied with tourism in their area.

RESULTS

For HVNP, Cronbach reliability alphas were 0.56 for a three-item institutional dimension, 0.65 for a three-item economic, 0.71 for a four-item ecological, and 0.75 for a six-item socio-cultural dimension (Table 1). For Chongdugou Village, alpha scores were 0.53 for the three-item ecological dimension, 0.59 for a four-item institutional, 0.64 for a three-item socio-cultural, and 0.70 for a five-item economic dimension. An additive index of was computed as the mean of items per dimension.

Table 1. Scale items for dimensions of sustainable tourism (Hoge Veluwe NP and Chongdugou China).

Dimensions of Sustainable Tourism	Hoge Veluwe[a] NP (n=142) α	Mean	Chongdugou[a] China (n=400) α	Mean
Institutional Dimension	.555	2.53	.588	2.76
Local inhabitants have influence on decision making process		2.2		---
Tourism contributes to better waste management of the region		2.5		---
There is good communication among parties involved in policy and decision making process		2.8		2.8
Participation is encouraged by local authorities		---		2.7
Feel I can access decision-making process to influence tourism development in the district.		---		2.3
Long-term planning by regional authorities can control negative impacts of tourism		---		3.2
Ecological Dimension	.712	3.37	553	2.84
Tourists cause pollution of environment (water, soil and air)*		2.9		2.8
The number of visitors results in disturbance of plants and animals*		3.3		2.9
Increasing exhaustion of water and energy resources was caused by tourist activities*		3.8		2.9
Tourism does not lead to the extinction of species in the region		3.5		---
Economic Dimension	.652	3.86	.704	3.71
Tourism brings more income to the local communities		4.0		---
Tourism increases the consumption of local products		3.6		---
Tourism creates job opportunities for local people		3.9		3.6
Tourism has resulted in local economic diversification		---		3.8
Products and services are better available generally since the development of tourism.		---		3.9
Region has better infrastructure (roads, electricity, water, public transport) due to tourism.		---		4.1
I have more education opportunities (vocational training) due to tourism development		---		3.2
Socio-cultural Dimension	.755	3.32	.644	3.34
There are too many tourists coming to the region*		3.2		---
Tourism development causes a change of local lifestyle and traditional habits*		3.0		---

Table 1. (Continued)

	Hoge Veluwe[a] NP (n=142)	Chongdugou[a] China (n=400)
Tourists annoy me*	3.9	---
Visitors to NP cause too much noise*	3.8	---
Changes in local lifestyles from tourism is positive	2.9	---
Tourism has increased the level of criminality, alcoholism, vandalism etc*	3.2	3.6
Tourism negatively influences norms and values in our area.*	---	3.2
Local traditions became less important because of tourism.*	---	3.3

Items measured on 5 point Likert agreement scale
* Items recoded to positive direction
[a] Dimensional scale means in bold/italic
α Cronbach's Alpha Reliability

Table 2. Mean comparisons between Hoge Veluwe NP examine differences between each dimensional and Chongdugou Village on each dimension of tourism sustainability.

Dimensions	Hoge Veluwe NP[a]	Chongdugou Village[a]	t-value	p-value
Institutional	2.5	2.8	3.27	.001
Ecological	3.5	2.8	-6.75	.001
Economical	3.9	3.7	-2.57	.01
Socio-cultural	3.3	3.3	.16	.87

We conducted an independent sample t-test to examine differences between each dimensional index and study location (Table 2). Scores for the institutional dimension were statistically higher (t = 3.27, p < 0.001) for Chongdugou (M = 2.8) than the HVNP (M = 2.5). Scores for both locations, however, indicated a general dissatisfaction with respondents' ability to participate in decision-making concerning tourism. Resident scores for the ecological dimension were higher (t = 6.75, p < 0.001) and positive for HVNP (M = 3.5) versus Chongdugou (M = 2.8). The Dutch residents did not view tourism to the HVNP as a threat to the environment while the Chongdugou village residents viewed tourism development negatively. Mean scores for the economical dimension were relatively positive for each location, however, higher for HVNP (M = 3.9) than Chongdugou (M = 3.7) (t = 2.57, p < 0.01). Residents from both locations believed tourism offered economic benefit. There were no differences (t = 0.16, p < 0.87) for the socio-cultural dimension; mean scores were the same (M = 3.3) and slightly positive with regard to the socio-cultural aspects of sustainable development.

A greater percentage of the Dutch residents (79%) than the Chongdugou Village residents (37%) were satisfied with tourism (Table 3). For HVNP, a majority of local residents (79%) were not directly involved with tourism for their livelihood; 21% of respondents were restaurant/hotel owners. Residents of the four sub-villages of Chongdugou all live within the boundaries of the agri-tourism project destination. Their daily lives are more directly influenced by tourism than residents near HVNP.

A logistic regression was conducted to determine the construct validity of each dimension to resident satisfaction. The logistic regression for Chongdugou Village correctly classified 70% of the responses (68%—No, 73%—Yes, 4). The model for Hoge Veluwe correctly classified 81% of the respondents (79%—No, 82%—Yes).

Table 3. Satisfaction with tourism.

	Hoge Veluwe NP		Chongdugou Village	
Satisfaction	Frequency	Percent	Frequency	Percent
No	27	21	192	63
Yes	102	79	112	37
Total	129	100	301	100

Table 4. Classification table—prediction of resident satisfaction with tourism.

	Study Location	
	Hoge Veluwe	Chongdugou
Satisfaction with Tourism	NP	Village
	%Correct	%Correct
No	78	68
Yes	82	73
Overall	81	70
Nagelkerke R^2	.55	.30

Two dimensions were statistically significant for the HVNP (Nagelkerke R2 = 0.55) and all four dimensions for Chongdugou Village (Nagelkerke R2 = 0.30) (Table 5). For HVNP, the socio-cultural (ExpB = 5.76) component was the strongest predictor followed by the institutional (ExpB = 3.34). For the Chongdugou Village, the institutional (ExpB = 3.17) index was the strongest predictor followed by the economic (ExpB = 2.38), ecological (ExpB = 1.73), and socio-cultural (ExpB = 0.519) dimensions.

CONCLUSIONS

Taken together, our findings support the hypothesis that all four dimensions can contribute to resident satisfaction with sustainable tourism as found for Chongdugou Village. As suspected, the relative contribution of each component varied depending on the situational specifics. The two study sites (Holland vs. China) represent distinctly different cultural environments. The institutional dimension was the strongest predictor of tourism satisfaction in the Chongdugou study, while the socio-cultural concept was the strongest at Hoge Veluwe. Examining the predictive contribution of each dimension at a tourism destination highlights which dimension has the greatest influence on resident attitudes about tourism development (Table 5).

Table 5. Predictors of resident satisfaction with sustainable tourism.

Dimensions	B	S.E.	Wald	df	Exp(B)	p-value
Chongdugou China						
Institutional	1.15	0.21	30.18	1	3.17	<.001
Ecological	0.55	0.18	9.04	1	1.73	<.003
Economical	0.87	0.25	12.24	1	2.38	<.001
Socio-cultural	-0.66	0.18	13.40	1	0.52	<.001
Constant	-6.45	1.21	28.16	1		<.001
Hoge Veluwe NP						
Institutional	1.20	0.57	4.50	1	3.34	<.034
Ecological	0.87	0.58	2.27	1	2.39	<.132
Economical	0.46	0.49	0.90	1	1.59	<.342
Socio-cultural	1.75	0.56	9.89	1	5.76	<.002
Constant	-11.54	2.75	17.57	1		<.001

From a theoretical perspective this study shows the importance of the institutional dimension versus the usual focus on the economic, ecological, and social dimensions; thereby supporting Eden et al. (2000) claim. Results clearly show that local resident ratings of their satisfaction with tourism depend on the institutional dimension, especially for the Chongdugou study. In this context (the importance of the institutional dimension), this study builds on Cutumisu's (2003) research arguing that sustainable tourism indicators depend on the specific social and institutional context of each study location. While encouraging, our findings point to the need for (1) refining the items used to measure institutional support; and (2) developing a more sophisticated set of indicators for resident satisfaction with sustainable tourism. Items for the institutional dimension were primarily participation in decision-making measures. The institutional dimension encompasses several sub-dimensions: access to decision-making, communication processes, politics, and democracy (Cutumisu, 2003; Spangenberg 2002; Valentin and Spangenberg, 2000). Further research is necessary to clarify an appropriate array of institutional indicators beyond our investigation. In addition, resident satisfaction with tourism was limited to a yes–no response. More precise levels of measurement are necessary to identify underlying aspects of satisfaction with tourism. Following the development of a valid and reliable set of sustainable tourism indicators, it is equally necessary to develop standards for each indicator. For example, what percent of local residents need to be satisfied with each dimension to claim that sustainable tourism has made a positive contribution to society? Development of indicator specific standards is only possible with continued monitoring of tourism development.

KEYWORDS

- **Chongdugou village**
- **Commission on sustainable development**
- **Hoge veluwe national park**
- **Socio-cultural**
- **World tourism organization**

Chapter 24

Subsistence, Tourism, and Research

Karen Gaul

INTRODUCTION

Overlapping designations of park, preserve, and wilderness are assigned to Lake Clark National Park and Preserve in south-central Alaska. The park was established in 1980 as a result of the Alaska National Interest Lands Conservation Act (ANILCA). Consisting of over 4 million acres, it includes homelands and hunting and fishing grounds for the inland Dena'ina, a northern Athabaskan-speaking people, who still engage in subsistence practices within the park. Dena'ina understandings of the environment include multiple spiritual dimensions. The park and preserve are also used by sport fishers and hunters, backpackers, rafters, and other park visitors who are in search of a variety of wilderness experiences. National Park Service (NPS) researchers conduct a range of research projects that contribute to efforts to monitor and protect cultural and natural resources in the area. In the midst of these multiple layers of designation, meaning and use, differences in perspective and value are constantly negotiated.

DENA'INA PEOPLE AND LAKE CLARK NATIONAL PARK

Telaquana Mountain is a site of special significance to the Dena'ina people. Ruth Koktelash (1981), a Dena'ina elder who passed away some years ago, relayed this creation story:

> "They went up on a mountain, and when they got to the mountain, they didn't see anything [no animals]...they didn't even see a ground squirrel. So they told a medicine man to look. When he looked, he saw mountain people. The mountain people put all the game on the mountain called Nduk'eyux Dghil'u, which means animals go on the mountain [Telaquana Mountain]. Ch'iduchuq'a [the shaman] went up and took the pica with him. There was no doorway. He took his cane and struck it on the top and then the door opened a little.
>
> Inside they saw every species of animal. People were singing and dancing. In his song Ch'iduchuq'a named each species of animal, and they went out through the door. That's why we've got wild game. All the wild animals out in the country, Ch'iguchuq'a let out," Ruth concludes.

This creation story has as its locus not some mythical place or unearthly realm, but features the very real and spectacular Telaquana Mountain (Figure 1) in what is now the wilderness area of Lake Clark National Park and Preserve. From Telaquana, according to this Dena'ina story, all the animals of the Earth tumbled out. This story represents just one set of meanings read into the complex and beautiful landscapes that now make up Lake Clark National Park and Preserve.

Figure 1. Telaquana Mountain is a site of special significance to the Dena'ina people (NPS photo).

Cultural resource specialists in the NPS have been increasingly attentive to the cultural history that is part of every national park, no matter how wild or remote. In this discussion, I consider the cultural use of the park, preserve and wilderness areas of Lake Clark National Park and Preserve in historical and contemporary times. Because Lake Clark National Park and Preserve was created by the ANILCA, cultural practices such as subsistence hunting, fishing, and gathering continue in the park. The majority of this mountainous park and preserve area is also designated wilderness, and park managers must respond to wilderness as well as to ANILCA legislation. In addition to the use of this area by Dena'ina people, there are multiple other interests and uses of the area: sport hunters and fishers, backpackers and river runners, sightseers and other tourists. Additionally, park staff assesses, measures, and monitors park lands according to their own systems of meaning, contributing to multiple "layers of significance" across the area. It is essential to keep these multiple interpretations in mind as we conduct research, manage and enjoy our wild lands.

Contemporary Dena'ina people live in Resident Zone Communities of Lake Clark National Park and Preserve in the villages of Iliamna, Lime Village, Newhalen, Nondalton, Pedro Bay and Port Alsworth. The Telaquana travel route that passes near Telaquana Mountain, of which Ruth Koktelash speaks, was one of many travel corridors across vast distances that Dena'ina people traveled in the area. We have numerous recordings of oral histories that refer to regular use and intimate knowledge of the Telaquana route by Dena'ina ancestors. Evidence of relatively recent Dena'ina occupation is visible at the Old (Telaquana) Village site, and at stopping spots along the way such as Votive Rock, where one can still find bits of rolled up birch bark, and hewn pieces of wood most likely used by travelers in the past for constructing shelter. These are cultural features tucked into the landscape that, if visitors know about them, can be read and appreciated as they travel along.

Lake Clark National Park and Preserve was established in December 1980, by section 201 (7) (a) of the ANILCA (94 Stat. 2383; Public Law 96-487). The park (2.6 million acres or 1,052,183 ha) and preserve (1.4 million acres or 566,560 ha) areas, consist of over 4 million acres (1.6 million ha) as of 2001, and of these, close to 2.5 million acres (1,011,714 ha) are designated wilderness. The park area is at the juncture of the Alaskan and Aleutian mountain ranges, which include a dynamic combination of glaciers and active volcanoes. ANILCA's mandate for Lake Clark National Park and Preserve was the preservation of all of these natural features, as well as sockeye salmon habitat and that of many other wildlife species.

The park area also encompasses homelands, and hunting, fishing, and gathering grounds for the inland Dena'ina, a northern Athabascan-speaking people. Prehistoric and historic Dena'ina settlements are found throughout what are now the Park and Preserve, and Yup'ik occupation runs along the southern portion of Lake Iliamna. Numerous archeological sites have been located along lakes, rivers, and coastal areas, and other strategic places. The Dena'ina lived along shorelines for easy fishing access and water transportation routes. They moved with the seasons across the tundra and into the high hills for hunting, trapping, berry picking, and other subsistence activities, and covered vast ranges of territory. The ANILCA provides for their continued ability to hunt and fish and gather plant resources in Lake Clark National Park and Preserve.

We have many oral accounts of Dena'ina people describing their traditional seasonal round. In the spring, they moved to spring fish camps to fish for whitefish and pike, to hunt waterfowl, and to trap muskrats (Ellanna and Balluta, 1992); following the breakup of the ice, they would move to summer fish camps at strategic locations along rivers, streams and lake edges to catch salmon, which came in species-specific waves throughout the spring and summer. Salmon was and is central to the Dena'ina people's sense of well being, and their sense of identity. There were countless ways to dry, store and prepare the many parts of the fish (Figure 2). One common way to dry the fish is to split the two large fillets away from the spine of the fish, make lateral cuts in the flesh, and hang it to dry or smoke it. The backs were fed to the dogs, during the period up until recently when people kept dogs for assistance in snow travel for hunting, trapping, packing wood, and other chores. Fish heads were boiled for their oil, fish skins were sewn into storage bags for fish oil or even sewn into boots.

Summertime also meant gathering blueberries, cranberries, salmonberries, and many others. Families still gather many gallons of different berries, and preserve them in a number of ways. One of the most popular traditional methods was to mix the blueberries with bear fat or other lard, and sugar, to make nivagi or Native "ice cream" (aguduc in Yup'ik) (Johnson et al., 1998).

Subsistence, Tourism, and Research   247

Figure 2. Dena'ina people describe their traditional seasonal movements from spring fish camps to summer fish camps. Mary Ann Trefon and daughter Katie with fish and furs (NPS Photo Archives H23).

People would then prepare for fall hunting, and move to camps up into the lands around their village sites where they might find moose, caribou, black bear, and ground squirrels. Late in October, the Dena'ina fished for spawned out salmon (or redfish), hunted Dall sheep and Brown bears. As the fall turned to winter, snow covered the ground and waterways froze up. Dena'ina would then trap fox, wolverine, mink, lynx and marten, and hunt moose (which have only been available since about the 1940s in the region) and caribou. They would set up winter camps for beaver trapping from January through April. By then, stores of fish for dogs and humans alike, as well as berries and meats may have been running quite low. Early spring fishing was always a welcome turn of the seasons, signaling a move into the flush times of rich summers of plenty of salmon.

Oral accounts record intricate details on how this mobile, subsistence lifestyle was maintained. People describe gathering and processing wood and hides to make snowshoes; how to make good spears or the packboard for tying on loads; the making of clothing; and many detailed accounts of how to catch, process, store, cook and eat fish, moose, berries and many other resources. And they talk of the travel, over lands that were rich with meaning, housed by spiritual beings in various dimensions, and how to live right in such a world. They have offered thousands of names that mark their landscape, guide their routes, and capture events that happened in particular places.

Cultural resource managers in the NPS are interested in identifying and documenting such associations people have with what are now park lands. We research and write ethnographic overview and assessments, or baseline documents on the cultural history and use of areas. We identify sacred sites and places of cultural and spiritual significance. We also conduct place-names studies that show the ways cultural meanings are inscribed on the landscape through the very way it was named and talked about. A study documenting Native place-names in Lake Clark National Park and Preserve is currently underway.

However, identifying culturally significant meanings inscribed on the landscape can prove a challenging undertaking, especially given the fact that people move, new layers of people move in, and new meanings are applied. We need to consider not simply the traditional use, associations, and meanings of an area, but layers of such associations, and uses.

In addition to the Dena'ina and Yup'ik associations to the Lake Clark area, new layers of significance came from Russian promyshlinniki or entrepreneurs, in the fur business, who made their way into these interior areas by the 1790s. These newcomers perhaps read the land as bountiful, rich in resources, and full of opportunity to make good money. It was a place from which to extract resources. The Native Dena'ina participated in fur trade endeavors and served as middlemen, facilitating the extraction and transport of fur animals from interior areas to the trade routes that started in local trade posts on Lake Iliamna (Figure 3), for example, and ended up in far away fashion shops in London or Moscow. Jointly, they re-crafted new sets of meanings on the landscape. Similarly, when gold prospectors entered the area, setting up staging camps at the Port Alsworth area for exploration in interior areas, some Dena'ina assisted and participated in gold prospecting as well. Commercial fishing and canning entered the area around the same time as gold prospecting (1890s), and many Dena'ina participated in that—and still do. The commercial approach to fishing was on a scale thousands of times larger than subsistence fishing, but it offered local people an opportunity to earn cash and to participate in a cash economy.

Figure 3. Native Dena'ina people participated in fur trade endeavors and served as middlemen, facilitating the extraction, and transport of fur animals from interior areas into the trade routes that started in local trade posts. Pictured here is Wilhelm Neilsen with his furs at Pete Anderson's house in Old Iliamna, circa 1908–1909 (NPS Photo Archives H1217).

Through these early interactions, Dena'ina people and some of the Russian and American newcomers married, had children and built family and community, merging cultural backgrounds, lifeways, and sets of understandings of place. As trappers, traders, prospectors, and explorers moved into the area, new languages and new names were assigned over the top of Dena'ina names. Lake Clark, for example, was previously called Qizhjeh Vena in the Dena'ina language, meaning "a place where people gathered." John W. Clark was a member of an exploration party in January of 1891, a group of explorers who traveled to the upper tributaries of the Nushagak River. They followed the Nushagak River to the Mulchatna River, and then followed the Chulitna to where it drained into a long lake. They named it in honor of John W. Clark, and the name has been mapped and called Lake Clark ever since.

OTHER MEANINGS OF LAKE CLARK NATIONAL PARK

Alaska—or the rights to it was purchased by the United States from Russia in 1867. Then followed many years of treaties and legislation that imposed new layers of meaning (and new rules about basic rights to lands). Alaska became a State in 1959.

After many years of debate, 1971 brought the Alaska Native Claims Settlement Act (ANCSA), which extinguished aboriginal title to 365 million acres (147.7 million ha) of land, conveyed 45 million acres (18.2 million ha) to Native corporations, and paid out $962.5 million to Native corporations (Case and Voluck, 2002). A decade later, ANILCA (1980) identified new Federal lands including national parks and preserves. Lake Clark National Park, as mentioned, is one such new "ANILCA" parks. The ANILCA also helped to designate Native allotments, and village and regional corporation lands. Even now, many lands remain unconveyed, so that the land status map around Lake Clark looks like a colorful patchwork.

We can view the inscription of the national park and preserve designation, and its wilderness designation, as yet more layers of meaning assigned to this area. Even though the ANILCA parks provide for recognition of resident zone peoples, and their continued subsistence, they also embody something of the identity of other big, western parks. That is, they extend the sense of the wild, wilderness, isolation, ruggedness, and a promise of solitude. Indeed, these are the very things that many visitors come to Lake Clark to seek out.

One key assumption underlying the national park idea in general, and the big western nature parks in particular, and particularly wilderness, is that nature is something fundamentally different and separate from human culture. Another is that nature started out pure, devoid of human influences, and it should be protected as such, returned to its pristine state. Nature, and nature parks, can serve as a sanctuary for us to enter into as a refuge from hectic urban life. Braun (2002: ix) describes this externalizing of nature in mainstream American thought, noting that nature is seen as: "a place to which one goes—the site of "resources," a stage for "recreation," a source for "spiritual renewal," and a scene for "aesthetic reflection." And, we might add, a laboratory for research. Indeed, these are the many reasons visitors come to Lake Clark: for river running, backpacking, camping, sport hunting, and so on. Because it is thought about in a number of ways and serves a variety of purposes for those who visit it, Braun (2002: p. 10) suggests that nature is always inherently social, and calls it "social nature" (see also Cronon, 1995).

Research is another set of meanings inscribed on or read from the landscape. Assessing plant and wildlife diversity and numbers is an activity that land managers deem important for resource management. The NPS, with its identification, inventorying and monitoring of natural and cultural resources, and its presentation of these resources to the public, promulgates its own sets of landscape meanings. But these landscape meanings are also multiple, as "wilderness" folks debate with "cultural resource" folks over issues such as what kinds of equipment archeologists can use to do their jobs within wilderness, or what forms of transportation are acceptable in wilderness. Such disputes wage at the agency level, even as subsistence users bristle and grumble about catch and release fishing, and sport hunters who are only after the trophy antlers.

We can easily see, even in this brief sketch, that layers of significance for this particular area are not of the same shape, size, and weight. The scale and reach are different. What Dena'ina subsistence users claim as their hunting and gathering grounds, and the reasons they claim it, lie pretty close to home. They are fairly local. Larger international claims or attachments of meaning such as those of Russian fur traders mean that the stretch of significance reaches pretty far. When a country like the US purchases the rights to the whole region of Alaska, sets of national claims and laws are assumed to apply to these lands. And when an area is set aside as a national park, it is defined as land belonging to the American public. Our lands and our national heritage.

Local interests are accommodated—and indeed, subsistence needs are given (nominally) a preference over commercial and sport hunting and fishing—but ultimately are subsumed under the goals and jurisdiction of a national entity. Native experience is codified into mandated management. People's lives, their history, their places now become the material of cultural resource management. Thus, multiple layers of meaning are held onto, and multiple experiences pursued, simultaneously. Certain definitions of or discourses about environments, or certain landscape ideas, take precedence over others. Thus, even for areas designated park, preserve or wilderness, there are political battles that necessarily link them to cultural agendas.

CONCLUSION

As park managers, or stewards, we must acknowledge these multiple and changing layers of significance. Wilderness is not unknown territory, but homeland well-known by people who have lived on it and traversed it, using countless plants, animals, water, and mineral resources for millennia. Subsistence practices—even as they have radically changed—represent a strong strand of continuity of connection Dena'ina have with the land (Figure 4). These ties are celebrated and strengthened as Dena'ina people themselves reinterpret their past and their traditions, and reinvigorate their language and culture through strong revitalization efforts.

In June of this year, I set off with our park historian, John Branson, and Samson Ferreira of the NPS Cultural Landscapes program, to walk the upper part of the Telaquana Trail near the mountain from which all of the world's animals are said to have emerged. We were there to photo document and record GIS data about cultural sites along the Telaquana travel corridor, which connected people from the Telaquana Lake area to the Kijik area. I loved being out on the Telaquana plateau, slogging through the brush, and boggy tundra and enjoying its hugeness. I am from Montana, but Montana's "Big Sky" seemed diminished compared to that over the wildness of Lake Clark National Park and Preserve. But what made the trip so rich for me was imagining Dena'ina women of 200 years ago packing their kids on their backs, or hunters with dogs cooking fresh caribou over campfires, building tent shelters from birch bark; or looking up at Telaquana Mountain and thinking of the shaman who tapped the mountain with his cane, and so many other ways Dena'ina and others interacted symbolically and materially with their environment. This is now "wilderness." But this rich cultural history should not disappear with new layers and designations of meaning, or with new names given to features on the landscape. ANILCA, even as we struggle to apply and interpret it 25 years later, recognized and kept central those cultural connections. In the ANILCA parks, wilderness was and must remain a peopled landscape.

Figure 4. The ANILCA recognizes and keeps central the cultural connections of people with the landscape in Alaska (photo by Dan Young, Lake Clark NP&P).

KEYWORDS

- **Alaska National Interest Lands Conservation Act**
- **Lake Clark National Park and Preserve**
- **National Park Service**
- **Telaquana Mountain**

Chapter 25

Biodiversity Science in South Africa

Michael Cherry

INTRODUCTION

In 1772, Carolus Linnaeus wrote a letter, now oft-quoted, to Ryk Tulbagh, the Governor of the Cape in which he envied Tulbagh's "sovereign control of that Paradise on Earth, the Cape of Good Hope, which the beneficent Creator has enriched with his choicest wonders." Two and a half centuries later, South Africa's biodiversity remains a great source of interest to the scientific community and for good reason. Plant biodiversity, with over 20,000 different species, is in the foreground: South Africa, which comprises less than 1% of the world's land surface, contains 8% of its plant species. Perhaps less well known is that the country also contains 7% of all bird, mammal, and reptile species, and 15% of known coastal marine species.

THE SOUTH AFRICAN NATIONAL BIODIVERSITY INSTITUTE

South Africa's new Biodiversity Act, signed on September 1, 2004, expands the mandate of the National Botanical Institute (NBI) to include responsibilities relating to the full diversity of the country's fauna and flora; it is now known as the South African National Biodiversity Institute (SANBI) (Pretoria, South Africa). Previously responsible for eight national botanical gardens and three herbaria, as well as botanical research centers in Pretoria and at its largest garden at Kirstenbosch on the slopes of Table Mountain, it now additionally should influence the prospects of all collections of specimens; coordinate research on indigenous biodiversity and its sustainable use; advise conservation agencies and municipalities with regard to planning decisions relating to biodiversity; coordinate the control of invasive species; and monitor the effect of any genetically modified organisms released into the environment.

Acting Chief Executive Officer Brian Huntley (Figure 1) admits openly that this is quite a brief. It is not difficult to see why it is the former NBI that has inherited this mantle, since it has become, over the past decade, by far the largest and most dynamic South African institution working in the biodiversity arena. Operating under the aegis of the Department of Environment Affairs, it was formed in 1989 through the amalgamation of what had previously been the National Botanical Gardens and the Botanical Research Institute. Currently supporting 680 staff, it has flourished particularly during Huntley's tenure, which has been characterized by an influx of externally funded projects, to the extent that external income $18 million per annum now exceeds the $16 million it receives from its parliamentary grant and from entrance fees paid by the million or so visitors to its gardens each year. Huntley is optimistic that this brief can succeed, although he concedes that in few countries does any single institution bear responsibility for research, information dissemination, and applications relating to biodiversity. But he believes that South Africa is a small enough country, with enough good intellectual capacity, for this model to work.

Figure 1. Cape Flowers in August (Photo: Peter Jones)

This view is echoed by Andrew Balmford of Cambridge University, who is spending a sabbatical at the Percy Fitzpatrick Institute for African Ornithology at the University of Cape Town. "While the obvious challenge is to link biodiversity conservation to development needs," he says, "there are very few developing countries which have the prospect of delivering jobs related to the conservation industry. South Africa has this prospect, not only because it is unbelievably diverse, but because of international goodwill towards the country."

Huntley's strategy will be to bring a sound scientific base to the enterprise, as he has already done with the NBI. There are several examples of this. One is the African Plants Initiative being led by the SANBI, Kew Gardens in the UK (London), and the United States Missouri Botanical Garden (St. Louis, Missouri, US) whose aim is to create an electronic library of the type specimens of all African plants: an estimated 300,000 accessions of 60,000 species. This includes scanned pictures of each individual specimen, the quality of which, according to Huntley, "is as good as if one were examining the specimen through a standard dissecting microscope." Another example involves placing the 2.5 million specimens in South Africa's herbaria on a computerized database, a task now 40% complete. A third example is the Southern African Botanical Diversity Network (Pretoria, South Africa), founded in 1996, which has, to date, trained 200 botanists in ten countries in the region.

By contrast, research on zoological diversity, traditionally the domain of the country's natural history museums, has lagged behind. The Iziko South African Museum in Cape Town, for example, one of the country's five national natural history museums, now has only seven research staff in natural history compared to the 16 it had in 1989. Why have they failed to capitalize on external funding in the way the NBI has done? One answer is that, unlike the three national herbaria, which all fell under the jurisdiction of the NBI, these five institutions have retained their institutional autonomy, and consequently have remained fragmented in their efforts. One, the South African Institute for Aquatic Biodiversity (Grahamstown, South Africa), is run by the National Research Foundation, while the other four are funded by grants from the department of arts and culture, which has tended to view them as educational, rather than research, organizations. Huntley emphasizes that the SANBI does not aspire "to do what other organizations are already doing well." With regard to natural history museums, he says that the first step will be to take the initiative in conducting a thorough review of their funding, and the "best practice of dealing with large and dispersed collections."

BIODIVERSITY AND THE SOUTH AFRICAN ECONOMY

The extraordinary diversity of habitats found on the southern tip of the African continent includes three globally recognized biodiversity hotspots: the temperate Cape Floristic Region (see Figure 2), the arid Succulent Karoo, and the subtropical Maputaland-Pondoland-Albany area. On account of its early colonization and relative wealth, South Africa has good universities, museums, and herbaria, and reasonably well-run conservation agencies at both the provincial and national levels. But in a country whose history has been characterized by fighting over land, the 6.6% of its land surface with formal conservation status (in other words, protected by the state) lags behind the global mean of 11.5%. By contrast, 17% of its coastline is formally protected. Protection is important for a number of reasons. A decade after the advent of democracy, the economy is booming at last, with the country currently experiencing the longest sustained period of growth in its history since the early 1960s. Rising levels of affluence have led to increased demand for housing, roads, and recreational facilities all developments that affect biodiversity. The benefits that biodiversity brings to the economy are increasingly being realized, notably through ecotourism. Tourism is the fastest growing sector of the economy, having risen to 7% of GDP in 2003, from only 2% a decade previously. The virtual abandonment of agriculture subsidies has led to much marginal agricultural land previously farmed essentially to generate subsidy being converted to private nature reserves, used either for ecotourism or for hunting, and sometimes for both. Such land now comprises 13% of the country's surface—more than twice the area protected by the state. There are also direct benefits associated with harvesting indigenous flora and fauna. Some are quantifiable, such as the fishing industry, worth just over half a billion US dollars last year. Others cannot be measured directly, but are no less important for that. For example, almost 20% of South Africa's plants, or 3,689 species, are used as traditional medicines, which still provide the first resource for primary health care to almost three-quarters of South Africa's population. The challenge of sustainable harvesting is difficult enough when yields are known, but even more daunting when they are undetermined.

Figure 2. Brian Huntley, Acting Chief Executive of the South African National Biodiversity Institute (SANBI).

Centers of Excellence in Biodiversity

Another related development is the recent announcement of the Department of Science and Technology that it will fund six centers of excellence nationally at South African universities, with effect from 2005. No fewer than three of these centers are focused on biodiversity: one at the Fitzpatrick Institute (Cape Town, South Africa), concerned with birds as models for understanding biodiversity processes; one at the University of Pretoria (Pretoria, South Africa), which will be concerned with pathogens on indigenous trees; and a third in the Faculty of Science at the University of

Stellenbosch, which will focus on invasion biology. All of the centers are based at the host institution, but can disburse funds to collaborators elsewhere in the country.

These centers of excellence, says Steven Chown (Figure 3), director of the Centre for Invasion Biology, "are a manifestation of the seriousness with which the South African government is taking science." Others are more skeptical. "I don't think that in the biodiversity field research is optimally conducted by large groups, but by smaller groups of collaborators," says David Ward of the School of Biological and Conservation Science at the University of KwaZulu-Natal (KwaZulu-Natal, South Africa). "Unlike fields like nuclear physics, in ecology costs are relatively low—large centers just incur additional administrative costs, without improving the quality of the science produced," he adds. Rob Slotow, from the same school, feels that the centers have confined their collaborative efforts to junior colleagues outside their own institutions. "There is very little real inter-institutional collaboration taking place at a senior level, which is disappointing," he says, as "the opportunity to kick-start a different level of funding for biodiversity research in the country the aim of the centers-of-excellence concept has been missed."

Figure 3. Steven Chown, Director of the Centre for Invasion Biology.

The research program of the Fitzpatrick Institute is based on two interlinking themes: understanding and maintaining avian biodiversity. Tim Crowe will lead a group investigating the processes responsible for the origins of African biodiversity, which will investigate how the process of speciation in birds occupying disjunct distributions in habitats ranging from montane forest to desert may have been influenced by past biogeographic corridors that shifted with changing climates many millions of years ago.

Understanding how relationships between organisms and their environments influence the form and functioning of biological systems is the core focus of a second grouping of researchers. For example, Phil Hockey is studying life-history traits and movement patterns of African Black Oystercatchers (Figure 4A, B), where research to date indicates that migration in juveniles is facultative, responding to body condition. Oystercatcher populations are increasing, primarily as a consequence of a ban imposed several years ago on four-wheel-drive vehicles on beaches. These increasing populations provide a unique opportunity to test the hypothesis that migration in stable habitats evolves initially in juveniles—in response to population density exceeding carrying capacity.

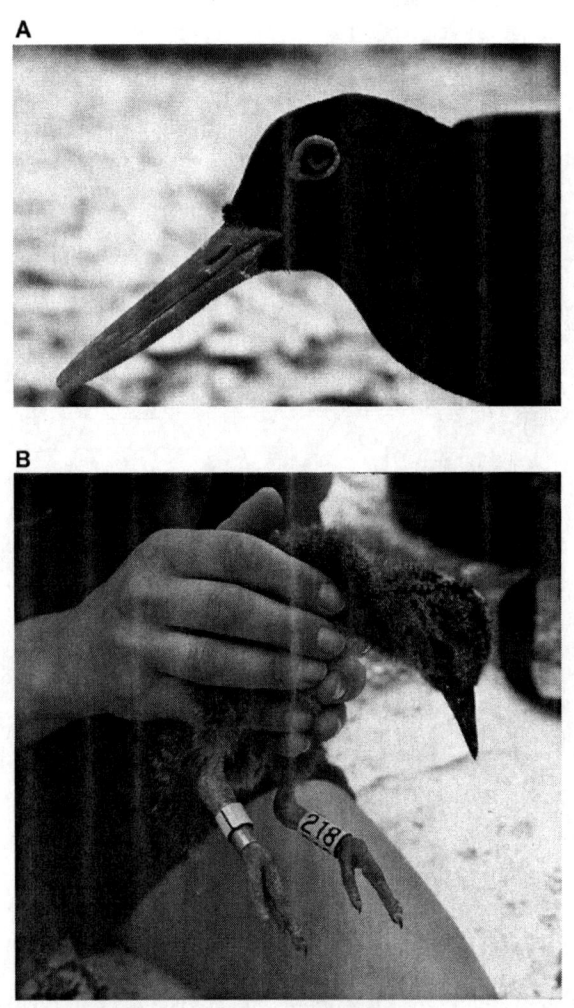

Figure 4. African Black Oystercatchers (A) Portrait of an adult African Black Oystercatcher. (Photo: Philip Hockey) (B) An African Black Oystercatcher chick with the numbered color rings that are used to follow its survival and migratory movements over several years. (Photo: Doug Loewenthal).

The Fitzpatrick Institute's teaching efforts have been impressive; its master's course in conservation biology has produced close to 150 graduates from 15 different African countries since its inception in 1992. But are birds really good models for understanding changes in patterns of biodiversity? Many would argue that they are not, since their mobility allows them to respond to environmental changes by colonizing new areas with relative ease. The center's director, Morné du Plessis, counters that "while birds are often not good indicators of environmental change, they are a group for which good baseline information exists, as well as being relatively easy to study."

The center for Tree Health Biotechnology forms part of the Forestry and Agriculture Biotechnology Institute at the University of Pretoria. The institute has to date focused largely on pathogens on trees used in commercial forestry, most of which are alien species, but according to its director, Mike Wingfield, the center will be devoted specifically to studying pathogens on indigenous trees. But the two, he adds, are closely related. "Alien trees used in commercial forestry are often able to thrive because they are distanced from their natural pathogens," he says, but "we are now observing natural pathogens of native trees switching hosts to alien species." This happens usually when alien and native trees are reasonably closely related. Wingfield believes that an example is the fungus causing *Cryphonectria canker*, which he and his collaborators have recently shown, on the basis of DNA sequences, to occur on both the native waterberry tree, *Syzgium cordatum*, and on the alien Eucalyptus (widely used for forestry in South Africa), from which it was first reported in 1989.

Similarly, native trees, which are often of importance to local communities, could be at risk from pathogens imported on alien species. The kiaat tree *Pterocarpus angolensis*, for example, is widely used by wood-carvers, as well as in traditional medicines. Trees are reported to be dying, but it is unknown whether this is on account of pathogens, climate change, or changing fire regimens. There have also been sporadic reports of dying baobabs (Figure 5) one of the icons of the African savannah over the past 15 years. Wingfield says that "while at the present time, there is no clear evidence that an unknown fungus is killing baobabs, these reports should not go unheeded." "Both kiaat and baobab deaths merit attention, which the center should now be able to provide," says Wingfield.

The Centre for Invasion Biology is somewhat different from the other two centers in that it focuses on a specific question, namely how invasions affect biodiversity and ecosystem functioning. Of its annual budget of $1 million, five-sixths will come from the government, with the remainder being provided by the University of Stellenbosch. Chown believes that this is a bargain, considering the magnitude of the problem: the global cost of addressing biological invasions is estimated to be $1.4 trillion annually about 5% of global GDP.

In South Africa, invasive plants are a particular problem. Apart from the threat they pose to indigenous diversity, they are a fire hazard in several ecosystems in which burning is part of the natural cycle and perhaps most importantly, they are a huge drain on water in a country in which this is a scarce commodity. This has led to a program certainly the largest of its kind in any developing country called working for water, in which unemployed persons have been hired to conduct alien clearances on a large scale. Chown's center will provide policy inputs to the program as part of a broad range of pure and applied research objectives.

Figure 5. African Baobab. The African baobab, Adansonia digitata, can reach up to 10 meters in diameter and can live more than 1,000 years. (Photo: Peter Jones).

The Centre for Invasion Biology will address both long-term studies of invasive organisms in different habitats and the outcomes of remediation program, which Chown views as large-scale ecological experiments whose effects need to be studied. "The Working for Water rehabilitation program provides excellent opportunities for understanding relationships between changes in species richness and changes in ecosystem function, and how alien invasion and clearance affects both phenomena," he says.

A second component will attempt to study invasions from the outset, as opposed to post hoc. Chown proposes to investigate concomitant climate and land-use changes in the Cedarberg Mountains, a range 200 km north of Cape Town. The predominant land-use patterns of agriculture and ecotourism are changing rapidly in the area, which he predicts will be accompanied by changes in the extent and identity of invasive species.

Additionally, climate-change models predict that this relatively arid part of the Fynbos Biome (the major vegetation type of the Cape Floristic Region) will be transformed within 50 years into a semi-desert system.

To what extent will these different ventures find a common purpose? There are some obvious links: Huntley sits on the board of the Fitzpatrick Institute, whose master's course in conservation biology has supplied many graduates to the NBI over the past 15 years. Chown sits on the board of the SANBI, together with representatives of the departments of Science and Technology, Agriculture and Environment Affairs, and David Mabunda, chief executive officer of South African National Parks. As the chief executive of the SANBI now exercises a huge degree of statutory influence over the nation's biodiversity, the answer to this question is closely related to that of who will replace Huntley, who is now 61. Huntley's tenure will be a hard act to follow, and the future of South Africa's biodiversity will lie largely in the hands of his successor.

KEYWORDS

- **Biodiversity**
- **Fitzpatrick Institute**
- **South African National Biodiversity Institute**
- **Tourism**
- **Tree health biotechnology**

Permissions

Chapter 1: Tourists' Satisfaction with Ecosystem Services as originally published as "The Providence of Nature: Valuing Ecosystem Services" in *International Journal of Environmental Science & Technology Vol. 1, No. 2, pp. 151–163, Summer 2004*. Reprinted with permission under the Creative Commons Attribution License or equivalent.

Chapter 2: Legal Implications for Nature-based Tourism was originally published as "Requirements of an International Legal Framework on Nature Based Tourism" in *International Journal of Environmental Science & Technology Vol. 1, No. 4, pp. 335–344, Winter 2005*. Reprinted with permission under the Creative Commons Attribution License or equivalent.

Chapter 3: Trends in Nature-based Tourism was originally published as "A Global Perspective on Trends in Nature-Based Tourism" in *PLoS BIOLOGY 6:30, 2009*. Reprinted with permission under the Creative Commons Attribution License or equivalent.

Chapter 4: Community Participation in Environmental Management of Ecotourism was originally published as "Research on Community Participation in Environmental Management of Ecotourism" in *International Journal of Business and Management Vol. 4, No. 3, March 2009*. Reprinted with permission under the Creative Commons Attribution License or equivalent.

Chapter 5: Environmental Issues and Best Practices for Ecotourism was originally published as "Environmental Issues and Best Practices for Ecotourism" in *USAID*. Reprinted with permission under the Creative Commons Attribution License or equivalent.

Chapter 6: Effect of Wind Power Installations on Coastal Tourism was originally published as "The Effect of Wind Power Installations on Coastal Tourism" in *Energies 2010, 3, pp. 1–22*. Reprinted with permission under the Creative Commons Attribution License or equivalent.

Chapter 7: Role for Local Communities in Biodiversity Conservation was originally published as "The Costs of Exclusion: Recognizing a Role for Local Communities in Biodiversity Conservation" in *PLoS BIOLOGY 10:23, 2007*. Reprinted with permission under the Creative Commons Attribution License or equivalent.

Chapter 8: Value of Rare Species in Ecotourism was originally published as "Rare Species are Valued Big Time" in *PLoS ONE 4:22, 2009*. Reprinted with permission under the Creative Commons Attribution License or equivalent.

Chapter 9: Rarity Value and Species Extinction was originally published as "Rarity Value and Species Extinction: The Anthropogenic Allee Effect" in *PLoS BIOLOGY 11:28, 2006*. Reprinted with permission under the Creative Commons Attribution License or equivalent.

Chapter 10: Parks and Tourism was originally published as "Parks and Tourism" in *PLoS BIOLOGY 6:30, 2009*. Reprinted with permission under the Creative Commons Attribution License or equivalent.

Chapter 11: The Conservation Business was originally published as "The Conservation Business" in *PLoS BIOLOGY 9:14, 2004*. Reprinted with permission under the Creative Commons Attribution License or equivalent.

Chapter 12: Ecological Sports Tourism Resources and its Industry was originally published as "Studies on Sustainable Development of Ecological Sports Tourism Resources and Its Industry" in *Journal of Sustainable Development Vol. 2, No. 2, July 2009*. Reprinted with permission under the Creative Commons Attribution License or equivalent.

Chapter 13: Ecotourism in the Northern Piedmont in the Qinling Mountains was originally published as "Study on Sustainable Development of Ecotourism in the Northern Piedmont in the Qinling

Mountains" in *Journal of Sustainable Development Vol. 3, No. 1, March 2010.* Reprinted with permission under the Creative Commons Attribution License or equivalent.

Chapter 14: Heritage Ecotourism in Micronesia was originally published as "Heritage Eco-tourism in Micronesia" in *Perceptions of Heritage Eco-tourism by Micronesian Decision Makers by Dirk R. Spennemann, David W. Look, Kristy Graham, Johnstone Centre, Charles Sturt University, Albury.* Reprinted with permission under the Creative Commons Attribution License or equivalent.

Chapter 15: Economic Value of Ecotourism in the Nigerian Rainforest Zone was originally published as "Economic Value of Ecotourism to Local Communities in the Nigerian Rainforest Zone" in *Journal of Sustainable Development Vol. 3, No. 1, March 2010.* Reprinted with permission under the Creative Commons Attribution License or equivalent.

Chapter 16: Visitor Access to Cumberland Island National Seashore, Georgia was originally published as "Wilderness Wilderness and Visitor Access to Cumberland Island National Seashore, Georgia" in *Proceedings of the 2008 Northeastern Recreation Research Symposium.* Reprinted with permission under the Creative Commons Attribution License or equivalent.

Chapter 17: Sustainable Development of China's Ecotourism was originally published as "A Study on the Strategies of the Sustainable Development of China's Ecotourism" in *International Journal of business and Management, Vol. 2, No. 5, 2009 at Publishing Center of IJBM, Australia.* Reprinted with permission under the Creative Commons Attribution License or equivalent.

Chapter 18: Ecotourism in Protected Areas in Cross River State, Nigeria was originally published as "A Critical Needs Assessment for Collaborative Ecotourism Development Linked to Protected Areas in Cross River State, Nigeria" in *Brooks, Jeffrey J.; Neary, John; Asuquo, Blessing E. 2007. A critical needs assessment for collaborative ecotourism development linked to protected areas in Cross River State, Nigeria. Final Report. Washington, DC: U.S. Department of Agriculture, Forest Service, International Programs Office p. 47.* Reprinted with permission under the Creative Commons Attribution License or equivalent.

Chapter 19: Kilim River Mangrove Forest Ecotourism Services was originally published as "Tourists' Satisfaction on Kilim River Mangrove Forest Ecotourism Services" in *International Journal of Business and Management, Vol. 4, No. 7, 2009 at CCSE.* Reprinted with permission under the Creative Commons Attribution License or equivalent.

Chapter 20: Wilderness Stewardship in the Kruger National Park, South Africa was originally published as "Balancing Conservation Management and Tourism Development with Wilderness Stewardship in the Kruger National Park, South Africa" in *Venter, F. J. (Freek) 2007. Balancing conservation management and tourism development with wilderness stewardship in the Kruger National Park, South Africa. In: Watson, Alan; Sproull, Janet; Dean, Liese, (comps.). Science and stewardship to protect and sustain wilderness values: Eighth World Wilderness Congress symposium; September 30-October 6, 2005; Anchorage, AK. Proceedings RMRS-P-49. Fort Collins, CO: U.S. Department of Agriculture, Forest Service, Rocky Mountain Research Station. pp. 109–111.* Reprinted with permission under the Creative Commons Attribution License or equivalent.

Chapter 21: Sustainable Tourism Development in Cross River State, Nigeria was originally published as "Patronage of Ecotourism Potentials as a Strategy for Sustainable Tourism Development in Cross River State, Nigeria" in *Journal of Geography and Geology Vol. 1, No. 2, November 2009 at CCSE.* Reprinted with permission under the Creative Commons Attribution License or equivalent.

Chapter 22: Conserving Biodiversity on Mongolian Rangelands was originally published as "Conserving Biodiversity on Mongolian rangelands: Implications for Protected Area Development and Pastoral Uses" in *Reading, Richard P.; Bedunah, Donald J.; Amgalanbaatar, Sukhiin 2006. Conserving biodiversity on Mongolian Rangelands: Implications for protected area development and pastoral uses. In: Bedunah, Donald J., McArthur, E. Durant, and Fernandez-Gimenez, Maria, (comps.) 2006. Rangelands of Central Asia: Proceedings of the Conference on Transformations, Issues, and Future Challenges. 2004 January 27; Salt Lake City, UT. Proceeding RMRS-P-39. Fort Collins,*

CO: U.S. Department of Agriculture, Forest Service, Rocky Mountain Research Station. pp. 1–17. Reprinted with permission under the Creative Commons Attribution License or equivalent.

Chapter 23: Predictors of Sustainable Tourism in Holland and China was originally published as "Predictors of Sustainable Tourism: Resident Perceptions of Tourism in Holland and China" in *Proceedings of the 2005 Northeastern Recreation Research Symposium*. Reprinted with permission under the Creative Commons Attribution License or equivalent.

Chapter 24: Subsistence, Tourism, and Research was originally published as "Subsistence, Tourism, and Research: Layers of Meaning in Lake Clark National Park and Preserve" in *Gaul, Karen 2007. Subsistence, tourism, and research: Layers of meaning in Lake Clark National Park and Preserve. In: Watson, Alan; Sproull, Janet; Dean, Liese, (comps.). Science and stewardship to protect and sustain wilderness values: Eighth World Wilderness Congress symposium; September 30-October 6, 2005; Anchorage, AK. Proceedings RMRS-P-49. Fort Collins, CO: U.S. Department of Agriculture, Forest Service, Rocky Mountain Research Station. pp. 29–34*. Reprinted with permission under the Creative Commons Attribution License or equivalent.

Chapter 25: Biodiversity Science in South Africa was originally published as "South Africa—Serious About Biodiversity Science" in *PLoS BIOLOGY 5:17, 2005*. Reprinted with permission under the Creative Commons Attribution License or equivalent.

ably
References

1

Adger, W. N., Brown, K., Cervigini, R., and Moran, D. (1995). Total economic value of forests in Mexico. *Ambio* **24**, 286–296.

Anyinam, C. (1995). Ecology and ethnomedicine: Exploring links between current environmental crisis and indigenous medical practices. *Soc. Sci.Med.* **40**, 321–329.

Balick, M., and Cox, P. (1996). *Plants, People, and Culture: The Science of Ethnobotany*. Scientific Publications, New York.

Balick, M. J. and Mendelsohn, R. (1992). Assessing the economic value of traditional medicines from tropical rain forests. *Conserv. Biol.* **6** (1), 128–130.

Burke, I. C., Yonker, C. M., Parton, W. J., Cole, C. V., Flach, K., and Schimel, D. S. (1989). Texture, climate, and cultivation effects on soil organic matter content in U.S. Grassland soils. *Soil Sci. Soc. Am. J.* **53**, 800–805.

Caniago, I. and Siebert, S. F. (1998). Medicinal plant ecology, knowledge and conservation in Kalimantan, Indonesia. *Eco. Bot.* **52**, 229–250.

Cox, P. (2000). Will tribal knowledge survive the millennium? *Science* **287**, 44–45.

Cox, P. A. (1999). *Nafanua: Saving the Samoan Rain Forest*. W. H. Freeman (Ed.). New York.

Daily, G. (1997). *Nature's Services: Societal Dependence on Natural Ecosystems*. Island Press, Washington, DC.

Fennell, D. (1999). *Ecotourism: An Introduction*. Routledge, London.

Gatto, M. and De Leo, G. (2000). Pricing biodiversity and ecosystem services: The never ending story. *BioScience* **50**, 347–355.

Godoy, R., Lubowski, R., and Markandya, A. (1993). A Method for the economic valuation of non-timber tropical forest products. *Eco. Bot.* **47**, 220–233.

Hoagland, P., et al. (1995). *A Methodological Review of Net Benefit Evaluation for Marine Reserves*. World Bank.

Hoevenagel, R. (1994). *The Contingent Valuation Method: Scope and Validity*. Thesis, Institute for Environmental Studies, Vrije Universiteit, Amsterdam.

Honey, M. (1999). *Ecotourism and Sustainable Development*. Island Press, Washington, DC.

Jungerius, P. D. (1998). Indigenous knowledge of landscape-ecological zones among traditional herbalists: A case study in Keiyo District. *Kenya, Geo-Journal* **44**, 51–60.

Kell, B. (2001). From the Shamen to the Clinic: The Role of Ethnobotany in Antiviral Research. *International Antiviral News* **9**, 123–124.

Krutilla, J. (1991). *Environmental Resource Services of Malaysian Tropical Moist Forest*. Resources for the Future, Washington DC.

Lebbie, A. and Guries, R. (1995). Ethnobotanical value and conservation of sacred groves of the kpaa mende in sierra leone. *Eco. Bot.* **49**, 297–308.

Levin, D. A. (1976). Alkaloid-bearing plants: An ecogeographic perspective. *Am. Nat.* **110**, 261–284.

Mendelsohn, R. and Balick, M. (1995). The value of undiscovered pharmaceuticals in tropical forests. *Eco. Bot.* **49**, 223–228.

Menkhaus, S. and Lober, D. (1996). International ecotourism and the valuation of tropical rainforests in Costa Rica. *J. Envir. Man.* **47**, 1–10.

Milliken, W., Miller, R. P., Pollard, S. R., and Wandelli, E. V. (1992). *The Ethnobotany of the Waimiri Atroari Indians of Brazil*. Royal Botanical Gardens, Kew.

Mitchell, R. C., and Carson, R. T. (1989). *Using Surveys to Value Public Goods: The Contingent Valuation Method*. Resources for the Future, Washington, DC.

Myers, N. (1997). Biodiversity's Genetic Library. In *Nature's Services*. G. C. Daily (Ed.). Island Press, Washington, DC, pp. 255–273.

Navrud, S. (1999). *Linking Weak and Strong Sustainability Indicators: Critical Loads and Economic Values*. John Wiley & Sons Ltd.

Pandey, A. K. and Bisaria, A. K. (1998). Rational Utilization of Important Medicinal Plants: A Tool for Conservation. *The Indian Forester* **124**, 197–202.

Peters, C., Gentry, A., and Mendelsohn, R. (1989). Valuation of an Amazonian rainforest. *Nature* **339**, 655–656.

Pitman, N. and Jorgensen, P. (2002). Estimating the size of the world's threatened flora. *Science* **298**, 989.

Principe, P. P. (1991). Valuing the biodiversity of medicinal plants. In *Conservation of Medicinal Plants*. O. Akerele, V. Heywood, and H. Synge (Eds.). Cambridge University Press, Cambridge.

Soejarto, D. D. and Farnsworth, N. R. (1989). tropical rain forests: potential source of new drugs? *Perspect. Biol. Med.* **32**, 244–256.

Urgent, D. (2000). Medicine, myths and magic: The folk healers of a mexican market. *Eco. Bot.* **54**, 427–43.

Voeks, R. and Nyawa, S. (2001). Healing flora of the Brunei Dusun. *Borneo Research Bulletin.* **32**, 178–195.

Voeks, R. A. (1996a). Tropical forest healers and habitat preference. *Eco. Bot.* **50**, 354–373.

Voeks, R. A. (1996b). Extraction and tropical rain forest conservation in Eastern Brazil. In *Tropical Rainforest Research—Current Issues*. D. Edwards, W. Booth, and S. Choy (Eds.). Kluwer, Netherlands, pp. 477–487.

Voeks, R. A. (1997). *Sacred Leaves of Candomblé: African Magic, Medicine, and Religion in Brazil*. University of Texas Press, Austin.

Voeks, R. A. and Leony, A. (2004). Forthcoming. Forgetting the forest: Assessing medicinal plant erosion in Eastern Brazil. *Eco. Bot.* **58**, 294–306.

Voeks, R. A. and Sercombe, P. (2000). The scope of hunter-gatherer ethnomedicine. Soc. *Sci. Med.* **50**, 1–12.

Wunder, S. (2000). Ecotourism and economic incentives an empirical approach. *Ecol. Eco.* **32**, 465–479.

2

Boyle, A. and Birnie, P. (2002). *International Law and the Environment*, 2nd edition (Ed.). Oxford University Press, Oxford.

Brundtland website. (2001). *Brundtland Report webpage*. Retrieved from the World Wide Web: http://www.brundtlandnet.com/brundtlandreport.htm

Bull, A. (1991). *The Economics of Travel and Tourism*. Pitman, London.

Ceballos-Lascurian, H. (1997). *Ecotourism: A Guide for Planners and Managers.* Ecotourism Society, II, North Bennington, VT, USA.

CSD website. (1999). *Decision 7/3*. UN. Retrieved, 2001, from the World Wide Web: http://www.un.org/esa/sustdev/sdissues/tourism/tour2.htm#doc

Fennell, D. (1999). *Ecotourism: An Introduction*. Routledge, London.

Giongo, F. (1993). *A Study of Visitor Management in the World's National Parks and Protected Areas*. Colorado State University, Fort Collins, Colorado City, USA.

Goodwin, H. (1996). In pursuit of ecotourism. *Biodiversity and Conservation*, **5**, 227–291.

Holden, A. (2000). *Environment and Tourism.* Routledge, London, New York.

Sands, P. (1995). *Principle of International Environmental Law*, 1st edition. Manchester University Press, I, Manchester.

Shackleford, P. (1995). *WTO/OMT Presentation*. Paper presented at the Lanzarote Conference, Lanzarote Spain.

Weaver, D. (2001). *Tourism in 21st Century*. Continuum, New York.

Weaver, D. and Lawton, L. (2001). Ecotourism in modified spaces. In *Encyclopedia of Ecotourism*. D. Weaver (Ed.). CABI Publishing, Wallingford, UK, pp. 315–326.

Whelan, T. (1991). *Nature Tourism: Managing for the Environment*. Island Press, Washington, DC.

WSSD website. (2002). *Plan of Implementation*. Retrieved from the World Wide Web: http://www.johannesburgsummit.org/html/documents/summit_docs/2309_planfinal.doc or www.un.org/esa/sustdev/documents/WSSDPOIPD/English/POIToc.htm

WTO/OMT (1998). *Tourism 2020 Vision*. World Tourism Organisation, Madrid.

WTO/OMT website 1 (2000). *Global Code of Ethics for tourism*. Retrieved from the World Wide Web: http://www.world-tourism.org/frameset/frame_project_ethics.html

WTO/OMT website 2 (2000). *Massage of Secretary General*. Retrieved from World Wide Web: http://www.world tourism.org/

WTO/OMT website (2002). *Quebec Summit Declaration*. Retrieved from the World Wide Web: http://www.world-tourism.org/sustainable/IYE-Main-Menu.htm

3

Anonymous (2007) *Rating the Parks*. Consumer Reports June, **1997**, 10–17.

Balmford, A., Clegg, L., Coulson, T., and Taylor, J. (2002). Why conservationists should heed Pokémon. *Science* **295**, 2367.

Balmford, A. and Cowling, R (2006). Fusion or failure? The future of conservation biology. *Conserv. Biol.* **20**, 692–695.

Barnes, S. (2007). *How to be Wild*. Short Books, London.

Boo, E. (1990). *Ecotourism: The Potentials and Pitfalls*. World Wildlife Fund, Washington, DC.

Bookbinder, M. P., Dinerstein, E., Cauley, H., and Rajouria, A. (1998). Ecotourism's support of biological conservation. *Conserv. Biol.* **12**, 1399–1404.

Buckley, R. (2004). Effects of World Heritage listing on tourism to Australian National Parks. *J. Sust. Tour.* **12**, 70–84.

Buckley, R., Robinson, J., Carmody, J., and King, N. (2008). Monitoring for management of conservation and recreation in Australian protected areas. *Biodivers. Conserv.* 17, 3589–3606.

Butler, R. (1980). The concept of a tourism area cycle of evolution. *Can. Geogr.* 42, 5–12.

Butynski, T. M. and Kalima, J. (1998) Gorilla tourism: A critical look. In *Conservation of Biological Resources*. E. J. Milner-Gulland and R. Mace (Eds.). Blackwell Science, Oxford, pp. 294–313.

Ceballos-Lascurain, H. (1993). *Ecotourism: A Guide for Planners and Managers*. K. Lindberg and D. E. Hawkins, (Eds.). The Ecotourism Society, North Bennington, Vermont, pp. 1–3.

Ceballos-Lascurain, H. (1996). *Tourism, Ecotourism and Protected Areas*. International Union for Conservation of Nature, Gland, Switzerland.

Cochrane, J. (2003). *Ecotourism, Conservation and Sustainability: A Case Study of Bromo Tengger Semeru National Park, Indonesia*. (Unpublished PhD thesis). University of Hull, Hull, UK.

Davenport, L., Brockelman, W. Y., Wright, P. C., Ruf, K., and Rubio del Valle, F. B. (2002). Ecotourism tools for parks. In *Making Parks Work*. J. Terborgh, C. van Schaik, L. Davenport, and M. Rao (Eds.). Island Press, Washington, DC, pp. 279–306.

Eagles, P. (2002). Trends in park tourism: Economics, finance and management. *J. Sust. Tour.* **10**, 132–153.

Eagles, P. F. J. (2009). Governance of recreation and tourism partnerships in parks and protected areas. *J. Sust. Tour.* 17, 231–248.

Fretwell, H. L. and Podolsky, M. J. (2003). A Strategy for Restoring America's National Parks. *Duke Environmental Law and Policy Forum* **13**, 143–186.

Goodwin, H. J. (1996). In pursuit of ecotourism. *Biodiv. Conserv.* **5**, 277–291.

Gossling, S. (1999). Ecotourism: A means to safeguard biodiversity and ecosystem functions? *Ecol. Econ.* **29**, 303–320.

Kahn, P. H. and Kellert, S. R., (Eds.) (2002). *Children and Nature*. MIT Press, Cambridge, Massachusetts.

Kareiva, P. (2008). Ominous trends in nature recreation. *Proc. Natl. Acad. Sci. USA* **105**, 2757–2758.

Kiss, A. (2004). Is community-based ecotourism a good use of biodiversity conservation funds? *TREE* **19**, 232–237.

Kruger, O. (2005). The role of ecotourism in conservation: Panacea or Pandora's box? *Biodivers. Conserv.* **14**, 579–600.

Louv, R. (2005) *Last Child in The Woods*. Algonquin, Chapel Hill, North Carolina.

Mastny, L. (2001). *Treading lightly: New Paths for International Tourism.* Worldwatch Institute, Washington.

Millennium Ecosystem Assessment (2005). *Ecosystems and Human Wellbeing: Biodiversity Synthesis.* World Resources Institute, Washington, DC.

Nabhan, G. P. and Trimble, S. (1994). *The Geography of Childhood: Why Children need Wild Places.* Beacon Press, Boston.

Pergams, O. R. W. and Zaradic, P. A. (2008). Evidence for a fundamental and pervasive shift away from nature-based recreation. *Proc. Natl. Acad. Sci. USA* **105**, 2295–2300.

Plummer, R. and Fennell, D. A. (2009). Managing protected areas for sustainable tourism: Prospects for adaptive co-management. *J. Sust. Tour.* **17**, 149–168.

Prosser, R. (1994). Societal change and the growth in alternative tourism. In *Ecotourism: A Sustainable Option?* E. Cater and G. Lowman (Eds.). John Wiley, Chichester, UK, pp. 19–37.

Pyle, R. M. (1993). *Thunder Tree: Lessons from a Secondhand Landscape.* Houghton Mifflin, New York.

Pyle, R. M. (2003). Nature matrix: Reconnecting people and nature. *Oryx* **37**, 206–214.

Reed, S. E. and Merenlender, A. M. (2008). Quiet, nonconsumptive recreation reduces protected area effectiveness. *Conserv. Lett.* **1**, 146–154.

Scholes, R. J. and Biggs, R. (2004). *Ecosystem Services in Southern Africa: A Regional Perspective.* Council for Scientific and Industrial Research, Pretoria.

Walpole, M. J. and Goodwin, H. J. (2000). Local economic impacts of dragon tourism in Indonesia. *Ann. Touris. Res.* **27**, 559–576.

Walpole, M. J., Goodwin, H. J., and Ward, K. G. R. (2001) Pricing policy for tourism in protected areas: Lessons from Komodo National Park, Indonesia. *Conserv. Biol.* **15**, 218–27.

Walpole, M. J. and Leader-Williams, N. (2001). Masai Mara tourism reveals partnership benefits. *Nature* **413**, 771.

Walpole, M. J. and Thouless, C. R. (2005). Increasing the value of wildlife through non-consumptive use? Deconstructing the myths of ecotourism and community-based tourism in the tropics. In *People and Wildlife: Conflict or Coexistence?* R. Woodroffe, S. Thirgood, and A. Rabinowitz, (Eds.). Cambridge University Press, Cambridge, pp. 122–139.

Wells, M. P. (1993). Neglect of biological riches—the economics of nature tourism in Nepal. *Biodivers. Conserv.* **2**, 445–464.

West, P., Igoe, J., and Brockington, D. (2006). Parks and peoples: The social impact of protected areas. *Ann. Rev. Anthropol.* **35**, 251–77.

Wilkie, D. S. and Carpenter, J. F. (2002). Can nature tourism help finance protected areas in the Congo Basin? *Oryx* **33**, 333–339.

Williams, N. (2008). Backs to nature. *Curr. Biol.* **18**, R136–137.

World Bank (2008). *World Development Indicators 2008.* World Bank Publications, Washington, DC.

World Conservation Union and United Nations Environment Programme-World Conservation Monitoring Centre (2007). *World Database on Protected Areas, version 2007.* United Nations Environment Programme-World Conservation Monitoring Centre, Cambridge.

World Tourism Organization (2002). *Tourism and Poverty Alleviation.* World Tourism Organization, Madrid.

World Travel and Tourism Council (2007). *The Global Travel and Tourism Summit.* World Travel and Tourism Council, London.

Zaradic, P. A. and Pergams, O. R. W. (2007). Videophilia: Implications for childhood development and conservation. *J. Dev. Proc.* **2**, 130–144.

4

Bian, X. Analysis on the relationship of ecotourism, biodiversity protection and local community in nature reserves (periodical style). *J. Beijing Second Foreign Lang. Inst.* **5**, 61–629 (In Chinese).

Design of Ecotourism (book style) (2006). China Forestry Publishing House, pp. 1–3 (In Chinese).

Guihua, Y., Linsheng, Z., and Qingzhong, M. (2000). *Ecotourism* (book style). Higher Education Press, Beijing, pp. 25–39 (In Chinese).

Hong, J. and Dongya, R. (2006). *Planning Design of Ecotourism* (book style). China Forestry Publishing House, pp. 1–3 (In Chinese) *Inter. J. Bus. Mgmt* March, 2009

Hongshu, W. and Min, T. (2005). *Ecotourism and Ecological Environment Protection* (book style). Northeast Forestry University Press, pp. 8–12 (In Chinese).

Jian-ping, Z. (2001). *Ecotourism—Theory and Practice* (book style). China Travel and Tourism Press, Beijing, pp. 196–197 (In Chinese).

Pearce, D. G. (1992). Alternative tourism: Concepts, classifications and questions, tourism alternatives, potentials and problems in the development of tourism (book style with paper title and editor). University of Pennsylvania Press, Philadelphia, pp. 15–20.

Tong M. (2006). *Study on Ecotourism Based on Community Participation of China* (book style). Northeast Forestry University Press, pp. 22–29 (In Chinese).

5

Campbell, L. M. (1999). Ecotourism in rural developing communities. *Annals of Tourism Res.* **26**(3), 534–54.

Honey, S. M. and Martha, S. (1999). Treading lightly? Ecotourism's impact on the environment. *Environment* **41**(5), 4–9.

IUCN (World Conservation Union) (1997). Chapter 4.22 Ecotourism. In *Beyond Fences: Seeking Social Sustainability in Conservation.* IUCN, Gland.

Volume 1 of this document presents guidelines for planning and implementing conservation activities, including ecotourism. The 2nd volume is an extensive reference book.

IUCN (World Conservation Union) (1998). Population and Parks. *PARKS Magazine* **8**(1).

A selection of case studies acknowledging the need to establish partnerships and encourage cooperation with neighbors and other stakeholders, promote stewardship, and other instruments which support protected areas objectives.

IUCN-WCPA (World Commission on Protected Areas). (2000). *Protected Areas: Benefits beyond Boundaries—WCPA in Action.* IUCN, Gland.

Lea, J. P. (2000). Ecotourism in the less developed countries. *Annals of Tourism Res.* **27**(1), 248–249.

Phillips, A. (Ed.) (2002). *Sustainable Tourism in Protected Areas: Guidelines for Planning and Management.* IUCN, Gland.

These guidelines focus on protected area tourism and its management. They provide theoretical underpinnings and practical guidelines for managers. Available for purchase online: http://www.iucn.org/bookstore.

Roe, D., Leader-Williams, N., and Dalal-Clayton, B. (1997). *Take Only Photographs, Leave Only Footprints: The Environmental Impacts of Wildlife Ecotourism Tourism.* Environmental Planning Group, International Institute for Environment and Development Wildlife and Development Series No. 10, October. Retrieved from: http://www.ecotourism.org/textfiles/roe.pdf

Sweeting, J., James, E. N., Bruner, A. G., and Rosenfeld, A. B. (1999). *The Green Host Effect: An Integrated Approach to Sustainable Tourism and Resort Development.* Conservation International, Washington, DC. (Digital copy provided.)

Wood, M. E. (2002). *Ecotourism: Principles, Practices and Policies for Sustainability.* UN Environment Programme, Division of Technology, Industry, and Economics and the International Ecotourism Society, Burlington, Vermont.

This publication, developed as a preparatory document for the World Ecotourism Summit in Quebec (May 2002), reviews the current status and trends in ecotourism globally and identifies future challenges and lessons learned in more than 15 years of ecotourism development. (Digital copy included: Part 1, Part 2.)

WTO (World Tourism Organization) (2001). *Tourism Highlights 2000.* WTO, Madrid.

WTO (World Tourism Organization) (2002). *Sustainable Development of Ecotourism: A Compilation of Good Practices.* WTO, Madrid.

This publication was prepared for the International Year of Ecotourism 2002 as a second edition of its series, Sustainable Development of Tourism: A Compilation of Good Practices. The

55 case studies from 39 countries present a wide range of successful ecotourism initiatives in a systematic form, describing stakeholders, objectives and strategies, funding, sustainability and monitoring, problems, and solutions.

6

Aitchison, C. (2004). *Fullabrook Wind Farm Proposal, North Devon: Evidence Gathering of the Impact of Wind Farms on Visitor Numbers and Tourist Experience.* University of the West of England, Bristol, UK, pp. 1–26.

American Wind Energy Association. (2009). *Wind Energy Grows by Record 8,300 MW in 2008: Smart Policies, Stimulus Bill Needed to Maintain Momentum in 2009.* AWEA Newsroom, Washington, DC, USA, Retrieved from: http://www.awea.org/newsroom/releases/wind_energy_ growth2008_27Jan09.html/ (accessed on September 26, 2009).

An Assessment of the Potential Costs and Benefits of Offshore Wind Turbines (2008). Global Insight Inc., Lexington, MA, USA, pp. 1–102.

Bishop, I. D. and Miller, D. R. (2007). Visual assessment of off-shore wind turbines: The influence of distance, contrast, movement and social variables. *Renewable Energy* 32, 814–831.

Booth, D. E. (2002). *Searching for Paradise: Economic Development and Environmental Change in the Mountain West.* Rowman & Littlefield Publishers, Lanham, MD, USA.

British Wind Energy Association (2006). *The Impact of Wind Farms on the Tourist Industry in the UK.* London, UK, pp. 1–23.

Carson, R. T. and Hanemann, W. M. (2005). Contingent Valuation. In *Handbook of Environmental Economics: Valuing Environmental Changes*, Volume 2. K. G. Maler and J. R. Vincent (Eds.). Elsevier B.V., Amsterdam, Netherlands, pp. 821–936.

Cook, G. (2004). *Renewable Energy Policy in Denmark—An Introduction.* Scottish Parliament Information Centre (SPICE), Edinburgh, UK, pp. 1–13.

Dalton, G. J., Lockington, D. A., and Baldock, T. E. (2008). A survey of tourist attitudes to renewable energy supply in Australian hotel accommodation. *Renewable Energy* 33, 2174–2185.

Devlin, E. (2002). *Factors Affecting Public Acceptance of Wind Turbines in Sweden.* Master's thesis, Lund University, Lund, Sweden.

Dillman, D. A. (2007). *Mail and Internet Surveys: The Tailored Design Method.* 2nd edition. John Wiley & Sons, Hoboken, NJ, USA.

Dudleston, A. (2000). *Public Attitudes Towards Wind Farms in Scotland: Results of a Residents Survey.* The Scottish Executive Central Research Unit. Edinburgh, UK, pp. 1–40.

Falk, J. M., Graefe, A. R., and Suddleson, M. E. (1994). *Recreational Benefits of Delaware's Public Beaches: Attitudes and Perceptions of Beach Users and Residents of the Mid-Atlantic Region.* Technical Report No. DEL-SG-05-94. University of Delaware, Sea Grant College Program, Newark, DE, USA, pp. 1–40.

Firestone, J. and Kempton, W. (2007). Public opinion about large offshore wind: Underlying factors. *Energ. Policy* 35, 1584–1598.

Firestone, J., Kempton, W., and Krueger, A. (2008). *Delaware Opinion on Offshore Wind Power, Final Report.* University of Delaware, Newark, DE, USA, pp. 1–66.

Firestone, J., Kempton, W., and Krueger, A. (2009). Public acceptance of offshore wind power projects in the USA. *Wind Energy* 12, 183–202.

Firestone, J., Kempton, W., Krueger, A., and Loper, C. E. (2005). Regulating offshore wind power and aquaculture: Messages from land and sea. *Cornell J. Law Public Policy* 14, 71–111.

Grijalva, T. C., Berrens, R. P., Bohara, A. K., and Shaw, W. D. (2002). Testing the validity of contingent behavior trip responses. *Amer. J. Agr. Econ.* 84, 401–414.

Gujarati, D. N. (2003). *Basic Econometrics,* 4th edition. McGraw-Hill/Irwin, New York, USA.

Harrington, M. (October 30, 2006). Wind power's payoff in Denmark: It's a global leader in the technology, and turbines are a common sight, but criticism and challenges persist, Newsday.

Houston, J. R. (2008). The economic value of beaches—A 2008 update. *Shore Beach* 76, 22–26.

How Important is Tourism to Delaware? (February 1, 2008). Global Insight Inc., Lexington, MA, USA, pp. 1–34. Retrieved from: http://www.dedo.delaware.gov/information/tourism/DelawareTSA-final_Feb2008.pdf (accessed on September 26, 2009).

How Important is Tourism in Delaware? The Tourism Satellite Account Perspective (June 9, 2005), Global Insight Inc., Lexington, MA, USA, pp. 1–38. Retrieved from: http://www.visitsoutherndelaware.com/media/2005_Economic_Impact_Global_Insight_Study.pdf (accessed on September 26, 2009).

Institut für Tourismus- und Bäderforschung in Nordeuropa (N.I.T.) (2000). *Touristische Effekte von On- und Offshore- Windkraftanlagen in Schleswig-Holstein.* Kiel, Germany, pp. 1–4.

Jarvis, C. M. (2005). *An Evaluation of the Wildlife Impacts of Offshore Wind Development Relative to Fossil Fuel Power Production.* Master's thesis. University of Delaware, Newark, DE, USA.

Kannen, A. (2005). The need for integrated assessment of large-scale offshore wind farm development. In *Managing European Coasts: Past, Present and Future,* J. Vermaat, L. Bouwer, K. Turner, and W. Salomons, (Eds.). Springer, Berlin, Germany, pp. 365–378.

Kempton, W., Archer, C. L., Dhanju, A., Garvine, R. W., and Jacobson, M. Z. (2007), Large CO_2 reductions via offshore wind power matched to inherent storage in energy end-uses. *Geophys. Res. Lett.* **34**, L02817.

Kempton, W., Firestone, J., Lilley, J., Rouleau, T., and Whitaker, P. (2005).The offshore wind power debate: Views from Cape Cod. *Coast. Manage.* **33**, 119–149.

Kent, L. K. and Jones, C. (2007). *The Economic Effects of a Five Year Nourishment Program for the Ocean Beaches of Delaware, Updated.* Report No. 2006-102. Chrysalis Consulting Inc., Alexandria, VA, USA, pp. 1–50.

Krueger, A., Firestone, J., and Parsons, G. Preferences for offshore wind power development: A choice experiment approach. *Land Eco.* (under review).

Krueger, A. D. (2007). *Valuing Public Preferences for Offshore Wind Power: A Choice Experiment* Approach. Doctoral Dissertation. University of Delaware, Newark, DE, USA.

Kuehn, S. (2005). Sociological investigation of the reception of horns Rev and Nysted offshore wind farms In *The Local Communities; Annual Status Report 2003.* Elsam Engineering, Fredericia, Denmark, pp. 1–25.

Ladenburg, J. (2009a). Attitudes towards offshore wind farms—the role of beach visits on attitude and demographic and attitude relations. *Energ. Policy* (in press).

Ladenburg, J. (2009b). Stated public preferences for on-land and offshore wind power generation—A review. *Wind Energy* **12**, 171–181.

Lieberman Research Group, Mills, D., and Rosen, H. (2006). *New Jersey Shore Opinions About Off-Shore Wind Turbines.* Great Neck, NY, USA, pp. 1–33.

Lilley, M. B. and Firestone, J. (2008). Wind power, wildlife, and the Migratory Bird Treaty Act: A way forward. *Environ. Law* **38**, 1167–1214.

Logan, J. and Kaplan, S. M. (2008). *Wind Power in the United States: Technology, Economic, and Policy Issues.* RL34546, Congressional Research Service. Washington, DC, USA, pp. 1–49.

Long, J. S. (1997). *Regression Models for Categorical and Limited Dependent Variables,* Vol. 7. Sage Publications, Thousand Oaks, CA, USA.

NFO WorldGroup (2003). *Investigation into the Potential Impact of Wind Farms on Tourism in Wales, Summary Report.* Project 013479. Edinburgh, UK, pp. 1–21.

Parsons, G. R. and Massey, D. M. (2003). A Random Utility Model of Beach Recreation. In *The New Economics of Outdoor Recreation.* Edward Elgar Publishing, Cheltenham, UK, pp. 241–267.

Roach, J. (2008). *U.S. leads world in windpower growth.* National Geographic News, April 21, 2008; Retrieved from: http://news.nationalgeographic.com/news/2008/04/080421-wind-power.html/ (accessed on September 26, 2009).

Santora, C., Hade, N., and Odell, J. (2004). Managing offshore wind developments in the United States: Legal, environmental and social considerations using a case study in Nantucket sound. *Ocean Coast. Manage.* **47**, 141–164.

Soerensen, H. C., Hansen, L. K., Hansen, R., and Hammarlund, K. (2003). *European Thematic Network on Wave Energy, Public Acceptability, Final Report.* NNE5-1999-00438, WP 3.4, pp. 1–23.

Strachan, P. A. and Lal, D. (2004). Wind energy policy, planning, and management practice in the UK: Hot air or a gathering storm? *Reg. Stud.* **38**, 551–571.

Strachan, P. A., Lal, D., and von Malmborg, F. (2006). The evolving UK wind energy industry: Critical policy and management aspects of the emerging research agenda. *Eur. Environ.* **16**, 1–18.

Southern Delaware Tourism, Beaches, Bays, and Waterways (2008). The Official Convention & Visitors Bureau of Sussex County Delaware. Georgetown, DE, USA. Retrieved from: http://www.visitsoutherndelaware.com/Beaches_Bays_and_Waterways.htm (accessed on September 26, 2009).

Thur, S. M. (2003). *Valuing Recreational Benefits in Coral Reef Marine Protected Areas: An Application to the Bonaire National Marine Park.* Doctoral Dissertation, University of Delaware, Newark, DE, USA.

Toepfer, K. (2002). Foreword: Signposts to sustainability. In *Wind Energy in the 21st Century: Economics, Policy, Technology and the Changing Electric Industry.* R. Y. Redlinger, P. D. Andersen, and P. E. Morthorst (Eds.). Palgrave Macmillan, Houndmills, UK.

US and China in Race to the Top of Global Wind Industry (2009). Global Wind Energy Council: Brussels, Belgium. Retrieved from: http://www.gwec.net/index.php?id=30&no_cache=1&tx_ttnews[tt_news]=177&tx_ttnews[backPid]=4&cHash=04fdc8c00a/ (accessed on September 26, 2009).

Visitor Profile Study: Sussex County (2008). Delaware Economic Development Office. Dover, DE, USA, pp. 1–17.

Wiser, R. and Bolinger, M. (2007). *Annual Report on U.S. Wind Power Installation, Cost, and Performance Trends: 2006.* Technical Report No: DOE/GO-102007-2433. National Renewable Energy Laboratory, Washington, DC, USA, pp. 1–23.

7

Ancrenaz, M., Gimenez, O., Ambu, L., Ancrenaz, K., Andau, P., et al. (2005). Aerial surveys give new estimates for orang-utans in Sabah, Malaysia. *PloS. Biol.* **3**(1), e3. doi:10.1371/journal.pbio.0030003.

Ancrenaz, M., Gimenez, O., Goossens, B., Sawang, A., and Lackman-Ancrenaz, I. (2004). Determination of ape distribution and population size with ground and aerial surveys: A case study with orang-utans in lower Kinabatangan, Sabah, Malaysia. *Animal Conserv.* **7**, 375–385.

Betz, W. (2001). Matschie's tree kangaroo (Marsupialia: Macropodidae, *Dendrolagus matscheie*) in Papua New Guinea: Estimates of population density and landowner accounts of food plants and natural history. University of Southampton.

Borrini-Feyerabend, G., Kothar, I. A., and Oviedo, G. (2004). *Indigenous and Local Communities and Protected Areas Towards Equity and Enhanced Conservation.* World commission in protected areas, Series number 11. IUCN Publications, Gland, Switzerland, p. 113.

Bubb, P., May, I., Miles, L., and Sayer, J. (2004). *Cloud Forest Agenda.* United Nations Environment Programme—World Conservation Monitoring Centre, Cambridge, UK.

Child, B. (2004). *Parks in Transition.* Earthscan, IUCN Publication, London, UK, p. 267.

Dabek, L., O'Neil, S., and Ross, T. (Eds.) (2007). *Biodiversity of the YUS Conservation Area—Survey Report.* In preparation.

Flannery, T. (1995). *Mammals of New Guinea.* Cornell University Press, Ithaca, New York, p. 568.

Hogkins, M., Stolton, S., Leverington, F., Dudley, N., and Courrau, J. (2006). *Evaluating Effectiveness: A framework for Assessing Management Effectiveness of Protected Areas,* 2nd edition. IUCN Publications, Gland, Switzerland, p. 121.

IUCN (2007). *IUCN List of Threatened Species: A Global Species Assessement.* IUCN, Gland, Switzerland.

Lascurain, H. C. (1996). *Tourism, Ecotourism and Protected Areas*. IUCN Publications, Gland, Switzerland.

Lea, D. (2004). *Customary Land Tenure in Papua New Guinea: What Does it Really Mean?* National Research Institute Printery, Boroko, Papua New Guinea, p. 88.

Mace, G. M., Balmford, A., and Ginsberg, J. R. (1998). *Conservation in a Changing World. Conservation Biology Series 1*. Cambridge University Press, Cambridge, UK, p. 308.

Mittermeier, R. A., Mittermeier, C. G., Gil, P. R., and Pilgrim, J. (2003). *Wilderness: Earth's Last Wild Places*. University of Chicago Press, Chicago, p. 576.

Oates, J. F. (1999). *Myth and Reality in the Rainforest: How Conservation Strategies are Failing in West Africa*. University of California Press, Berkeley, California, p. 297.

Phillips, A. (2003). Turning ideas on their heads: The new paradigm for protected areas. *The George Wright Forum* **20**(2).

Rajaratnam, R., et al. (2007). Ecotourism and indigenous communities: The lower Kinabatangan experience. In *Tourism at the Grassroots: Villagers and Visitors in the Asia Pacific*. J. Connell and B. Rugendyke (Eds.). Routledge, Abingdon, Australia (in press).

Woodroffe, R., Thirgood, S., and Rabinowitz, A. (2005). People and wildlife: Conflict or coexistence? *Conservation Biology Series 9*. Cambridge University Press, Cambridge, UK, p. 497.

8

Bain, D. E. (2002). A model linking energetic effects of whale watching to killer whale (*Orcinus orca*) population dynamics. *Friday Harbor*. University of Washington Press, Washington.

Barnes, J. I. (1996). Changes in the economic use value of elephant in Botswana: The effect of international prohibition. *Ecolog. Eco.* **18**, 215–230.

Brook, B. W. and Sodhi, N. S. (2006). Rarity bites. *Nature* **444**, 555–557.

Clark, C. W. (1990). *Mathematical Bioeconomics: Optimal Management of Renewable Resources*. Wiley, Hoboken, New Jersey.

Courchamp, F., Angulo, E., Rivalan, P., Hall, R., Signoret, L., et al. (2006). Rarity value and species extinction: The anthropogenic Allee effect. *PLoS Biology* **4**(12), e415. doi: 10.1371/journal.pbio.0040415.

Duarte-Quiroga, A. and Estrada, A. (2003). Primates as pets in Mexico City: An assessment of the species involved, source of origin, and general aspects of treatment. *Amer. J. Primatolog.* **61**, 53–60.

Gault, A. and Meinard, Y. (2008). Courchamp. FConsumers' taste for rarity drives sturgeons to extinction. *Conservation Lett.* **1**, 199–207.

Hall, R. J., Milner-Gulland, E. J., and Courchamp, F. (2008). Endangering the endangered: The effects of perceived rarity on species exploitation. *Conservation Lett.* **1**, 75–81.

Jepson, P. and Ladle, R. J. (2005). Bird-keeping in Indonesia: Conservation impacts and the potential for substitution-based conservation responses. *Oryx* **39**, 442–448.

Martín-López, B., Montes, C., and Benayas, J. (2007). The non-economic motives behind the willingness to pay for biodiversity conservation. *Biolog. Conservation* **139**, 67–82.

Ojea, E. and Loureiro M. L. (2007) Altruistic, egoistic and biospheric values in willingness to pay (WTP) for wildlife. *Ecolog. Eco.* **63**, 807–814.

Rivalan, P., Delmas, V., Angulo, E., Rosser, A. M., Bull, L. S., et al. (2007). Can bans stimulate wildlife trade? *Nature* **447**, 529–530.

SAS Institute Inc. (2004). *SAS, 9·1·3, Help and Documentation*. SAS Institute Inc., Cary, N.C, USA.

Slone, T. H., Orsak, L. J., and Malver, O. (1997). A comparison of price, rarity and cost of butterfly specimens: Implications for the insect trade and for habitat conservation. *Ecolog. Econim.* **21**, 77–85.

StatSoft Inc. (2001). Data Analysis Software System, version 6. Retrieved from: http://www.statsoft.com.

Torgler, B. and García-Valiñas, A. (2007) The determinants of individuals' attitudes towards preventing environmental damage. *Ecolog. Eco.* **63**, 536–552.

Yi-Ming, L., Zenxiang, G., Xinhai, L., Sung, W., and Niemela, J. (2000). Illegal wildlife trade in the Himalayan region of China. *Biodiv. Conserv.* **9**, 901–918.

9

Bain, D. E. (2002). *A model Linking Energetic Effects of Whale Watching to Killer Whale (Orcinus orca) Population Dynamics*. University of Washington Press, Friday Harbor, Washington, p. 23.

Bulte, E. H. (2003). Open access harvesting of wildlife: The poaching pit and conservation of endangered species. *Agric. Econ.* **28**, 27–37.

California Department of Fish and Game (2005). *Abalone Recovery and Management Plan*. California Department of Fish and Game-Marine Region.

Capercaillie Action Programme. (October 12, 2006). Retrieved from http://www.rspb.org.uk/scotland/action/capercaillie/program.asp

Clark, C. W. (1990). *Mathematical Bioeconomics: Optimal Management of Renewable Resources*. Wiley, Hoboken, New Jersey, p. 386.

Courchamp, F., Clutton-Brock, T., and Grenfell, B. (1999). Inverse density dependence and the Allee effect. *Trends. Ecol. Evol.* **14**, 405–410.

Courchamp, F. and Macdonald, D. W. (2001). Crucial importance of pack size in the African wild dog *Lycaon pictus*. *Anim. Conserv.* **4**, 169–174.

Davis, G. E., Haaker, P. L., and Richards, D. V. (1998). The perilous condition of white abalone *Haliotis sorenseni*, Bartsch, 1940. *J. Shellfish. Res.* **17**, 871–875.

Donaldson, T. J. and Sadovy, Y. (2001). Threatened fishes of the world: *Cheilinus undulatus* Rüppell, 1835 (Labridae). *Environ. Biol. Fishes* **6**, 428–428.

Dulvy, N. K., Sadovy, Y., and Reynolds, J. D. (2003). Extinction vulnerability in marine populations. *Fish and Fisheries* **4**, 25–64.

Ekelund, R. B. J. and Hebert, R. F. (1997). *A history of economic theory and method*. McGraw-Hill, New York, p. 704.

Festa-Bianchet, M. (2003). Exploitative wildlife management as a selective pressure for life-history evolution of large mammals. In *Animal behavior and Wildlife Conservation*. M. Festa-Bianchet and M. Apollonio (Eds.). Island Press, Washington, District of Columbia, pp. 191–207.

Fuller, E. (1999). *The Great Auk*. N. Harry (Ed.). Abrams, New York.

Gordon, H. S. (1954). The economic theory of a common property resource: The fishery. *J. Polit. Econ.* **62**, 124–142.

Hobday, A. J. and Tegner, M. J. (2000). *Status Review of White Abalone (Haliotis sorenseni) Throughout its Range in California and Mexico*. U.S. Department of Commerce, National Oceanic and Atmospheric Administration.

Jacobson, S. K. and Lopez, A. F. (1994). Biological impacts of ecotourism–tourists and nesting turtles in Tortuguero National Park, Costa-Rica. *Wildlife Soc. Bull.* **22**, 414–419.

Pikitch, E. K., Doukakis, P., Lauck, L., Chakrabarty, P., and Erickson, D. L. (2005). Status, trends and management of sturgeon and paddlefish fisheries. *Fish and Fisheries* **6**, 233–265.

Raymakers, C. (2002). International trade in sturgeon and paddlefish species—The effect of CITES listing. *Int. Rev. Hydrobiol.* **87**, 525–537.

Raymakers, C. and Hoover, C. (2002). Acipenseriformes: CITES implementation from range states to consumer countries. *J. Appl. Ichthyol.* **18**, 629–638.

Rosser, A. M. and Mainka, S. A. (2002). Overexploitation and species extinctions. *Conserv. Biol.* **16**, 584–586.

Sadovy, Y. and Cheung, W. L. (2003). Near extinction of a highly fecund fish: The one that nearly got away. *Fish and Fisheries* **4**, 86–99.

Sekercioglu, C. (2002). Impacts of birdwatching on human and avian communities. *Environ. Conserv.* **29**, 282–289.

Slone, T. H., Orsak, L. J., and Malver, O. (1997). A comparison of price, rarity and cost of butterfly specimens: Implications for the insect trade and for habitat conservation. *Ecol. Econ.* **21**, 77–85.

Stephens, P. A. and Sutherland, W. J. (1999) Consequences of the Allee effect for behavior, ecology and conservation. *Trends. Ecol. Evol.* **14**, 401–405.

Stuart, B. L., Rhodin, A. G., Grismer, L. L., and Hansel, T. (2006). Scientific description can imperil species. *Science* **312**, 1137.

Tegner, M. J. (1993). Southern California abalones: Can stocks be rebuilt using marine harvest refugia? *Can. J. Fish Aquat. Sci.* **50**, 2010–2018.

Thomas, M., Elliott, G., and Gregory. R. (2001). The impact of egg collecting on scarce breeding birds 1982–1999. *RSPB Conserv. Rev.* **13**, 39–44.

10

Balmford, A., Beresford, J., Green, J., Naidoo, R., Walpole, M., et al. (2009). A global perspective on trends in nature-based tourism. *PloS Biol.* **7**(6), e1000144. doi:10.1371/journal.pbio.1000144.

Balmford, A., Bruner, A., Cooper, P., Costanza, R., Farber, S., et al. (2002). Economic reasons for conserving wild nature. *Science* **297**, 950–953.

Balmford, A., Gaston, G. J., Blyth, S., James, A., and Kapes, V. (2003). Global variation in conservation costs, conservation benefits, and unmet conservation needs. *Proc. Natl. Acad. Sci. USA* **100**, 1046–1050.

Balmford, A. and Whitten, T. (2003). Who should pay for tropical conservation, and how could the costs be met? *Oryx* **37**, 238–250.

Bruner, A., Hanks J., and Hannah, L. (2003). How much will effective protected area systems cost? Retrieved from: http://www.conservation-finance.com/Documents/CF_related_papers/PA_Costs2.pdf (Accessed March 29, 2009).

Buckley, R. C. (1994). Values, benefits, costs and funds in biodiversity conservation. *Aust. Biol.* **7**, 46–48.

Buckley, R. C. (1999). An ecological perspective on carrying capacity. *Ann. Tour. Res.* **26**, 705–708.

Buckley, R. C. (2004a). *Environmental Impacts of Ecotourism*. CABI, Oxford.

Buckley, R. C. (2004b). The effects of World Heritage listing on tourism to Australian national parks. *J. Sust. Tour.* **12**, 70–84.

Buckley, R. C. (2008a). World wild web: Funding connectivity conservation under climate change. *Biodiversity* **9**, 71–78.

Buckley, R. C. (2009). *Ecotourism Principles and Practices*. CABI, Oxford.

Carpenter, S. R., Mooney, H. A., Agard, J., Capistrano, D., DeFries, R. S., et al. (2009). Science for managing ecosystem services: Beyond the Millennium Ecosystem Assessment. *Proc. Natl. Acad. Sci. USA* **106**, 1305–1312.

Costanza, R., d'Arge, R., Groot, R. D., Farber, S., Grasso, M., et al. (1997). The value of the world's ecosystem services and natural capital. *Nature* **387**, 253–260.

Eagles, P. (2002). Trends in park tourism: Economics, finance and management. *J. Sust. Tour.* **10**, 132–153.

Ehrlich, P. R. and Pringle, R. M. (2008). Where does biodiversity go from here? A grim business-as-usual forecast and a hopeful portfolio of partial solutions. *Proc. Natl. Acad. Sci. USA* **105**(Suppl), 111579–111586.

Ferraro, P. J. and Kiss, A. (2002). Direct payments to conserve biodiversity. *Science* **298**, 1718–1719.

Ghazoul, J. (2009). Bailing out creatures great and small. *Science* **323**, 460.

Ingraham, M. W., and Foster, S. G. (2008). The value of ecosystem services provided by the US National Wildlife Refuge System in the contiguous US. *Ecol Econ* **67**, 608–618.

Jacobs, M. H. and Manfredo, M. J. (2008). Decline in nature-based recreation is not evident. *Proc. Natl. Acad. Sci. USA* **105**, E40.

James, A., Gaston, K., and Balmford, A. (1999). Balancing the earth's accounts. *Nature* **401**, 323–324.

Kareiva, P. (2008). Ominous trends in nature recreation. *Proc. Natl. Acad. Sci. USA* **105**, 2757–2758.

Kleijn, D. and Sutherland, W. J. (2003). How effective are European agri-environment schemes in conserving biodiversity? *J. Appl. Ecol.* **40**, 947–969.

Littlefair, C. and Buckley, R. C. (2008) Interpretation reduces ecological impacts of visitors to World Heritage Areas. *Ambio.* **37**, 338–341.

McDonald-Madden, E., Gordon, A., Wintle, B. A., Walker, S., Grantham, H., et al. (2009) "True" conservation progress. *Science* **323**, 43–44.

Pergams, O. R. W. and Zaradic, P. A. (2007). Evidence for a fundamental and pervasive shift away from nature-based recreation. *Proc. Natl. Acad. Sci. USA* **105**, 2295–2300.

Pergams, O. R. W. and Zaradic, P. A. (2008). Reply to Jacobs and Manfredo: More support for a pervasive decline in nature-based recreation. *Proc. Natl. Acad. Sci. USA* **105**, E41–42.

Pimm, S. L., Ayres, M., Balmford, A., Branch, G., Brandon, K., et al. (2001). Can we defy nature's end? *Science* **293**, 2207–2208.

Sinclair, A. R. E., Ludwig, D., and Clark, C. W. (2000). Conservation in the real world. *Science* **289**, 1875.

Varghese, G. (2008). Public-private partnerships in South African national parks: Rationale, benefits and lessons learned. In *Responsible Tourism: Critical Issues for Conservation and Development*. A. Spenceley (Ed.). Earthscan, London, pp. 69–84.

Watson, A. E. and Borrie, W. T. (2003). Applying public-purpose marketing in the USA to protect relationships with public land. In *Nature-based Tourism, Environment and Land Management*. R. C. Buckley, C. M. Pickering, and D. B. Weaver (Eds.). CABI, Oxford, pp. 25–33.

11

Balmford, A., Gaston, K. J., Blyth, S., James, A., and Kapos, V. (2003). Global variation in terrestrial conservation costs, conservation benefits, and unmet conservation needs. *Proc. Natl. Acad. Sci. USA* **100**, 1046–1050.

Conrad, J. C. and Ferraro, P. J. (2001). *Habitat Conservation: The Dynamics of Direct and Indirect Payments.* Environmental Policy Working Paper Ser. Georgia State University: 2001–2005.

Retrieved from: http://epp.gsu.edu/pferraro/docs/ConradFerraroWorkingPaper2001Distrib.pdf via the Internet (Accessed July 21, 2004).

du Toit, J. T., Walker, B. H., and Campbell, B. M. (2004). Conserving tropical nature: Current challenges for ecologists. *Trends Ecol. Evol.* **19**, 12–17.

Ferraro, P. J. and Kiss, A. (2002). Direct payments to conserve biodiversity. *Science* **298**, 1718–1719.

Kiss, A. (2004). Is community-based ecotourism a good use of biodiversity conservation funds? *Trends Ecol. Evol.* **19**, 232–237.

12

Liu, F. Y. (2005). Sports ecotourism and the countermeasures for its sustainable development. *J. Shenyang Phys. Educ. Institute* **24**(1), 17–19.

Song, D. L. (2005). Exploitation on human resource of ecological sports tourism in southwest of Zhejiang province. *China Sports Sci. Tech.* **42**(4), 75–78.

Wang, D. H. (2005). Exploitation on human resource of ecological sports tourism in southwest of Zhejiang province. *J. Wuhan Institute Phys. Educ.* **38**(1), 29–31.

Zhao, Y. Y. (2006). Investigation and analysis of development of ecological sports in mount Tai tourism area. *J. Taishan University* **28**(6), 90–94.

Zheng, X. X. (2005). Connotation and characteristics of ecology sports. *J. Chengdu Sport University* **30**(2), 43–46.

Zhu, P. F. (2001).Take advantage of resources and characters, construct ecological industry example in Zhuhai. *Special Zone Economy* **145**(2), 13–15.

13

Buckley, R. (2008). *Environmental Impacts of Ecotourism.* CABI Publishing, Wallingford, Oxfordshire.

JIUSAN Society Shaanxi Province Committee. (2009). To Formulate long-term plans, to Deepen Institutional innovation and to feasibly carry forward sustainable development of eco-tourism district in the North Piedmont of Qinling Mountains. *JIUSAN Society Shaanxi Province* (4), 4–6.

Wang, S. and Wang, R. (March 18, 2009). *The Great Qinling Mt: The First "National Central Park"?* Shaanxi Daily.

Wearing, S. and Neil, J. (2009). *Ecotourism.* Butterworth-Heinemann, Sydney.

Weaver, D. B. and Lawton, L. J. (2007). Twenty years on: The state of contemporary ecotourism research. *Tourism Management* **28**(5), 1168–1179.

Xiao, L., Wang, S., Zhang, J., et al. (2008). Investigation and assessment on the water quality of main rivers in the North Piedmont of Qinling Mountains. *Arid Land Res. Env.* **1**, 74–78.

Zhang, Q. (2001). Studies on the composition, characteristics and geographic element of the family of seed plant Flora in Qinling Mt. *Bulletin of Botanical Research* **21**(4), 535–546.

14

A full presentation and discussion of all findings can be found in Dirk, H. R. Spennemann, Look, D. W., and Graham, K. (2000). *Perceptions of Heritage Eco-tourism by Micronesian Decision Makers.* Johnstone Centre Report 174. Charles Sturt University, Albury, NSW. The Johnstone Centre. The report is available for free download in pdf format at the following site: http://life.csu.edu.au/marshall/Reports/RotaAttitudes.pdf [This is not yet available on the web].

Kristy Graham has a degree in eco-tourism and is currently is a research student at School of Environmental and Information Sciences at Charles Sturt University in Albury, Australia. Her current research focuses on the interaction between cultural heritage managers and natural disaster managers in New South Wales, Australia.

Look, D. W. AIA, is Chief, *Cultural Resources Team, Pacific Great Basin Support Office, National Park Service,* San Francisco, California.

Spennemann, D. H. R. Ph.D. is an associate professor at Charles Sturt University in Albury, Australia, where he teaches cultural heritage management courses in the Parks Management and Eco-tourism degrees. His primary research interests are the management of human impacts and natural disasters on cultural heritage sites; German colonial history and heritage in the Pacific; and cultural heritage policy in Australia and Oceania, especially Micronesia.

The lack of a pretesting opportunity revealed an unexpected problem. A number of respondents did not rank the responses properly and assigned the same number (commonly the top rank) to a number of options. These multiple responses were excluded in the analysis. Hence the response rate for this section is lower.

15

Abbot, J. I. O., Thomas, D. H. L., Gardner, A. A., Neba, S. E., and Khen, M.W. (2001). Understanding the links between conservation and development in the Bamenda Highlands, Cameroon. *World Development* **29**, 1115–1136.

Baral, N., Stern, M. J., and Bhattarai, R. (2008). Contingent valuation of ecotourism in Annapurna conservation area, Nepal: Implications for sustainable park finance and local development. *Ecolog. Eco.* **66**, 218–227.

BirdLife International. (2009). *Important Bird Area factsheet.* Cross River National Park, Okwangwo Division, Nigeria. Retrieved from: www.birdlife.org (accessed on October 3, 2009).

Boman, M., Norman, J., Kindstrand, C., and Mattsson, L. (2008). On the budget for national environmental objectives and willingness to pay for protection of forest land. *Can. J. Forest Res.* **38**(1).

Boo, E. (1990). *Ecotourism: The Potentials and Pitfalls,* Vols. 1 and 2. World Wildlife Fund, Washington, DC.

Bowler, J. M., English, D. B. K., and Cordell, H. K. (1999). Outdoor recreation participation and consumption: Projections 2000–2050. In *Outdoor Recreation in American life: A National Assessment of Demand and Supply Trends.* H. K Cordell, C. J. Betz, and J. M. Bowker (Eds.). Segamore press Inc., Champagne, IL, pp. 323–350.

Brander, L. M., Florax, R. J. G. M., and Vermaat, J. E. (2006). The empirics of wetland valuation: A comprehensive summary and a meta-analysis of the literature. *Environ. Resource Eco* **33**(2), 223–250.

Carson, R. (2004). *Contingent Valuation: A Comprehensive Bibliography and History*. Edward Elgar, Cheltenham, UK and Northampton, MA.

Champ, P. A., Boyle, K., and Brown, T. C. (Eds.) (2003). *A Primer on Non-market Valuation*. Kluwer Academic publishers, Boston.

Coldecott, J. O., Oates, J. F., and Ruitenbeek, H. J. (1990). *Cross River National Park (Okwangwo Division)*. Plan for developing the park and its support zone Goldalming, WWF-UK.

Cross River State Government. (June 23, 2008). Facts and figures about Cross River state.

Eraqi, M. I. (2008). Ecotourism economics: The case of Egypt. *Inter. J. Ser. Oper. Mgmt* **4**(2), 165–180.

Floro, M. S. and Miles. M. (2003). Time use, work and overlapping activities: Evidence from Australia. *Cambridge J. Eco.* **27**(6), 881–904.

Foot, D. K. (1990). The age of outdoor recreation in Canada. *J. Appl. Recreation Res.* **15**(3), 159–178.

Foot, D. K. (2004). Leisure futures: A change in demography? In *The Tourism and Leisure Industry: Shaping the Future*. K. Weiermair and C. Mathies (Eds.). The Haworth hospitality press, Binghamton, New York, pp. 21–33.

Garrod, G. and Willis, K. G. (1999). *Economic Valuation of the Environment*. Edward Elgar, Cheltenham, UK.

Greene, W. (2003). *Econometric Analysis*. Prentice Hall, New Jersey.

Hall, M. (2006a). Extreme tourism: Lessons from the world's Cold Water Island. In *Stewart Island*. G. Baldacchino (Ed.). Elsevier, Amsterdam, pp. 219–232.

Hökby, S. and Söderqvist, T. (2003). Elasticity of demand and willingness to pay for environmental services in Sweden. *Environ. Resource Eco.* **26**, 361–383.

Isaacs, J. C. (2000). The limited potential of ecotourism to contribute to wildlife conservation. *The Ecologist* **28**(1), 61–69.

Ite, U. E. (2004). The challenges and imperatives of conservation with development in Cross River national park, Nigeria, (accessed on October 30, 2006).

Kamauro, O. (1996). *Ecotourism: Suicide or Development?* Voices from Africa No. 6: Sustainable Development, UN Non-Governmental Liaison Service. United Nations News Service.

Kimmel, J. and Connelly, R. (2007). Mothers' Time choices: Caregiving, leisure, home production, and paid work. *J. Human Resources* **42**(3), 643–681.

Lindberg, K. and Hawkins, D. E. (Eds.) (1993). Ecotourism: A guide for planners and managers. *North Bennington V.T.* The Ecotourism Society.

Lindsey, P. A., Alexander, R. R., Du Toit, J. T., and Mills, M. G. L. (2005). The potential contribution of ecotourism to African wild dog *Lycaon pictus* conservation in South Africa. *Biological Conservation* **123**, 339–348.

Loomis, J. B. (1993). *Integrated Public Lands Management: Principles and Applications to National Forests, Parks, Wildlife Refuges and BLM Lands*. Columbia University Press, New York.

Maharana, I., Rai, S. C., and Sharma, E. (2000). Valuing ecotourism in a sacred lake of the Sikkim Himalaya, India. *Environ. Conserv.* **27**(3), 269–277.

Majid, I., Sinden, J. A., and Randall, A. (1983). Benefit evaluation of increments to existing system of public facilities. *Land Economics* **59**, 377–392.

Marsh, J. (2000). Tourism and national parks in polar regions. In *Tourism and National Parks-issues and Implications*. R. Butler and S. Boyd (Eds.). Chichester, Wiley, pp. 127–136.

Mitchell, R. C. and Carson, R. T. (1989). Using surveys to value public goods: The contingent valuation method. *Resources for the Future*. Washington, DC.

Nickerson, N. P. (2000). *Travel and Recreation Outlook 2000: Focusing on Demographics*. Montana Business Quarterly, Spring.

Nuva, R. and Shamsudin, M. N. (2009). Willingness to pay towards the conservation of ecotourism resources at Gunung Gede Pangrango National

Park, West Java, Indonesia. *J. Sustainable Develop.* **2**(2), 173–186.

Oates, J. F., White, D., Gadsgy, E. L., and Bisong, P. O. (1990). Conservation of gorilla and others. Appendix 1 of Cross River national park (Okwangwo Division): Plan for developing the park and its support zone. Goldalming, WWF-UK.

Pate, J. and Loomis, J. (1997). The effect of distance on willingness to pay values: A case study of wetlands and salmon in California. *Ecolog. Eco.* **20**, 199–207.

Ratz, T. (2002). Residents' perceptions of sociocultural impacts of tourism at Lake Balaton, Hungary. In *Tourism and Sustainable Development*. G. Richards and D. Hull (Eds.). Routledge, London.

TIES (The International Ecotourism Society). (1990). Retrieved from: http://www.ecotourism.org/site/c.orLQKXPCLmF/b.4835303/k.BEB9/What_is_Ecotourism__The_International_Ecotourism_Society.htm

Tobin, J. (1958). Estimation of relationships for limited dependent variables. *Econometrica* **26**, 24.

Weiler, S. and Seidl, A. (2004). What's in a name? Extracting econometric drivers to assess the impact of national park designation. *J. Regional Sci.* **44**, 245–262.

White, D. (1990). Okwangwo Division species lists. *Appendix 9 of Cross River National Park: Plan for Developing the Park and Support Zone*. Goldalming, WWF-UK.

Yacob, M. R., Radam, A., and Shuib, A. (2009). A contingent valuation study of Marine Park' Ecotourism: The case of Pulau Payar and Pulau Redang in Malaysia. *J. Sustainable Develop.* **2**(2), 95–105.

16

Bonnicksen, T. M. and Robinson, T. S. (1981). Constraints on the development of national seashores and lakeshores: A political perspective. *Public Administration Review* **41**(5), 550557.

Dawson, C. P. and Watson, A. E. (2000). Measures of wilderness trip satisfaction and user perceptions of crowding. In *Wilderness Sciences in a Time of Change Conference* (RMRS-P-15, Vol. 4). N. Cole, S. F. McCool, W. T. Borrie, and J. O'Loughlin (Eds.). USDA Forest Service, Ogden, UT, pp. 93–98.

Dilsaver, L. M. (2004). *Cumberland Island National Seashore: A History of Conservation Conflict*. University of Virginia Press, Charlottesville.

Fitzsimmons, A. K. (1976). National parks: The dilemma of development. *Science* **191**(4226), 440444.

Freimund, W. A. and Cole, D. N. (2001). Use density, visitor experience, and limiting recreational use in wilderness: Progress to date and research needs. *Visitor use Density And Wilderness Experience*. Proceedings, June 1–3, 2000; Missoula, MT. Proc. RMRS-P-20. W. A. Freimund and D. N. Cole, (comps.). U.S. Department of Agriculture, Forest Service, Rocky Mountain Research Station, Ogden, UT, pp. 3–8.

Georgia Conservancy (n.d.). *Cumberland Island National Seashore Transportation Management Plan*. Retrieved February 21, 2007 from: www.georgiaconservancy.org/News/TransportationPlanLetter.pdf.

Hartrampf, Inc. and Jordan, Jones, and Goulding, Inc. (2006). Summary public scoping comments for transportation management plan and environmental assessment. In *Cumberland Island National Seashore*. Atlanta, GA.

Ike, A. F., and Richardson, J. L. (1975). *Estimating Carrying Capacity for Cumberland Island National Seashore*. Institute of Community and Area Development, University of Georgia.

Mace, B. L., Marquite, J. D., and Kay, R. (2006). Six years of mandatory shuttle use in Zion National Park: A longitudinal analysis of the visitor experience. *Presentation at the 12th International Symposium for Society and Resource Management*. Vancouver, BC.

Miller, C. A. and Wright, R. G. (1999). An assessment of visitor satisfaction with public transportation services at Denali National Park & Preserve. *Park Science* **19**(2), 1821.

National Park Service (1984). *Cumberland Island National Seashore General Management Plan*. Retrieved March 15, 2007 from: http://www.nps.gov/cuis/parkmgmt/upload/GMP.pdf

National Park Service (2007). *The National Park System: Caring for the American Legacy.* (Online). Retrieved July 25, 2007 from: http://www.nps.gov/legacy/mission.html

Sax, J. L. (1980). *Mountains without Handrails.* The University of Michigan Press, Ann Arbor.

Shelby, B. (1980). Crowding models for backcountry recreation. *Land Economics* 56(1), 4355.

Sims, C. B., Hodges, D. G., Fly, J. M., and Stephens, B. (2005). Modeling visitor acceptance of a shuttle system in the Great Smoky Mountain National Park. *J. Recrea. Park Admin.* 23(3), 2544.

White, D. D. (2007). An Interpretive Study of Yosemite National Park Visitors' Perspectives Toward Alternative Transportation in Yosemite Valley. *Environmental Management* 39(1), 5062.

17

Chen, L. (2006). A study on status quo and strategy of China's ecotourism. *Jiangsu Business Forum* 158(9), 84.

Liang, X. (2006). On sustainable development of China's ecotourism. *Policy-making Consultancy Reportage* 73(3), 7274.

Lu, Y. and Wang, J. (2001). *Ecotourism.* Tour Education Press, Beijing, p. 213.

Luo, M. (2002). Sustainable development of ecotourism: Commentary on Asia-Pacific conference at ministerial level. *Tourism Tribune* 17(3), 78.

Song, W. (2003). Ecotourism: The main orientation of sustainable development of China's tourism. *J. Zhongnan University of Economics and Law* 139(4), 5559.

Tu, X., Hou, L., and Zhao, L. (2002). Analysis of countermeasures on the sustainable development of ecotourism. *Environmental Protection Science* 113(28), 40.

Zhao, C. (2006). Analysis of sustained growth of ecological tourism. *J. Harbin University of Commerce* 90(5), 87.

Zhao, Z. (2006). Probing into the problems of sustainable development of China's ecotourism. *Economist* 208(6), 149.

Zhou, X. and Wang, L. (2007). Revelations of sustainable development practices on ecotourism in Canada. *China Environmental Protection Industry* 177(1), 51.

18

Adams, W. M. and Hulme, D. (2001). If community conservation is the answer in Africa, what is the question? *Oryx.* 35(3), 193–200.

Andersen, D. L. (1993). A window to the natural world: The design of ecotourism facilities. In *Ecotourism: A Guide For Planners And Managers.* K. Lindberg and D. E. Hawkins (Eds.). The Ecotourism Society, North Bennington, VT, pp. 116–133.

ARD BIOFOR Consortium. (2004). Sustainable practices in agriculture for critical environments. *Draft Design and Implementation Plan.* ARD Inc., Burlington, VT, p. 37.

Beebe, J. (1995). Basic concepts and techniques of rapid appraisal. *Human Organization* 54, 42–51.

Brooks, J. J., Bujak, A. N., Champ, J. G., and Williams, D. R. (2006). Collaborative capacity, problem framing, and mutual trust in addressing the wildland fire social problem: An annotated reading list. *General Technical Report.* RMRS-GTR-182, CO, U.S. Department of Agriculture, Forest Service, Rocky Mountain Research Station, Fort Collins, p. 27.

Buckley, R. (2001). Environmental impacts. In *The Encyclopedia of Ecotourism.* D. B. Weaver (Ed.). CAB International, pp. 379–393.

Ceballos-Lascurain, H. (2006). *Tourism, Ecotourism and Protected Areas.* IUCN, Gland, Switzerland.

Chaskin, R. (2001). Defining community capacity: A definitional framework. *Urb. Affair. Rev.* 36, 295–323.

Cross River Environmental Capacity Development Coalition. (2006). *Report: Cross River State Forestry-community Consultation Results.* ONE SKY-Canadian Institute of Sustainable Living, p. 69.

Drumm, A., Moore, A., Soles, A., Patterson, C., and Terborgh, J. E. (2004). *Ecotourism Development: A Manual for Conservation Planners and*

Managers. Volume II: The business of ecotourism development and management. The Nature Conservancy, Arlington, VA, p. 111.

Dunn, R. and Otu, D. (1996). A community forest inventory for productive forest management in Cross River State, Nigeria. In *Recent Approaches to Participatory Forest Resource Assessment.* J. Carter (Ed.). Overseas Development Institute, London, pp. 33–55.

Edom, T., Chapman, K., and Eyamba, P. (2006). *DRAFT Policy brief: Ecotourism on the roof of Cross River State.* Calabar, Nigeria: Cross River Environmental Capacity Development Project, Nigeria Canada Coalition, ONE SKY-Canadian Institute of Sustainable Living, p. 6.

Endter-Wada, J., Blahna, D., Krannich, R., and Brunson, M. (1998). A framework for understanding social science contributions to ecosystem management. *Ecol.App.* **8**(3), 891–904.

Generon Consulting. (2001). *An Overview of Multi-stakeholder Civic Scenario Work.* Retrieved, December 13, 2006 from: http://www.generonconsulting.com/publications/papers

Hochachka, G. and Liu, S. (2005). *Case study: Ecotourism in Cross River State, Nigeria.* Calabar, Nigeria: Cross River Environmental Capacity Development Project, Nigeria Canada Coalition, ONE SKY-Canadian Institute of Sustainable Living, p. 21.

Innes, J. E. and Booher, D. E. (2003). The impact of collaborative planning on governance capacity. *Paper presented at the Annual Conference of the Association of Collegiate Schools of Planning*; 2002 November 21–24; Baltimore, MD. Working Paper 2003–03. University of California Berkeley, Institute of Urban and Regional Development, Berkeley, CA, p. 31.

Ite, U. E. (1996). Community perceptions of the Cross River National Park, Nigeria. *Env. Conser.* **23**(4), 351–357.

Ite, U. E. and Adams, W. (2000). Expectations, impacts and attitudes: Conservation and development in Cross River National Park, Nigeria. *J. Inter. Develop.* **12**, 325–342.

Kahane, A. (2004). *Solving Tough Problems: An Open Way of Talking, Listening, and Creating New Realities.* Berrett-Koehler, San Francisco, CA, p. 149.

Kaplan, A. (2000). Capacity building: Shifting the paradigms of practice. *Development in Practice* **10**(3, 4), 517–526.

Keough, H. L. and Blahna, D. J. (2006). Achieving integrative, collaborative ecosystem management. *Conserv. Biol.* **20**(5), 1373–1382.

Knudson, D. M., Cable, T. T., and Beck, L. (2003). *Interpretation of Cultural and Natural Resources.* Venture, State College, PA, p. 411.

Lindberg, K. and Hawkins, D. E. (Eds.) (1993). *Ecotourism: A Guide for Planners and Managers.* The Ecotourism Society, North Bennington, VT, p. 175.

Meludu, N. T. (2004). Assessment of income generating activities that influence sustainable livelihoods of forest communities in Nigeria: Implications for policy enhancement in Nigeria. In *Proceedings of Human Dimensions of Family, Farm, and Community Forestry International Symposium.* D. M. Baumgartner (Ed.). Washington State University Extension Report MISC0526. Washington State University, Pullman, WA, pp. 291–295.

Moore, S. A. and Lee, R. G. (1999). Understanding dispute resolution processes for American and Australian public wildlands: Towards a conceptual framework for managers. *Env. Manag.* **23**(4), 453–465.

National Park Service. (1999). *National Park Service Decree Number 46, Establishing the National Parks Service and the Workings Thereof.* Lagos, Nigeria: Published by Authority of the Federal Military Government of Nigeria and printed by the Ministry of Information and Culture, Printing Department.

Nigeria Business Info. (2005). TINAPA: A unique tourism vision for Africa. Retrieved, October 19, 2006 from: http://www.nigeriabusinessinfo.com/tinapa171005.htm

Oates, J. F. (1999). *Myth and Reality in the Rainforest: How Conservation Strategies are Failing in West Africa.* University of California Press, Berkeley, CA, p. 310.

Oates, J. F., McFarland, K. L., Groves, J. L., Bergl, R. A., Linder, J. M., and Disotell, T. R. (2003). The Cross River gorilla: Natural history and status of a neglected and critically endangered subspecies. In *Gorilla Biology: A*

Multidisciplinary Perspective. A. B. Taylor and M. L. Goldsmith (Eds.). Cambridge University Press, Cambridge, UK, pp. 472–497.

Sarmiento, E. E. and Oates, J. F. (2000). *The Cross River Gorillas: A Distinct Subspecies, Gorilla Gorilla Diehli Matschie 1904*. American Museum Novitates. Number 3304. American Museum of Natural History, New York, p. 55.

Scheyvens, R. (1999). Ecotourism and the empowerment of local communities. *Tourism Mgmt.* **20**, 245–249.

Schuett, M. A., Selin, S. W., and Carr, D. S. (2001). Making it work: Keys to successful collaboration in natural resource management. *Env. Mgmt.* **27**(4), 587–593.

Schusler, T. M., Decker, D. J., and Pfeffer, M. J. (2003). Social learning for collaborative natural resource management. *Soc.Nat. Res.* **15**, 309–326.

Spicer, C. (1997). *Organizational Public Relations: A Political Perspective*. Erlbaum, Mahwah, New Jersey, p. 324.

Stringer, E. T. (1999). *Action Research*. Sage, Thousand Oaks, CA, p. 229.

Toman, E., Shindler, B., and Brunson, M. (2006). Fire and fuel management communication strategies: Citizen evaluations of agency outreach activities. *Soc.Nat. Res.* **19**, 321–336.

Wearing, S. (2001). Exploring socio-cultural impacts on local communities. In. *The Encyclopedia of Ecotourism*. D. B. Weaver (Ed.), CAB International, pp. 395–409.

Western, D. (2003). Conservation science in Africa and the role of international collaboration. *Conserv. Biol.* **17**(1), 11–19.

Wildlife Conservation Society. (2006). Investigating a recent report of the killing of "gorillas." *Gorilla J.* **32**, 14–15.

19

Arlen, C. (May 29, 1995). Ecotour, Hold the Eco. *US News and World Report* **118**, 61–63.

Benitez, S. (2001). *Visitor Use Fees and Concession Systems in Protected Areas: Galapagos National Park Case Study*. Unpublished report prepared for The Nature Conservancy, Arlington, Virginia.

Guide to Best Practice for Sustainable Tourism in Tropical Forests Lodging Businesses. (2003). Conservation International, Ecuadorian, Ecotourism Association (ASEC) and Programme for Belize (PfB). Rainforest Alliance, New York.

Mulaik, S. A. and Millsap, R. E. (2000). Doing the four-step right. *Structural Equation Modeling* **7**, 36–73.

20

Freitag-Ronaldson, S., Kalwa, R. H., Badenhorst, J. C., Erasmus, J. P., Venter, F. J., and Nel, F. J. (2003). Wilderness, wilderness quality management, and recreational opportunities zoning within Kruger National Park, South Africa. A. Watson and J. Sproull (comps.). *Seventh World Wilderness Congress symposium: Science and Stewardship to Protect and Sustain Wilderness Values*. November 2–8, 2001, Port Elizabeth, South Africa. Proc. RMRS-P-27. U.S. Department of Agriculture, Forest Service, Rocky Mountain Research Station, Fort Collins, CO, pp. 39–49.

21

Campbell, L. M. (2002). Ecotourism in rural developing communities. *Annals Tourism Res.* **26**(3), 534553.

Coppock, J. P. and Duffiod, B. A. (1980). Recreation in the country side. *A Spatial Analysis.*

Eboka, O. A. (1999). *Man and Leisure: A Philosophy of Recreation*. C. K. Bright Bill (Ed.). Green Wood Press.

Hall, C. M. (2003). *Politics and Place: An Analysis of Power in Tourism Communities*. Oxford, England, pp. 99114.

Lynch, B. C. (1975). *Tourism Economic Physical and Social Impacts*. Routledge, London.

Ojo, G. J. (1976). *Nigeria National Park and Related Reserves.*

Ormsby, A. and Mannle, K. (2006). Ecotourism benefits and the role of local guides at Masola National park, Madagascar. *J. Sustainable Tourism*, **14**(3), 271287.

Prentice, R. (2007). Strategic management for tourism countries: Bridging the gaps. *Tourism* **23**, 363377.

Robinson, H. (2006). *Geography of Tourism*. MacDonald and Evans, London.

Ukpana, S. (2005). *Tourism Development in Nigeria*. Macmillan, Lagos.

UNESCO. (1979). Final report of sub-regional training. *Workshop on Environmental Education Programme Nekedem*, Owerri.

22

Agriteam Canada. (1997). *Study of Extensive Livestock Production Systems TANo.2606-MON*. Report submitted to the Asian Development Bank, Agriteam Canada Consulting Ltd, Calgary, Alberta.

Amgalanbaatar, S. and Reading, R. P. (2000). *Altai argali*. In *Endangered Animals: Conflicting Issues*. R. P. Reading and B. Miller (Eds.). Greenwood Press, Westport, Connecticut, USA, pp. 5–9.

Amgalanbaatar, S., Reading, R. P., Lhagvasuren, B., and Batsukh. N. (2002). Argali sheep (*Ovis ammon*) trophy hunting in Mongolia. *Prineos* **157**, 129–150.

Anonymous. (2003). *Assessment of Biological Diversity Conservation Capacity of Mongolia*. Ministry for Nature and Environment, Global Environment Facility, World Bank, and Mongolia Nature and Environment Consortium, Ulaanbaatar, Mongolia.

Anonymous. (2004). *Bridge to Nowhere*. Economist January 29.

Ariuna, C. and Mashbat, O. (2002). *Selected Commercial Laws of Mongolia*. The Legal Information Center, Ulaanbaatar, Mongolia.

Bazargur, D., Shiirevadja, C., and Chinbat, B. (1993). *Territorialorganisation of Mongolian Pastoral Livestock Husbandry in the Transition to a Market Economy*. PALD Research Report No. 1. University of Sussex, Institute of Development Studies, Policy Alternatives for Livestock Development in Mongolia, Brighton, England, p. 14.

Bedunah, D. J. and Miller, D. J. (January 18, 1995). Sustainable livestock grazing in Mongolia: Socio/political characteristics, grazing ecosystems and rangeland issues. In *Proceedings of the 1995 International Rangeland Development Symposium*. J. Powell (Ed.). Phoenix, AZ.

Bedunah, D. J. and Schmidt, S. (2004). Changes in communal use of a recently established protected area in Mongolia. *Development and Change* **35**, 167–191.

Birdlife International. (2003). *Saving Asia's Threatened Birds: A Guide for Government and Civil Society*. BirdLife International, Cambridge, UK.

Brooke, J. (October 3, 2003). The following article appeared in the New York Times. *Mongolia Is Having a Mine Rush*. New York Time.

Bruun, O. (1996). The herding household: Economy and organization. In *Mongolia in Transition*. O. Bruun and O. Odgaard (Eds.). Nordic Institute of Asian Studies, Studies in Asian topics. No. 22. Curzon Press, Ltd., Richmond Surrey, Great Britain, pp. 65–89.

Bruun, O. and Odgaard, O. (1996). A society and economy in transition. In *Mongolia in Transition: Old patterns, New Challenges*. pp. 23–41.

Chimed-Ochir, B. (1997). Protected areas of Mongolia in past, present and future, p. 51–55. In Second Conference on National Parks and Protected Areas of East Asia: Mobilizing Community Support for National Parks and Protected Areas in East Asia, June 30–July 5, 1996, Kushiro, Hokkaido, Japan. Japanese Organizing Committee for the Second Conference on National Parks and Protected Areas of East Asia, Tokyo, Japan.

Enebish, D. and Myagmasuren, D. (2000). *Special Protected Areas of Mongolia*. Government Regulatory Agency of Mongolia, Environmental Protection Agency of Mongolia, and GTZ Nature Conservation and Buffer Zone Development Project. Ulaanbaatar, Mongolia.

Farrington, J. D. (2005). The impact of mining activities on Mongolia's protected areas: A status report with policy recommendations. *Integrated Environmental Assessment and Management* **1**(3), 283–289.

Ferguson, R. (2003). In the wake of economic transition: Mongolia's new environmental challenges. *Biodiversity Briefings from Northern Eurasia* **2**(1), 5–7.

Fernandez-Gimenz, M. E. (1999). Sustaining the steppes: A geographical history of pastoral land use in Mongolia. *The Geographical Review* **89**, 316–342.

Finch, C. (1996). *Mongolia's Wild Heritage: Biological Diversity, Protected Areas, and Conservation in the Land of Chingis Khan.* Mongolia Ministry for Nature and the Environment, United Nations Development Programme-Global Environmental Facility, and World Wide Fund for Nature, Avery Press, Boulder, CO.

Frazier, J. G. (1997). Sustainable development: Modern elixir or sack dress. *Environmental Conservation* **24**, 182–193.

Germeraad, P. W. and Enebish, Z. (1996). *The Mongolian Landscape Tradition: A Key to Progress* (Nomadic tradition and their contemporary role in landscape planning and management in Mongolia).

Gilberg, R. and Svantesson, J. -O. (1996). The Mongols, their land and history. In *Mongolia in Transition: Old Patterns, New Challenges*. O. Bruun and O. Odgaard (Eds.). Nordic Institute of Asian Studies. Curzon Press, Ltd., Richmond, UK, pp. 5–22.

Gunin, P. D., Vostokova, E. A., Dorofeyuk, N. I., Tarasov, P. E., and Black C. C. (Eds.) (1999). *Vegetation of Mongolia*. Kluwer Academic Publishers, Boston, Massachusetts.

Henwood, W. D. (1998a). Editorial—the world's temperate grasslands: A beleaguered biome. *Parks* **8**, 1–2.

Henwood, W. D. (1998b). An overview of protected area in the temperate grasslands biome. *Parks* **8**, 3–8.

Hilbig, W. (1995). *The Vegetation of Mongolia.* SPB Academic Publishing, Amsterdam, The Netherlands.

Humphrey, C. (1978). Pastoral nomadism in Mongolia: The role of herdsmen's cooperatives in the national economy. *Development and Change* **9**, 133–160.

Jagchid, S. and. Hyder, P. (1979). *Mongolia's Culture and Society.* Westview Press, Boulder, CO.

Johnstad, M. D. and Reading, R. P. (2003). Mongolia's protected areas system. *Biodiversity Briefings from Northern Eurasia* **2**(1), 8–11.

Kennett, G. (2000). *Land Use-range Management Report.* Gobi regional economic growth initiative. US Agency for International Development, Ulaanbatar, Mongolia.

Lhagvasuren, B., Dulamtseren, S., Amgalan, L., Mallon, D., Schaller, G., Reading, R., and Mix, H. (1999). Status and conservation of antelopes in Mongolia. *Scientific Research of the Institute of Bio. Sci.* **1**, 96–108.

Mallon, D. P., Bold, A., Dulamtseren, S., Reading, R. P., and Amgalanbaatar, S. (1997). Mongolia. In *Wild Sheep and Goats and their Relatives: Status Survey and Action Plan for Caprinae*, D. Shackleton and the IUCN.SSC Caprinae Specialist Group (Eds.). IUCN, Gland, Switzerland, pp. 193–201.

Mearns, R. (2004). Sustaining livelihoods on Mongolia's pastoral commons: Insights from a participatory poverty assessment. *Development and Change* **35**(1), 107–139.

Mineral Resources Authority of Mongolia. (2004). *Mongolia: Discovering New Minerals Opportunities*. Mineral Resources Authority of Mongolia, Ulaanbaatar, Mongolia.

Minjigdorj, Baljiriin. (July 23–28, 1995). Different ways of protecting animals from unfavourable natural conditions. N. E. West (Ed.). Proceedings of Fifth International Rangeland Congress, *"Rangelands in a sustainable biosphere: proceedings of the 5th International Rangeland Congress."* Salt Lake, Utah. 1995. Society for Rangeland Management, Denver, Colorado, USA, pp. 375–375.

Mix, H., Reading, R. P., Blumer, E. S, and Lhagvasuren, B. (2002). Status and distribution of wild Bactrian camels in Mongolia In *Ecology and Conservation of Wild Bactrian Camels (Camelus bactrianus ferus)*. R. P. Reading, D. Enkhbileg, and T. Galbaatar (Eds.). Mongolian Conservation Coalition and Admon Printing, Ulaanbaatar, Mongolia, pp. 39–48.

Mix, H., Reading, R. P., and Lhagvasuren, B. (August 1995). A systematic census of various large mammals in Eastern and Southern Mongolia. *Proceedings from the Conference on Asian Ecosystems and Their Protection.* Ulaanbaatar, Mongolia, (In Russian).

MNE (Ministry of Nature and Environment). (2001). *State of the Environment—Mongolia 2002.* United Nations Environment Programme, Klong Luang, Thailand.

Mooza, M. (2003). (UMENGO) Union of Mongolian Environmental Non-governmental Organizations: A source for environmental change and civil society development in Mongolia. *Biodiver. Brief. North. Eur.* **2**(1), 19–21.

Muller, F. -V. and Bold, B. -O. (1996). On the necessity of new regulations for pastoral land use in Mongolia. *Appl. Geog. Develop.* **48**, 29–51.

Natsagdorj, T. and Batbayar, N. (2002). The impact of rodenticide used to control rodents on Demoiselle Crane (*Anthropoides virgo*) and other animals in Mongolia. *Proceedings of a Conference on Brandt's Voles.* WWF—Mongolia, Ulaanbaatar, Mongolia, p. 8.

NSO (National Statistical Office)—Mongolia. (2004). *Mongolian Statistical Yearbook 2003.* National Statistical Office, Ulaanbaatar, Mongolia.

Pimbert, M. P. and Pretty, J. N. (1995). Parks, people and professionals: Putting "participation" into protected area management. *United Nations Research Institute for Social Development Discussion Paper* **57**, 1–59.

Pratt, D. G., MacMillan, D. C., and Gordon, I. J. (2004). Local community attitudes to wildlife utilization in the changing economic and social context of Mongolia. *Biodiv. Conserv.* **13**, 591–613.

Reading, R. P., Amgalanbaatar, S., Kenny, D., Onon, Yo., Namshir, Z., and DeNicola A. (2003). Argaliecology in Ikh Nartiin Chuluu Nature Reserve: Preliminary findings. *Mongolian J. Biol. Sci.* **1**(2), 3–14.

Reading, R. P., Johnstad, M., Amgalanbaatar, S., Batjargal, Z., and Mix, H. (1999). Expanding Mongolia's system of protected areas. *Nat. Areas J.* **19**(3), 211–222.

Reading, R. P., Mix, H., Blumer, E. S., Amgalanbaatar, S., Galbaatar, T., Wingard, G., Tuya, T. S., Johnstad, M. D., Namshir, Z., and Lhagvasuren, B. (2002). Wild ungulate conservation in Mongolia. *Proceedings of the Institute of Biology of the Mongolian Academy of Sciences (Mammalogical Studies in Mongolia and Its Adjacent Territories)* **24**, 120–132.

Reading, R. P., Mix, H., Lhagvasuren, B., Feh, C., Kane, D., Dulamtseren, S., and Enkhbold, S. (2001). Status and distribution of khulan (*Equus hemionus*) in Mongolia. *J. Zool. (London)* **254**, 381–389.

Reading, R. P., Mix, H. M., Blumer, E. S, Amgalanbaatar, S., Galbaatar, T., Wingard, G., Tserenbataa, T., Johnstad, M. D., Namshir, Z., Lhagvasuren, B., and Kane. D. (November 3–4, 2000). Wild ungulate conservation in Mongolia. *Proceedings of the Conference on Mongolian Paleoclimatology and Environmental Research.* Lamont-Doherty Earth Observatory and Columbia University, Palisades, NY.

Sanders, A. J. (1996). Foreign relations and foreign policy. In *Mongolia in Transition: Old Patterns, New Challenges.* O. Bruun and O. Odgaard (Eds.). Nordic Institute of Asian Studies. Curzon Press, Ltd., Richmond, UK, pp. 217–251.

Schuerholz, G. (2001). *Community Based Wildlife Management (CBWM) in the Altai Sayan Ecoregion of Mongolia Feasibility Assessment: Opportunities For and Barriers to CBWM.* Report to WWF-Mongolia, Ulaanbaatar, Mongolia.

Sheehy, D. (1996). Sustainable livestock use of pastoral resources. In *Mongolia in Transition: Old Patterns, New Challenges.* O. Bruun and O. Odgaard (Eds.). Nordic Institute of Asian Studies. Curzon Press, Ltd., Richmond, UK, pp. 42–64.

Sneath, D. (1999). Spatial Mobility in Inner Asian Pastoralism. In *The End of Nomadism? Society, State and the Environment in Inner Asia.* C. Humphrey and D. Sneath (Eds.). Duke University Press, Durham, North Carolina, p. 218–277.

Swift, J. and Mearns, R. (1993). Mongolian pastoralism on the threshold of the twenty-first century. *Nomadic Peoples* **33**, 3–7.

UNDP (United Nations Development Programme). (2000). *Human Development Report:*

Mongolia 2000. Government of Mongolia and United Nations Development Programme, Ulaanbaatar, Mongolia.

Western, D. and Wright, R. M. (1994). *Natural Connections: Perspectives in Community-Based Conservation.* Island Press, Washington, DC.

Wingard, J. R. and Odgerel, P. (2001). *Compendium of Environmental Law and Practice in Mongolia.* GTZ Commercial and Civil Law Reform Project and GTZ Nature and Conservation and Buffer Zone Development Project, Ulaanbaatar, Mongolia, pp. 409.

Wondolleck, J. M. and Yaffee, S. L. (2000). *Making Collaboration Work: Lessons from Innovation in Natural Resources Management.* Island Press, Washington, DC.

World Bank. (2003). *Mongolia Environment Monitor, 2003: Land Resources and Their Management.* World Bank Office, Ulaanbaatar, Mongolia, p. 34.

Zahler, P., Lhagvasuren, B., Reading, R. P., Wingard, J. R., Amgalanbaatar, S., Gombobaatar, S., and Onon, Yo. (2004). Illegal and unsustainable wildlife trade in Mongolia. *Mongolian J. Biol. Sci.* **2**, 23–32.

23

Ankersmid, P. and Kelder, L. (2000). Long live Manuel Antonio and Texel. Unpublished Masters Thesis. *Socio-spatial Analysis.* Wageningen University, The Netherlands.

Berg, C. van den and Bree, F. van. (2003). *PAN Parks Principles: Crosscultural or Site Specific?* Unpublished Masters Thesis. Department of Socio-spatial Analysis. Wageningen University, The Netherlands.

Berg, C. van den, Bree, F. van, and Cottrell, S. P. (June 2004). *PAN Parks Principles: Cross-Cultural Comparison-Poland/Slovakia.* T. Sievänen, J. Erkkonen, J. Jokimäki, J. Saarinen, S. Tuulentie, and E. Virtanen, (Eds.). Policies, methods and tools for visitor management proceedings of the second International Conference on Monitoring and Management of Visitor Flows in Recreational and Protected Areas, June 16–20, 2004, Rovaniemi, Finland. Retrieved from http://www.metla.fi/julkaisut/workingpapers/2004/mwp002-32.pdf, pp. 227–234.

Coccossis, H., Collovini, A., Konstandoglou, M., Mexa, A., and Parpairis, A. (2001). Defining, measuring, and evaluating carrying capacity in European Tourism destinations. *Athens, Environmental Planning Laboratory.*

Cottrell, S., Berg, C. van den, and Bree, F. van. (2004). Abstract-PAN Parks implementation process: Cross Cultural Comparison-Bieszczady & Slovenski Raij National Parks. *2nd International Conference on Monitoring and Management of Visitor Flows in Recreational and Protected areas*, June 16–20, 2004, Rovaniemi, Finland.

Cottrell, S. P. and Duim, R. v.d. (2003). Sustainability of tourism indicators: A tourist perspective assessment in Costa Rica and The Netherlands. *The Environment Paper Series* **6**(1), 2–9.

Cutumisu, N. (2003). *The Synergy Between Nature Conservation and Development: A Framework for Analyzing the Impact of the Sustainable Tourism Development Strategy in Natura.* Unpublished Masters Thesis. Department of Socio-spatial Analysis. Wageningen University, The Netherlands.

Dymond, S. (1997). Indicators of sustainable tourism in New Zealand: A local government perspective. *J. Sustainable Tourism* **5**(4), 279–293.

Eden, M., Falkheden, L., and Malbert, B. (2000). The built environment and sustainable development: research meets practice in a Scandinavian context. *Planning Theory and Practice.* **1**(2), 260–272.

Fujun, S. (2004). *Agritourism Sustainability in Mountain Rural Areas in China: Chongdugou Happy-In-Farmhouse Case Study.* Unpublished Masters Thesis. Department of Socio-spatial Analysis. Wageningen University, The Netherlands.

Hughes, G. (2002). Environmental indicators. *Annals of Tourism Research* **29**(2), 457–477.

Innes, J. E. and Booher, D. E. (2000). Indicators for sustainable communities: A strategy building on complexity theory and distributed intelligence. *Planning Theory and Practice* **1**(2), 173–186.

Miller, G. (2001). The development of indicators for sustainable tourism: Results of a Delphi survey of tourism researchers. *Tourism Management* **22**(4), 351–362.

Sirakaya, E., Jamal, T. B., and Choi, H. S. (2001). Chapter 26. *Developing Indicators for Destination Sustainability.* The Encyclopedia of Ecotourism. D. B. Weaver and CAB International (Eds.). pp. 411–432.

Spangenberg, J. H. (2002). Environmental space and the prism of sustainability: Frameworks for indicators measuring sustainable development. *Ecological Indicators* **57**, 1–15.

Spangenberg, J. H. and Valentin, A. (1999). Indicators for Sustainable Communities. *Wuppertal Institute for Climate, Environment and Energy.* A. f. Retrieved from http://www. foeeurope.org/sustainability/sustain/t-content-prism.htm. 2003, The Prism of sustainability.

Twining-Ward, L. and Butler, R. (2002). Implementing STD on a small island: Development and use of sustainable tourism development indicators in Samoa. *J. Sustainable Tourism* **10**(5), 363–387.

Valentin, A. and Spangenberg, J. H. (2000). A guide to community sustainability indicators. *Environmental Impact Assessment review* **20**, 381–392.

WCED. (1987). *Our Common Future.* Oxford University Press, Oxford.

Yuan, W., James, P., Hodgson, K., Hutchinson, S. M., and Shi, C. (2003). Development of sustainability indicators by communities in China: A case study of Chongming county, Shanghai. *J. Env. Mgmt.* **68**(3), 253–261.

24

Braun, B. (2002). *The Intemperate Rainforest: Nature, Culture and Power on Canada's West Coast.* University of Minnesota Press, Minneapolis, p. 347.

Case, D. and Voluck, D. (2002). *Alaska Natives and American laws.* University of Alaska Press, Fairbanks, p. 515.

Cronon, W. (1995). The trouble with wilderness: or, gettingback to the wrong nature. In *Uncommon Ground: Toward Reinventing Nature.* W. Cronon (Ed.). Norton, New York, pp. 69–90.

Ellanna, L. and Balluta, A. (1992). *Nuvendaltin Quht'ana: The People of Nondalton.* Smithsonian Institution Press, Washington, DC, p. 354.

Johnson, D., Hunn, E., Russell, P., Vande Kamp, M., and Searles, E. (1998). Subsistence uses of vegetal resources in and around Lake Clark National Park and Preserve. *Technical Report NPS/CCWSOUW/NRTR-98-16.* U.S. Department of the Interior, National Park Service, Seattle, WA, p. 568.

Koktelash, R. (1981). *Oral History Recording with Priscilla Russell Kari.* Tape 71 (1), oral history collections at Lake Clark National Park and Preserve, Anchorage, Alaska.

Index

A

Afolami, C. A., 129–139
Alaska National Interest Lands Conservation Act (ANILCA), 244
Amgalanbaatar, S., 212–235
Ancrenaz, M., 73–82
Angulo, E., 83–91, 92–102
Aniah, E. J., 203–211
ANILCA. *See* Alaska National Interest Lands Conservation Act (ANILCA)
Anthropogenic Allee effect (AAE), 92–93
　demonstration of, 94
Asuquo, B. E., 154–188
Averting Expenditure Method (AEM), 5–6

B

Balmford, A., 30–37
Bedunah, D. J., 212–235
Beresford, J., 30–37
Best management practices (BMPs), 233
Biodiversity conservation, local communities
　challenges, 73
　efforts, 73
　Kinabatangan Orangutan
　　activities and assistants research, 75–77
　　challenges, 75
　　ecological fieldwork, 75–76
　　ecotourism, 77
　　encroachments, 76
　　environmental problems, 75
　　floodplain, 75
　　nature-based tourism, 77
　　Pongo sp., 73–74
　　wide array of wildlife, 81
　　working, 81
　modern, 73
　substantial, 73
BMPs. *See* Best management practices (BMPs)
Brooks, J. J., 154–188
Buckley, H., 103–105
Bull, L., 92–102

C

Cherry, M., 253–261
China's ecotourism
　actuality and problems
　　blindly developing and utilizing resources, 148–149
　　economic benefits, 150
　　legal system and management, 149
　　managing level of, 149
　　pollution, 149–150
　　right comprehension, lacking, 148
　　seriously superfluous and overstep, 149
　　threats, 149
　　tourist objects, 148
　development of, 147
　idea of, 147
　problems in, 147
　strategies of
　　consciousness and ecological protection education, 151
　　culture and philosophy backgrounds, 152
　　economic benefits of relative principle parts, 152
　　financing methods, 150–151
　　law of, 150
　　legal system, 150

Index   289

management system of, 150–151
regulations of nature reserves, 150
scientific building layout, 151
scientific content of, 152–153
sustainable development culture, 152
Chinese medicinal herb storehouse, 118
Clearing house mechanism (CHM), 21, 28
Coastal tourism, wind power installations
  approved and cape wind, 54
  contingent behavior
    fossil power plant, 59
    research design and methods, 59–60
  demographic and trip characteristics
    effects of wind power, 63
    mean desirability of beach features, 63
    sample population, 62
  experimental turbines, 54
  local economic importance
    bluewater, 55
    effect on, 55
    offshore wind power, 55
    potential impact of, 55
  offshore wind power and tourism, 56
  PPA, 54
  reported changes in beach visitation
    acceptance of offshore wind, 67
    contingent behavior modeling, 67–69
    descriptive statistics, 65
    out of sight, 64
    surveys of Delaware residents, 66
    variables and diagnostics, 70
    wind farm distances, 64–65
  research objectives
    purpose of, 56
  response rates, and weighting, implementation
    adult beachgoers approached, 61
    sampling location, 61
    sampling strategy and pretesting approaches, 60
  survey development
    instrument, 58
    wind farms, 59
  wind turbines, 54, 56, 57, 63
Commission on Sustainable Development (CSD), 18, 237
Commonwealth of Northern Mariana islands (CNMI), 125
Conservation business
  biodiversity, 106
  buzzwords, 106
  costs and benefits
    expenditure, 107
    Kenya boasts, 106
    Masai Mara National Park, 106
  distraction
    approach, 107–108
    community-based ecotourism, 107
    direct payment, 108
    ecologically noble savage, 107–108
    ecotourist paradise, 108
    forest protected, 109
    Galápagos sea cucumber, *Stichopus fuscus*, 108–109
    hypothetical model, 110
    quantitative data and analysis, 107
    spin-off, 109
  paying in perpetuity
    approach, 110
    charity-based conservation, 110
    indirect and direct payment, 110
  test
    conservation biologists, 111
    land tenure, 111
Conservation of Mongolian rangelands, 234
Contingent Valuation Method (CVM), 4

Cottrell, S., 236–243
Courchamp, F., 83–91, 92–102
Cross River National Park (CRNP), 154
Cross River State Forestry Commission (CRSFC), 154
Cross River State Government (CRSG), 154
CRS tourism bureau (CRSTB), 155
CSD. *See* Commission on Sustainable Development (CSD)
Cumberland island national seashore, Georgia
   cultural history, Dungeness, 141
   ecology, 141
   management, 141
   moving toward the future
      national parks, 146
      NPS transportations systems, 146
      society, 146
   NPS involvement
      legislation, 142
      managers, 142
   TMP, 140
      decision-making process, 145
      development, 144–145
      electric vehicles, 143
      factor, 143–144
      issue, 143
      NPS mission, 143
      Plum Orchard, 144
   wilderness, 140
CVM. *See* Contingent Valuation Method (CVM)

D

Dabek, L., 73–82
Degradation, 228
Delaware economic development office (DEDO), 60

E

Ecological sports tourism resources
   countermeasure for sustainable development
      irregular distribution, 117
      novel protection and utilization of, 116
      theory and method system, 116
   planning and design
      evaluation of, 115
      index system, 115
      industrialization specific items, 116
      objective feasibility analysis, 115
      principles of, 115
   regional planning
      application of modern technological, 113–114
      development of, 114
      industrial policy, 114–115
      scientific comprehensive investigation, 113–114
      survey of, 113–114
   research directions developed, 112
   resource analysis of
      Chinese traditional and ethnic sports, 113
      industry, 113
      natural ecological environment, 113
      spontaneous mass, 112–113
      Western or Chinese sports, 112
Ecology theory, 147
Ecosystem services, 1
   direct estimation methods, behavioral linkage approach
      CVM, 4
      political referendum method, 4
      WTP and WTA, 4–5
   ecotourism and nature's economic services, 10–12

Index   291

indirect estimation methods, behavioral linkage approach
   AEM, 5–6
   TCM and HPM, 6
methodological approaches
   direct method, 3
   HPMs, 4
   indirect method, 3–4
   three-step process, 3
nature valuation with, 2
petty resource extraction, economics, 8–10
social and cultural impacts of nature's goods and services
   coastal and marine biomes, 12–13
   coastal marine environments, 14
   deserts and tundra, 16
   grasslands/rangelands, 15
   inland lakes and rivers, 15–16
   open oceans, 14
   temperate/boreal forests, 14–15
   terrestrial biomes, 13
   tropical forests, 14
   wetlands and floodplains, 15
theoretical framework
   GDP, 2–3
   primary environmental benefit, 2
total value of nature's services, 16
valuing local plant pharmacopoeias, 6–7
   medicinal plant, economic projections, 7
   potential drug plants, economic projections, 7–8
Ecotourism
   and community participation
      assimilation, 41
      destination, 41, 42
      financial source acquirement, 41
      internal convergence, 42
      local inhabitants, 41
      model of, 41
      predatory management, 42
      social morality, 42
      tourist destination, 41
   connotation and essence, prominence, 39
   and ecological environment
      development model, 40–41
      materials production, 40
      natural tourism pattern, 40
      scenic spots, 40
      unified ecological, 41
      virtuous circle, 40
Ecotourism services, Kilim River mangrove forest, 189
   AMOS output, 195
   business ethics, 195
   conceptual model 1-4, 192–194
   environmental management, 195
   finding of micro study, 189
   marketing practices, 196
   methodology
      AMOS output, 191–192
      basic information, 189
      data analysis, 191
      data collected, 189
      logic of SEM, 191
      research tested, 191
      sample subjects, 190
      survey questionnaires, 190
   money tourists paid, 195
   raising tourists, 195
   rapid global growth, 189
   rules of thumb, 195
   services exceeding, 195
   standardized total effects, 196
   variables
      in business ethics, 196
      in environmental management, 190–191
      in marketing, 196

Environmental issues in ecotourism
   management plans
      ecological assessment, 48
      permissible-lodges, 48
      tourism concession programs, 48
   mitigation and monitoring, 49–53
   potential environmental impacts
      natural contours, 46
      soil erosion/compaction, 46
   program design
      acceptable use, limits, 47
      economic integrity, 46
      national tourism plan, 46
      nature conservancy, 45
      potential environmental impacts, 46
      tourism services, concessions, 47
Environmental management of ecotourism
   artificial sceneries, 38
   biological diversity, 38
   community participation, measures
      fragile and protection, 42
   ecological safety, 39
   establish decision-making mechanism, 43
   eutrophication, 38
   protection type, life style
      destruction, 43
      natural reserve, 43
   resources degradation, 39
   sustainable development, 38, 40, 41
Ezebilo, E. E. E., 129–139

F

Fatimah Mohd Saman, 189–197
Federal Government of Nigeria (FGN), 154
Firestone, J., 54–72
Fitzpatrick Institute, 259
Fujun Shen, 236–243

G

Gaul, K., 244–252
Geographic Information System (GIS), 199
German Wuppertal Institute, 236
Government officials, 234
Graham, K., 125–128
Green, J., 30–37
Gross domestic product (GDP), 2–3, 208

H

Hall, R. J., 92–102
Hedonic pricing methods (HPMs), 4, 6
Holland and China, predictors of sustainable tourism
   classification table, 242
   construct validity, 236
   greater percentage, 241
   indicators of, 237–239
      common structure, 238
      earth summit, 237
      physical indicators, 238
      purpose, 239
      study settings, 238–239
   logistic regression, 242
   mean comparisons, 241
   methods, variables measured, 239
   predictors of resident satisfaction, 243
   prism of sustainability, 237
   resident satisfaction, 243
   sample t-test, 241
   satisfaction with tourism, 242
   scale items for dimensions, 240–241
   strongest predictor, 242
Hongmei Dong, 118–123
Hongshu Wang, 38–44
HPMs. *See* Hedonic pricing methods (HPMs)
Hypothesized factors, 189

I

Institute for Aquatic Biodiversity, 254
The International Ecotourism Society (TIES), 122
International Labour Organization (ILO), 26

K

Kamaruzaman Jusoff, 189–197
Kempton, W., 54–72
Kinabatangan Orangutan conservation project (KOCP), 75

L

Lake Clark national park, 244
Lilley, M. B., 54–72
Look, D. W., 125–128

M

Manica, A., 30–37
Mattsson, L., 129–139
Mean willingness to contribute (MWTC), 135
Meinard, Y., 92–102
Micronesia, heritage ecotourism
    archeological and natural landscapes, 128
    aspect of, 125–126
    CNMI, 125
    cultural heritage tourism, 125
    impacts of
        environmental problems, 126–127
        sacrificial area, 127
        softer, 126–127
    opinions, 128
    priorities of
        cultural heritage sites, preserve, 127
        preserve local plants and animals, 127
    profiling
        definition, 126
        integral factors, 126
        questionnaire posited, 126
    questionnaire, 128
    ranking opportunities
        cluster, 127
        participants, 127
    strongly agree, 125
Miller, C. A., 140–146

Min Tong, 38–44
Mohammad Zaki Ayob, 189–197
Mongolian rangelands, conserving biodiversity, 212
    anthropogenic impacts, 212
    change in
        distribution of herd sizes over time, 221
        percentage of each type, 221
    changes in
        distribution of herd sizes over time, 221
        indices of, 223
        indices of Mongolian herder wealth over time, 223
        percentage, 221
    context of
        biodiversity, 213–215
        culture and conservation, 223–225
        livestock numbers, 219–223
        pastoralism, 217–219
        protected areas, 215–217
    designations, 216
    flora and fauna, 213
    free market system, 212
    improving prospects
        grazing reform, 232–233
        integrated solutions and conflict reduction, 234
        strengthening protected area management, 231–232
        tourism, 232
        wildlife management, 233–234
    increase in area and number of protected areas, 216
    livestock
        losses in, 222
        trends, 220
    livestock losses in, 222
    livestock trends, 220

Mongolian protected area designations, 216
number of herders, 221
pastoralist and conservation, 212
prospects
    grazing reform, 232–233
    integrated solutions and conflict reduction, 234
    protected area management, 231–232
    tourism, 232
    wildlife management, 233–234
protected areas, 216
socioeconomic changes, 212
strengthening protected area, 212
threats and challenges
    conflicts between pastoralism and conservation, 227–229
    conservation capacity, 229–231
    lack of conservation capacity, 229–231
    natural resources exploitation, 225–227
transition, 212
Mongolia's steppe, 234

N

Naidoo, R., 30–37
National Botanical Institute (NBI), 253
National multi-stakeholders body (NMB), 25–26
National Park Service (NPS), 140, 244
Nation's livestock, 223
Nature-based tourism areas (NBTA), 25
Nature-based tourism (NBT)
    absolute attendance, 35
    apparent paradox, 30
    biodiversity-rich areas, 35
    broad-scale variation, 36
    cross-sectoral policy, 18
    definition, 18–20
    international instrument, legal bases, 23–25
        principles on, 24
    international instrument, needs/characteristics, 22
    literature review, 21–22
        sustainable tourism, 20
    local downturns, 37
    materials and methods, 31–32
    methodology, 18
    pervasive shift, 30
    plausible, 34
    protected areas (PAs), 29
    Quebec summit, 18, 21
    required innovations
        awards, 28
        CHM, 28
        compensation mechanism, 27–28
        compliance measure mechanism, 29
        criteria for sustainability, 28
        EIA procedures, 27
        IMB, 26
        NMB, 25–26
        providing local community with major roles in, 26
        tourism industry involvements/rights/obligations, 26–27
        tourism seasonality, 28
    Rio activities, 17
    sedentary, 31
    spatial heterogeneity, 36
    tangible financial flows, 35
    vulnerability, 35
NBI. *See* National Botanical Institute (NBI)
Neary, J., 154–188
NFO World Group's, 58
Nicholls, H., 106–111
Nigeria, ecotourism in protected areas in CRS, 154

and activities of mission
   assessment of related needs for, 156
   collaborative, 155
   facilities for, 156–157
   during mission activities, 156
   planning and operating, 157
   policies, 156–157
   principles of, 156
   site visits to, 156–157
   three community-centered projects, 157
   USFS/IP team, 155–156
   written report, 156
method of assessment, 157–160
   critical needs for protected areas, 159–160
   CRSTB, need of, 158
   enhancing capacity for collaborative, 160
   forestry commission, 160
   national and international visitors for, 157–158
   USFS short-term, technical assistance, 158–159
national park system, 154
natural resources, 154
objectives of mission, 155–157
   assessment of related needs for, 156
   collaborative, 155
   facilities for, 156–157
   during mission activities, 156
   planning and operating, 157
   policies, 156–157
   principles of, 156
   report, 156
   site visits to, 156–157
   three community-centered projects, 157
   USFS/IP team, 155–156
purpose of mission, 155–157
   assessment of related needs for, 156
   collaborative, 155
   facilities for, 156–157
   during mission activities, 156
   planning and operating, 157
   policies, 156–157
   principles of, 156
   site visits to, 156–157
   three community-centered projects, 157
   USFS/IP team, 155–156
   written report, 156
Nigerian National Park Service (NNPS), 154
Nigerian rainforest zone, economic value of ecotourism
   annual disposable income, 134
   benefits of, 129
   contingent valuation format
      hypothetical market scenario, 131–132
   data collection
      pre-test interviews, 131
      survey, 131
   environmental conservation group, membership, 135
   gender, bread-winners, 134
   local communities, 130
   natural areas, 129
   occupation, 134
   Okwangwo Division, respondent's residence
      ecotourism activities, 134
   respondents education, 129, 134
   study site
      Calyptocichla serina, 130
      Gorilla gorilla diehli, 130
      Picathartes oreas, 130
   theoretical framework and statistical analysis
      definition of variables, 133–134
      linear and Tobit models, 132–133

willingness to contribute, 132
  WTC values, 133
willingness to contribute, respondents characteristics
  coefficient, 137
  environmental conservation group, 138
  OLS and Tobit models, 136
  social and cultural changes, 138
  WTC estimate and sample, description MWTC of, 135
Nigeria, sustainable tourism development in Cross River State, 203
  amount suspended by tourist as fare to Ranch, 210
  basic social amenities, 203
  economic development, 203
  environmental conservation, 203
  leisure activity, 203
  map of Cross River State study area, 205
  methodology, 205–206
    chi-square, 206
    patronage of, 205
  mountain savannah of
    Ogoja and Obudu, 204
  Obudu Ranch Resort
    chi-square, 203
    domestic and international patronage, 203, 208–209
    major tourism attractions and facilities in, 209–210
    tremendous facilities, 203
  patronage, 209
  physical environmental features, 203
  population threshold of communities, 204
  study area, 204–205
  tourism in theory and practice, 206–208
    cognizance survey, 207
    democratic republic accounted, 208
    development, 207
    Hall analyses, 208

individual's educational background, 206
likelihood, 207
physical relationship, 207
socio-economic development, 206
statement of Ukpana, 206
study opines, 208
tropical climate, 207
tourist's preference of Obudu Ranch Resort, 210
tourist visit to Ranch, 208
Non-governmental organizations (NGOs), 154
Northern piedmont in Qinling Mountains
  Chinese medicinal herb storehouse, 118
  countermeasures and recommendations, 118
    advantages of tourism resources, 122
    development and construction of ecotourism, 123
    ecological agriculture and atmosphere, 124
    environmental protection project, 123
    forest, 123–124
    medium and long-term project, 123
    poverty relief and capital investment, development, 124
    scientific experts, 122
    TIES, 122
  ecotourism, status quo problems development
    disordered management, 121
    environmental protection facility, 120–121
    exploitation of tourism resources, 121
    geological landform resources, 120
    pollution, 120–121
    scenic spots, 119–120
    seeking for new life, 120

talents and inefficient management, 121–122
tourist attractions, 119–120
humanistic ecotourism resources
  dynasties of, 119
  kingdom of animals and plants, 118
  Kuan-Chung Plain, 118–119
  natural ecotourism resources
    biological, 119
    forest parks, 119
    Kingdonia uniflora, 119
  rural ecotourism resources, 119
  tourism resources, 118–119
NPS. *See* National Park Service (NPS)

O

Obudu Ranch Resort, 203
Offshore wind
  economic development associate
    avoidance of beaches, 71
    effect of, 71
    potential benefit, 70–71
  installations, 56
  power and tourism, 56
  turbines, 56
Okwangwo division (OD), 130
O'Neil, S., 73–82
Ordinary least squares (OLSs), 129
Organization for Economic and Co-operation Development (OECD), 36
Otu, J. E., 203–211

P

Parks and tourism
  biologists, 103
  commercial nature, 104
  conservation, 103, 105
  ecosystem services, 103
  industry, 104
  issues, 104–105
  parks agencies, 104
  pergams and zaradic, 105
  politics, 103
  relationship marketing, 104
  videophilia, 104
  visitors, 104
Parsimony ratio (PRATIO), 192
Participatory Research Method (PRM), 206
Percy Fitzpatrick Institute, 254
Poor environmental, 230
Power purchase agreement (PPA), 54
PPA. *See* Power purchase agreement (PPA)
PRM. *See* Participatory Research Method (PRM)

R

Rahmatian, M., 1–16
Rarity value and species extinction
  AAE, 92–93
  collections
    of butterflies in Papua New Guinea, 96
    Pinguinus impennis for, 96
    of wildlife, 96
  ecotourism ventures
    Capercaillie *(Tetrao urogallus),* 100
  empirical examples
    assumption of AAE, 95–96
  exotic pets
    article reports, 98
    CITES status of, 99
  human-generated feedback loop, 92–91
  luxury items
    Cheilinus undulatus, 97
    white abalones, 97–98
  model and results theoretical framework
    assumptions, 93
    rate of change of hunting effort, 93
    of supply and demand theory, 94–95

traditional medicine use
　　Chinese bahaba *(Bahaba taipingensis),* 100–101
　　trophy hunting, SCI, 96–97
Reading, R. P., 212–235
Revenue generator, 189
Rivalan, P., 92–102
Root mean square of approximation (RMSEA), 192

S

Sabah wildlife department (SWD), 75
Safari Club International (SCI), 96–97
SEM. *See* Structural Equations Modeling (SEM)
Severe Avian Respiratory Syndrome (SARS), 232
Sharp, R. L., 140–146
Signoret, L., 92–102
Soleimanpour, H., 17–29
South Africa, biodiversity science, 253
　　African Baobab, 260
　　African Black Oystercatchers, 258
　　Cape Flowers in August, 254
　　centers of excellence in
　　　　biogeographic corridors, 257
　　　　departments of, 261
　　　　development, 256
　　　　disappointing, 257
　　　　Fitzpatrick Institute, 256
　　　　indigenous diversity, 259
　　　　invasion biology, 257
　　　　Pterocarpus angolensis, 259
　　　　relationships, 258
　　　　unique opportunity, 258
　　　　water rehabilitation program, 260
　　coastal marine species, 253
　　economy
　　　　challenge of sustainable harvesting, 256
　　　　global mean of, 255
　　　　habitats, 255
　　　　virtual abandonment of, 256
　　institute, 255
　　　　dynamic, 253
　　　　indigenous, 253
　　　　influx of, 253
　　　　optimistic, 253
　　　　research centers, 253
　　　　responsibility for, 254
　　　　zoological diversity, 254
　　scientific community, 253
South Africans National Biodiversity Institute(SANBI), 253
South Africa, wilderness stewardship in KNP, 198
　　aesthetic impacts, 200
　　areas/zones, 200, 201–202
　　　　back-to-basics, 202
　　　　basic essentials, 201
　　　　future generations, 201
　　　　human habitation, 201
　　　　legalize, 201
　　　　minimum-impact, 201
　　　　obligation, 201
　　　　remote areas, 201
　　　　return-to-roots, 202
　　attributes and biodiversity, 202
　　biophysical, 200
　　commercial poaching, 198
　　consolidation process, 200–201
　　human population explosion, 198
　　methods, 199–200
　　　　appropriate buffer distance, 199–200
　　　　generic zoning system, 199
　　new legislation and opportunities, 199
　　　　act, 199
　　　　area designated, 199
　　　　human habitation, 199
　　spiritual and experiential, 202
　　undiluted to diluted, 202
　　war-ridden Mozambique, 198

Index   299

wildlife diseases, 198
zoological and botanical gardens, 202
Spennemann, D. H. R., 125–128
Structural Equations Modeling (SEM), 189
Subsistence, tourism and research, 244
   Big Sky, 251
   celebrated and strengthened, 251
   Dena'ina people and lake clark national park, 244–249
      creation story, 244
      entrepreneurs, 248
      fall hunting, 248
      gold prospecting, 249
      layers of significance, 245
      nivagi, 246
      oral histories, 245
      plenty of salmon, 248
      Qizhjeh Vena, 249
      read and appreciated, 246
      resource, 245
      Telaquana Mountain, 244
      transportation routes, 246
      trap muskrats, 246
   Dena'ina people describe their traditional seasonal, 247
   Native Dena'ina people participated, 249
   other meanings of
      accommodated, 251
      act, 250
      aesthetic reflection, 250
      Alaska, 249
      ANILCA parks, 250
      promulgates, 250
      recreation, 250
      resources, 250
      spiritual renewal, 250
      wilderness, 250
   Telaquana Mountain, 245

T

TCM. *See* Travel Cost Method (TCM)

TKCP. *See* Tree Kangaroo Conservation Program (TKCP)
TLI. *See* Tucker-Lewis Index (TLI)
Tourism behavior
   Denmark, 57
   effect on, 57
   European Union, 56
   potential changes
      broader evidence, 57–58
      effect of, 57
   wilderness experience, 57
Transportation management plan (TMP), 140
   development, 144–145
   electric vehicles, 143
   factor, 143–144
   issue, 143
   NPS mission, 143
   Plum Orchard, 144
Travel Cost Method (TCM), 6
Tree Kangaroo Conservation Program (TKCP)
   Dendrolagus matschiei, 78
   education projects, 80
   Gabriel Porolak of PNG prepares, 78–79
   interest, 80
   inventories, 78
   issues, 77
   wildlife banks, 80
   working, 78
Tucker-Lewis Index (TLI), 192

U

UNESCO park, 189
United Nations Conference on Trade and Development (UNCTAD), 18
United Nations Environment Programme (UNEP), 18
United states agency for international development, 107

United States Government (USG), 155
Ushie, M. A., 203–211

V

Value of rare species in ecotourism
   anthropogenic allee effect, 83
   attractiveness of photographs of
      IP number and program, 88
   automatically coded IP number, 85
   and endangered species, exploitation of, 83–84
   photographs
      patience awaiting for, 90–91
      perseverance to see, 91
   slideshow
      attractiveness of each type, 85
      behavior of visitors, 89
      experiment
         by contacting large newsgroups in, 88
      experiment design, 84
      patience awaiting for each, 85–86
      perseverance for each, 86
      with photographs, 83
      rarity affected time spent waiting for, 87

visitors choice, 87
Vaske, J. J., 236–243
Venter, F. J., 198–202
Voeks, R. A., 1–16

W

Walpole, M., 30–37
Wei Chen, 147–153
Wenpu Wang, 147–153
Wildlife Conservation Society (WCS), 155
Wildlife management agency, 233
Willingness to accept (WTA), 4–5
Willingness to pay (WTP), 4–5
World Commission on Environment and Development (WCED), 19
World Summit On Sustainable Development (WSSD), 18
World Tourism Organization (WTO), 18, 21, 22, 25, 237

Z

Zaliha Hj Hussin, 189–197
Zhu, P., 112–117